CONQUERING THE PAST

CONQUERING THE PAST

Austrian Nazism
Yesterday & Today

EDITED BY F. PARKINSON

 Wayne State University Press   Detroit   1989

Library of Congress Cataloging-in-Publication Data

Conquering the past : Austrian Nazism yesterday and today / edited
by F. Parkinson.
p.   cm.
Includes bibliographies and index.
ISBN 0-8143-2054-6   ISBN 0-8143-2055-4 (pbk.)
1. National socialism. 2. Austria—Politics and government—20th
century. I. Parkinson, F.
DP97.C65 1989   88-31328
324.436'038—dc19   CIP

To the memory of
Franz Jägerstätter—
Austrian war hero

Contents

7

Contributors

Evan R. Bukey, Professor of History, University of Arkansas, Fayetteville

Dr. Tone Ferenc, Edvard Kardelj Institute of History, University of Ljubljana, Yugoslavia

Reinhold Gärtner, Institute of Political Science, University of Innsbruck, Tyrol

Ernst Hanisch, Professor of History, University of Salzburg

Dr. Blair R. Holmes, Department of History, Brigham Young University, Provo, Utah

Robert H. Keyserlingk, Professor of History, University of Ottawa, Canada

Helmut Konrad, Professor of History, Karl-Franzens University, Graz

Dr. Andreas Maislinger, Institute of Political Science, University of Innsbruck, Tyrol

Dr. F. Parkinson, Institute of Latin American Studies, University of London

Bruce F. Pauley, Professor and Head, Department of History, University of Central Florida, Orlando

Anton Pelinka, Professor and Head, Department of Political Science, University of Innsbruck

9

Dr. Jerry W. Pyle, History Department, Southern Arkansas University, Magnolia

Max E. Riedlsperger, Professor and Chair, Department of History, California Polytechnic State University, San Luis Obispo

Robert Schwarz, Professor and Head, Department of Philosophy, Florida Atlantic University, Boca Raton

Dr. Alan Sked, Department of History, London School of Economics

Dr. Karl Stuhlpfarrer, Institute of Contemporary History, University of Vienna

Dr. Melanie A. Sully, Department of Humanities, North Staffordshire Polytechnic

Dr. Maurice Williams, Dean of Mathematics and Science and member of the Department of History, Okanagan College, Kelowna, B.C., Canada

Introduction

F. PARKINSON

Enormous efforts were made during the war by the Allied Powers to highlight the evil nature of the Nazi regime. In the end, the Nazi state had to be battered down by sheer superiority in men and *matériel de guerre*.

In view of this one would have expected historians of all nationalities to jump at the opportunity to write and document the history of Nazism in all its aspects. As regards the subject of Germany that expectation has largely been fulfilled, but so far as Austria is concerned there has been almost complete silence. As the correspondent of the London *Times* reported from Vienna recently, "Austrians grow up increasingly ignorant of the events of their country's history. One Austrian historian recently wrote that basic school history texts used throughout the country contained dozens of omissions and errors concerning the inter-war period. One of the most ominous of these was the lack of any reference to the fact that Austrian Right-wing Federal Chancellor Engelbert Dollfuss was assassinated by the Nazis in 1934."[1]

Amazingly, it was not before 1981 that an attempt was made by an English-language historian to trace out the history of what he rightly called "the forgotten Nazis," that is, of Austria.[2] Yet Austria was well known to have been a breeding ground of Nazism.

What were the reasons for this reluctance? Was it perhaps because, all outward professions to the contrary notwithstanding, it was considered that the power of Germany, rather than the ideology of the Nazi movement, constituted the truly objectionable factor? If that was the case, then it stood to reason that anything likely to curb the power of a postwar Germany was welcome and had to be promoted.

One such element was the resurrection of an independent Austria irrespective of the wishes of the Austrians themselves. Self-determination was to be subordinate to diplomatic expediency. In that event, an image had to be projected and cultivated of an Austria brutally invaded and annexed by an imperialist Germany bent on conquest in 1938; an Austria, moreover, whose population, though pressed into the service of the German cause by all manner of means, was straining at the leash to be liberated and, when actually so liberated, behaved in a way that differed in no material respect from that of other liberated countries, such as Czechoslovakia, France, Poland, Belgium, or Greece.

If it was seen as politic to promote such an image, were the new Austrian government, the Austrian political parties, let alone the Austrian population at large, expected to protest against such preferred treatment in the name of abstract historical accuracy? Could they seriously be expected to conduct an inquest into their own very recent past, especially in respect of their allegedly close connection with the sinister phenomenon of Nazism? And were Austria's historians to be encouraged in those circumstances to enter a political minefield that portended almost certain professional death? All this at a time when all concerned – the Allies, the Austrian government, and the Austrain population at large – found it perhaps not the better side of wisdom but rather the better side of expediency to derive the maximum relief and comfort from such a favorable if entirely fortuitous turn of events?

In the short run positions like these were tenable, but in the long run history cannot be cheated, and the day could not be put off indefinitely when serious and possibly disturbing attempts would have to be made to reveal the picture in its historical fullness.

Efforts have been undertaken to attribute the succumbing of Austria to Nazism to the letdown by the great powers who sacrificed the country on the altar of their policies of appeasement.[3] The thesis implicit in this line of reasoning answers some but by no means all the questions that may be asked. For, at least prima facie, it could still be argued that, with the notable exception of the Jews, the mass of Austrians would have been broadly sympathetic to Nazism whatever the nature of the international politics of the period.

This volume is not concerned primarily with fixing the guilt of Nazi Germany in suborning and ultimately conquering the state of Austria. This task has been discharged repeatedly, and frequently with distinction, by others.[4] What has been left undone is the task of determining the attitudes adopted by the Austrians themselves towards Nazism. It was in pursuit of that latter objective that the present editor assembled a team of historians and political scientists drawn predominantly from North America (the United States and Canada) and Britain, but including some Austrian colleagues of the younger generation with no axe to grind, as well as a distinguished Yugoslav scholar, to conduct a scholarly inquiry covering all ramifications of Nazism in Austria, wide enough to comprehend not only the activities and attitudes of those in power but of all sections of the population, whether in Vienna or the provinces, whether organized in political parties or professing certain creeds, throughout the country before and after the *Anschluss*.

The task was to be achieved by the scrupulous avoidance of a priori scholarship committed to defending a particular thesis. As in the case of the parallel history of Germany, this has raised methodological problems connected with steering a line betwen empathetic "historicist" understanding on the one hand and moral relativism on the other. The problem was resolved in accordance with Martin Broszat's advice—endorsed by Robert Knight in a review of a collection of his essays—to retain "a critical moral sensitivity, even while remaining essentially in sympathy with the historicist aspiration."[5]

One point deserves special mention. The idea of embarking on the present task came to this editor gradually over a couple of decades—long before the Reder and Waldheim crises burst upon an unsuspecting world—and the decision to act was most certainly not taken in response to the latter.

NOTES

1. Richard Bassett, *The Times*, 11 April 1987.

2. Bruce F. Pauley, *The Forgotten Nazis. A History of Austrian National Socialism* (Chapel Hill, 1981).

3. One of the latest attempts of that genre was made by Max Löwenthal-Chlumecki, "Der Westen schaute zu—'Was wollen Sie allein?'", *Die Presse*, 28 February 1987, concentrating on an analysis of the visit to Paris in 1937 by Austria's Under-Secretary of State, Guido Schmidt.

That Britain was unwilling to act was attested by Sir Nevile Henderson, former Ambassador to Berlin, in connection with the second anniversary of the Nazi seizure of power in Austria. In an article in the *Daily Herald* of 11 March 1940, he claimed that two years before the case against Hitler had not yet been "iron-cast."

4. See, for instance, N. Schausberger, *Der Griff nach Österreich* (Vienna and Munich, 1979).

5. H. Graml and K.-D. Henke (eds.), *Nach Hitler. Der schwierige Umgang mit unserer Geschichte* (Munich, 1987). Cited by Robert Knight in the *Times Literary Supplement*, 15 May 1987.

I

Austria and Germany

The Growth of an Inferiority Complex?

ALAN SKED

AUSTRIA AND GERMANY, 1815–1918

The relationship of Austria to Germany has always been an ambiguous one, but at no time was this more true than in the nineteenth century. It began with the Habsburgs still in possession of the German Crown as Holy Roman Emperors, and, for half a century after 1815, still witnessed their diplomats presiding over the Germanic Confederation. Yet with their defeat at Königgraetz in 1866, the Austrians were forced by Prussia to surrender their claims to leadership in Germany. The Emperor Franz Joseph appeared ready to dispense with his Germanic obligations altogether, writing to his wife that "we are pulling out of Germany completely, whether this is demanded or not; after the experiences I have had with our dear fellow-members of the German Confederation, I consider this a good fortune for Austria."[1] Not all his German-speaking subjects, on the other hand were to adopt the same attitude nor, indeed, had he himself as yet abandoned all hope of regaining German leadership. With Prussia's victory over France and the proclamation of the German Empire in 1871, on the other hand, he had to reconcile himself to the fact that his imperial ambitions would henceforth have to be restricted to the Balkans. Even there, however, he was to discover that his Empire no longer possessed the resources necessary to maintain a position of dominance. By the 1880s the military advice he received was that only with German support could he undertake a war. His army, short of money and manpower, could not, it was reckoned, risk fighting alone. This meant that Austria-Hungary had become dependent on Berlin for its survival as a great power. No longer was it the "European necessity" of Metternich's era but in the last resort a client state of the Hohenzollerns. This was indeed an ironic twist of fate, but one which was clearly demonstrated in both the Bosnian crisis of 1908–1909 and in July 1914.

Conrad von Hötzendorf, the Chief of the General Staff in 1914, hoped that the First World War would restore Austria's diplomatic freedom. He said, "if the War ends in victory, then Austria-Hungary will be so much strengthened that she will be able to face Germany as an equal."[2] On the other hand, his own military blunders in 1914, not to mention the neglect of the armed services beforehand, meant that by 1915 the Austrians were already totally dependent on the Germans to win the war. On all fronts, battles and campaigns were won only with German participation. Where there were no Germans, as a rule there were no victories. Austria-Hungary also became dependent on Germany for food and hard currency. The inevitable result was that, in the diplomacy of wartime, Germany called all the shots. To Vienna's bewilderment, Berlin insisted that—since German armies had won the campaigns against Russia and Romania—Germany, not Austria, would be the cartographer for East and Central Europe. By the summer of 1918, therefore, Austria-Hungary had had to agree to both the establishment of an independent Ukraine and to her own participation in some future form of *Mitteleuropa*. As Conrad put it, "it was our evil fate (that the Germans) mixed operational requirements with their post-war aims: territorial expansion, economic and political hegemony over their own Allies."[3] In the words of one historian, "Austria-Hungary, far from reaching her own goal, had to supply the cannon-fodder to achieve Germany's."[4] When Germany failed to win the war, Austria-Hungary ceased to exist.

THE NATURE OF THE RELATIONSHIP

It should be immediately apparent even from this brief survey that relations with Germany literally were of vital importance to Austria. Indeed, they were so close, so crucial that Austrian historians have always had to ask themselves whether Austria ever really enjoyed an existence separate from that of Germany. Should Austrian history be considered part of German history or something sui generis? This has always been an extremely difficult question to answer. Certainly there is a shared historical experience: the colonization of Eastern Europe; the Holy Roman Empire; the

German Confederation; the war of 1864 against Denmark; the First World War. Yet there was also historical dividing lines: the Counter-Reformation; the Seven Years' War; the Austro–Prussian War; the Nazi period. Austrian historians today argue over whether Austria was settled first of all by German tribes or by Slavs, whether there was a separate Austrian musical tradition, whether *Biedermeier* or *Cafehaus* culture was peculiarly Austrian or merely parochial versions of German life-styles. If even today there are doubts regarding Austria's heritage, it is little wonder that nineteenth century Austrians and Germans were even more confused. But it is only with this confusion in mind, as well as a knowledge of Austro–German relations, that we shall begin to understand the true nature of the relationship that developed between the Austrians and the Germans.

Austrian liberal opponents of the Metternich system were convinced of their German nationality. Schuselka, the author of several pamphlets on this theme, wrote, "If Austria ceases to be German, she ceases altogether to be Austrian."[5] In this he was echoed by Baron Viktor von Adrian-Warburg, author of the famous two volumes entitled *Austria and Its Future (Österreich und dessen Zukunft)*, who wrote that Austria was "a purely imaginary name, which signifies no self-contained people, no country, no nation, a conventional usage for a complex of sharply distinct nationalities. There are Italians, Germans, Slavs, Hungarians, who together constitute the Austrian Empire, but there is no Austria, no Austrian, no Austrian nationality, nor has there ever been any save for a strip of land around Vienna."[6] In spite of this, however, prominent Germans seemed to be aware of differences. Goethe, for example, was writing of an "Austrian nation" in 1792 and was later to describe Austria, from the point of view of Germans, as "intellectually a foreign country" (*geistiges Ausland*).[7] Friedrich Schlegel wrote in 1819 to his wife "How can you make the strange error of believing that Vienna is located in Germany or that it has the least to do with Germany? They are separated by entire continents, and one could hardly think of more polar opposites."[8] Metternich for his part did not believe in German political nationalism for either Austrians or Germans. Like Italy, Germany for him was a "geographical expression," an area ruled by a variety of sovereign princes, including foreign ones like the king of the Netherlands, the king of Denmark, and until 1837, the king of England. The Austrian Chancellor, therefore, denounced *Teutonismus*, asserting that the Austrian Empire was not a German State, but an "agglomeration of nationalities."[9]

GERMAN AND NON–GERMAN "AUSTRIANS"

The existence of other nations within the confines of the Habsburg Monarchy was of course an obstacle to any attempt to define it purely as a German State. Habsburg emperors were aware of this more than anybody else. Thus when Francis I heard of someone being described as an "Austrian patriot," he dismissed the phrase, asking "But is he a patriot for me?"[10] As far as the dynasty was concerned, the duty of its subjects was allegiance to their sovereign not to any nationality and certainly not to the German one. Habsburg emperors, in their quest for power and prestige, were willing to reign over subjects of any nationality and expected undivided loyalty in return. Like Napoleon, they had long discovered that ruling one piece of land was much like ruling any other. A rather saccharine version of this outlook was once articulated by the Archduke Albrecht when he said "In a polyglot Empire inhabited by many races and peoples the dynasty must not allow itself to be assigned exclusively to one of these. Just as a good mother, it must show equal love for all its children and remain foreign to none. In this lies the justification for its existence."[11] The key to Habsburg thinking therefore was the presumption of a special bond between subject and ruler which transcended nationality. Hence the Archduchess Sophie, the mother of Franz Joseph, paradoxically, could even approve of Bismarck. She wrote, "While I completely disapprove of the pernicious policy of Bismarck towards Austria, I cannot refuse him my admiration for the great and admirable courage with which he pleads the cause of his sovereign and of the real welfare of his country and indeed the cause of all sovereigns."[12]

Habsburg dynastic values, however, were rooted in illusion rather than reality. If subjects, on the one hand, were expected to be loyal, their reward, on the other, was to be merely the appearance of imperial impartiality. The Austrian Foreign Minister, Stadion, for example, had to be told this during the Napoleonic Wars. The Archduke John, who had been born in Florence and who knew Stadion well, took the latter aside in 1808 and let him know that his imperial brother Francis, thought himself as German as he did."[13] The Archduke John, it is true, was himself something of a German nationalist—certainly he acquired this reputation in the 1840s—and in 1848, as German *Reichsverweser*, was greatly distrusted by the rest of the family (*Onkel Reichsvermoderer* was the pun employed by the young Franz Joseph),[14] yet even Mitternich himself was no enthusiast for anything other than apparent national equality. He, too, believed in the superiority of the German element within the Monarchy, commenting on the Galician situation after the massacres in 1846, that what was needed was its "promotion" there. He explained:

> One race of people can only be transformed into another with the help of time—and under altogether particular circumstances. The promotion of the German element must be sought through its continued presence and influence by means of the help immediately available, that is through its civilization in the truest sense of the word. The means to this end lie in increasing

the sales of feudal estates to Germans, in encouraging the growth of the German city population, in promotion and spreading the use of German in schools, and in other ways.[15]

This then was to be the reward of the Galician Poles for their loyalty to the dynasty. Metternich in fact, saw his task not merely as giving the illusion of strength to Austria in foreign affairs but in giving the illusion of impartiality to the nationalities in domestic ones. His so-called reform schemes of 1817 were designed to achieve this by creating separate "chancelleries" for certain national groups under the aegis of a uniform ministry of the interior; likewise, his support for local diets extended only to tolerating them in the most emasculated form rather than abolishing them altogether. Basically, like all Habsburgs and their servants after 1749 he favored running the Monarchy through an efficient, centralized bureaucracy, one that would use German as its language of internal communication and that would depend on the Germans of the Monarchy and other States for recruitment. During the whole period 1815–1918, therefore, the Monarchy's German subjects were aware that they were the main beneficiaries of Habsburg rule. This, according to Peter Katzenstein, was the simple reason why, even after 1866 or the Badeni crisis of 1897, they rejected the alternative Pan-German program of integration into the *Reich* of the Hohenzollerns.[16]

The extent of German dominance within the Empire can be judged from the following figures, culled from Katzenstein's compelling study:[17] In 1914, in the cental ministries of Cisleithania, 76 percent of the civil servants were German, and in the joint ministries that linked the eastern and western parts of the Dual Monarchy, the corresponding figure was still as high as 56 percent. (Germans formed only 24 percent of the population of the Monarchy as a whole and only 36 percent of that of Cisleithania). They were overrepresented in the top posts to an even greater degree. In 1910, for example, German-Austrians filled 81 percent of the top six grades of the Finance Ministry, which was widely thought to be well disposed to the claims of candidates of other ethnic groups. In the Foreign Ministry, the figure was only 65 percent, but that was still more than twice the proportion of German-Austrians in the total population. As in the civil service, so, too, in the army. In 1910 roughly two-thirds of the officer corps were German Austrians, the figure being 85 percent in the western part of the Empire. As far as Parliament was concerned, 66 percent of the Reichstag members were German-Austrians in 1873, 52 percent in 1885, and even after the introduction of universal suffrage in 1907, the proportion was 44 percent. Since civil servants tended to dominate the cabinet in Cisleithania, there, too, the German-Austrians predominated. In 1900, the Koerber cabinet was almost exclusively filled with them. Industry and finance, fi-

nally, was also dominated by German-Austrians. In terms of industrial production, the Alpine provinces and the Sudetenland predominated, whereas
Vienna, the financial hub of the Empire, controlled 80 percent of share capital in 1900 and 67 percent in 1914. Hence Katzenstein concludes:

> Until 1918 Empire-wide institutions like the bureaucracy and army con-
> tinued to offer the German-Austrians opportunities for upward social mo-
> bility (especially at the centre of the empire) which they could hardly expect
> to find in Germany. Furthermore, the German character of these institutions
> provided symbolic and actual reassurance, and strengthened the sentimental
> commitments of the German-Austrians to the Empire. From both an instru-
> mental and a sentimental perspective, in the eyes of the German-Austrians,
> the Empire continued as a going concern; and when it finally collapsed under
> the cumulative impact of internal and external strains and stresses, the German-
> Austrians were the last ethnic group to abandon it.[18]

THE AUSTRIAN IDEA

The Germans of the Habsburg Monarchy, therefore, found it difficult
to have straightforward feelings with regard to nationality. That they identified with their cultural brethren in the German States and later in Bismarck's
Reich cannot be questioned; Schuselka and others did so almost exclusively. Yet they were also loyal to their Habsburg ruler and realized that,
within his Empire, they enjoyed a position with regard to the other nationalities that they could not hope to secure in a purely German Empire
dominated by Prussians, Bavarians, and other exclusively German-speaking
natives. Both self-interest and sentimentality, therefore, conspired to keep
them loyal to their dynasty, a situation they could afford to remain com-
placent about so long as the Monarchy remained the principal power in
Germany. The rise of German nationalism, however, with its demand for
a German nation-state, was to impose strains on this complacency, although
it never really succeeded in undermining it.

The Austrian response was simply the "Austrian Idea," or in A. J. P.
Taylor's phrase, "the best of both worlds."[19] Austria presented herself as the
power best able to protect German interests, both through her leadership
of Germany and through her role in spreading German culture in Eastern
Europe. In this way the German-Austrians could be associated both with
their fellow-Germans outside the Monarchy and continue to lord it over
the Slavs and Hungarians inside it. Things, in other words, would best be
left as they were. This was the basis of the Habsburg policy of preserving
an eternal status quo, a policy pursued most consciously by Prince Metternich after 1815. Yet as the century wore on and as it became increasingly
clear that Prussia was the leading economic and military power in Germany,

the first part of the Austrian Idea became ever less convincing. Worse still, the rise of nationalism affected the Monarchy's other nationalities. No longer were they satisfied to be mere recipients of German culture but demanded the right to pursue cultural activities of their own. After 1848, therefore—indeed before then in several cases—the second part of the Austrian Idea was also wearing thin. Still, only by following the history of this ideal can we hope to understand the relationship of Austrians and Germans before 1918.

THE AUSTRIAN IDEA, 1815–1866

In the age of Metternich, there was little for Austria to worry about. She had emerged from the Congress of Vienna of 1815 with the leadership of Germany as president of the new Germanic Confederation. Inside the Monarchy itself there was little opposition to government policies save from the Hungarians and Italians, opposition that was easily contained and that found little echo among German-Austrians, apart from a few students and intellectuals. Things only got out of hand in 1848, thanks largely to the loss of nerve of the imperial family and the power vacuum created by the dismissal of Metternich. Until then the Austrian Idea seemed a perfectly rational one. The Confederation acted much as Austria desired and functioned not as a national assembly of any kind but as an instrument for Metternich to use against the revolution. Indeed, this practically became its only function, its constitution having been designed to limit its authority over the individual States. For example, a unanimous vote was required on the most important issues which came before it. Since this obviously restricted the agenda, only sixteen meetings of the general assembly (sixty-eight instructed delegates) took place between 1816 and 1866. Important diplomatic business was therefore often conducted outside its auspices—for example, the signing of the Elbe, Weser, and Rhine conventions of 1821, 1823, and 1831 or the establishment of the German Customs Union (or Zollverein.) As a result, the Confederation never needed to employ more than twenty-seven officials. Its main business was conducted by its Executive Council that examined a relatively small number of petitions each year (they varied in number between 20 and 123) and that under Metternich's guidance helped formulate the restrictions on the press, universities, and local diets, which constituted his only response to the threat of revolution. The Carlsbad Decrees of 1819, the Final Act of the Vienna Conference of 1820, the Six Acts of 1832 are both personal monuments to Metternich and the major part of the record of work of the Confederation.

Metternich's obsession with the threat of revolution is well known.

He cherished an unshakeable belief in conspiracy theories and was utterly convinced that a directing committee of revolutionaries planned to over-throw governments all over Europe. He also believed, incidentally, that Europe's Jews were involved in this conspiracy, a sign perhaps that he had picked up the anti-Semitism already prevalent in Austria. He wrote "In Germany . . . the Jews accept what is virtually the principal role and are revolu-tionaries of the highest class. They have writers, philosophers, poets, orators, political journalists, bankers, and over their head as well as in their heart the full weight of their ancient ignominy. One day they will give Germany something to fear, after which Germany may well do the same to them."[20] Yet, his fear of revolution was the one thing that the German princes shared, so that his leadership in resisting it ensured him the leading voice in Ger-man affairs.

Austria's relations with Germany during the Metternich period were, otherwise, less than intimate. As is well known, she refused to participate in the *Zollverein*, a decision that many historians have seen as portentous, and one that Metternich himself regretted. It would, he predicted, become "a State within a State," something that Prussia would exploit "to weaken the influence of Austria" in Germany and "to make Austria appear a foreign country." He feared lest "the links which bind Austria to the other States of the Germanic Confederation [would] gradually become loosened and in the end break entirely, thanks to this barrier . . . and to those machina-tions which tend to change a material into a moral and political separation."[21] There were other ways, too, in which Austria did not seem to enjoy as close a partnership with the German States as might have been the case. For ex-ample, in 1828 only five of the seventy-one foreign consulates in Austria were German, as opposed to thirty-two that were Italian. Likewise Austria accredited only four consuls to the German States, compared with twenty-four in Italy.[22] Again, "Austria . . . was tardy in its attempt to establish railway connections with southern or central Germany."[23] The first link was finally opened in 1849 only after years of negotiations and most future develop-ments took place later in the century; however, according to one historian "the great acceleration in later developments merely underlines Austrian in-difference to the forging of durable links with southern and central Ger-many at a time when it matter most, during the early years of the railway age."[24] Finally, foreign students (including German ones) were forbidden to study in Austria after 1825, and after 1829 Austrian students were for-bidden to study abroad.[25] All this has led Katzenstein to conclude that "Pre-occupation with the consolidation of the Empire at home and indifference to the amalgamation of Germany abroad went hand in hand."[26]

Yet, this sort of criticism is misplaced. For a start, Metternich did not desire any amalgamation of the German States nor in fact did the majority of the German princes. Likewise, historians have greatly exaggerated the significance of the *Zollverein* for the development of German unity. In parts of Germany it was simply unpopular; in any case, when it came to the crunch, the majority of its members supported Austria against Prussia (in 1850 and 1866, for example); besides, Austrian industrialists consistently refused to support Austria's entry into it, despite Metternich's and later Bruck's desire that they should do so. Katzenstein is simply wrong to write of an "Austrian quest for isolation".[27] The fact of the matter is that Metternich took it for granted that Austria was the leading German State, by virtue of the active policy against the revolution that she pursued with the support of all the others. The high number of non-Austrian Germans, moreover, who filled the top decision-making posts in the Austrian government (31 percent in the foreign office, 35 percent in the central administration, and 35 percent in the army in 1848[28]) would also have confirmed this. At the level of elitism, therefore, the only one that mattered as far as Metternich was concerned, Austria still enjoyed leading Germany, and her leadership was recognized by the other German States.

There was no room for complacency, however, regarding Austria's position. It *was* being undermined by a number of developments, although not the ones already mentioned. The economic factors of importance here were the following: relative economic backwardness, lack of credit, huge State debt, and balance of payments problems. By 1847, Kolowrat, Metternich's rival and the man in charge of economic and budgetary policy within the Empire, was confessing that, due to lack of funds, nothing could be done to help the poor survive the economic crisis. A large part of the problem, according to Kolowrat, was the cost of the army to support of Metternich's active policy of counterrevolution. This was why the State debt was so high. The trouble was that everybody else knew this, hence Metternich's unpopularity and the run on the banks in 1848 after the declaration of martial law in Lombardy–Venetia. The fall of King Louis Philippe in France and the establishment of a republic there, opening up the prospect of a European war, only further undermined confidence in the Austrian currency. Thus, economically Austria's position was inherently a weak one, especially in comparison with Prussia, which did not suffer from any of these problems. Moreover, despite her military expenditure, Austria also experienced difficulties regarding her armed forces. For a start, they were never as large as they appeared to be on paper–in untroubled times one-third to one-half of them were usually on leave. Miserable levels of pay (for officers and men), appallingly brutal disciplinary measures, nationality problems, and lack of proper training also meant that morale was extremely low. Indeed, when Metternich approached the Archduke Charles in 1830 about a possible campaign against France, the Habsburg military hero advised him to forget the idea. The Emperor himself explained to Radetzky why nothing had happened: "I held a camp this year near Münchendorf where my troops displayed themselves so badly and apathetically, that the Prussians voiced their dissatisfaction. We therefore recognized Louis Philippe as the King of France at the same time as England. *Isolated, I could not undertake war.*"[29] The situation therefore had already arisen and would arise again after 1880; indeed, it really applied throughout the whole of the century. Austria needed Prussian support to act in defence of her own or German interests. Prussia, for her part, could act more on her own. In both 1830 and 1840 (when there was another war scare with France), she offered to contribute more troops to the campaign than Austria. In 1848, moreover, the Tsar would write to her urging the deliverance of Germany. Yet so long as Austria presided over the German Confederation, she would never concede to Prussia the official military command of Germany. The sense of grievance this created on the part of Prussia would one day be portentous, but during the Metternich period, at least, there were few disputes between the two States. Metternich wrote in 1823 what he could have written at any time until 1848: "The mental superiority that we enjoy over the Prussian Government is so decisive that I have yet to see that Government fail to go back on what it has too often advanced with great rapidity and frivolity, once it is sure that our point of view differs from its own."[30] As late as December 1850, even Bismarck could extol the role of Austria in Germany. He said:

> I seek Prussia's honour in this . . . that whatever Prussia and Austria judge sensible and politically right after common and independent reflection, will be carried out jointly by Germany's two protecting powers who enjoy equal rights. It is a rare modesty that people cannot decide to consider Austria a German power . . . but I recognise in Austria the representative and heir of an old German power, which often and gloriously commanded Germany's armies.[31]

Bismarck's tone, however, was not quite the tone of Metternich. If the latter had always worked for a partnership with Prussia in the Confederation and in diplomacy generally against the forces of revolution, he did not have in mind an equal partnership. Bismarck, on the other hand, thought of nothing less, and once he perceived that this was not on the cards, he resolved that Prussia not Austria should dominate Germany. By the end of 1850, however, many others had already reached that conclusion.

The revolutions of 1848 had thrown the whole of Europe into turmoil. There were fears of social and national revolution, as well as hopes of a new dawn. In Central Europe, however, whatever the initial fears of social revolution, the basic issue soon became a dynastic one. Which dynasty was to rule in Italy, in Hungary, and finally, in Germany? In Italy and Hungary, the issue was resolved by force of arms in favor of the Habsburgs. In Germany, a military decision was avoided only at the last moment by the climb-down of Prussia at Olmütz in December 1850. The story leading up to this is well known, but a few remarks should be made here. That there would have to be some kind of decision in Germany was made inevitable by the actions of the Frankfurt Assembly, whose constitutional committee in October 1848 voted that any State which desired to belong to a united Germany might only retain a connection with non-German territories through a personal union of its head of State. This meant that the Habsburg Monarchy would have to be dissolved if German unity were to be attained – a price that neither the Austrian delegates nor the Austrian government was willing to pay. Nor were they willing to back a compromise worked out by the President of the Assembly, Heinrich von Gagern, which foresaw a united Monarchy linked loosely with a united Germany. Matters came to a head, however, in 1849 when Schwarzenberg dissolved the Kremsier Reichstag and imposed a constitution on the Empire that made it a centralized and unitary state. This meant that Austria could only join a new, united Germany, so long as her non-German territories were also included. It postulated, in fact, a Greater Austria, rather than a Greater Germany. The result was that the crown of Germany was offered by the Assembly to the king of Prussia, who nevertheless rejected it. He believed that he could only accept it from his peers – Germany's kings and princes. And when he arranged for them to do this – through the so-called Erfurt Union – the struggle for mastery in Germany began.

Austria's attitude to the Erfurt Union scheme was quite simple. She was not going to allow Friedrich Wilhelm IV of Prussia to wear some new version of the German crown that had belonged to the Habsburgs for a thousand years. She would not, in short be expelled from Germany. Yet, what did Schwarzenberg propose instead? At first he merely recalled the Germanic Confederation into life as a counter to the Erfurt Union. The clash between these two bodies then took place over events in Hesse-Kassel. The outcome was the Prussion climb-down at Olmütz, when the Prussian statesman Manteuffel agreed to dissolve the Erfurt Union, demobilize the Prussian army, and meet with all the German princes at Dresden, under Austria's presidency, to discuss Germany's future. It was here that Schwarzenberg and Bruck, his trade minister, made their famous bid to create a *Reich of seventy millions*. Austria, in short, demanded that all her territories be allowed to enter both the Confederation and the *Zollverein* and that the executive of the Confederation be reorganized to ensure an anti-Prussian majority. There is much debate concerning the motives behind these proposals, particularly Schwarzenberg's, yet the point to note is that they were never implemented. All Schwarzenberg secured was a return to the status quo and confimation that the German States would not accept the whole of Austria as German territory. Nonetheless, a treaty was signed between Austria and Prussia that committed both to oppose revolution, and in 1853, after Schwarzenberg's death, a commercial treaty was signed between Austria and the *Zollverein*, which allowed free access to 70 percent of Austrian goods, the rest of them entering with tariffs averaging only 7 percent.[32] The final outcome of the economic negotiations of this period was therefore much better than historians have traditionally allowed. Yet, the political legacy of 1848 was to prove ominous.

Here, the results were not as good as they looked. Despite the victories achieved in Italy, Hungary, and Germany, the outcome was merely the return to the status quo, save that there was now huge discontent in Hungary and Italy and resentment in Prussia and elsewhere. All this meant huge economic costs for an already overburdened economy, since large armies of occupation and inflated civil services were needed to run large parts of the Monarchy. The Empire's new monarch was Franz Joseph, a boy of eighteen when he succeeded to the throne in December 1848, for whom participation in the Italian and Hungarian campaigns had brought both an overweening sense of dignity and an overconfidence in the abilities of the Austrian army. Schwarzenberg's success over Prussia had also led him to believe that the proper policy to pursue in any crisis was a forceful one.

As is well known, the crises were not long in coming. The first was the Crimean War, the second the Italian War, the third was the crisis over German unification, which subsumed the Danish and Prussian wars. There is no need for us to go into any of the details. The point to note is that in all of these Franz Joseph simply expected the German States (including Prussia for most of the time) to follow his leadership almost blindly. There was never any question of either concessions or flexibility. During the Crimean War, he expected the German States not merely to back his ultimatum to Russia to withdraw from the Danubian Principalities—itself an astonishing decision—but also to back the conditions to be imposed on Russia for ending the war. When Prussia refused—she had already been forced to risk war with Russia for the sake of German unity over territories of no vital interest to her—Franz Joseph wrote to the king of Prussia that he found his lack of support "incredible."[33] The same lack of coordination came in 1859. Now, the Prussians were expected to support Austria in Lombardy-Venetia, to save her from the consequences of yet another ultimatum, sent, naturally without prior notice to Prussia, this time to Sardinia, who turned out to have a secret alliance with France. When Prussian aid was not forthcoming, Franz Joseph wrote to his mother, "our position is difficult . . . we have a numerically superior, very brave enemy . . . to whom even the most despicable means are welcome, who has revolution as his ally . . . we are everywhere betrayed in our own country. . . . I hope that perhaps after all Germany and that ignominious scum of Prussia will come to our aid at the last moment."[34] Prussia did mobilize but too late to prevent Austria's defeat.

In view of Austria's dependence on Prussian diplomatic and military aid, it might have been wise for her to have offered some inducements. Yet, despite Prussia's claims to the military command in Germany, Franz Joseph was willing to offer her only what he had offered his Italian subjects: absolutely nothing. The differences in outlook between the two powers are summarized perfectly in the memoranda prepared for a meeting between Franz Joseph and the Prince Regent of Prussia in 1860. The Prussian one included the following passage: "It is well to be clear that it is Austria who needs help, whereas Prussia can easily find allies and is not dependent on Austrian help. . . . If . . . Austria asks us to regard an attack on the Mincio as an act of war (i.e., if France and Sardinia were to attack Venetia), then we would have to explain the reasons which prevent us from complying with this request if our aspirations in Germany are not taken into account."[35] The equivalent Austrian memorandum ran:

> The Prince Regent must understand that the Imperial Court, even with the best will to further the influence, the prestige and the very power of Prussia, cannot but feel the most legitimate reluctance at this juncture in sacrificing its rights and its position in Germany. Austria has fought honourably against Germany's hereditary enemy, has suffered losses and money, has had to sacrifice a province in Italy, has seen the minor branches of the Imperial House being illegally dethroned in the peninsula: and now she is expected to retrace her steps in Germany too! The Prince must understand, as a friend of Austria, that he cannot ask such a thing, which would have a disastrous effect internally for the Habsburg Monarchy and cause it to lose face throughout Europe.[36]

Franz Joseph, instead, made a bid to increase his own prestige by attempting to secure the German Crown again for Austria with the support of the German Princes in 1863. This maneuver, however, was defeated by Bismarck, who since the early 1850s had decided to expel Austria from Germany and succeeded in doing so in 1866. With Prussia's victory at König-graetz, therefore, followed by the proclamation of the German Empire in 1871, the first part of the Austrian Idea, came to an end. Henceforth, the role of German-Austrians could only be to dominate the other nationalities of the Habsburg Monarchy. Their task for Germandom would now be restricted to their self-proclaimed civilizing mission in Eastern Europe and the Balkans.

THE AUSTRIAN IDEA, 1866–1918

Yet, things went wrong. In the first place, the new constitutional arrangements agreed to by Franz Joseph meant that the German-Austrians lost control of the Monarchy. The *Ausgleich* of 1867 gave control of Hungary and all its inhabitants to the Magyars. This meant that the Germans, for the most part, could expect to lord it over only the Czechs. Yet, even here, they lost control. So strong was Czech resistance to German hegemony that the dynasty made concessions to them: the franchise was extended; a separate Czech university was created in Prague; the citizens of Bohemia were even allowed to communicate with the bureaucracy in Czech. Then in 1897 came the crunch. In order to secure agreement with the Hungarians over the renewal of the so-called economic *Ausgleich*, the imperial government under Count Badeni agreed to make the Czech language equal with German in the bureaucracies of Bohemia and Moravia. This meant that German civil servants there would have to learn Czech, something that threatened the livelihood and ambitions of millions of families. German Austria revolted. There were riots in every German town, many of which had to be put down by force. In Parliament, obstructionism became the order of the day. Worse still, Berlin intervened on the German-Austrian side, so that Pan-Germanism acquired support. Badeni's ordinances were, therefore, withdrawn. Austria's German population could still retain its priviliged position within Cisleithania, but never again would it trust the dynasty to look after its interests in the old, automatic fashion. Meanwhile, the Empire, as has been seen, was forced to rely on German support in foreign affairs and in 1914 decided on war, partly because it was afraid that German support over the Balkans might not be forthcoming in the future.

By the First World War, therefore, the Austrian Idea was looking very threadbare. No longer did the Monarchy have any role to play in German affairs; it even required German support to fulfill its self-styled, civilizing role in the Balkans. The First World War would show how totally dependent it had become on German arms. Meanwhile, in domestic affairs, too, the predominant position of the German population in the western part of the Monarchy could no longer be taken for granted. The Linz Program of 1882 – a call by German nationalist politicians of left, right, and center to separate Dalmatia, Galicia, and the Bukovina from the hereditary German-speaking provinces and to make German the sole official language in the rest of Cisleithania – had already indicated the growing mistrust between German-Austrians and their governments. The Pan-German agitation of von Schönerer, who toasted the Hohenzollerns in the Reichstag and called upon the Germans of the German Empire to invade the Monarchy to save their German-speaking brethren within it from Pan-Slavism, was a much cruder reminder of the same. However, the withdrawal of the Badeni ordinances and German support over the Bosnian crisis restored German faith in the Monarchy to a certain degree before 1914. So, too, did electoral compromises with the Slavs in Moravia (1905), and the Bukovina (1911) which seemed at least to stabilize the German position and offered the hope of creating precedents for a similar deal in Bohemia. Finally, the conclusion of an economic compromise with Hungary in 1907, which was unusually satisfactory from the Austrian point of view, also served to restore faith in the Monarchy among its German population. However, in spite of all these developments, the Austrian Idea was no longer credible. The German-speaking population of the Monarchy might still wish to have the best of both worlds, but in fact, they depended on imperial Germany to safeguard their position both internally and externally, whatever their loyalty to the Habsburgs. Franz Joseph himself realized this and in his will instructed his daughter to keep her personal fortune in Berlin, just in case the Monarchy did not survive his death.[37]

Imperial Germany naturally was aware of this situation, although there was no concern to absorb the Monarchy in any hurry. Straightforward absorption, in any case, would bring the same problem that now faced the Habsburgs—what to do about their Slav subjects? The feelings of the future Emperor Wilhelm II on Austria were discovered in 1887 by the Archduke Rudolph, who reported them to the Austrian military attaché in Berlin: "he remarked that things were going well only in Prussia, in Austria the whole State was rotten, near to dissolution, that it would break up, that the German provinces would fall like ripe fruit into Germany's lap, that [Austria], as an insignificant duchy, would become even more dependent on Prussia than Bavaria was."[38] Wilhelm had added: "The Emperor of Austria, can, if he wishes live out his life as an insignificant monarch in Hungary. Prussia will do nothing to bring this about quickly, it will happen in any case by itself." In 1898, German Chancellor Bülow made the same point. It was in Germany's interest, he claimed, to preserve Austria-Hungary, and he stressed

> That interest demands of us, that we take care not to encourage destructive tendencies in Austria, whether they come from the Czech, Polish or *German* side. The German Austrians should be in no doubt that so long as their struggle for German interests concerns preserving Germandom as a cement for the internal cohesion and future existence of the Austrian State in its present guise, we shall support their efforts to the greatest extent, but they should have to reckon with our opposition, should they take as their objective, the separation of the German parts from Austria and a return to the situation before 1866.[39]

On a popular level, however, most Reich Germans simply did not think about their Austrian counterparts.[40] Passau in Bavaria declared itself the most easterly German city. Theodor Mommsen joked that Bavarians were halfway between Austrians and human beings. Imperial German factory owners in Bohemia had no objections to employing Czech labor. Only the imperial Pan-Germans kept hoping for amalgamation—for example, R. Tannenberg, in his 1911 study, *Greater Germany* (*Grossdeutschland*). With the First World War, however, Pan-German ideas would grow in strength, and after 1918, with the dissolution of the Monarchy, few alternatives would be available. Only the Allies would be able to resist their implementation— and only then until 1938.

NOTES

1. Brigitte Hamann, "Die Habsburger und die deutsche Frage im 19. Jahrhundert" in Heinrich Lutz and Helmut Rumpler (eds.), *Österreich und die deutsche Frage im 19. und 20. Jahrhundert. Probleme der politisch-staatlichen und soziokulturellen Differenzierung im deutschen Mitteleuropa* (Munich, 1982), pp. 212–30, quote from p. 225.

2. Quoted by W. W. Gottlieb, *Studies in Secret Diplomacy During the First World War* (London, 1957), p. 263.

3. Ibid., p. 277.

4. Ibid.

5. Adam Wandruszka, "Grossdeutsche und kleindeutsche Ideologie, 1840–1871" in Robert A. Kann and Friedrich Prinz (eds.), *Deutschland und Österreich: ein bilaterales Geschichtsbuch* (Vienna and Munich, 1980), pp. 110–42, quote from p. 113.

6. Quoted in Berthold Sutter, "Die politische und rechtliche Stellung der Deutschen in Österreich, 1848 bis 1918," in A. Wandruszka and P. Urbanitsch (eds.), *Die Habsburgermonarchie 1848–1918*, vol. III/I, *Die Völker des Reiches* (Vienna, 1980), pp. 154–339, quote from p. 164.

7. Sutter, ibid., p. 158. The expression *geistiges Ausland* is quoted by Peter J. Katzenstein, *Disjointed Partners, Austria and Germany since 1815* (Berkeley, Los Angeles and London, 1977), p. 52.

8. Katzenstein, ibid., p. 59.

9. Sutter, p. 161.

10. The quote appears to be apocryphal but is used in all the standard textbooks.

11. Hamann, p. 222.

12. Ibid., p. 224.

13. Sutter, p. 159.

14. Hamann, p. 215.

15. Sutter, pp. 161–62. He does not believe that Metternich, however, believed in "Germanization."

16. This is the theme of Katzenstein's book.

17. Ibid, pp. 111–16.

18. Ibid, 113–14.

19. A. J. P. Taylor, Introduction to Heinrich Friedjung, *The Struggle for Mastery in Germany, 1859–1866* (London, 1935), p. xiii.

20. Quoted in G. de Bertier de Sauvigny, *Metternich and his Times* (London, 1962), pp. 169–70.

21. Quoted in E. L. Woodward, *Three Studies in European Conservatism* (London, 1929), p. 86.

22. Katzenstein, p. 42.

23. Ibid., p. 45.

24. Ibid., p. 47.

25. Ibid., p. 57.

26. Ibid., p. 45.

27. Ibid., p. 42.

28. Ibid., p. 49.

29. J. H. Blumenthal, "Vom Wiener Kongress zum Ersten Weltkrieg," in *Unser Heer, 300 Jahre österreichisches Soldatentum in Krieg und Frieden* (Vienna, Munich and Zürich, 1963), p. 216.

30. Quoted in Bertier de Sauvigny, p. 176.

31. Quoted in Walter Hubatsch, "Österreich und Preussen, 1740–1848," in Kann and Prinz (eds.), p. 109.

32. See Thomas F. Huertas, *Economic Growth and Economic Policy in a Multinational Setting. The Habsburg Monarchy, 1841–1865* (New York, 1977), pp. 34–35.

33. Quoted in Bernhard Unckel, *Österreich und der Krimkrieg. Studien zur Politik der Donaumonarchie in den Jahren 1852–1856* (Lübeck and Hamburg, 1969), p. 140.

34. Quoted in Franz Schnurer (ed.), *Briefe Kaiser Franz Josephs I an seine Mutter, 1838–1872* (Munich, 1930), p. 292.

35. Quoted in Franco Valsecchi, "European Diplomacy and the Expedition of the Thousand: the Conservative Powers," in Martin Gilbert (ed.), *A Century of Conflict, 1850–1950, Essays for A. J. P. Taylor* (London, 1966), pp. 60–61.

36. Ibid.

37. See Adam Wandruszka, "Finis Austriae? Reformpläne und Untergangsahnungen in der Habsburgermonarchie," *Der Österreichisch-Ungarische Ausgleich von 1867. Seine Grundlagen und Auswirkungen* (Munich, 1968), pp. 112–23.

38. Quoted in Georg Markus, *Der Fall Redl* (Vienna, 1984), p. 109.

39. Quoted in Stephan Verosta, *Theorie und Realität von Bündnissen, Heinrich Lammasch, Karl Renner und der Zweibund (1897–1914)* (Vienna, 1971), p. 190.

40. See Sutter, pp. 203–6.

The Austrian Nazi Party before 1938

Some Recent Revelations

BRUCE F. PAULEY

Since the Second World War it has been fashionable – particularly within Austria – to characterize that country as the "first victim of Nazi aggression." This idea originated in November 1943 with an Allied Declaration in Moscow as a means of encouraging Austria to separate from the Third Reich. The idea was reinforced by the government of the United States when it issued a postage stamp during the war displaying the Austrian flag and calling the country a "captive nation." As a propaganda ploy, at a still critical stage of the war, describing Austria as a Nazi victim had some utility. As a historical fact, however, it was, like the infamous "war guilt clause" (Article 231) of the Treaty of Versailles of 1919, a gross and misleading exaggeration. To be sure, Austria was the first sovereign state taken over by Nazi Germany with the help of the German armed forces. The Moscow Declaration ignored, however, the long history of native Austrian Nazism and the central role the Austrian Nazi party played in the so-called *Anschluss*, or union of Austria and Germany, in March of 1938. Far from being imported or imposed from the outside, Nazism was a thoroughly Austrian phenomenon, having been founded in the Habsburg Empire, not in Germany. Indeed, its ideology, social composition, structure, and propaganda were not even unique within the Austrian political scene.[1]

Not only did Nazism in Austria precede the *Anschluss*, it also antedated the establishment of the First Republic in 1918. Georg Ritter von Schönerer (1842–1921), who is often cited as the father or perhaps the grandfather of Nazism, was an ardent advocate of two of its more important ingredients: Pan-Germanism and violent anti-Semitism.[2] Like Hitler, Schönerer used the title *Führer* and considered himself a messiah; in his case, his mission was to save the German-Austrians from denationalization.[3] Even his followers anticipated the groups that would follow the Nazi banner after the Great War: the middle and lower-middle classes who felt threatened by industrialization and Jewish competition, and university students who saw their hopes of entering the liberal professions blocked by well-established Jews.[4] Schönerer's inability to capture the support of the two largest social groups in the Habsburg Empire, the peasants and the factory workers, condemned his movement to the status of a tiny minority. Nevertheless, more than any one else, he was responsible for radical, racial anti-Semitism penetrating both the masses and the intellectual élite by the turn of the century.

The role of direct forerunner of the Austrian Nazi party belongs not to Schönerer's Pan-German party but instead to the German Workers' Party. Founded in 1903, it was one of many parties that profited from the nationalistic clash of German and Czech workers in Bohemia. Even after the party enlarged its name in May 1918 to German National Socialist Workers' Party (DNSAP), it continued to appeal to a lower-middle class population consisting of government employees such as railroad workers, artisans, academically trained professionals, and after the World War I, veterans.[5] Other civil servants hard hit by inflation or among the 25,000 pensioned off in the austerity measures of Federal Chancellor Ignaz Seipel, joined the DNSAP in late 1922 or early 1923.[6] Geographically, most of the membership was concentrated, especially before the war, in ethnically mixed provinces like Bohemia, Moravia, Austrian Silesia, Styria, Carinthia, Trieste, Carniola, and Küstenland. The exceptions were Upper Austria and especially Salzburg. Because the majority of these provinces were awarded to Czechoslovakia, Yugoslavia, and Italy in the Treaty of St. Germain (1919), only a fraction of the party's membership remained in the new Republic of Austria.

THE EARLY YEARS OF THE PARTY:
GROWTH AND IDEOLOGY

Although the Austrian Nazi Party would benefit in the long run from the economic misery produced by the breakup of the Austrian Empire, especially its effect on the country's middle class, in the short run the Nazis were unable to exploit the situation and grew at only a modest rate. In the first postwar parliamentary elections held in February 1919, the NSDAP could muster just 27,690 votes or a scant 0.78 percent of the almost 3 million cast.[7] Only in the province of Salzburg, where the Nazis garnered 7382 votes,[8] could they regard the results as in any way encouraging. Although the growth of the Austrian Nazi Party was more rapid on a per capita basis than its German counterpart, which had not been founded until January 1919, it was nevertheless disappointing. Not even numerous speaking engagements by leading Nazis, such as Adolf Hitler in 1920 and 1921 and Julius Streicher in 1923, made a dramatic difference.[9]

The Nazis' lack of success can be attributed in part to their relatively late arrival on the Austrian political scene. The country's two most important parties, the Social Democratic Workers' Party (SDAP) and the Christian Social Party (CSP), had both been founded about 1890 and consistently attracted around 75 percent of the vote in parliamentary elections between 1919 and 1930. The SDAP appealed to skilled industrial workers and intellectuals, especially Jewish intellectuals, and the CSP drew its strength from the Roman Catholic peasantry and petty bourgeoisie. The remaining 25 percent was divided among various Pan-German parties with the lion's share usually going to the Greater German People's Party (GDVP).

Perhaps even more crucial to the Nazis' frustrations during the 1920s was the absence of any originality in the Party's ideology. Until 1933, all the political parties of Austria advocated a union with Germany, albeit with varying degrees of enthusiasm,[10] the CSP being the most tepid and the GDVP the most enthusiastic.

Anti-Semitism, whether religious, racial, or cultural, was also no monopoly of the Nazis. To be sure, the SDAP confined its anti-Semitism to "Jewish capitalists."[11] The official CSP programs of 1926 and 1932 objected to the "destructive" and revolutionary influence of the Jews in both intellectual and economic affairs,[12] but the party usually tolerated Jews who had converted to Catholicism.[13]

When it came to racial anti-Semitism, however, the Nazis could scarcely surpass the virulence of the GDVP and the League of anti-Semites (Anti-Semitenbund).[14] According to the GDVP's official program of 1920, the Jews were to be treated as a separate nation and their influence over the country's economic and public life was to be greatly reduced.[15]

At most, the Nazis were merely somewhat more boisterous in voicing their objections to "Jewish influence" in comparison to other anti-Semitic groups as was seen, for example during the Nazi-led demonstrations against the meeting of the World Zionist Congress in Vienna in July 1925.[16] Even the Nazis' love of uniforms and marching, and their hatred of democracy and Marxism could be matched by the paramilitary Heimwehr (Home Guard).[17]

DIVISION AND DEBTS, 1923–1929

After reaching a early peak around August 1923, the Austrian Nazi Party entered a long period of decline and stagnation that did not end until 1930. The Party's fate in these years and beyond was closely tied to that of its brother party in Germany. Thus, the failure of the Beer Hall Putsch in Munich in November 1923 had a profound impact on the Austrian party. Austrian Nazis provided refuge for top Nazis fleeing from Munich such as Hermann Göring, Hermann Esser, Ernst Hanfstängl, and Alfred Rosenberg. For a time, the Nazi newspaper of Salzburg, *Volksruf,* was smuggled into Bavaria and illegal Nazi propaganda was organized in the city of Mozart.[18] If the Austrians expected Hitler's gratitude for this assistance, however, they were soon to be disappointed.[19] Although not suffering such catastrophic losses as the German Nazis, the Party did decline in 1924, especially in Salzburg.[20] On the other hand, it picked up some support in local elections held in Styria in May of the same year.[21] Being heavily in debt the Party lacked money for effective propaganda during the 1920s. Only at the end of February 1925, two months after Hitler's release from prison, did attendance at Nazi meetings momentarily improve. For example, 1,700 people turned out to hear Julius Streicher speak in Vienna on 12 March.[22]

If the decline in the Party's fortunes after the Beer Hall Putsch can be traced to Germany, much of the reason for the Party's stagnation between 1923 and 1930 had strictly domestic origins. Foremost among the woes was the split in 1925–26 over the question of whether or not to accept Adolf Hitler's dictatorial leadership. About half the Party, generally those who were younger and more academically trained, enthusiastically supported the Führer, whereas older members, most of whom were government employees and skilled workers, continued to follow the democratically elected Austrian leader, Karl Schulz.[23]

Between 1926 and 1931, the Hitlerian faction of the Austrian Nazi Party (known as the Hitler-Bewegung [HB] or Movement), mostly vegetated in a *führerlos* condition. Hitler almost certainly preferred this arrangement so that his own authority would not be challenged again by a powerful native leader the way it had been between 1923 and 1926 by Karl Schulz and his predecessor, the Viennese lawyer Dr. Walter Riehl. So for five years the Austrian Nazis had no *strong* centralized leadership and sometimes no centralized leadership at all. In 1928 Alfred Proksch, the Gauleiter of Upper Austria, was promoted to business manager of the Hitler Movement and in 1930 became its administrative head but with no political authority. Probably his only important achievement was liquidating a party debt of 30,000 schillings (about $3750).[24]

FRAUENFELD, HABICHT, AND THE
NAZI RESURGENCE, 1930–1933

Fortunately for the Austrian Nazis, local success did not entirely depend on a strong central leadership. As in Germany, there was an elaborate party hierarchy, which gave local leaders, especially the Gauleiter, considerable powers. One of the more successful of these local leaders was Alfred Frauenfeld, who was confirmed by Hitler as Gauleiter of Vienna in January 1930.

With the help of 2000 political leaders in the twenty-one districts of Vienna, Frauenfeld pursued his new task with seemingly inexhaustible energy. In three years he participated in over 1000 propaganda meetings, about 140 of which were in Germany. A one-time actor, he boasted that he did not give dry lectures but was careful to spice up his speeches with anecdotes and jokes while describing Nazi accomplishments. He also used his severance pay as a bank official to found an official party newspaper, *Der Kampfruf*, in 1930. By 1932 he had established four daily and four weekly newspapers in *Gau Wien* and had twenty-five editors working for him whose only source of income was their unemployment benefits.[25] Prior to the critical local elections of April 1932, Frauenfeld organized as many as thirty meetings a day.[26] The Gauleiter's efforts, along with the impact of the Great Depression, produced spectacular results; the Nazi vote in Vienna rose from 27,000 in the national parliamentary elections in November 1930 to over 201,000 in April 1932. Still more evidence of the growing popularity in Vienna came in the fall when Frauenfeld organized a Gauparteitag, or local party rally, in which perhaps as many as 150,000 spectators (by his own estimate) attended the final demonstration.[27]

Frauenfeld's impressive achievements, however, only aroused the envy of the other Austrian Gauleiter. Although the Reichsleiter of the NSDAP in Munich, Gregor Strasser, along with Hitler Youth leader Baldur von Schirach, favored elevating Frauenfeld to state leader (Landesleiter) of the whole Austrian party in March 1931, Hitler preferred keeping the Austrian Nazi headquarters in "racially pure" Linz, where it had been since 1928. According to Hitler, out of a population of 1.8 million in Vienna, only 800,000 were Germans. "The rest [were] Czechs, Jews, and Polacks."[28]

Consequently, as a compromise, Strasser chose Theo Habicht of Wiesbaden to be the new leader (Landesgeschäftsführer, later Landesinspekteur) of the Austrian Nazi Party in July 1931. The disappointed Frauenfeld wrote years later that "Habicht's appointment was a psychological mistake about which he [Habicht] could do nothing. Austrians are a visual people . . . the outward appearance of Habicht was undoubtedly disadvantageous. I have to say, [however], that Habicht was not only very intelligent, but also of extraordinarily high character, dutiful, and personally, brave."[29]

Although far from universally liked, during his three-year administration, Habicht gave the Austrian Nazi party the strong leadership and the direction it had so desperately needed. Within a few months he reorganized the Party along German lines by dividing the central administration (Landesleitung) into eight agencies for the formulation of economic, agricultural and labor policies, and for the management of party leadership, legal affairs, finance, recruitment, and propaganda. This organization was then repeated for the seven Austrian *Gaue*, 110 districts (*Bezirksleitungen*), and the almost infinite number of *Ortsgruppen, Sprengl,* and *Zellen* throughout the Alpine State. With Hitler's approval, Habicht also moved the central offices of the Hitler Youth, SA, and the SS from Vienna to Linz.[30]

PROPAGANDA AND PROGRESS

Habicht and Frauenfeld were not the only ones involved in political and propagandistic activities during the critical Depression years of the early 1930s. According to a police report some eighty Nazi speakers came to Austria from Germany between 1927 and September 1932. Many of these men were personally invited by Frauenfeld, who had close connections with major German Nazi leaders. Josef Goebbels, for example, told a Viennese crowd in November 1931 that former Federal Chancellor Ignaz Seipel was a "traitor to his people and country," presumably for signing the Geneva Protocols which extended for ten years the Allied prohibition of an Austro-German Anschluss.[31]

One major Nazi leader in Germany who did *not* visit Austria in these years was Adolf Hitler. It was not, however, because he was unwanted. In May 1932, Frauenfeld broached the idea to Habicht of inviting Hitler to speak at the Vienna Gauparteitag scheduled for that fall. Frauenfeld was sure that 300,000 Viennese would turn out to hear the Führer; that show of strength in turn would force Dollfuss to hold new parliamentary elections.[32]

The possibility of a visit by Hitler placed the Austrian government in an awkward position. Hitler had been forbidden entry into Austria since 1924, ostensibly because of his uncertain nationality but in reality because of his radical politics. Although the Austrian Nazi Party had been trying since 1927 to obtain permission for Hitler to speak in Austria, he had been allowed only two unofficial entries: to visit the grave of his niece (Geli Raubal) in September 1931 and to attend a concert in Salzburg in his honor in 1932, a visit that never materialized.

But conditions were far different in the summer of 1932 than they had been in 1924. Hitler was now the leader of the largest party in Germany rather than a small and obscure one. It was possible that he might one day

become the Reich Chancellor of Germany and would recall a snub by the
Austrian government with unpleasant consequences for the latter. It would
have been doubly hard to deny entry to Hitler after a visit to Vienna by
the Soviet commissar, Maxim Litvinov, in November 1932. Moreover, to
deny Hitler the right to speak in Vienna could have resulted in stormy
demonstrations and a propaganda victory for the Nazis, or so the government reasoned.[33]

At a cabinet meeting held on 20 August the minister of justice and
future Federal Chancellor, Kurt von Schuschnigg, favored allowing Hitler
to enter the country but forbidding a speech "on the grounds of public security, peace and order." The cabinet eventually agreed to let Federal Chancellor Dollfuss to make the final decision.[34] Dollfuss must have been cool
to the idea, however, because Hitler never attended the party rally.

When in March 1933 the Austrian government forbade the Nazis from
holding political meetings, the Landesleitung in Linz sent explicit instructions
to Gaupropagandaleiter on how to hold "nonpartisan lecture evenings." In the
provincial capitals and larger towns such talks were to be held on historical,
philosophical, or economic subjects. Only speakers thoroughly familiar
with these themes were to be used. Through comparisons between Austria
and Germany, satire, and humor, the talks would achieve their propagandistic purpose. The opposition press was to be closely monitored for all signs
of differences within the government and these differences were to be exploited. All economic problems were to be blamed on the Dollfuss government. The accomplishments of Nazis in public office were to be publicized
in door-to-door propaganda and leaflets. Their public speeches were also
to be reprinted in Nazi newspapers and quoted in posters if they had propagandistic value. Radio speeches from Germany were also to be reprinted in
Nazi newspapers and whenever possible broadcast into inns and private
homes. Personal canvassing (which the Nazis regarded as one of their most
effective forms of propaganda) was also to be pursued as much as possible.[35]

These efforts at "public enlightenment" were not made in vain. Whereas
they had gained a mere 111,000 votes in the parliamentary elections of
1930, or just 3 percent of all votes cast, in the provincial and municipal
elections of April 1932 the Nazis attracted 378,000 of the 3,149,000 votes
cast, of 16.4 percent,[36] mostly at the expense of the GDVP. A year later,
the Nazis achieved still more impressive results when they amassed 41.2 percent of the votes in municipal elections held in Innsbruck and 37.6 percent
in nearby Landeck. Consequently, Gau Tyrol-Vorarlberg in westernmost
Austria jumped from last to third place in membership among the seven
Austrian *Gaue*.[37] Only in Upper Austria, where Christian Socials and Social
Democrats continued their tacit alliance, did the Nazis fail to make significant progress by the spring of 1933.[38]

MEMBERSHIP AND SOCIAL COMPOSITION

Although the Austrian Nazi Party grew rapidly between 1930 and 1933, and somewhat more slowly in subsequent years, it should not be imagined that new members always came from the same social groups as the *Altkämpfer* (old-time fighters). The Nazis grew at their fastest pace during the first half of 1933, after Hitler's takeover of power in Germany on 30 January and before Federal Chancellor Dollfuss outlawed the party on 19 June. During this period their membership rolls grew from 43,000 to 68,000.[39] During the next thirteen months the party added only 20,000 members. From 1934 to July 1936, during which time the Party remained outlawed and many of its members imprisoned, growth was minimal. However, in the final twenty-one months before the *Anschluss* another 60,000 Austrians joined the party.[40]

The early party had consisted largely of low-level government workers; a decade later, however, it was more common to find professionals, shopkeepers, and skilled workers.[41] Austrian historian Gerhard Botz has calculated that in 1933, 3 percent of the Austrian Nazis were university-age students, 6 percent were members of the free professions, 17 percent were civil servants, 14 percent were employees, 33 percent were laborers, and 8–10 percent were independently employed or peasants.[42] Private employees who were somewhat overrepresented in the Party's early years, declined in number after 1936.

The biggest change after the outlawing of the Party occurred among peasants and workers, who suffered from the German trade boycott after May 1933 and from extremely high unemployment. Their numbers increased substantially, whereas those of civil servants (who feared being dismissed from their jobs for belonging to an illegal party) and employees engaged in trade and commerce declined.[43] Unemployed factory workers became increasingly important to the Party, especially after the outlawing of the Social Democratic Party in February 1934. However, the Austrian NSDAP remained a predominantly middle-class party.[44]

Although not enormous in absolute numbers, university students and members of the liberal professions were important elements of the Austrian Nazi Party since the founding of the Hitler-Bewegung in 1926, being four to six times overrepresented.[45] In student government elections held in February 1931, Nazi students won 1164 of 2417 votes cast at the Technical Institute; 530 of 947 votes at the Institute for World Trade, and 2335 of 6249 votes at the University of Vienna. At all three institutions the percentage of eligible voters participating was over 75.[46] Nazi students were frequently ringleaders of vicious assaults on Jewish students. There was so much terror at Austrian universities that lectures were frequently interrupted and Jewish students seriously injured.[47] If anything, Nazi activities may have been even more common at the University of Innsbruck than in Vienna. Until 1933, 60 to 65 percent of the students in the Tyrolean capital were from Germany although they declined to a still substantial 37 percent in 1934.[48]

Not just students but young people in general were disproportionately numerous in Nazi ranks. Seventy-three percent of SA and SS men in Austria were under the age of twenty-five, and 87 percent were under thirty.[49] For all Austrian Nazis, the average age in 1931 was 29.4 although that figure tended to increase between 1930 and 1938.[50] As in other fascist movements of interwar Europe, most Austrian Nazis had been born between 1893 and 1912.[51]

If young people, especially students, along with urban professionals, peasants, and unemployed workers were represented in the Party far beyond their percentage of the general population during the 1930s, employed workers, practicing Catholics, and women were underrepresented.[52] Employed workers usually remained loyal to the Social Democratic Party, even after it was outlawed in 1934, or at most shifted their allegiance to the Communist Party. Believing Catholics continued to support the governments of Dollfuss and his successor, Kurt von Schuschnigg, although there were exceptions to this rule; the women were far more likely to support the CSP than the NSDAP.

Until 1932, fewer than 10 percent of Nazi Party members were women; by 1938 it was still only about one in four.[53] The Nazis did considerably better with women in elections than in membership rolls. Even so, in the parliamentary elections of October 1920 there were only 850 female voters for every 1000 males who voted for the Nazis.[54] In the April elections of 1932 in Vienna just 14.3 percent of female voters cast ballots for the Nazis compared to virtually 17 percent for the males.[55] An important reason for the reluctance of many women to vote for the NSDAP was probably the banning of women from leadership roles in both the German and Austrian parties in 1921.[56]

HITLER, DOLLFUSS, AND THE OUTLAWED AUSTRIAN NAZI PARTY, 1933–1934

Although there were many parallels between the German and Austrian Nazi Parties up to the beginning of 1933, the similarities largely ended with Hitler's appointment as Reich Chancellor on 30 January 1933. On a per capita basis the electorate of the Austrian Party was not much smaller than that of its German partner in the spring of 1933. Nevertheless, the Austrian government under Federal Chancellor Engelbert Dollfuss refused to step aside in favor of the Nazis or even accede to their demand for new parliamentary elections. Indeed, in early March Dollfuss allowed the Austrian Parliament to "dissolve itself" and thereafter ruled by decree. When the Nazis responded by bombing government installations and public officials, Dollfuss counterattacked by arresting almost 2500 Nazi leaders on the mere suspicion of treason, sending hundreds of them to prison, and sealing Nazi offices throughout the country.[57] Finally, the party was outlawed on 19 June and the Austrian civil and military services were purged of Nazi party members and sympathizers.

Hitler, who had hoped that the Austrian Nazi party could achieve power on its own without German intervention, felt constrained on 26 May 1933 to put pressure on the Austrian government by ordering a trade boycott with Austria and virtually prohibiting German tourism in the Alpine Republic by charging 1000 Reichsmarks for an exit visa from the Third Reich. In the Tyrol, traditionally heavily dependent on German tourism, the number of overnight visitations dropped from 760,000 in 1932 to 340,000 in 1933, most of them undoubtedly coming before the imposition of the 1000-reichsmark fee.[58] Only Upper Austria, which had a surplus of productive agricultural land and not much foreign trade, managed to survive the middle 1930s in reasonably good economic shape. In 1937, the last full pre-*Anschluss* year, unemployment still stood at only 7.13 percent compared to 20.3 percent federally.[59]

The German trade boycott seriously damaged the already pathetically weak Austrian economy, and the bombing of government electrical works, bridges, and railroad lines did considerable damage. Neither policy, however, seriously undermined the Dollfuss government. The acts of terror may have actually had the opposite effect.

Throughout the first half of 1934 the position of Federal Chancellor Dollfuss appeared to the Nazis to be getting steadily stronger. In a speech to the Reichstag on the first anniversary of his coming power, Hitler declared that a solution of the Austrian problem by force was out of the question. The Austrian Nazis would have to make their own way.[60] In February, Dollfuss easily crushed a three-day uprising by the Social Democrats' paramilitary Republican Defense Corps (Schutzbund).[61] In early March, Hitler ordered a new policy according to which "all direct attacks on the Austrian Government in the press and radio [were] to be strictly avoided."[62] Finally, in a meeting between Hitler and Mussolini in Venice on 14 June, the Duce refused to back away from his support of the Austrian chancellor.[63] By the summer of 1934, with elections abolished and the NSDAP and its propaganda outlawed, the Austrian Nazis were growing increasingly frustrated at their inability to achieve power. The only alternate route to success, for many Austrian Nazis, appeared to be a putsch.

Rumors of a putsch first reached the German Legation in Vienna on 26 July 1933, one day less than a year before a putsch was actually attempted and only five weeks after the Austrian NSDAP had been outlawed.[64] The rumors subsided in the fall and winter months of 1933 and early 1934, only to resume again in late January. By May, radical members of the party, particularly the paramilitary SA and SS formations, wanted action, and they wanted it soon. As mostly unemployed young men, they had no desire, and saw no need, to wait several years while the German evolutionary policy of subtle, subversive propaganda had time to run its course. They were either ignorant of or indifferent to the German requirement of peaceful relations between Germany and Austria until Hitler had time to rebuild the armed forces.

HITLER AND THE JULY PUTSCH:
THE QUESTION OF RESPONSIBILITY

The question of who made the final decision to go ahead with the July Putsch of 1934 has never been definitively answered. Recent revelations, however, make it possible to eliminate most of the mystery. The evidence, on balance, points to Theo Habicht and Alfred Frauenfeld. Since the beginning of the year Habicht's position as de facto leader of the Austrian Nazis had been growing increasingly precarious. He found himself caught between the radical SA, which demanded more action, and relatively moderate individuals like Walter Riehl, who believed Habicht's policies were already too extreme and preferred a strictly native leadership. Even Hitler was unhappy about Habicht's leadership and the recent slow progress of the party.[65] Habicht knew that to cling to power he had to do something quickly and decisively.[66]

Habicht's exact role in the decision-making process remains unclear. Frauenfeld, in his memoirs published posthumously in 1978, maintains that Hitler was kept constantly informed about the putsch plans and that neither he [Frauenfeld] nor Habicht undertook the putsch without Hitler's approval. Frauenfeld, moreover, denied the Nuremberg testimony of Hermann Göring that Habicht deceived Hitler by pretending that the Austrian army would take part in the action: "On the contrary, contact with high army officers established that they were not only sympathetic with the NSDAP, but would also remain neutral during the action and would cooperate in maintaining law and order after the success of the putsch. We wanted and expected nothing more from them than that."[67]

Frauenfeld is scarcely a disinterested witness, however. By arguing that Hitler was kept fully informed of the putsch plans the former Viennese Gauleiter in effect shifted at least part of the blame for the putsch's failure from himself and Habicht to the Führer. Moreover, arguing that some high officers in the Austrian army knew of the putsch plan–which is perfectly plausible–does not prove that they all did. Far from remaining neutral, the Austrian army from the outset actively suppressed the action. Frauenfeld and Habicht may not have deliberately deceived Hitler, but they certainly deceived themselves into thinking they could count on the army's neutrality.

The recently published English-language edition of the memoirs of Hitler's close associate, Otto Wagener, provide fascinating insight into Hitler's thinking about the wisdom of putsches in general. At the time the Führer appointed him SA chief of staff in August 1929, Hitler told him:

> Most especially you must on all accounts prevent the idea from arising . . . that someday the SA itself might be charged with staging a putsch. That is not its purpose. Nor can it be. A putsch requires arms. The SA has no weapons and is not meant ever to obtain any, unless they are issued by the government. Even then it is better that the SA not receive weapons, for its members are not trained in weaponry. Rather, should things come to such a pass, the SA would simply assign the appropriate men to the army of police.[68]

The German historian, Martin Broszat, has pointed out that "Hitler practiced no direct or systematic leadership but from time to time jolted the government or Party into action, supported one or the other initiative of Party functionaries. . . . Thus in all those areas of policy with which Hitler never or seldom bothered, the absolute supremacy of the Führer spawned a growing system of rival power centers, all trying to put forward schemes in the name of Hitler, all trying to get access to him and to get Führer commands to back them up."[69]

Broszat's analysis is confirmed by Wagener who wrote that Hitler "never issued binding instructions on any matter."[70]

Based on this evidence our safest assumption about Hitler's role in the July Putsch is that he did not order it, let alone take the initiative in planning it. On the other hand, he almost certainly knew that something was afoot. By eschewing the issuance of a formal command he probably thought he could dissociate himself if anything went awry. The likelihood of this scenario is again supported by Otto Wagener:

> Hitler had a weakness that was grounded precisely in this manner of working. Whenever anything was carried out on the basis of conversations and general

remarks he claimed its success for himself. . . . But if it was carried out along a different line, he mercilessly put the responsibility on whoever had committed the action. Furthermore, depending on the importance and significance of the matter, especially if it damaged the public welfare or even just public opinion, he drew the necessary conclusions. The person in question was transferred to another position.[71]

THE JULY PUTSCH: COURSE AND CONSEQUENCES

The events of the July Putsch itself are too familiar to deserve more than a brief mention here. In Vienna, 154 members of the SS "Standarte 89", all recently released from the Austrian army because of their Nazi associations, tried to capture Dollfuss and his entire cabinet which was meeting at the Chancellery on the Ballhausplatz. The attempt was foiled, however, when Dollfuss learned of the plot shortly before its implementation, and ordered his cabinet to disperse. The Federal Chancellor himself was mortally wounded, however, under still unexplained circumstances.

Uprisings by the SA were supposed to occur simultaneously in the provinces, but in fact began on 27 July, two days after the putsch had already ended in Vienna. The fighting in Styria and Carintha lasted for three days because the putschists there appear to have been well armed with machine guns and machine pistols and had an ample supply of trucks.[72]

Elsewhere, however, the Nazis were far less prepared. In Upper Austria they had no prior knowledge of Habicht's plans and neither the local SA nor the SS had drawn up any operational plans of their own and in any event had insufficient supplies of arms.[73] The SA and SS of Tyrol and Vorarlberg, which were supposed to come to the aid of the Carinthians, did not even become involved because of the great military superiority of the local Austrian executive and its Heimwehr supporters.[74] Altogether, some 260 people were killed in the putsch, 133 of them Nazis. Thirteen participants were executed in August, and 5,300 tried in courts.[75]

The putsch failed for any number of reasons. Foremost, however, was the overconfidence of Habicht and Frauenfeld in the willingness of the Austrian executive forces to join the putsch or at least stay neutral. They did neither. Equally important was the total lack of coordination between the SA and SS—greatly aggravated by the Röhm Purge fewer than four weeks earlier—and between the paramilitary formations in the provinces and those in Vienna.

For the Austrian Nazi Party the July Putsch was an unmitigated disaster. Of those putschists who did not succeed in fleeing the country, more than five thousand were sent to the Wöllersdorf detention camp near Wiener Neustadt. Moreover, the disclosure of complete membership lists enabled the government to suppress hitherto clandestine Nazi cells and to destroy the party's Political Organization.

The outcome of the putsch was not only materially damaging but also psychologically demoralizing. In secret meetings held in and around Innsbruck in December 1934, Nazis from the provinces angrily accused the Viennese Nazis of making insufficient preparations for the putsch and thus ruining their local organizations. German representatives at the meetings complained about the "spineless behavior of the SA and SS" during the putsch, accusations that were vehemently rejected by the Austrians.[76]

The internal quarrels of the Austrian Nazi Party were made all the worse by Hitler's determination to sever nearly all formal ties between the German and Austrian parties. Habicht was dismissed from his post as Landesinspekteur and the Austrian Landesleitung, which had been in Munich since the Party was outlawed in June 1933, was dissolved.[77] Only the Austrian SS, which remained under the direct control of Heinrich Himmler, and a charitable *Hilfswerk*, retained formal ties with Germany.[78]

The divisions and recriminations of the Austrian Nazi Party proved to be a godsend to the hard-pressed government of the new Federal Chancellor, Kurt von Schuschnigg. With the country's largest political faction, the Social Democrats, thoroughly alienated by the harsh repression of the civil war in February 1934 and by the subsequent prohibition of the party and its trade unions, the government's base of popular support had grown precariously narrow. Only the former members of the now also dissolved Christian Social Party, the country's Roman Catholic hierarchy, 200,000 Jews, especially Jewish war veterans, and the Catholic, pro-Italian wing of the Heimwehr, could be counted on as loyal supporters of the regime. The Heimwehr's military strength proved to be a vital counter force to the Nazis' SA and SS until the Heimwehr was absorbed into the government's Fatherland Front in 1936. United States historian Evan Bukey has made the observation that the Dollfuss-Schuschnigg regime was a throwback to the absolutism of the mid-nineteenth century Habsburg Empire with the important difference, however, that now there was no father figure to replace the emperor and resolve conflicts.[79]

THE ILLEGAL NAZI PRESS

With receiving little material help and still less leadership coming from Germany after the July Putsch, the Austrian Nazis were forced to rely on their own resources. Like the German Nazis after the Beer Hall Putsch, their strategy was to come to power by slowly winning converts through propaganda while renouncing violence.[80]

Because their public meetings were outlawed, the Nazis were forced to rely to a large extent on their underground party press. Newspapers had never been the Nazis' strong suit either in Austria or Germany. Hitler had made it very clear in *Mein Kampf* that he considered the spoken word to be far more effective than the written one.[81] This policy, of course, included newspapers. Although Hitler later softened his contempt of newspapers, it would be safe to say that they remained the stepchild of Nazi propaganda. As late as 1932, the fifty-nine Nazi dailies had a total circulation in Germany and Austria of only 780,000.[82]

In Austria, Nazi newspapers were censored in the spring of 1933 and banned altogether after the Party was outlawed, only to reappear for a time under different names. After the failure of the July Putsch, even these newspapers were temporarily shut down, along with almost every other form of Nazi propaganda, if we can assume that the Tyrolean example is representative.[83] But by April 1935, there were once again eight illegal Gau newspapers, although they sometimes did not appear for months at a time. Every Bezirk also had its own mimeographed paper. In January 1936, all but one of the twenty-one districts of Vienna had their own illegal Nazi newspaper.[84]

The illegal newspapers were strikingly similar. All were produced with a small format, in part because of a scarcity of paper and in part because of a fear that larger newspapers could more easily be discovered; smaller ones were easier to pass from one person to another.[85] In April, a government informant noted that the contents of illegal Nazi newspapers in Vienna were so similar that it was obvious there had to be a common editor.[86] After July 1936, there was an illegal Nazi newspaper, the *Österreichischer Beobachter*, whose 45,000 copies circulated throughout the whole country every week or two. Provincial editions of the *ÖB* also carried news of local interest.[87] Nazi subsidiaries, such at the SA, the Hitler Youth, and the Nationalsozialistische Betriebsorganisationen for workers, all had their own newspaper in the illegal period.[88]

It is far easier to describe Nazi propaganda than it is to evaluate its effectiveness. It would be a mistake, however, to assume that its sole or even primary purpose was to win converts. There can be no doubt, as Austrian officials themselves admitted, that it helped to maintain the morale of the Party members while sowing distrust among government loyalists.[89]

THE TRIUMPH OF THE SS

A reversal in the dismal fortunes of the Austrian Nazi Party following the July Putsch came less from its own exertions than from a revolution in the international constellation. At a time when Germany was still militarily weak it required only a show of strength by the Italian army on the Brenner Pass to discourage Hitler from sending any military help to the Austrian Nazi putschists.

Mussolini's dream of creating an Italian empire in Ethiopia completely changed the balance of power in Central Europe after October 1935. Italy, hampered economically by the sanctions of the League of Nations, became economically and politically dependent on Germany. The quid pro quo was Italy's abandonment of its protectorate over Austria.

This new state of affairs was formalized by the July Agreement in 1936 between Austria and Germany. Austria gained a formal German declaration recognizing Austrian sovereignty, as well as an end to the trade boycott, but Germany gained the right to send propaganda into Austria, the release of most Nazis from detention camps, and a promise that members of the "National Opposition" would be taken into the Austrian government. The Austrian economy benefited from this agreement; but now both Nazi Germany and the Austrian Nazi Party resumed their subversion of the Austrian government and society.[90]

The nineteen-month period between the signing of the July Agreement and the Hitler-Schuschnigg meeting at Berchtesgaden in February 1938 was marked by continued rivalries within the Austrian Party and between it and the parent German NSDAP. Although the period began with the Austrian SA, led by Captain Josef Leopold, controlling a new Landesleitung in Vienna, it ended with the dismissal of Leopold and the triumph of the SS.

The Austrian SS had never been under the jurisdiction of the Political Organization of the Austrian Nazi Party or the Austrian SA; rather it was directly subordinate to Heinrich Himmler. The Austrian SS therefore developed a sense of independence vis-à-vis the Austrian Party. After the July Putsch the SS in Austria was purged of 40 percent of its members by a special commission in Munich. Those who survived the purge were organized into two groups and given three tasks: to maintain a surveillance of all Nazi leaders including those in the Political Organization, SA, and Hitler Youth; to report on political developments and the Austrian security system; and to infiltrate the highest circles of Austrian society. The second SS group, in addition to supporting the first one, was responsible for subverting the army, gendarmerie, and the police.[91]

In January 1937, the six-foot, seven-inch Upper Austrian lawyer and future leader of the German secret police, Ernst Kaltenbrunner, was named by Himmler to be leader of the Austrian SS. As the United States historian Peter Black revealed in his recent biography, Kaltenbrunner had joined the Heimwehr in 1929 because of its anti-Semitic, anti-Marxist, and antidemocratic ideology. After just fifteen months he quit, however, because he found the organization's leadership insufficiently pro-*Anschluss* and too willing to compromise with the system. In 1931, he transferred his allegiance to the Austrian Nazi Party because of its more ardent *völkisch* ideology and charismatic leadership. Membership in the party alone was not enough for the twenty-eight-year-old Kaltenbrunner. In order to be a 100 percent Nazi he also became a member of the SS.[92]

Although Kaltenbrunner's SS career was interrupted by a six-month prison sentence in 1935 for belonging to the illegal organization, his rise to prominence began soon after his release. In part, his success may have resulted from the removal of so many of his Austrian SS superiors by death or imprisonment. He was finally appointed leader of the Austrian SS because his predecessor, Karl Taus, had been unable to keep his subordinates in line. Himmler was convinced that Kaltenbrunner, with his strong personality, would not have the same problem and would therefore be able to prevent a repetition of the kind of fiasco that had occurred in July 1934. Kaltenbrunner, moreover, had already succeeded in establishing good relations with SS leaders and Nazi moderates all over Austria, as well as with major Nazi leaders in Germany. Finally, by early 1937 Himmler had come to regard Kaltenbrunner as an expert in intelligence operations.[93]

Although Kaltenbrunner did not play a major role in the final *Anschluss* drama of February–March 1938, he helped shift the Nazi internal balance of power from the SA to the SS. This transformation can perhaps be said to have begun in July 1937 when Hitler appointed the German industrialist and State Secretary, Wilhelm Keppler, to supervise relations between the German and Austrian Nazis and particularly to keep an eye on Josef Leopold and his SA who were eager to come to power on their own, if necessary by force.[94] This process was completed in late February 1938 when Hitler dismissed Leopold as the Austrian Landesleiter. By lining up with the Carinthian SS leader Friedrich Rainer and the Viennese lawyer and pro-Nazi Arthur Seyss-Inquart, Kaltenbrunner was able to wage a secret campaign in Berlin by enlisting the support of Himmler, Heydrich, Göring, and Keppler, as well as the German Foreign Office, which had never cared for the Landesleiter.[95]

It was not simply his SS rivals, however, which proved to be Leopold's undoing. He was also his own worst enemy by not realizing that he had committed one unforgivable sin: he had defied the Führer by attempting to build up a following of his own. Leopold was not the first or last Nazi to learn that what Hitler "demanded from party members was unconditional and speechless obedience."[96]

THE AUSTRIAN NAZI PARTY AND THE *ANSCHLUSS*

In the final analysis, however, it was not changes within the Austrian Nazi Party alone which ended Austria's independence but the transformation in the international setting which had occurred by early 1938. Germany's rapidly growing military strength made Hitler's foreign policy far less cautious than it had been between 1933 and 1937. Moreover, Mussolini had abandoned his protectorate of Austria, and Britain and France were relatively indifferent to Austria's plight.

Nevertheless, returning to this paper's original thesis, it would be completely false to imagine that the final *Anschluss* was due entirely to German machinations. To be sure, Hitler's intimidation of Schuschnigg at Berchtesgaden on 12 February 1938 and in his 20 February speech to the Reichstag set the *Anschluss* machinery in motion. As a result of the Berchtesgaden agreement Schuschnigg had to release still more imprisoned Nazis and appoint Seyss-Inquart to be Minister of the Interior. Hitler's Reichstag speech gave encouragement to the Austrian Nazis by demanding self-determination for the German-speaking people of Austria and the Sudetenland.

Probably not even Hitler, however, expected the *Anschluss* to come as quickly as it did. Starting in Styria and then spreading to other provinces, Nazi demonstrations took place which neither the Austrian authorities nor even the Nazi leaders could control. Fearing that the whole country would soon be Nazified if he did not do something drastic, Federal Chancellor Schuschnigg, on 9 March, suddenly called for a countrywide plebiscite on the question of Austrian independence. The familiar story of how this was prevented by Hermann Göring, using Seyss-Inquart as his "telephone operator" to pass on demands to Schuschnigg and President Wilhelm Miklas, need not be repeated here. The point is that it was the activities of home-grown Austrian Nazis which compelled Schuschnigg to call for his plebiscite in an act of desperation.

Ironically, however, the Austrian Nazis wanted only the *threat* of a German invasion in order to gain power for themselves. What they got, the actual invasion of 12 March and the complete incorporation of Austria into the Third Reich the next day, was more than most of them had bargained for. Not even Ernst Kaltenbrunner, whose 700 SS-troops were surrounding the Austrian Federal Chancellery at the time of Schuschnigg's farewell radio address, was entirely satisfied with the German invasion and annexation.[97]

FINAL THOUGHTS

Although most Austrian Nazis probably wanted neither the German invasion nor the complete destruction of their country's independence, they had in fact helped to bring about both. Aside from their wanting a certain amount of autonomy for their country so that they could get the choicest administrative positions, the history, ideology, size, and social composition of the Austrian Nazi Party did not differ significantly from its German counterpart.

Indeed, in some respects Nazism in Austria was more deeply rooted and extreme than in Germany. It antedated the founding of the German NSDAP by nearly sixteen years. Like the Party in Germany, it attracted elements of every social class, although there may have been an even higher representation among the intelligentsia than in the Reich. Until at least 1924 it was larger on a per capita basis than the German Party. Its growth in the late twenties was somewhat slower than in Germany, but by the spring of 1933 it had nearly caught up, if the elections in the Tyrol are any indication. Its willingness to resort to terror in 1933 and 1934 needed no prompting from Germany. In fact, Hitler and the German Foreign Office devoted more time to restraining the Austrian Nazis than to provoking them. In their fanatical anti-Semitism the Austrian Party was far ahead of the German Nazis, as was clearly seen at Austrian universities and in the streets of Vienna immediately after the *Anschluss*.

Only in the effectiveness of their leadership did the Austrians not measure up to the Germans. Their most successful leader, Habicht, was from Germany. Their own leaders such as Proksch, Riehl, Schulz, Leopold, and Seyss-Inquart could not command much respect outside their home province or social class. This lack of leadership probably had as much to do with keeping the Austrian Nazis out of power as did the statesmanship or popular support of Federal Chancellors Dollfuss or Schuschnigg.

After 1938, the Austrian Nazis were largely forgotten at home and abroad. By a strange quirk of fate both Hitler and the Allies, not to mention the Austrians themselves, found it politically expedient to credit or blame Germany, rather than the Austrian Nazis, for the *Anschluss*. Not until the Waldheim affair, nearly half a century after the Anschluss, did the world take much note of Austria's Nazi past.

NOTES

Abbreviations

AVA   Allgemeines Verwaltungsarchiv; General Administrative Archive, Vienna
BKA   Bundeskanzleramt; Federal Chancellery, Vienna
DAP   Deutsche Arbeiter-Presse, Vienna

Dötz   *Deutsch-österreichische Tages-Zeitung*, Vienna
IdVF   *Informationsdienst der Vaterländischen Front*, Vienna
NSP   Nationalsozialistische Parteistellen; National Socialist party archives, Gau
       Vienna (located in the AVA)
Vkst   *Volksstimme*, Linz

1. The Austrian Nazi Party is far too broad a topic to cover in any detail in a scholarly article. Rather than seeking comprehensiveness this chapter will therefore emphasize new information derived from the author's recent research and from books which have appeared since 1980 when the author completed research for his book *Hitler and the Forgotten Nazis: A History of Austrian National Socialism* (Chapel Hill, NC, 1981). Those readers seeking a more complete picture of the Austrian Nazi party should consult *Forgotten Nazis* or other works cited in its bibliography.

2. For the best and most recent biography of von Schönerer, see A.G. Whiteside, *The Socialism of Fools: Georg von Schönerer and Austrian Pan-Germanism* (Berkeley, Los Angeles, London, 1975).

3. *Ibid.* pp. 6, 264, 280.

4. *Ibid.*, pp. 43, 311; F.L. Carsten, *Fascist Movements in Austria: From Schönerer to Hitler* (London and Beverly Hills, CA, 1977), p. 19; P. G. Pulzer, *The Rise of Political Anti-Semitism in Germany and Austria* (1964), pp. 279–81.

5. For the most recent studies of the social composition of the Austrian Nazi party, see G. Botz, "Strukturwandlungen des Österreichischen Nationalsozialismus (1904–1945)," in I. Ackerl, W. Hummelberger, and H. Mommsen (eds.), *Politik und Gesellschaft im Alten und Neuen Österreich. Festschrift fuer Rudolf Neck zum 60. Geburtstag* (1981), pp. 163–93; and G. Botz, "Die Österreichischen NSDAP Mitglieder," *Historisch-Sozialwissenschaftliche Forschungen* 9 (1980): 98–136. On the NSDAP in Salzburg, see E. Hanisch, "Zur Frühgeschichte des Nationalsozialismus in Salzburg (1913–1925)," *Mittleilungen der Gesellschaft für Salzburger Landeskunde* 117 (1977):371–410.

6. Botz, "NSDAP Mitglieder," p. 104. On Seipel's economic policies, see K. von Klemperer, *Ignaz Seipel: Christian Statesman in a Time of Crisis* (1972), pp. 179–219, especially p. 217.

7. *DAP*, 22 February 1919, p. 1; G. Botz, "The Changing Patterns of Social Support for Austrian National Socialism (1918)" in S. V. Larsen et al.(eds), *Who Were the Fascists? Social Roots of European Fascism* (1980), p. 202.

8. J. Hawlik, "Die politische Parteien Deutschösterreichs bei der Wahl zur Konstituierenden Nationalversammlung 1919" (Diss., University of Vienna, 1971), p. 485.

9. Hanisch, pp. 403–404; report of Einberger to the Dept. 14 in Vienna, 1 September 1923, BKA Inneres 1923 #52.921, AVA, p. 1.

10. Hanisch, p. 399.

11. G. Fellner, *Antisemitismus in Salzburg 1918–1938* (1979), p. 124.

12. *Ibid.*, pp. 72–73.

13. For the exceptions, see F. Heer, *Gottes erste Liebe: 2000 Jahre Judentum und Christentum; Genesis des österreichischen Katholiken Adolf Hitler* (Munich, 1967), p. 363.

14. Published information on the Antisemitenbund is scarce, but see Fellner, pp. 102, 128, 131–133, and K. Peter, *Der Antisemitismus* (Vienna, 1936), 24 pp.

15. K. Berchtold (ed), *Österreichische Parteiprogramme, 1868–1966* (Vienna, 1967), pp. 70–72.

16. See, for example, *Dötz* for 8, 14, and 23 Aug. and 3 Sept. 1925.

17. For recent general works on the Heimwehr, see C. E. Edmondson, *The Heimwehr and Austrian Politics, 1918–1936* (Athens, GA, 1978), and my own *Hahnenschwanz und Haken-*

kreuz: steirischer Heimatschutz und österreichischer Nationalsozialismus, 1918–1934 (Vienna, Frankfurt, Zürich, 1972).

18. Hanisch, p. 408.

19. *DAP*, 21 August 1926, p. 11.

20. Hanisch, p. 381.

21. *DAP*, 6 June 1934, p. 2.

22. Report with an illegible signature (Schober?) to the BKA Dept. 14 in Vienna. Vienna, 17 March 1925, BKA Inneres 1925, #64135–25, AVA, 5 pp.

23. For details on the party split, see B. Pauley, *Forgotten Nazis*, pp. 38–51.

24. E. B. Bukey, *Hitler's Hometown: Linz, Austria, 1908–1945* (Bloomington, 1986), p. 93.

25. A. E. Frauenfeld, *Und trage keine Reu': vom Wiener Gauleiter zum Generalkommissar der Krim. Erinnerungen und Aufzeichnungen* (Leoni am Starnberger See, 1978), pp. 30–31, 37, 45.

26. *Dötz*, 4 April 1932, p. 1.

27. Frauenfeld, p. 75.

28. Bukey, p. 95. See also, Frauenfeld, p. 84.

29. Frauenfeld, p. 85.

30. Bukey, p. 101.

31. Police report by O. Braude to the BKA Generaldirektion für die öffentliche Sicherheit in Vienna, 14 September 1932, BKA Inneres, #209.793-32, AVA, 6 pp.

32. Letter of Frauenfeld to Habicht, Vienna, 30 May 1932, NSP-6 (folder Habicht), AVA, 1 p.

33. Vortrag für den Ministerrat, 11 August 1932, BKA Inneres, #196.455-32, AVA, 4 pp.

34. Auszug aus dem Ministerratsprotokoll vom 20. August 1932, Beilage 1, BKA Inneres, #201.948-32, AVA, 2 pp.

35. Circular instructions on principles of propaganda activity sent to the Gauleitungen of the NSDAP from the Landesleitung für Österreich of the NSDAP, Linz, 11 March 1933. Signed by Heixelbanning, NSP-16 (Propaganda Manuskripte), AVA, 3 pp.

36. *Vkst.*, 14 May 1933, p. 5. The Nazis drew their largest vote in Salzburg, where they won 29 percent of the total, followed by 17 percent in Vienna, and 14 percent in Lower Austria. In the provincial election of November 1932 in traditionally democractic Vorarlberg, the Nazis gained only 11 percent of the vote. See G. Botz, "NSDAP Mitglieder," p. 108.

37. *Vkst.*, 30 April 1933, p. 5; H. Walzer, "Die illegale Tätigkeit der NSDAP in Tirol (1933–1938): Darstellungen und Dokumente" (Hausarbeit aus Geschichte, University of Innsbruck, 1977), pp. 20–21.

38. Bukey, p. 110.

39. Anonymous, membership list drawn up in 1938, Sammlung Schumacher, 303 folder I, Bundesarchiv in Koblenz.

40. Botz, "Changing Patterns," p. 215.

41. Bukey, p. 159.

42. Botz, "Strukturwandlungen," p. 187.

43. Botz, "Changing Patterns," p. 221.

44. Botz, "Strukturwandlungen," p. 192.

45. Ibid., p. 186.

46. *Dötz*, 2 February 1931, p. 1.

47. *Festschrift zur Feier des 50-jährigen Bestandes der Union österreichischer Juden* (Vienna, 1937), pp. 96–97.

48. Walser, p. 61.

49. G. Botz, *Gewalt in der Politik: Attentate, Zusammenstösse, Putschversuche, Unruhen in Österreich 1918 bis 1938*, 2nd ed. (Munich, 1983), p. 327.

50. G. Botz, "Social Causes for Nazi Success in Austria" (unpublished manuscript, 1982), p. 9.

51. P. H. Merkl, "Comparing Fascist Movements," in *Who Were the Fascists,* p. 769.

52. For a more detailed description of these groups, see Botz, "Changing Patterns," pp. 221–222 and Pauley, *Forgotten Nazis,* pp. 97–102.

53. Botz, "Strukturwandlungen," p. 184.

54. Botz, "NSDAP Mitglieder," p. 104.

55. R. Danneberg, *Die Wiener Wahlen 1930 und 1932: statistische Betrachtungen* (Vienna, 1932), p. 51.

56. Bukey, p. 90.

57. *Dötz,* 17 June 1933, pp. 1–2.

58. Walser, p. 8.

59. Bukey, p. 96.

60. P. R. Black, "The Austrian National Socialists and the Destruction of the Austrian State" (unpublished M.A. thesis, Columbia University), p. 69.

61. For the most recent research on this subject, see Bukey, pp. 124–137.

62. "The Director of Department II to the Minister in Austria," 15 March 1934, United States Department of State, *Documents on German Foreign Policy 1918–1945,* series C, vol. 2 (Washington, 1958), p. 615.

63. Black, pp. 85–86.

64. G. Jagschitz, *Der Putsch: die Nationalsozialisten 1934 in Österreich* (Vienna, Cologne, 1976), p. 153.

65. Ibid., p. 80.

66. Botz, *Gewalt in der Politik,* p. 268.

67. Ibid.

68. H. A. Turner, Jr. (ed.), *Hitler—Memoirs of a Confidant.* Translated by R. Hein (New Haven and London, 1985), p. 8.

69. *The Hitler State: the foundation and development of the internal structure of the Third Reich* (London and New York 1981), p. xi.

70. Turner, p. 147.

71. Ibid., pp. 178–179.

72. Botz, *Gewalt in der Politik,* p. 273.

73. Bukey, p. 155.

74. Walser, p. 74.

75. Botz, *Gewalt in der Politik,* p. 274.

76. Information über den Verlauf einer Führerbesprechung der illegalen NSDAP . . . , Vienna, 6 January 1935, BKA Inneres #301.117-35, AVA, pp. 1–2.

77. For details, see Pauley, *Forgotten Nazis,* p. 135.

78. On the Hilfswerk, see Maurice Williams, "Aid, Assistance, and Relief: German Nazis and the Austrian *Hilfswerk,*" *Central European History* 14, no. 3 (September 1981): 230–42.

79. Bukey, pp. 139, 144.

80. Information Über den Verlauf einer Führerbesprechung der illegalen NSDAP . . . , Vienna, 6 January, BKA Inneres #301.117-35, AVA, pp. 3–6.

81. *Mein Kampf,* trans. Ralph Mannheim (1943), p. 469.

82. Broszat, p. 46.

83. I. Trabe, "Illegale nationalsozialistische Presse in Österreich (1933–1938)," in *Presse und Pressepolitik 1933–1945* (proseminar of the Institut für Publizistik, University of Vienna, 1977), p. 3; Walser, p. 76.

84. *IdVF*, 6 April 1935, BKA Inneres #382374-35, AVA, p. 6; Trabe, pp. 13–14.

85. J. Lewonig, "Die nationalsozialistische Bewegung und ihre illegale Presse in der Steiermark von 1933 bis 1918" (Seminararbeit, Institut für Publizitik und Kommunikationswissenschaft, University of Vienna, 1978), pp. 21, 23.

86. *IdVF*, 20 April 1935, BKA Inneres #382474-35, AVA, p. 10.

87. Trabe, p. 15; Lewonig, p. 22.

88. Trabe, pp. 6–8.

89. Monatliche Lageberichte des BKA/Generaldirektion für die öffentliche Sicherheit, Vienna, March 1935, p. 1.

90. For details, see Pauley, *Forgotten Nazis*, pp. 163–71.

91. Anonymous six-page report on conditions within the Austrian NSDAP, Vienna, 14 December 1934, BKA Inneres, NSDAP Allgemeines, #303.514–35.

92. P.R. Black, *Ernst Kaltenbrunner: ideological soldier of the Third Reich* (Princeton, 1984), pp. 56, 60, 65, 84.

93. Ibid., pp. 79, 86, 93, 284.

94. Black, "Austrian National Socialism," pp. 95, 136, 150.

95. Black, *Ernst Kaltenbrunner*, pp. 92–93.

96. W. S. Allen (ed.), *The Infancy of Nazism: the memoirs of ex-Gauleiter Albert Krebs, 1923-1935* (New York, 1976), p. 189.

97. Black, *Ernst Kaltenbrunner*, p. 97.

Captain Josef Leopold

Austro-Nazi and Austro-Nationalist?

MAURICE WILLIAMS

T he roots of contemporary Austrian nationalism are not easy to discern, for as in most countries they spring from numerous sources. They could be said to originate in the disillusionment following the *Anschluss* in 1938, the terror of the Third Reich administration, and the ten years of foreign occupation. Equally well, they might stem from the struggles of Karl Renner for an independent state, the economic achievements of the country since 1955, and the stability of a modern democratic government. When looking to the roots of this present-day nationalism, the logical and popular sources have been examined—the Renners, the Figls, the Kreiskys—but what about the darker, somewhat unsavory origins?

PRE-1938 AUSTRO-NAZISM

One area that has not been scrutinized closely in attempting to understand contemporary Austrian nationalism is the attitude and outlook of Austro-Nazis prior to 1938. Examinations have been clouded by the fact that after 1945 the victorious Allies made being a Nazi a crime; returning emigrés reinforced this notion by characterizing all Nazis as traitors to the Austrian State. In contrast to Germany where Nazism was considered an integral part of the domestic history, in Austria it was not. It was viewed more as a national betrayal or, more often, it was ignored. Yet Austrian Nazism and its leaders should not be neglected if a complete picture of contemporary Austrian nationalism is to be obtained.

This author has previously explored the idea that an influential number of Austro-Nazis had demonstrated during the 1930s that they were more Austrian than Nazi.[1] Had they acquired power at that time they would have sought to reconcile their loyalty to their country with their party beliefs. Bruce Pauley has shown in *Hitler and the Forgotten Nazis* that it is misleading and unfair to divide prewar Austrians into the Schuschnigg "patriots" and the pro-Nazi "traitors." None of the indigenous Nazi leaders wanted their country absorbed into an expanded German Reich. As Pauley writes, "Not even the most rabid and misguided of the Nazis thought of themselves as being in any sense traitors. They naively thought they could reconcile their loyalty to Austria with their loyalty to Party."[2]

Josef Leopold: A Contradiction?

In the negotiations of Josef Leopold, the acknowledged head (Landes-leiter) of the indigenous Nazis, with Kurt von Schuschnigg's regime in late 1936, Leopold attempted to reconcile these loyalties. He styled himself as a politician attempting to gain power legitimately, a man trying to reverse his party's status as an illegal organization. He tried to create an association for Austrian Nazis, hoping to use it as a means of influencing the Schuschnigg regime. As he saw it, legal recognition of his association would lead eventually to a role in a coalition government; in time, political involvement might allow a *Gleichschaltung* as had occurred in Germany.[3] Leopold's objective was simple and straightforward: he wanted to make Austria into a "National Socialist" state with himself and his party in power. That he failed is well known; what has not been as well understood is that he saw no contradiction between his Nazi affiliations and his loyalties to Austria. This paper thus briefly examines Leopold's attempt to gain a legitimate position and to play a political role in the First Republic and considers whether indigenous Nazism and Austrian nationalism were mutually exclusive or might have coexisted.

A NEW BEGINNING FOR LEOPOLD

Austro-German Agreement of 1936

An opportunity was offered to Leopold by the July 1936 treaty of friendship signed by the Schuschnigg and Hitler regimes. Acknowledging the sovereignty of its neighbor, the Reich government noted that the issue of Austrian "National Socialism" was a domestic matter over which Germany would attempt neither direct nor indirect influence. The Austrians for their part committed themselves to pursue policies befitting the "second German State," and agreed to accept two "national" sympathizers into the cabinet; they also promised amnesty for imprisoned Nazis. As a consequence Leopold was released from the concentration camp where he had spent the previous twelve months. After reasserting his authority as head of the Austrian Nazi Party, he set about interpreting the new treaty to his best advantage. He chose to accept at face value the notion that the activities of the Nazi Party (NSDAP) were a strictly domestic concern; more precisely he saw the July accord as an opportunity for the Austro-Nazis to obtain legal standing, probably by attaching the Party en masse to the Fatherland Front, the government's all-embracing league for patriots. Leopold affirmed, then, that Austrian Nazism was a legitimate political cause, a movement that would participate in local affairs and would seek power legally on its own merits.[4]

Earlier Schemes at Legality

Leopold's views and subsequent efforts were actually similar to earlier schemes. Ever since May 1933 and the founding of the Fatherland Front, the so-called nationals had sought recognition, either as a separate entity or as part of the main body. The *Nationale Kampffront* (spring 1933), the *Nationalständische Front* (summer 1933), the *Nationalfaschistische Front* (early 1934), and the *Nationale Front* (summer 1934) had all been attempts to gain acceptance. Leopold now added his efforts to those of his predecessors. He set about forming an association of Nationals, a group that in his case, would attract not only his own "National Socialists," but also supporters of the so-called conscientious Nationals, Austrians sympathetic to Germany who were anxious to reduce the tension between the two lands. Initially Leopold saw his association operating outside the Fatherland Front, but once organized, he envisioned a corporate entry into that organization. Although others had failed, Leopold was confident of success.[5]

Leopold's optimism

The Landesleiter had some reason for his optimism. He believed that the relationship between the Nationals, the Nazis, and the government had changed dramatically as a result of the July accord, and thus he now had a real opportunity to gain recognition. He also believed that he represented more than one segment of the population, since he had made contact with the leaders of the earlier *Land* League and Great German Peoples' Party and persuaded them to recognize him as head of a united National Opposition. Most significantly, and the real key to his accomplishments over the next several months, was the support and protection he received from two members of cabinet, Edmund Glaise-Horstenau, Minister without Portfolio after July 1936, and Odo Neustädter-Stürmer, Minister of the Interior in early November and named Minister of Public Security on October 10.[6] Glaise-Horstenau, a respected National, had little difficulty rationalizing his effects to help, especially when Leopold advised him thus:

> Herr Minister, I am introducing myself to you as the spokeman for the National Socialists of Austria. I beg you to impart to the Chancellor of the Federal Republic our position. We National Socialists recognize the Treaty of 11 July 1936 between the German Reich and Austria. We want to pursue our policies on the basis of this treaty, and are prepared to share in the affairs of our country publicly, and to cooperate in the reconstruction as long as one treats us as equal citizens.[7]

In addition Leopold would have endeared himself to the two Ministers when, in late August, he commented on the uniqueness of the Austrian Nazi Party and affirmed its separateness: "Adolf Hitler has ordered strict non-interference. . . . Such non-interference is a *vital necessity* for us, and after all, also a matter of honor. . . . We will achieve our goal unaided."[8]

Leopold also had other reasons for his optimism. Franz von Papen, the German ambassador, held similar views regarding a corporate entry into the Fatherland Front. Since the *Anschluss* was years, probably decades away, the ambassador felt that members of the illegal movement should work with the present government and its officials. To ensure a commonality of approach, in late September, Papen arranged for Leopold to travel to the Reich, where he met with Rudolf Hess, Heinrich Himmler, and Hitler. After long hours of discussion with these men, Leopold returned with their support and the understanding that he would seek, with Papen's help, Austrian governmental agreement to the collective entry of the party into the Fatherland Front. Further assistance in his quest for legality was provided by the Counselor of the German Legation in Vienna. He advised Schuschnigg that "Leopold was a patriotic, upright, and in my opinion also a capable leader." He suggested that the Austrian Chancellor ought to make the personal acquaintance of the head of the National Opposition.[9]

Growing Contacts with the Government

With so many signs of support, it was no wonder Leopold and his collegues felt confident. One of the Landesleiter's chief lieutenants, Gilbert in der Maur, summed up their feelings when he wrote that the Austro-Nazi Party was most optimistic about the domestic situation. He noted that the organization was fully intact; it had shown its strength in several public demonstrations, had countless new members and supporters, and most importantly, had growing contact with officials in the Schuschnigg regime.[10]

Cabinet Ministers' Support. Throughout the weeks of late 1936 Leopold and his entourage held numerous conferences and discussions with Neustädter-Stürmer and Glaise-Horstenau, talks designed to find some means of legal recognition. The openness with which the Nazis met with government ministers was significant in itself. The talks proceeded because of a split within the cabinet, the Chancellor and one group calling the Nazis major enemies of the State, while others[11] spoke sympathetically for contact and understanding. Initially, discussions centered on the government's ability to carry through the amnesty as outlined in the July accord, but more and more they turned to how to overcome the special laws against establishing new associations, a most important consideration as Leopold could not organize his new group until the laws were altered. The culmination of this first round of talks came at year's end (1936). The sympathetic ministers won approval for a cabinet committee to examine the legislation and submit proposals on how the decrees could be removed. Shortly thereafter Neustädter-Stürmer made the talks public. In a widely circulated newspaper interview, he spoke of the need for domestic peace, and he became the first cabinet minister to call openly for the Nationals to work with the government.[12]

Government Contact Diversified. After these events the contact between Leopold, his staff, the German Embassy, and the Austrian government intensified. On 8 January 1937, after meeting with Glaise-Horstenau, Leopold had an hour's private conversation with the Vice-Chancellor, Lt. Field-Marshal Ludwig Hülgerth, followed by talks with interested leaders in industry. Papen and Glaise-Horstenau meanwhile met on January 9 and agreed upon the necessity of a "German-minded" association, one composed of all elements of the National Opposition, including followers of the illegal party. On 12 January 1937, in der Maur spoke with State Secretary for Security Michael Skubl, discussing Austro-German relations, the desires and goals of the National Opposition, and the solidarity of the NSDAP in Austria. Skubl closed the conversation by saying, "So we work together for peace, law and order; greet Captain Leopold."[13]

AUSTRO-NAZI INDEPENDENCE

To ensure that there was no misunderstanding of his position Leopold forwarded a memorandum to Schuschnigg in which he outlined the reasons for entering into negotiations and the resolutions necessary for domestic peace. He struck an early note of Austro-Nazi independence: "We wished to prove above all that we could conduct the struggle singlehanded, that we had conducted it for a long time without foreign influence and help, and that we were proud of this fact."[14]

Leopold especially emphasized the reasons why domestic peace was so important: a large, youthful, and enthusiastic portion of the population supported Nazism, whereas a significant segment, one that adhered to Marxist thought, had to be won away. Leopold added that the common desire for domestic peace should begin with a "solemn declaration in favor of common racial stock as the purpose of the political life of the State," whereas an adherence to Christianity would serve as the basis for morality. The Nazi leader then outlined the measures that would bring internal political peace. In addition to the expected full amnesty and assured civil and political rights for Nazis, there should be freedom for cultural and national activities, a close military alliance with Germany, a plebiscite to determine the form of the State and the *Anschluss*, prohibition of the Jewish press, and the appointment of men to the cabinet who enjoyed the confidence of all groups. He concluded:

> Of course, when these measures are started the National Opposition and particularly the illegal National Socialist Party . . . will change. It will . . . support not only the proposed measures, but any other reconstructive activity of the Government as well, and will reserve to itself merely the right of objective, positive, criticism. . . . It will, though without legal recognition, especially stand on the ground of facts and of the Constitution of 1934. It will refrain from any kind of cultural struggle in view of the fact that Austria is a predominantly Catholic State.[15]

GERMAN SOCIAL PEOPLE'S LEAGUE

After completing this memorandum Leopold turned his attention to another task, also designed to promote his quest for power and legality. On 13 January 1937 he met with his closest advisors to work out the particulars of the proposed cultural association. The group quickly expanded to include the liaison to Glaise-Horstenau, Egbert Mannlicher, and the two representatives of Neustädter-Stürmer, Ferdinand Wolsegger and Stefan Berghammer. By 20 January, the men had completed their outline and presented it directly to the two cabinet ministers.[16]

DSVB Organization

The proposed association, the Deutschsozialer Volksbund (DSVB) or German Social Peoples' League, was presented in some detail. It was designed to attract a wide following of "national-minded" persons: some Party members, others well-known Nationals. Since the terms of reference were quite liberal, even Austrians with strong religious beliefs could join without feeling they were betraying the Church. The association, of course, would work only as a cultural entity and would avoid political commitments. But as its founders (especially Leopold) envisioned, as the organization grew, it would demonstrate the strength of the movement. Membership would become in effect, a plebiscite, allowing Austrians an opportunity to support the "nationalistic" movement. Additional thought was given to the actual procedure for establishing the association. Plans called for a broadly based proposal committee to make the formal approach for a charter. By signing a petition, men from all areas of work, interest, profession, and geography would become members of the proposal committee. In turn a smaller working body of twenty men (fourteen Nazis and six Nationals) would guide the actual incorporation. Here then was the association that would serve as the springboard to a role in government.[17]

Notwithstanding that many in the Austrian regime had highly critical views of the Nazis and their colleagues, Leopold and his associates felt confident that the new association would be allowed to organize. After all, the federal courts had recently permitted the establishment of a similar regional organization in Graz.[18] The plan also had the support and organizing energies of two cabinet ministers and could count on pressure for such an association from industrial circles.[19]

DSVB Support

With the cultural union becoming a reality, Leopold and his staff began to solicit backing and signatures. On 24 January 1937 the Landesleiter briefed his Gau leaders and their deputies and received their support. Then, while Leopold traveled to Berlin to outline the scheme to Hitler and in der Maur sought help from the Italian ambassador, another associate of the Landesleiter, Leopold Tavs, organized the collection of signatures throughout Austria. Although Leopold found the Germans cool and in der Maur found the Italians decidedly neutral, Tavs received overwhelming support. For four days he traveled throughout the western provinces collecting signatures; he also met representatives from Lower Austria, Burgenland, and Vienna who passed on their signatures to him. By February 4

Tavs had promises of nearly 500 names supporting the establishment of the DSVB.[20]

THE COMMITTEE OF SEVEN

At this point Leopold agreed to a change of tactics in his plan to establish an association. Upon the advice of both Glaise-Horstenau and Papen, the Landesleiter charged a small group with the responsibility of pursuing the peace effort. This "Committee of Seven" was composed of the three Nazis (Hugo Jury, Tavs, and in der Maur, all representing Leopold) and Mannlicher, Wolsegger, and Berghammer (acting for the two sympathetic ministers). These six then agreed upon a seventh member, Oswald Menghin, the Rector of the University of Vienna and a member of the Catholic-National circle. On 5 February 1937 this new committee met first with Glaise-Horstenau, the then Neustädter-Stürmer, and finally with Papen to work out specific terms of reference for their work. All agreed that in the first place the group would handle all peace efforts and initiatives as a plenary, and second, that its activities would not serve as a collecting point for Nazis (although the government said it would not use a committee member's background against him). With these terms settled and tacitly accepted by the government (Glaise-Horstenau reported to Schuschnigg that evening), Leopold acquired de facto recognition of his peace efforts.[21]

Opposition

But, if Glaise-Horstenau and Neustädter-Stürmer had convinced the Federal Chancellor to recognize the Committee and if Schuschnigg had agreed to deal with this small group, others among government circles objected strenuously. Mayor Richard Schmitz of Vienna argued that the cultural association scheme was not a method of putting out a fire but only a means of starting another one. Many among the press, led by the *Reichspost*, called the plan an impossible dream.[22]

Committee Approaches Schuschnigg

With opposition growing, the Committee had to act quickly. On 8 February it handed Neustädter-Stürmer a copy of the DSVB statutes, along with the petition signed by prominent public and business figures. It requested that the association be founded and asked that all documentation, including the petition, be handed to Schuschnigg. As Glaise-Horstenau later reported, when the Federal Chancellor saw the materials he was most impressed, especially since many of the signatories were influential Austrians. When the Committee met the next day with the two sympathetic ministers, it heard welcome news. Schuschnigg was ready to consider the wishes of the National Opposition and was prepared to begin conversations with a small group (specifically, Jury, Mannlicher, and Menghin). To help inaugurate the talks, he forbade the press from discussing the question of the peace action. The two ministers commented further that the completed petition, now with 493 names, was an influential factor in these decisions, especially since it indicated a widespread support for the DSVB idea.[23]

Schuschnigg Is Favorably Disposed

Over the next several days there was a flurry of activity. On the evening of 10 February Menghin met with Schuschnigg for the first time, outlining the objectives of the group. The next evening Jury and Mannlicher joined him, until Schuschnigg dismissed all save Jury. The Federal Chancellor and Leopold's close advisor then had an extensive private conversation in which they discussed the specific requests of the National Opposition. Schuschnigg first asked Jury not to insist on discussing the statutes of the DSVB for the moment. It would be best to wait for a more opportune occasion, when they could be reintroduced. Meanwhile, the Federal Chancellor would give de facto recognition to the Committee of Seven, maintain contact with it, and allow it to work unimpeded by government intervention. Schuschnigg also spoke favorably of appointing contact men for the Fatherland Front to act as liaison "in national matters" and to make possible collaboration with the Nationals. He also indicated he was prepared to release another 145 Nazis and drop any proceedings that were pending in the courts. "Defamation and discrimination because of membership in the NSDAP would cease." Past expulsion of civil servants with Nazi associations would be investigated sympathetically. Finally, the Federal Chancellor commented that government officials who were particularly objectionable to the National Opposition would be removed gradually.[24]

After these favorable discussions, the Committee of Seven met on 12 February, first with Leopold and then with the two ministers, Glaise-Horstenau and Neustädter-Stürmer. It decided to continue the talks with Schuschnigg but also agreed for the moment to relinquish the idea of establishing the association. The eventual creation of the DSVB was most important, especially since it was the only way to enable the illegal Nazis to work lawfully; but for now the Committee (and Leopold) would wait.[25]

Leopold Meets Schuschnigg

On the same evening, 12 February, contact between Schuschnigg and the committee continued. This time Jury proposed that Leopold be called in to meet the Federal Chancellor. Schuschnigg agreed. The resulting conversation brought a confirmation of the proposals made the previous evening: the release of imprisoned Nazis, momentary cessation of the request for an association but protection for the committee to work, the establishment of formal contacts between the Fatherland Front and the National Opposition, and some specific discussions on removing objectionable government officials.[26] Then, as an indication of their agreement, Jury, speaking for Leopold and the Nazis, made the following statement: "I declare that for reasons of *Realpolitik* we take cognizance of the independence of Austria, and shall act in accord with it. This statement also applies to the Constitution of 1934 and to the law concerning the Fatherland Front, beyond which we wish to form no additional political Party."[27]

This meeting and the understandings that followed became the high points in Leopold's leadership of the Austro-Nazis, as well as the pinnacle of his quest for a political role in his homeland. The planned association and the Committee of Seven were not the Party; but as the NSDAP Gau Salzburg pointed out, the Party now carried weight and influence through its involvement in the DSVB projects. As Leopold saw it, his negotiations with Schuschnigg were a great step forward. They showed clearly the unity within the movement and the government's de facto recognition of his position as leader of that movement. In der Maur wrote that the Nazis of Austria, as well as their sympathizers, had procured a leading post and had gained influence. What occurred, however, was not the end to their differences, just a beginning. Only if both sides remained loyal to the ideas would peace emerge.[28]

TALKS COLLAPSE

In der Maur's final point was telling. Both sides had to honor the agreement, but since neither did, the political atmosphere of compromise and the possibility of internal peace disappeared. Leopold was the first to suffer. Over the next several months, his prestige plummeted so that by the summer of 1937 the Landesleiter was struggling just to keep his head aloft. Schuschnigg, of course, continued to walk his tightrope in Central Europe, surrounded by Hitler's Third Reich, Mussolini's Italy, and Horthy's Hungary, while at home he continued the futile effort to fashion a one-party State in a three-factioned country.

The reasons for Leopold's downfall are obvious. In the first place, there was significant opposition to his activities; not all his comrades understood his motives and tactics, so his agreements and conversations with Schuschnigg were interpreted as an abandonment of some party doctrines. This sentiment led directly to mutinies in Vienna and Styria. Although Leopold overcame the challenges to his leadership, his credibility was damaged. Second, Schuschnigg faced significant opposition among his own supporters, which meant he could not pursue the February agreement. Richard Schmitz, the influential mayor of Vienna and a mainstay of the Fatherland Front, led a group that demanded a different approach. So intense was the dissatisfaction that some talked openly of replacing Schuschnigg with Schmitz. For several weeks this group badgered the Chancellor to break all ties with the Nazis. It especially objected to Schuschnigg's support of Neustädter-Stürmer as Minister of Public Security; the group saw this minister's endorsement of the DSVB as the first step toward legalizing the Nazi Party. As a means of appeasing his opposition, and in an effort to strengthen his own position, Schuschnigg dropped Neustädter-Stürmer from the cabinet on 21 March. With this change the DSVB project floundered and collapsed; it had lost its major champion within the government.[29]

Leopold suffered other losses of prestige and support. Not only did Schuschnigg back away from further contact, he soon had the Landesleiter, the Committee of Seven, and their respective headquarters under close watch. The surveillance culminated in May 1937, when the police raided and seized incriminating evidence of antigovernment activity. Leopold lost what little confidence the government still had in him. Meanwhile Schuschnigg was dividing the National Opposition. He had found an alternative to the Leopold projects in the ideas and advice of Arthur Seyss-Inquart. After some discussion, Schuschnigg and Seyss-Inquart agreed that supporters of the National Opposition ought to enter the government on an individual basis not as members of any group. Leopold's contacts with the government and his schemes had collapsed totally.[30]

SOME REFLECTIONS

That Leopold failed in his efforts to exert an effective leadership in political circles is self-evident. However, in looking at the activities of late 1936 and the early months of 1937, Leopold appears to have attempted to blend party allegiance with Austrian loyalties. The Landesleiter was one of those indigenous Nazis who did not disagree that Austria was German but thought his country had an identity of its own and his Party an independent heritage. Loyalty to Austria was a significant consideration.

After all, Leopold had supported the publication of a brochure that noted that the pride of the Nazi Party was its ability to find its way alone, over-coming all obstacles in the struggle for a free German State. He also sup-ported a newspaper article that identified the NSDAP with a free and in-dependent Austria. At no time did Leopold and his associates anticipate that they would have to choose between Hitler's Nazism and their Austrian loyalty; they thought the two compatible. That they were not did not become totally clear to Leopold until he was summoned by Hitler in Feb-ruary 1938 to reckon for his independent policies.[31]

Leopold is obviously not Everyman's image of an ideal Austrian or a respected political leader. The vision and dream for his country's future may have been questionable; but there is no evidence he wanted to turn it over to the Reich Germans any more than did Schuschnigg, the Social Democrats, the Communists, or the Heimwehr. He may have desired the *Anschluss*, but then so did many in Austria in the 1920s and 1930s. One should recall that the goal was a partnership with Germany not an occupation by the Reich. The ties that Leopold obviously had to his country, the maneuver-ing that he undertook in late 1936 and 1937, the proclamations that he made for the record, and his struggle to obtain legal recognition were all efforts to amalgamate party and country loyalties; the ultimate objective, as he saw it, was always to better the fortunes of his homeland.

The Landesleiter was not an Austrian in the contemporary sense. He was a petty tyrant and a political bully, the leader of a small party that used violence and terror. But where do the roots of today's right-wing activities in Austria come from? It is important to recognize that national identities do not originate in all that is sweetness and light; Canada has its Louis Riels, its Maurice Duplessis, its Jim Keegstras and the United States has its Joe McCarthys, its George Wallaces, and its Joseph Calleys. Austria cer-tainly has its Josef Leopolds. However distasteful the philosophy and ac-tivities of the man and his entourage, the loyalties they had to their country may be seeds of an identity that today has become Austrian. Contemporary Austrianism should be recognized as the product of many factors—a sound democratic government, a pride in economic stability, the struggles to end four-power control, the reaction to the terror of German occupation, the disillusionment over union, and conceivably, the efforts of some indige-nous Nazis to plan the future of their homeland. Leopold, the most un-likely of the Austrians, advocated a change in government, not necessarily a change in countries.

NOTES

Abbreviations

AA	Auswärtiges Amt, Bonn
AVA	Allgemeines Verwaltungsarchiv, Vienna
BA	Bundesarchiv, Koblenz
BKA, GD	Bundeskanzleramt, Generaldirektion fuer die öffentliche Sicherheit
BMJ	Bundesministerium fuer Justiz
DOW	Dokumentationsarchiv des österreichischen Widerstandes, Vienna
NPA	Neues Politisches Archiv, Österreichisches Staatsarchiv, Vienna
Ö	Österreich
USNA	United States National Archives, Washington, D.C.

1. See Maurice Williams, "Reflections on Austro-Nazis and Their Brand of Nationalism Before and After the Anschluss," *Canadian Review of Studies in Nationalism* 12 (Fall 1985): 285–306; "Delusions of Grandeur: The Austrian National Socialists," *Canadian Journal of History* 14 (December 1979):417–36; "Austrian National Socialism: A German Branch or an Austrian Movement?" Paper read before the Canadian Historical Association, Learned Societies, University of New Brunswick, June 1977.

2. Bruce Pauley, *Hitler and the Forgotten Nazis; A History of Austrian National Socialism* (Chapel Hill 1981), p. 179.

3. Ibid., pp. 173, 177–80.

4. Text of the July 1936 Gentlemen's Agreement, *Documents on German Foreign Policy, 1918–45*, Series D, *1937–45*, Vol. 1: *From Neurath to Ribbentrop (September 1937–September 1938)* (Washington, 1949), pp. 278–81; USNA, Department of State, Decimal Files 1930–9, 863.00/1332, Legation of the United States of America (Messersmith) to the Secretary of State, 27 January 1937, Vienna (hereafter cited as Messersmith, 27 January 1937). AA, Ö PO 29, Bd. II, 475664-5, Aufzeichnung (Altenburg), 22 September 1936, Berlin; BA, NS 10, #281, Josef Leopold an Hitler, 22 August 1937, Krems, Niederösterreich; BA, Seyss-Inquart, #1, Memorandum des Hptm. Leopold an den Kanzler, "Zur inneren Befriedung Österreichs," January 1937; Friedrich Rainer, "Rede von Gauleiter Dr. Friedrich Rainer vom 11. März 1942 über den Nationalsozialismus in Österreich vom 25. Juli bis zum 11. März 1938," 4005-PS, *Der Prozess gegen die Hauptkriegsverbrecher vor dem Internationalen Militargerichtshof; Nürnberg (14. November 1945–1. Oktober 1946)* (46 vols.; Nuremberg, 1949), vol. 34, pp. 16–18.

5. Wolfgang Rosar, *Deutsche Gemeinschaft. Seyss-Inquart und der Anschluss* (Vienna 1971), p. 108; Messersmith, 27 January 1937; DOW, #6184b, BKA, GD, Lagebericht über den Monat Oktober 1936, GD368.393 (hereafter cited as Lagebericht Oktober 1936.) USNA, Microfilm No. T84, Rl6, 44254; Untitled memorandum (Odilo Globocnik?), May 1938.

6. Lagebericht Oktober 1936; Rosar, *Deutsche Gemeinschaft*, pp. 98, 109; Friedrich Rainer, "Report on the Events in the NSDAP of Austria Since the Beginning of the Last Stage of Battle Until the Seizure of Power on the 11th March 1938," 812-PS, *Nazi Conspiracy and Aggression* (10 vols.; Washington, 1946), vol. 3, p. 592.

7. AVA, BMJ, VIe, Österreich. Beobachter 1937-8, "Erschienen im 'Virradat', Budapest, am 18. Oktober 1937, Hauptmann Leopold über die innenpolitische Lage," *Österreichischer Beobachter* (Sonderausgabe, November 1937?).

8. AA, Ö PO 29, Bd. II, 475676-7, Weisungsblatt 9, der Landesleitung der NSDAP in Österreich, 30 August 1936, Vienna.

70

MAURICE WILLIAMS

9. BA, NS 10, #50, Papen an Hitler, 1 September 1936, Vienna; DOW, #6184b, BKA, GD, Lagebericht über den Monat November 1936, GD374.855; Josef Leopold quoted in Friedrich Funder, *Als Österreich den Sturm Bestand: aus der Ersten in die Zweite Republik* (Vienna 1957), pp. 270–71; Rosar, *Deutsche Gemeinschaft*, p. 101; NPA, Liasse Österreich, Fasz 148, Österreichisches Generalkonsulat, An das BKA, Auswärtige Angelegenheiten, 13 October 1936, Munich; NPA, Liasse Österreich, bsz 308, 616, BKA, Bundespressedienst, Bericht über die Aussprache zwischen Hauptmann Leopold und den Wiener Bezirksleitern der NSDAP, in der Vorwoche, 20 April 1937, Vienna (hereafter cited as Bundespressedienst, Bericht, April 1937). AA, Politik 5, Österreich, Bd. 5, 44819-20, Aufzeichnung (Freiherr von Stein), 29 November 1936, Vienna.

10. USNA, Microfilm No. T77, R798, 529265, OKW, Abteilung Inland, Aufzeichnung ueber ein Gespräch des Hauptmanns von Heimburg mit dem k.u.k. Rittmeister a.D. Gilbert in der Maur, 3 December 1936, Berlin (hereafter cited as Aufzeichnung [Heimburg], 3 December 1936).

11. Glaise-Horstenau, Neustädter-Stürmer, Ludwig Hülgerth (Vice-Chancellor), and Wilhelm Taucher (Commerce).

12. Messersmith, 27 January 1937; Aufzeichnung (Heimburg), 3 December 1936; NPA, Liasse Österreich, Fasz 468, 369a, BKA, Befehle und Weisungen der Gauleitung der NSDAP Salzburg, Exposé ueber die österr. Innenpolitik, 21 April 1937, GD322.292; AA, Handakten Megerle, Bd. NSDAP 5/5, 351563, Bericht I, (Berichtszeitraum: ab Jahresbeginn), 19 January 1937, Vienna (hereafter cited as Bericht I, 19 January 1937).

13. Bericht I, 19 January 1937; Rosar, *Deutsche Gemeinschaft*, p. 110.

14. AA, Handakten Megerle, Bd. NSDAP 5/5, 351723-32, Memorandum des Hauptmann Leopold an den Kanzler, "Zur inneren Befriedung Österreichs," (January 1937) (hereafter cited as Leopold, "Zur inneren Befriedung Österreichs").

15. Ibid.; an English translation appears as an enclosure to USNA, Department of State, Decimal File 1930–9, 863.00/1328, Messersmith to Secretary of State, 18 January 1937, Vienna.

Leopold drafted his seven page, closely typed memorandum for an anticipated meeting with Schuschnigg on 11 January. Although the meeting was cancelled, the memorandum was received by the Austrian authorities. Schuschnigg certainly saw it and was aware of its contents (note attached to Leopold, "Zur inneren Befriedung Österreichs").

16. Bericht I, 19 January 1937.

17. Ibid.; Messersmith, 27 January 1937. See also Bundespressedienst, Bericht, April 1937.

18. The Grossdeutschen (Pan-Germans) had attempted to establish a regional cultural organization for nationally minded persons as early as September 1936. The authorities, however, had forbidden its organization, because officials saw it as a threat to Austrian sovereignty. But when the Grossdeutschen appealed to the federal courts, since they had the blessing of Glaise-Horstenau, the courts upheld the right to organize. On 14 January 1937, the Ostmärkischer Volksverein was formally founded in Graz. Its purpose was to attract nationally minded individuals, including Nazis. The founders also planned branches outside Graz, so that when they were strong enough they could demand admission to the Fatherland Front.

Although Leopold was not linked directly to the founding of the Ostmärkischen Volksverein, Papen's name was mentioned freely in addition to Glaise-Horstenau. (Rosar, *Deutsche Gemeinschaft*, p. 110; Bericht I, 19 January 1937; Messersmith, 27 January 1937.)

19. Messersmith, 27 January 1937; BA, NS 10, #50, 313, Botschafter des Deutschen Reiches, Österreichreferat an die Reichskanzlei (Wiedemann), Zur Lage in Österreich, Vertraulicher Bericht, 14 January 1937.

20. USNA, Microfilm No. T77, R798, 529277-8, OKW, Abteilung Inland, Vortrags-

notiz, Bericht der NSDAP Österreich über Verhandlungen mit Bundeskanzler Dr. Schuschnigg über die Gründung des Deutsch-Sozialen Volksbundes (In der Maur or Egon von Pflügl), 9 March 1937, Berlin; AVA, BKA, GD1334.413, Bericht II über die Zeit vom 24.I bis 14.II (In der Maur), Illegale NS Landesleitung in Wien II, Helferstorfersstrasse Nr. 5, Aufdeckung durch die BPD in Wien, 2 June 1937 (hereafter cited as Bericht II, 24.I bis 14.II). Rosar, *Deutsche Gemeinschaft,* pp. 112–13.

21. Bericht II, 24.I bis 14.II.

22. Ibid.

23. Ibid.; BA, R43II, 1473a, 376328-33, Papen an Hitler, 13 February 1936 (sic 1937), Vienna.

24. Bericht II, 24.I bis 14.II; NPA, Liasse Österreich, Fasz 468, 366-7, N.S.D.A.P. Gau Salzburg, Bericht, Befehle und Weisungen der Gauleitung der NSDAP Salzburg, Exposé über die österr. Innenpolitik, 26 May 1937, Vienna (hereafter cited as Gau Salzburg, Bericht).

25. Papen an Hitler, 13 February 1936 (sic 1937), Vienna; Bericht II, 24.I bis 14.II.

26. Schuschnigg seemed prepared to recall the Director of Security for Salzburg (Bechanie) but not Michael Skubl of Vienna or Director Gautsch from Lower Austria. (Papen an Hitler, 13 February 1936 [sic 1937], Vienna.)

27. There is some question as to when this statement was made. Papen said that Jury made it on 11 February and that Leopold confirmed and repeated it on 12 February. In der Maur, however, claimed that it was made on the evening of 12 February. (Papen an Hitler, 13 February 1936 [sic 1937], Vienna; Bericht II, 24.I bis 14.I.)

28. Gau Salzburg, Bericht; BA, NS 10, #281, Leopold an Hitler, 22 August 1937, Krems, Niederösterreich; Bericht II, 24.I bis 14.II.

29. USNA, Microfilm No. T120, R751, 3450553, Wolfgang Scholz an Papen, 25 June 1937, Vienna; DOW, #1460, Alfred Persche, "Hauptmann Leopold. Der Abschnitt 1936–1938 der Geschichte der nationalsozialistischen Machtergreifung in Österreich" (unpublished manuscript, 1947?), p. 122 (hereafter cited as Persche, "Hauptmann Leopold"). Bericht II, 24.I bis 14.II; AA, Ö PO 29, Bd. V, 321–32, Bericht IV vom 27.I bis 23. März 1937 (In der Maur?), Dr. Paul Rauscher an das AA, April 1937, Berlin; USNA, Microfilm No. T77, R798, 55295-6, OKW, Abteilung Inland, Vortragsnotiz, Lage in Österreich (Scheller), 14 April 1937, Berlin; Walter Goldinger, *Geschichte der Republik Österreich* (Vienna, 1963), p. 233; Rosar, *Deutsche Gemeinschaft,* p. 117.

30. NPA, Liasse Österreich, Fasz 308, 528-42, Auszugsweise Zusammenstellung der Beweisstücke für die fortgesetzte Einmischung reichsdeutscher NSDAP-Stellen in inner-österreichische Angelegenheiten, BKA, Sammelakt, Ausgang aus dem bei der Aushebung der illegalen Landesleitung der österr. NSDAP in der Helferstorferstrasse in Wien beschlagnahmtes Material, 28 July 1937, Vienna; AVA, BMJ, Sign VIe, Österreich. Beobachter, 1937–1938, Sonderausgabe des Österreich. Beobachter, n.d. (November 1937?); AA, Handakten Megerle, Bd. NSDAP 5/5, 351755-7, Lagebericht VI vom 19. Juni 1937; Pauley, *Hitler and the Forgotten Nazis,* p. 184.

31. Persche, "Hauptmann Leopold," pp. 359–60; BA, R43II, 1479, Abschrift: für Österreichs Freiheit und Recht, enclosure in Franz von Papen, Neue Verfolgungswelle gegen die NSDAP Österreichs, 22 June 1935, Vienna; AVA, BMJ, VIe, Österreichischer Beobachter 1936–1937, "Unsere Antwort," *Österreichischer Beobachter* 1 (September 1936).

Austrian Patriotism

Alternative to the *Anschluss*

JERRY W. PYLE

Austrian history from 1918 to 1934 has been stereotyped as a period almost devoid of individuals who believed in Austrian independence. The Austrian State created at the end of the war was supposedly peopled only by irate Germans who were forcibly prevented from seeking unification with their German brethren to the north. It was widely assumed that, if the Allied Powers should so much as waver in their vigilance, these embittered people would seek an immediate *Anschluss* with their true Fatherland.

To prove the supposed nonexistence of Austrian patriots, historians have repeatedly cited the almost unanimous vote of the Provisional National Assembly (of 21 October 1918) for union with Germany. Little weight should actually be assigned to that decision. The body was not truly representative of the new Austrian State. Many delegates represented such areas as the Sudetenland and the South Tyrol, which would never legally be part of German-Austria. These phantom legislators were some of the most outspoken advocates of the *Anschluss*, since their only other alternative was domination by non-Germans. Since all the legislators had been elected seven years earlier, in an essentially different era with totally different issues, it is doubtful whether they had any mandate from the people. Thousands of individuals who had come of age after 1911 had no voice at all. The extent of distorted representation is reflected in the following statistics: The Pan-Germans held 44 percent of the seats in Parliament in October

72

1918, compared with only 15.3 percent after the first postwar election in 1919. The Social Democrats, on the other hand, who had traditionally supported a Danubian Confederation, increased their representation from 18.1 to 40.8 percent.

PUBLIC OPINION AND THE *ANSCHLUSS*

Public opinion about the *Anschluss* can best be gauged by examining the attitudes of the Christian Socials and the Social Democrats, the two parties who actually represented the overwhelming majority of the Austrian people in the postwar Austrian Republic. On the eve of vote on the *Anschluss* resolution, a large delegation of Christian Socials had assured Emperor Charles of their undying opposition to the *Anschluss*. Following his unexpected abdication, however, only three of their numbers voted against the *Anschluss*.

A few days before the *Anschluss* vote, the Social Democrats were seriously exploring other alternatives to union with Germany. Viktor Adler, the grand old man of the party, explained:

> The German people of Austria is now to establish its own democratic State . . . which will decide in full freedom the nature of its relationship with its neighbors and with the German Reich. It may unite with the neighboring peoples to form a league of free nations—if this is the people's will. Should, however, the other nations reject such a union, or only be prepared to agree to it on conditions which do not meet the economic and political requirements of the Austrian people, then German-Austria will be compelled to attach herself to the German Reich as a federal unit, as, left on her own, she would not be an economically viable state.[1]

Although the Social Democrats preferred a Danubian Confederation, their reservations concerning the *Anschluss* to Germany essentially disappeared with the abdication of Emperor Wilhelm of Germany and the creation of the German Republic, soon to have a Social Democratic government. The change in the status of Germany prompted Adler to give his belated blessing to the proposal. He justified his decision by explaining that Germany and Austria "will have to come together again one day: it will be best for them."[2]

The *Arbeiter-Zeitung* immediately launched a campaign to win the workers over to the idea of the *Anschluss*:

> We must, therefore, seek union where we belong on the basis of our history, language and culture. . . . It is the red, the proletarian, the socialist Germany with which we wish to unite and will unite. German-Austria is a poor mountainous land, with inadequate agriculture, backward industry, and with masses

of conservative peasants, who, if left to themselves, would not be ready for
a socialist society. . . . *Anschluss* with Germany is *Anschluss* with socialism.
As an integral part of Germany, German-Austria can and will become what,
if left to herself, she would not become for a long time—a socialist community.[3]

Not all socialists agreed with this new policy. Franz Rothe, a member
of the extreme left-wing of the party, accused Renner and Bauer of leading
the Social Democrats into a nationalistic "hell." He also accused Bauer of
dictating his own personal desires with respect to the *Anschluss*, while "robbing" the people of their right of self-determination. As a consequence of
his criticism, Rothe was—not surprisingly—denied access to the pages of
Der Kampf.[4] Two statements by Karl Renner offer striking evidence that
the *Anschluss* lacked the wholehearted support of the Austrian people. On
4 April 1919 he told an official of the United States: "Botho Wedel, the
German Minister, had just left me and what I told him he is even now wir-
ing to his Government. It was that we would join with the Reich. I was
quite frank with him and told him that we were doing it without any enthusiasm; I made it quite plain that the lessons derived from our relations
during the war were too fresh in our memories for that. What else was I
to do?"[5] Later, on 6 April, he declared: "Few of our people are enthusiastic
about union with North Germany. We have learned to know these people
both in war and peace."[6]

On several occasions, moreover, Social Democratic leaders even acknowledged that union with Germany lacked the support of the majority
of the people. For example, in his book, *The Austrian Revolution*, Otto
Bauer stated that the "Republic was imposed on the overwhelming majority of the German-Austrian bourgeoisie by force in 1918. The tradition
of the vast majority of the German-Austrian bourgeoisie is old Austrian,
Habsburgian."[7]

To overcome the objections of the Catholic peasants to the *Anschluss*,
Social Democratic leaders frequently relied more heavily on German nationalism than on Marxist philosophy. Articles in the leftist press emphasized nationalistic motifs, sometimes to the point of virtually omitting all
Marxist trappings. During the period from 1926 until 1932 many leftists
unequivocally equated German nationalism with Marxism. Although the
Social Democrats' stratagem was temporarily successful, it created the impression among Austria's future patriots that most, if not all, Social Democrats were traitors to their Austrian fatherland. In their effort to drum up
support for the *Anschluss*, the Social Democrats also attacked many traditions and concepts that were essential to the development of patriotism in
the first Austrian Republic. As Kurt von Schuschnigg put it:

> Every reminder of other days was sternly proscribed. An absurd icono-
> clasm, a state of mind which did not stop short even of inscriptions as harm-

less as street-names, if they recalled historical characters or events, best characterized the confusion of minds which then prevailed. Any impulse of patriotism
was alien to the spirit of the hour and was rejected offhand as the embodi-
ment of reactionary opinions.[8]

Or, as he put it elsewhere, "Everything that recalled Austria, her history
or her symbols, was persecuted with demonic hatred."[9]

Even Ignaz Seipel, the future stalwart of Austrian independence, fell
victim to the doom and gloom that permeated the republic at the time.
When Charles appointed him to his cabinet in October 1918, Seipel was an
idealist committed to the reorganization of Austria-Hungary along federal
lines. When his plans were dashed to the ground by the decision of the
various Slavic nationalities to establish their own independent nation-
states, he became despondent about this cruel trick of fate. Late in November he gloomily suggested that perhaps *Anschluss* with Germany would be
the best course of action for Austria. He insisted, however, that the two
states be joined by means of an equal union rather than through the humiliating declaration of a parliament that had declared that German-Austria was
an "integral part of Germany." Reflecting upon his frustrated dreams, Seipel
then whimsically suggested that perhaps the obvious economic solution for
Austria was not the final solution, since the Austro-Germans still attached
considerable importance to the question of where "they could best serve
the German people."[10]

The Social Democratic Party swept to an easy victory in February 1919,
as the opponents of the *Anschluss* made little pretense of trying to rally
despairing patriots to support the Austrian fatherland. Leopold Kunschak,
editor of the weekly *Christlichsoziale Arbeiter-Zeitung*, charged that the margin of defeat had been determined by the failure of responsible leaders to
disprove the Social Democratic accusations that the Christian Socials had
been responsible for the war and that they favored the return of the monarchy and the old military power structure.[11]

Kunschak's counteroffensive was dealt a near-fatal blow by the Czech
occupation of the Sudetenland and the Paris Peace Conference of the same
year. The Austrian people were particularly incensed by the *Anschluss* ban
and the clause of the treaty that stipulated that the word *German* must be
removed from the official title of the Austrian State. Angered by the dictatorial nature of the treaty, the Social Democrats, the Pan-Germans, and
the Christian Socials all joined together to denounce the peace settlement.
Many individuals who had formerly opposed union with Germany now
questioned the wisdom of their previous advice. For instance, Kunschak,
who was later praised for his "eternal Austrianism," responded angrily to the
terms of the treaty by asking his fellow legislators "And what gives the men
in Paris the right so categorically to put the blame for the outbreak of the

World War on us, just the inhabitants of German-Austria . . . The day will come when the world will clearly see that one can force the body into servitude, but one can never clap the spirit and soul in chains."[12]

"GERMAN" AUSTRIA

The eternal defiance that Kunschak and the other legislators had vowed proved to be of brief duration. In September 1919 as the food crisis became critical, the National Assembly finally decided to ratify the detestable treaty. As an eternal symbol of their "unbroken spirit," Austria's parliamentary leaders, however, changed the forbidden phrase *German-Austria* to read the *German people of Austria*, thereby preserving the intent of the original words.

In October 1919 the first indication of internal Austrian opposition to the *Anschluss* surfaced during a rather vitriolic session of the National Assembly. Dr. Straffner, a Pan-German deputy, angrily insisted that he was convinced that the *Anschluss* ban "was dictated not so much in St. Germain as in Vienna." Such an insinuation was not entirely without foundation. Recent evidence indicates that in February Otto Bauer, the Foreign Minister, had come into possession of a remarkable letter written by Seipel on 17 December 1918 that provided what he considered to be irrefutable proof of the prelate's complicity in the matter. Hoping to embarrass the Christian Socials, Bauer unsuccessfully sought permission from his diplomatic source to publish the letter. According to Seipel's letter, the *Anschluss* could produce only unhappiness in Austria at that time. Not only would Bohemia be incorporated into Czechoslovakia but the German South Tyrol would be permanently lost, since the Allied Powers would never sanction German control of the Brenner Pass. Instead of being partitioned as a consequence of the *Anschluss*, Seipel believed that the Tyrol and Voralberg would much prefer to become small neutral States. Seipel was firmly convinced that the ideal solution for the entire German nation and German-Austria in particular was the revival of "Old Austria" or the creation of a Danubian Confederation. In any event, he believed that union with Germany was impractical until the Berlin government had triumphed over its own political instability. Moreover, Seipel insisted that he would never support the *Anschluss* as long as a Social Democratic government was in power in Germany.[13]

Seipel's clandestine opposition to the *Anschluss* was clearly based on his hopes for the creation of a Danubian Confederation and his hatred of Marxism. Only after April 1922 when Eduard Beneš permanently halted discussions on any form of Central European association did Seipel begin to think the unthinkable—a small independent Austrian State. Meanwhile, as the successor States turned to economic nationalism, Austria began to wither on the vine. She survived only by virtue of the charity doled out by the international community. Within a year after the peace treaty was signed, and the danger of an *Anschluss* between Austria and Germany no longer seemed imminent, all foreign assistance from the European powers ceased. As economic deprivation encroached on the country, internal momentum began to build for *Anschluss* with Germany. In April 1921 Tyrol announced that it intended to conduct a plebiscite on the question of *Anschluss* with Germany. As threats were hurled at this upstart province from every corner of Europe and from Vienna, 98 percent of the Tyrolese defiantly voted in favor of union with Germany. Probably no other event in Austrian history has been misinterpreted as greatly as the Tyrolese plebiscite. The Christian Socials who were the dominant party in the region had been actively campaigning against the *Anschluss* until France demanded an end to all *Anschluss* agitation there. At that point they reportedly reversed their position and urged the people to vote in favor of the proposed union.[14] In the final analysis the plebiscite should probably be viewed more as a manifestation of the extent of local Francophobia than as an accurate barometer of sentiment favoring an *Anschluss*.

By 1923 after four years of devastating inflation, Austria had seemingly reached the end of the road. Almost everyone was predicting the immediate demise of this ill-begotten State. Everyone, that is, except Ignaz Seipel. In a last desperate attempt to save his fatherland, he formed a new cabinet. He wasted no time in explaining his motives: "the German people in Austria . . . must live, and we who are flesh of its flesh and blood of its blood must do everything which stands in our power that it may live."[15] Seipel had now come to believe that his country had entered into a new dimension in the postwar period. Although he had labored for the past four years to recreate the old Habsburg State, that was not what God had ordained. Austria had been assigned a new "spiritual mission" for the twentieth century: to lead the states of Europe away from the horrors of integral nationalism. Although she was little more than a rump-state compared with her previous status, Austria could still exercise supremacy in the world of ideas. As long as Austria existed, whether large or small, the Austrian idea would be alive.

Seipel also aided the cause of Austrian patriotism immeasurably by convincing the Austrian people that the repudiation of the *Anschluss* was not a repudiation of the German nation. He constantly explained that nation, State, and Church were coequals and that each provided an essential service in a different dimension. He asserted, moreover, that nationalism, or the union of nation and State, was a passing phenomenon that contradicted God's master plan for the universe. He also pointed out that the State and the nation had each achieved some of their greatest accomplishments during the Middle Ages, when they had been independent of one another. Finally, Seipel reminded the German people of Austria that if they successfully executed the Austrian mission with which they had been entrusted they would bring glory not only to the Austrian Republic but to the German nation as well. By implication, he suggested that if they shunned their appointed task, they would disgrace not only themselves but the entire German nation.[16]

Seipel realized that in the final analysis the success or failure of his divine mission depended entirely upon his ability to win the overwhelming support of the people. Not only would he have to refute the attempts of the Social Democrats to root out the last vestiges of the Habsburg heritage, which was, after all, intimately connected with the Austrian mission; he would also be compelled to find a solution to Austria's financial problems. In his inaugural address he tried to revive faith in the Austrian fatherland. Describing himself as an eternal optimist, he sternly denounced the insinuation of the Social Democrats that he would be the last minister of the Republic just as he had been the last minister of the Empire, and boldly proclaimed that as Federal Chancellor he had "no intention of presiding over a second dismemberment of Austria." To the Catholic masses the priest-chancellor proudly asserted that "God had led me to this place." As for the financial problems of the State, Seipel explained that the problems could more likely be solved by a person who believed in its viability. He asserted that union with Germany could be viewed only in the light of *Realpolitik* and must wait until a more favorable opportunity.[17] He then unveiled a financial program designed to shore up the Austrian economy, to encourage foreign loans, and to foil the *Anschluss*. He soon discovered to his dismay, however, that the international banking community and the European powers would not lift a finger to help Austria escape from her economic quagmire.

THE GENEVA PROTOCOLS

Undaunted by the indifference shown him, Seipel launched one of the most brilliantly conceived diplomatic gambits of the twentieth century. He startled the world by mentioning a "practical solution" to his country's problems. Lest anyone fail to recognize his euphemism for the *Anschluss* a few days later he provocatively stated that if Austria should find it necessary to associate with a single neighboring State, Germany quite naturally was an obvious choice. Having vaulted dramatically to the center stage of world politics, Seipel continued to drop key phrases and innuendos in the major European capitals.

Seipel's "survival diplomacy" worked to perfection. By means of skillful diplomacy, suggestive press conferences, and the inevitable speculation of the press, the Austria's Federal Chancellor brought Europe to the brink of war – all within the span of two weeks. While Italy and Yugoslavia mobilized their troops, the League of Nations summoned its members to deal with the Austrian crisis. At Geneva, Austria's spokesmen outlined their country's position very succinctly. Unless the League came up with some meaningful financial assistance, Austria would play the "role of Mrs. O'Leary's cow and set all of Central Europe aflame."[18] Rumors abounded about Seipel's immediate plans. Although the possibility of an *Anschluss* with Germany was not taken too seriously in most circles, there was a great deal of apprehension about an alleged combination with either the Little Entente or the more probable association with Italy. Since any form of union with any of her neighbors would only excite the others and exacerbate an already dangerous situation, the League agreed to arrange a massive infusion of capital into Austria. The details of the financial package were spelled out in the Geneva protocols signed on 4 October 1922. Seipel was elated. With tears in his eyes he explained that Austria had wanted to live from the very beginning and now the League of Nations had made it possible for her to do so. He said that he eagerly awaited the day when an Austrian Federal Chancellor could finally say that "Austria is rehabilitated."[19]

Seipel's exuberance was not shared by the Social Democrats. They had believed that he would fail to solve Austria's financial problems like everyone else. They had reasoned that, once he admitted defeat, the last major obstacle to the *Anschluss* would be removed. Having wearied of the continual subsidies necessary to maintain the independence of Austria, the Allied Powers would finally drop their opposition to the *Anschluss*. They had not reckoned on the success of Seipel's blackmail diplomacy.

Anticipating Seipel's failure, the *Arbeiter-Zeitung* had already attempted to marshall public opinion on behalf of the *Anschluss*. It had complained that not even Seipel had known what he wished to accomplish in either Prague or Berlin. Only one point was absolutely clear, Seipel had traveled to Berlin only to pacify the conscience of the Pan-Germans. The newspaper had predicted his early failure to gain financial assistance. Its editorial page had snarled: "We will know within a few days how well founded the hopes of Herr Seipel are. . . . With 15 million pounds sterling in hand any jackass could save our economy."[20] The newspaper saw a definite alternative to Seipel's plans: "A final solution of the German-Austria problem is possible only through *Anschluss* to Germany. As long as *Anschluss* cannot be consummated, we must defend our independence by every possible means."[21] On numerous occasions the *Arbeiter-Zeitung* reminded its readers that the *Anschluss* was unlikely to take place as long as Seipel was Federal Chancellor.

Seipel was portrayed as an advocate of Austrian independence, filled with "inner disgust" at the mere thought of *Anschluss* with Germany. Instead of trying to escape from the prison of "independence" in which the Austrian people had been placed in 1918, Seipel could envision "no other remedy than submission to foreign control."[22]

The *Reichspost* urged its readers to disregard the critical comments of the Social Democrats. Any person not blinded by party prejudice could clearly see that in this time of great crisis Seipel was the right man—"the man who had freed Austria from her isolation as a scarcely noticed beggar state and has placed her in the mainstream of European politics." Furthermore, it concluded, Seipel had "given this people confidence and unanimous faith in this state."[23] When Seipel returned to Vienna he was greeted by Jodok Fink, the chairman of the Christian Social Party, who spoke of the great success which Seipel had achieved for his fatherland. Fink asserted that if everyone "will fulfill his duty, we may hope that, with God's help, we will face better times for our fatherland and Volk."[24] When Seipel surveyed his large audience of well-wishers, he urged them to join him in his efforts to save Austria. He quickly reminded everyone that the fatherland was only at the beginning of the road to salvation—not at the end. However, with the active support of the populace, he was able to visualize a time when "we can hope to lead a normal political and economic life." After cautioning the people not to underestimate the difficulties that still lay ahead, Seipel shouted to the appreciative crowd, "Our fatherland, may it live again!"[25]

Seipel's moment of glory in the Westbahnhof marked the beginning of a patriotic revival throughout Austria. Kurt von Schuschnigg, a quiet, withdrawn individual, was one of the many thousands of individuals affected by Seipel's contagious patriotism. As he later explained in his memoirs:

> I was a young assistant lawyer when I heard Chancellor Seipel speak for the first time. It was a meeting at Innsbruck, just after his first journey abroad, when he became an international figure. The lucid, quiet, convincing words in which he formulated his confession of faith in Austria moved us deeply. At last a man had come forward, courageously seized the helm, and without ifs and buts, but without stipulation, recognized the Fatherland. . . . he summoned us to share in his determination to re-create Austria.[26]

Like Schuschnigg, Heinrich Mataya, a member of Seipel's cabinet, traced his renewed sense of patriotism to the Geneva Protocols. Seipel had more than satisfied the "indispensible prerequisite for the salvation of Austria."[27]

The *Arbeiter-Zeitung* quickly expressed its displeasure with Seipel: "Thanks for the treaty which sacrificed the *Anschluss* with Germany. Congratulations for the treaty which permitted the Italians and the Czechs to establish a dictatorship on German soil. And the whole bourgeois press, Jew and Christian without distinction, agrees with him."[28] By 11 October, the Social Democrats had decided to bring down the Seipel coalition by demonstrating the hypocrisy of his Pan-German allies on the *Anschluss* issue. A year earlier the Pan-Germans had pulled out of the governing coalition when Schober had introduced the Treaty of Prague, which contained an anti-*Anschluss* clause. It insisted that the passage of time had obviously produced a major change in the objectives of the Pan-German Party. Their political leaders had apparently abandoned their most sacred campaign slogan, the *Anschluss*, without receiving a single concession from the Christian Socials.[29]

Although they had been accused of disloyalty to the German nation many times in the past, the Christian Socials were no longer hesitant to admit publicly that Austrian patriotism must take precedence over any commitment to German nationalism. On 12 October, Leopold Kunschak admonished the members of the Nationalrat that the ratification of the Geneva Protocols provided everyone with an opportunity to vote either for "the collapse or the salvation of this land." He urged his fellow legislators to make his concluding words a reality: "Long live our fatherland! Long live Austria!"[30]

Another patriotic lawmaker proclaimed: "It is fine and it is necessary for us to make some sacrifices for the salvation of our fatherland. We want to live. We want to create a future for our people. And today is that fateful hour. Here is the place and now is the time when we can begin again."[31]

"AUSTRIAN" AUSTRIA

After a year of austerity measures and League control, the time had come to permit the Austrian electorate to voice their approval or disapproval of Seipel's efforts to rehabilitate Austria. In order to give the voters a clear choice, the Christian Socials insisted that the only significant issue in the campaign was whether the Austrian people preferred political independence to *Anschluss* with Germany. Although other minor issues did crop up from time to time to obscure the issue, in the words of the *Reichspost*, "Next to the question of the existence of Austria all other questions and party differences" lost "their actual importance."[32] In order to make their position perfectly clear, the Christian Socials used the expression *the Austrian people* instead of the term *German-Austrian*. Whenever they used the word *German*, it was only as an adjective. For instance, the Christian Social Union of Austria headed their appeal to the people: "Christians! Austrians!" and Seipel made extensive use of the word *Austrian* in almost all of his campaign addresses. Throughout the 1923 campaign the Christian Socials used this terminology specifically to indicate that the German-speaking populace of the small Alpine Republic of Austria was entitled to a political identity separate from that of the German-speaking people who lived in Germany.[33] Also throughout the campaign the Christian Socials constantly derided the *Anschluss*. Seipel taunted the Social Democrats with the slogan "*Anschluss* to the Mark?" and cited Germany as an example of how far Austria could have fallen. In similar fashion, the *Reichspost* wrote that no one "wants to entrust the leadership of the State to a party which advocates *Anschluss* to the mark."[34] Kunschak likewise boldly stated that the "old black-yellow hostility towards the *Anschluss* which timidly concealed itself in 1919 can now venture into the light." He also voiced the opinion that his viewpoints were shared not only by the "blackest of the blacks" but also by four-fifths of the middle class. In fact, Kunschak was so confident of the approval of public opinion that he taunted Bauer with the questions, "Herr Dr. Bauer, what say you now? Now do you still have the courage to speak of the 'high treason' of Prelate Seipel?"[35]

The commitment of the Christian Socials to Austrian independence perhaps is best revealed in the campaign addresses of Seipel and other leading figures of the Christian Social Party. At Amstetten, to the vigorous applause of a crowd of 10,000, Seipel declared: "If we all remain faithful to our land and are resolved to work for this land, then Austria cannot go under." That same day at St. Pölten, before another crowd of 10,000, Carl Vaugoin reinforced Seipel's previous remarks by declaring: "The people want to remain faithful to our fatherland and to our Federal Chancellor and therefore will vote Christian Social on October 21." At Jennersdorf, in the Burgenland, Dr. H. K. Zessner-Spitzenberg, a candidate for the National Assembly, introduced Seipel to the thousands of people who had waited for hours to see "the deliverer of Austria." Explaining why Seipel commanded the trust of the masses, Zessner-Spitzenberg asserted: "Because he caused us to regain our faith in our homeland, to regain our will for Austrianism and for the land of our fathers." At Feldbach, in Styria, the Federal Chancellor affirmed his conviction that the "Austrian people want to see the salvation of the fatherland."[36]

The extent of Seipel's commitment to Austrian patriotism is readily apparent in an important speech that he delivered at Zell-am-Ziller, Tyrol, on 1 October 1923. Two years earlier, Seipel explained, almost everyone had been filled with despair. At that time he was among the very small handful of Austrians who believed that the "piece of the homeland left by the so-called peace treaty" could survive. At a time when almost all the provincial leaders wished to dissolve their ties with Vienna, he had asserted all his influence to persuade the party chieftains to give Austria one more chance.

They had not only yielded to his request but elected him Party Chairman. Since that day the future of Austria had been assured. The reason for this dramatic reversal, Seipel asserted, was not due to foreign aid but to the efforts of the Austrians themselves. The economic problems of the past had been due solely to the "fact that the Austrian did not believe in himself, the land, God or the future." If the people would only maintain the will to preserve Austria, Seipel promised, then the State could not perish. "We struggle to preserve our Austrian fatherland, not only for us but also for those who are now young, the children who will come after us. . . . I am no stranger in the Tyrol because I am an Austrian, just as the Tyrolese are no strangers in Vienna. This fact will never change because you are Austrians and will remain so for eternity."[37]

The Christian Socials had based their political campaign almost exclusively on the issue of Austrian patriotism and came within one seat of winning an absolute majority in the Austrian National Assembly–a feat no other political party in the first Austrian Republic was ever able to duplicate. The decision of the Social Democrats late in the campaign to concentrate exclusively on economic issues while backpedaling on the *Anschluss* theme is perhaps the most telling commentary on the election. Austrian patriotism was, at least temporarily, in the ascendancy. Assured that he had set Austria on a safe course, Seipel removed himself from the helm of the Austrian State following a near fatal attempt on his life in 1924. He retained the powerful position of Party Chairman to ensure that no major change in foreign policy could be implemented without his approval. After a brief outburst of pro-*Anschluss* sentiment by two members of his caretaker government, the ringmaster halted the performance to reiterate his position: "I am not against a union [with Germany], but I do not see a solution to Austria's Europe[;] . . . if not in a political sense at least in an economic sense."[38]

If the majority of the Austrian people did not agree with Seipel's dictum on union with Germany, the prospect of Hindenburg's election as President of Germany in 1925 seemed likely to accomplish that end. One week before election day, the *Arbeiter-Zeitung* insisted that the German presidential campaign would ultimately "determine the future of Austria." The newspaper then explained for the benefit of all interested persons in both Germany and Austria: "Whoever wants the *Anschluss* must reject Hindenburg; whoever votes for Hindenburg works against the union of the entire German nation in a united Europe." The *Reichspost* and Seipel's faction of the Christian Social Party likewise seemed convinced that Hindenburg's election would virtually destroy the *Anschluss* movement in the Austrian Republic.[39] Austrian opponents of the *Anschluss* consequently were in a jubilant mood when Hindenburg defeated Wilhelm Marx, the Social Democratic candidate, by a margin of over a million votes. In its analysis of the German presidential election, the *Reichspost* somewhat gloatingly observed that "the prospects for the *Anschluss* have unquestionably been considerably diminished." The Catholic paper theorized that at long last the Social Democrats of Austria would finally repudiate their goal of union with Germany.[40] However, much to the consternation of Seipel and other Austrian patriots, the Social Democrats refused to disavow *Anschluss* with Germany. The *Arbeiter-Zeitung* reported: "Already the Black-Yellows sneer 'Now that Hindenburg rules in Germany, surely the yearning of the Austrian Social Democrats for the *Anschluss* will cease.' The gentlemen err! We have confidence in the power of German Democracy." It then insisted that "if Austria had been a part of Germany, Hindenburg would never have been elected. More than four-fifths of the Austrian people opposed Hindenburg—less than one-fifth supported him."[41]

The Christian Socials were not easily dissuaded by the seemingly instransigent attitude of the Social Democrats on the the *Anschluss* issue. The *Reichspost* published an article with the banner headline "Seipel and Marx." The accompanying text, which covered two-thirds of the front page and one-third of the next page, pointed out how Seipel and Wilhelm Marx, the Presidential candidate of the German Social Democrats, had both done so much for their respective countries. It concluded that Austria would obviously benefit if the Socialists and Catholics would cooperate as they had done in Germany. A few days later the *Reichspost* spoke favorably of Ferdinand Lassalle, one of the founders of the German Social Democratic Party.[42] As an additional inducement to the Social Democrats, Seipel tried to lay to rest the issue of monarchy. He explained that the new Austria was completely different from the old Habsburg Empire. However, in order to create a viable State, it was necessary to use the only readily available building materials: the tradition of the great Austrian past and the foundation of the old State. It would be impossible to build a new fatherland totally from scratch. It was simply a question of using the available material or not building at all; there were no other alternatives.[43]

The conciliatory gestures of Seipel and the Christian Socials, however, failed to evoke a favorable response from the Social Democrats. Convinced that their political adversary harbored ulterior motives and that he remained at heart an incorrigible monarchist, they stood steadfast in their loyalty to the German State.

Wearied from his unaccustomed flirtation with the Social Democrats, Seipel soon sought solace in the arms of fascism. Hoping to garner enough additional seats in the Austrian National Assembly to enact a constitutional amendment that would cripple the power of the Social Democratic Party in Austria, Seipel assumed the lead in the formation of a bourgeois block in 1927. He tried to justify his party's "questionable association" with the monarchists and the fascists by explaining that when one's "house is burning, one does not ask the man from the fire-brigade his position on the race question; one lets him extinguish it."[44] Seipel's grandiose political strategy proved to be surprisingly inept. Not only did the supposed rout of the Social Democrats fail to materialize, they picked up three additional seats whereas the Christian Socials lost nine. To compound his misfortune further, three months later—at the time of the blaze of the Palace of Justice in 1927—fascism would elude its would-be-master and overnight grow large enough to threaten to destroy everything that Seipel and his friends had tried to create.

THE CUSTOMS UNION ISSUE

By 1930 Seipel had been forced to relinquish control of Austria to a political coalition composed of Pan-Germans, the Landbund, and some rural elements of his own party. When this group announced a proposed Austro-German Customs Union, surprisingly strong internal opposition suddenly materialized. The *Reichspost,* for instance, disputed its government's contention that the project was simply an innocent economic arrangement between neighboring States and pointedly explained that economic cooperation might be indistinguishable from political cooperation. On 10 April, the *Niederösterreichische Zeitung*, a clerical newspaper with close ties to Seipel, printed a scathing attack on the Federal Chancellor and the proposed Customs Union.[45] Schober angrily turned on his internal critics, accusing them of "high treason." His charge elicited a rapid response from the Viennese chapter of the Christian Social Party, which insisted Schober's ill-advised choice of words had undoubtedly confirmed the suspicions of the French and the Czechs that the entire project was primarily political.[46]

Although the *Reichspost* and the Viennese Christian Socials were quite relieved to see the French quash the proposed Austro-German Customs Union, they denied any responsibility for the failure of Schober's foreign policy. They insisted that Schober should have realized from the very beginning that the French would never tolerate the creation of a Customs Union between the two Germanic States. If Schober had simply practiced *Realpolitik* Austria would never have been brought to her knees at "Canossa." The *Reichspost*, moreover, argued that Schober's proposal was illogical, since the Federal Chancellor had suggested an unnatural association. If Austria must form closer economic ties with another State, then Hungary was the most logical choice because the industrial and agrarian interests of the two States complemented each other. Finally, if Schober had wished to cre-

86 JERRY W. PYLE

ate a nucleus around which a united Europe could develop, a union between Hungary and Austria would have been more sensible because the
French government would have been more likely to give its consent to the
formation of an Austro-Hungarian Customs Union than one between Germany and Austria.[47]

The *Arbeiter-Zeitung* provided a totally different critique. It insisted
that from the very beginning the Seipel-Schmitz wing of the Christian
Social Party had tried to destroy the dream of German economic unity
by encouraging the French government to oppose the proposed union.
The Social Democrats concluded that the ultimate realization of "the goal
which history had set for itself with the destruction of the central European
monarchy" could never be achieved through a bourgeois government that
was only half-heartedly committed to an *Anschluss* between Austria and
Germany.[48]

The bickering over the foiled customs union project obscured one of
the most promising developments in the history of the Austrian Republic.
On 19 June 1931 Seipel asked Otto Bauer to accept the office of Vice-
Chancellor in a nonpartisan cabinet. Although the recent upsurge of Nazi
strength in Germany certainly made Seipel's offer fairly attractive, Bauer po-
litely declined. The odds of a possible rapproachement between the Christian Socials and the Social Democrats nonetheless suddenly looked better
than any time since the creation of the Austrian Republic. Cooperation between the two parties seemed more imperative than ever following provincial elections in April 1932. The Nazis polled 16 percent of the votes in
Vienna, 18 percent in Lower Austria, and 22 percent in Salzburg. The vast
majority of these Nazi votes were cast by former members of the Pan-
Germans and the various fascist groups. The only Pan-Germans who survived the provincial elections were those whose terms had not yet expired.

The champions of Austrian independence would achieve one last hur-
rah before Hitler's final assumption of power in Germany. Rocked by the
collapse of the Creditanstalt in 1931, Engelbert Dollfuss, the new Austrian
Federal Chancellor, had negotiated the Lausanne loan in the last desperate
attempt to keep the Austrian economy afloat. When it was announced that
the agreement would prohibit the *Anschluss* for another twenty years, the
Pan-Germans and the Social Democrats did everything in their power to
block ratification. Despite their combined opposition, the measure was approved by the Austrian National Assembly by a margin of two votes.

AN ANTI-NAZI COALITION?

A patriotic revival swept Vienna and much of Austria following Seipel's
death on 2 August 1932. At the Central Cemetery, 100,000 mourners

gathered to pay their last respects to the "father of Austrian patriotism." His countrymen heaped patriotic oratory on the fallen Caesar. Vaugoin hailed him as a "man of whom one can say that for him one thing mattered above all else: 'His love for our Austria.'" Seipel, he insisted, deserved to be remembered as "the father of Austria because, had he not lived, there would no longer be an Austria." In similar vein President Wilhelm Miklas urged the people never to "forget what it owes to Dr. Seipel, who was the savior of our fatherland."[49] The most significant obituary at the time was by Otto Bauer. Although Bauer was understandably critical of Seipel's anti-Marxist policies, he nonetheless spoke very kindly of his lifelong archenemy. He specifically praised him for his efforts to form a Christian Social–Social Democrat coalition in April 1932.[50] The fact that Bauer's conciliatory words followed on the heels of a dramatic Nazi victory in Germany, in which the Nazis increased their representation from 120 to 230 in the Reichstag, should not be underemphasized. Bauer was seemingly now willing to make common cause against the "brown" menace.

Certain individuals in Germany acted quickly to prevent the death of Seipel from becoming a catalyst to bring the Christian Socials and the Social Democrats together. Franz von Papen asserted that Seipel was not an advocate of Austrian independence, as everyone in Germany had always assumed, but a champion of *Anschluss* between Germany and Austria. Seipel, he aruged, was simply trying to preserve his country's integrity until it became feasible to consummate a union between the two Germanic countries. His financial policies, moreover, were designed strictly to ensure that when the day of reunion finally came, Austria would not be compelled to come to Germany as a " helpless bankrupt."[51] The Big Lie about Seipel subsequently was enhanced by Franz Riedl, a correspondent for von Papen's newspaper, who was arrested in 1933 for his anti-Austrian activities. Riedl contended that Seipel had concluded in 1928 that union with Germany was inevitable and had consequently dropped his previous objections to the *Anschluss*. He insisted that Seipel had become such a staunch supporter of German nationalism that at the time of his death he was in the process of revising his book, *Nation und Staat*, to emphasize the ever-increasing importance of the new nationalism, that is, Nazism.[52] Seipel's reputation would never completely recover from the Nazi smear.

Although the ensuing rancor over the ratification of the Lausanne Protocols had destroyed an immediate likelihood of a united Austrian front against the Nazis, the situation changed dramatically after Hitler was sworn in as Reich Chancellor of Germany. After the Austrian Social Democrats dropped the *Anschluss* plank from their Party platform, Friedrich Adler proclaimed on behalf of the Social Democrats: "We have worked for an *Anschluss* to the German Republic—but we refuse an *Anschluss* to a fascist prison."[53]

Dollfuss, however, turned a deaf ear to the Social Democrats. Undaunted by his latest rejection of their support, they again proffered assistance in September. This time the chairman of the Christian Social Party, Carl Vaugoin, urged Dollfuss to end his bitter feud with the Social Democrats. For his efforts, Vaugoin was dropped from the cabinet. The one coalition that could have put a stop to the Nazis' designs on Austria was destined never to be. Engelbert Dollfuss was now irreconcilably alienated from the Marxists.

As the likelihood of German intervention in Austria became more real in 1934, Dollfuss heeded the advise of his new mentor, Mussolini, and attempted to short-circuit the electrifying appeal of Nazism for may Austrians by launching "a frontal attack on the Social Democrats." For four days in February 1934 the Social Democrats were bombarded with heavy artillery until they finally sued for peace. When the shooting finally ended, hundreds of workers were dead and thousands of others were wounded. The most prominent casualty of the military assault was Austrian patriotism. Karl Renner summed up the horrible consequences:

> The workers turned away in resignation from their own state and came to the conclusion that if fascism was unavoidable, the anti-clerical variety of the Germans was preferable to that oriented towards Italy and the Catholic Church. That meant, in terms of foreign policy, that four years later the mass of the workers allowed annexation to take place without objection and also were soon taken in by the dazzling successes of Hitler. Without Dollfuss in 1934, Hitler would never have been able to achieve such a stupefying easy success in Austria in 1938.[54]

Following the assassination of Dollfuss by the Nazis in July 1934, the streets of Vienna once again echoed with patriotic eulogies. Among the most moving was that of the *Reichspost*:

> It is only a few hours, since Dr. Dollfuss has closed his eyes forever. He has fallen for his Austrian fatherland and for the freedom of the Austrian people whom he loved with all his heart. . . .
>
> In death the mouth of our beloved chancellor is silenced, but his words still ring forth: *Österreich über alles, wenn es nur will! And we will!*[55]

The only obituaries that really counted, however, were the ones that were never penned. Karl Renner and Otto Bauer remained silent. The formation of a united front in behalf of Austrian independence would be impossible until after the end of World War II.

NOTES

    1. As quoted in Julius Braunthal, *Victor und Friedrich Adler: Zwei Generationen Arbeiterbewegung* (Vienna, 1965), pp. 261–62.

2. Ibid., p. 259; Karl R. Stadler, *The Birth of the Austrian Republic, 1918–1919* (Leyden, 1966), p. 65.

3. *Arbeiter-Zeitung*, 12 November 1918, p. 1.

4. Franz Rothe, "Die Arbeitsgemeinschaft revolutionärer Sozialdemokraten Deutschösterreichs: eine Erwiderung an Otto Bauer," *Der Kampf* 13 (September 1920):326–35.

5. As quoted in Stephan Bonsal, *Unfinished Business* (Garden City, 1944), p. 88.

6. Ibid., p. 137.

7. Otto Bauer, *Die österreichische Revolution* (Vienna, 1965), p. 277.

8. Kurt von Schuschnigg, *My Austria* (New York, 1938), pp. 56–57.

9. Ibid., p. 48.

10. *Reichspost*, 23 November 1918, p. 1. See also Seipel's article "Das Recht des Volkes," *Reichspost*, 19 November 1918, pp. 1–2.

11. *Christlichsoziale Arbeiter-Zeitung*, 22 February 1919, p. 1.

12. Ibid., 20 September 1919, p. 4.

13. Viktor Reimann, *Zu gross für Österreich. Seipel und Bauer im Kampf um die Erste Republik* (Vienna, 1968), pp. 176–180; Klemens von Klemperer, *Ignaz Seipel. Christian Statesman in a Time of Crisis* (Princeton, 1972), pp. 115–116.

14. *Neue Freie Presse*, 24 April 1921, Morning edition, p. 6.

15. Ignaz Seipel, "Die erste Regierungserklärung, Vienna, May 31, 1922," in Josef Gessl (ed.), *Seipels Reden in Österreich und anderwärts* (Vienna, 1926), p. 21.

16. Ibid., pp. 17–21. See also Reimann's *Zu gross für Österreich*, pp. 193–201; and Paul R. Sweet, "Seipel's Views on *Anschluss* in 1929. An unpublished exchange of letters, '45," *Journal of Modern History* (December 1947): 320–24, and Klemperer, *Ignaz Seipel*, p. 161. Also useful is Richard Schmitz's personal recollection of Seipel in his *Ignaz Seipel: Denkblätter* (Vienna, 1946).

17. Seipel, "Die erste Regierungserklärung," pp. 17–21.

18. *The New York Times*, 2 September 1922, p. 4.

19. Speech by Seipel, Geneva, 4 October 1922, in Gessl, pp. 34–36.

20. *Arbeiter-Zeitung*, 30 August 1922, p. 1.

21. Ibid., 24 August 1922, p. 1.

22. Ibid., 19 August 1922, p. 1; 22 August 1922, p. 1; and 27 August 1922, p. 1.

23. *Reichspost*, 15 September 1922, p. 1.

24. Ibid., 8 October 1922, p. 1.

25. Ibid.

26. Schuschnigg, pp. 65–66.

27. *Reichspost*, 15 October 1922, p. 1.

28. *Arbeiter-Zeitung*, 8 October 1922, p. 1.

29. Ibid., 12 October 1922, p. 1.

30. *Reichspost*, 13 October 1922, p. 1.

31. Ibid.

32. Ibid., 1 October 1923, p. 1.

33. *Christlichsoziale Arbeiter-Zeitung*, 22 September 1923, p. 1; and 22 December 1923, p. 2. *Reichspost*, 15 October 1923, p. 5; 1 October 1923, p. 2; 4 October 1923, p. 8; and 7 October 1923, p. 10.

34. *Christlichsoziale Arbeiter-Zeitung*, 23 June 1923, p. 1.

35. Ibid., 2 June 1923, p. 1.

36. *Reichspost*, 1 October 1923, p. 2; 7 October 1923, p. 5; and 15 October 1923, p. 5.

37. Ibid., 4 October 1923, pp. 8–9.

38. *The New York Times*, 17 April 1925, p. 4.

39. *Arbeiter-Zeitung*, 9 April 1925, pp. 1–2; *Reichspost*, 9 April 1925, pp. 1–2.

40. *Reichspost*, 28 April 1925, p. 1.

41. *Arbeiter-Zeitung*, 19 April 1925, p. 1.

42. *Reichspost*, 24 April 1925, pp. 1–2; and 30 April 1925, p. 2.

43. Ignaz Seipel, "Unser Bekenntnis zum Vaterland," *Reichspost*, 29 May 1925, pp. 2–3. See also Sweet, pp. 320–24.

44. *Reichspost*, 12 April 1927, p. 2.

45. Ibid., 24 March 1931, p. 1. See also Adam Wandruszka, "Aus Seipels letzten Lebensjahren. Unveröffentlichte Briefe aus den Jahren 1930 und 1931," *Mitteilungen des Österreichischen Staatsarchiv* 9 (1956):566–68.

46. *The New York Times*, 13 April 1931, p. 11.

47. *Reichspost*, 4 September 1931, p. 1.

48. *Arbeiter-Zeitung*, 2 September 1931, p. 1; 4 September 1931, p. 1.

49. *Reichspost*, 3 August 1932, pp. 2, 12.

50. *Arbeiter-Zeitung*, 3 August 1932, p. 3.

51. Von Papen's article was reprinted in the *Reichspost*, 4 August 1932, p. 3. See also *Documents on German Foreign Policy, 1918–45* (11 vols., Washington, 1937–45), ser. D, vol. 1, p. 263.

52. Franz Riedl, *Kanzler Seipel: ein Vorkämpfer volksdeutschen Denkens* (Saarbrücken, 1935). Interested readers may profitably study pp. 27, 31, 47, 49, 58, 81, 125, 133, 137, 154, 187, and especially pp. 139–41.

53. Stadler, p. 79.

54. Karl Renner, *Denkschrift über die Geschichte der Unabhängigkeitserklärung Österreichs* (Vienna, 1945), p. 15.

55. *Reichspost*, 26 July 1934, p. 1.

The Austrian Monarchists, 1918–1938

Legitimism versus Nazism

BLAIR R. HOLMES

The significance of Austrian monarchism (legitimism) in inter-war Europe was its opposition to Nazism and support of Austrian independence in the face of German domination. The growth of Austrian monarchism during the 1930s largely resulted from the anti-Nazi position of the legitimists and the political value of a possible Habsburg restoration in countering German encroachment. Prior to the Great Depression and the threat of Nazism, the monarchist movement was unimportant. The failures in 1921 of Emperor Charles to seize the Hungarian throne virtually eliminated any political capital monarchism possessed. During most of the succeeding decade the movement was innocuous, limited in support and opposed to the new Austrian State. Legitimists considered the new State to be illegal, oppressive, and a violation of imperial traditions.

Gradually, as legitimists recognized the unlikelihood of recreating the Habsburg Empire, they changed their view to support the new Austria. They conceded that failure to preserve Austria would end all possibility of restoring the monarchy, whereas an attempt to resurrect the Empire would likely result in war. The only viable choice was to operate within the boundaries of Austria. By 1930 the preservation of "Little Austria" was an integral part of legitimist goals,[1] and their primary aim was to create a monarchical version of the Austrian Idea.

Contemporary with this evolution in legitimist thought was the resurgence of the *Anschluss* movement in Austria and Germany. The difficulties of the Great Depression had convinced many Austrians that their country was not viable, politically or economically. A tradition of political authoritarianism and the fear of social revolution inclined others to favor a state based on fascist principles. These views were reinforced after the Nazi assumption of power in Germany in 1933. Proponents of the *Anschluss* pointed to Hitler's Reich as the model of order and efficiency, whereas those desirous of preserving Austrian independence and avoiding Nazi domination cast about for means to counter the German threat. One of the supports for a free Austria was the monarchist movement.

The legitimists were in the forefront of early Nazi opposition, precisely because they knew that an annexation would end all possibility of a restoration. From the monarchist point of view, an *Anschluss* would be "more severe than any plague, worse than any war." The boundary between the two states was defined as the only difference between life and death for the Austrians.[2] In addition, annexation by Germany would lead to hostilities with France.

Otto Guenther, the Vice-President of the *Kaisertreue Volkspartei* and a leader in the initial legitimist opposition to Nazism, warned that Austrian parties and politicians were underestimating the Nazis.[3] The Austrian League (*Reichsbund der Österreicher*), also an early antagonist of Nazism, maintained that "National Socialism in Austria is not an Austrian movement. It denies that Austria is a national and political concept. It demands the incorporation of Austria into a unitary Germany."[4]

PARAMILITARISM AND THE DEFENSE OF AUSTRIA

The first arena of the conflict between monarchists and the burgeoning Nazis was paramilitarism. Because the brutality of Austrian politics made it essential that groups holding meetings have paramilitary units, monarchists played major roles in the development of Austria's largest paramilitary groups. Founded in 1919, the *Bund für Ordnung und Wirtschaftschutz* was part of the original nuclei of the the Heimwehr and the Union of Front Fighters (*Frontkämpfervereinigung*).[5] Monarchist paramilitary units were small, but numerous legitimists were in nonmonarchist organizations. In most cases, the monarchists were welcomed because they opposed Nazism and the Social Democrats. The Union of Front Fighters, one of Austria's larger paramilitary organizations, never endorsed a restoration but retained strong monarchist sympathies and enrolled numerous legitimists.

Throughout its existence, the Heimwehr was a conglomeration of groups each seeking its own ends. Some party segments wanted to take part in elections, whereas others sought to seize power and rule by dictatorship.[6]

Because of the diversity of its members, there was no comprehensive philosophy or political program during the history of the organization. Monarchists recognized the importance of the Heimwehr and attempted to use it for their own cause.[7] The first Heimwehr group in Tyrol was created by legitimists.[8] As late as 1933 legitimists in the Linz Heimwehr were so numerous that one troop was known as the "monarchists."[9] Like most early Heimwehr members, the legitimists were involved to combat the forces of the Left and to change the form of government.[10] By 1927 the Heimwehr had grown significantly but remained an amorphous movement with no common bond to unify its members who were drawn from legitimists, Nazis, clericals, Jews, ruffians, students, and a wide array of others.[11]

As the Republic entered its second decade, Nazism expanded its strength within the Heimwehr, and the influence of the monarchists was increasingly limited. Karl Werkmann, a leading monarchist who often spoke out sharply against the Brown Shirts, noted in 1931 that he and the meetings he addressed frequently were attacked by Nazi thugs.[12] Aware of the threat that extreme German nationalism posed to legitimism, prominent monarchists helped persuade Prince Ernst Rüdiger Starhemberg to become the leader of an Austrian-nationalist wing of the Heimwehr. The legitimists hoped that Starhemberg would defend monarchist interests and prevent the increasing influence of the Nazis from becoming dominant within the Heimwehr.[13]

The growth of Nazi influence soon led to a split within the ranks of the Heimwehr and, by some factions, to heightened activity against legitimism. In 1932 the leader of the Lower Austrian Heimwehr declared that "there may be no legitimist politics in the *Heimatschutz*, because our greatest principle is the welfare of the German people in Austria and a partnership with our German brothers."[14] The persistence of antimonarchist sentiments led the inspector of the Nazi Party to declare in 1934, that "the split of the *Heimatschutz* into a legitimist and nationalist faction is becoming more and more evident."[15]

Nazi opposition within the Heimwehr stemmed from fear that the movement might become the instrument of those favoring the Habsburg cause. A *Heimwehr* group in Linz resolved "not to let ourselves be used as a tool of dynastic interests."[16] Many Heimwehr members, though, were not opposed to legitimist participation so long as the monarchists supported Austrian-national and Christian aims and made no attempt to restore the Habsburgs. Under those conditions, monarchists were welcome allies in warding off attacks from the extreme Left and Right. An agreement was reached with the national leaders of the Heimwehr in 1931 at which the monarchists conceded that their "participation in the *Heimwehr* . . . was made possible when they clearly declared themselves to be above parties, forbade every party activity and limited their goals so that the feelings and convictions of the legitimists were not touched upon." On the basis of this agreement, "numerous adherents of the legitimist ideas took part in the *Heimwehr* movement and prevented any legitimist propaganda within the *Heimatschutz*."[17]

The Heimwehr factions led by Emil Fey and Prince Starhemberg were the most receptive to monarchists, refused to make the legitimist question a matter of discussion, and viewed "each of its members who are legitimists and renounce an application of their inner political convictions within the *Heimatschutz* as comrades against whom no accusations can be made and no hindrance laid in front of because of their political attitude."[18] The alignment of these Heimwehr factions with the legitimists and their subsequent backing of the revocation of the Habsburg Exclusion Laws were not policies aimed toward restoration. Starhemberg perceived that political realities dictated the need to gain monarchist support, but noted that the restoration was "an international problem which must be handled with great tact and caution."[19]

The Nazis were abominable to the legitimists for many reasons, but what rankled most were the defections from monarchist ranks of those who cast their lot with the swastika-bearing adversary. Included among some of the earliest notable defectors from legitimism were national leaders of the Party of Austrian Monarchists.[20] Several prominent Nazis, including Eduard Frauenfeld, the Gauleiter of Vienna, and Arthur Seyss-Inquart, the Nazi replacement for Schuschnigg in 1938, at one time had paid allegiance to monarchism.

The continued growth of Nazism inside and outside the Heimwehr persuaded many monarchists to join the largest nonmonarchist paramilitary group with pronounced legitimist sympathies: the Ostmärkische Sturmscharen. The creation of Kurt Schuschnigg, this group was, in part, an attempt to promote the monarchist cause in order to weaken the appeal of the Nazis and the Heimwehr. Schuschnigg needed to rely on legitimists because he would not cooperate with either the Social Democrats or Nazis and the Heimwehr was not entirely reliable. The Federal Chancellor sought a loyal group of supporters, some of whom could be gained promoting legitimism.[21] At a parade in Vienna in 1935 over 15,000 uniformed members of the organization (not all legitimists) participated.[22] Such overt courting of Austrian legitimists during the second decade of the Republic increased their membership greatly and accorded them greater influence in Austrian politics. Official approval and statements by government officials and foreign journalists also promoted the illusion in Austria and Germany that a future restoration was possible.

As a result of partisan animosity, Austrian politics reached the stage where "the opponent was never seen as a partner with whom one might exchange the command post . . . a partner one could trust not to change the basic rules of the game. Here the political opponent was always the enemy to be destroyed."[23] Such a situation increased the vigor of the monarchists in supporting the idea of an independent Austria and vilifying those who opposed it. Arguments that the Republic was not viable were met with sharp criticism from legitimists, who maintained that Austria was as capable as Switzerland, Belgium, and Holland in achieving a state of stability and prosperity.[24]

Although the legitimists never ceased hoping for an eventual restoration of the monarchy, by the early 1930s their political emphasis was on the preservation of the Republic. They argued that the well being of the Austrian people and State were much more important than the temporary form of government and made efforts to demonstrate their loyalty to Austria, hoping thereby to quell fears that they were awaiting an opportunity to overthrow the government.[25] Count Bethlen reflected monarchist sentiment when he declared that "it is not the question of the monarchy that is of importance in the present political disputes. . . . We have to pursue *Realpolitik.*"[26] Eugenio Morreale, the Italian press attaché in Vienna, believed that the monarchists were one of the three foremost groups battling for Austria's existence and representing the "will for independence" of the Austrian people.[27] Such monarchist sentiments and tactics did not go unnoticed in official governmental circles.

Monarchist opposition to ties with Germany accelerated and received increased surveillance in 1930, when Austria concluded a Customs Union with her northern neighbor. Chronic financial problems had made government officials receptive to closer ties with Germany in the hope that such an arrangement would rescue the Austrian economy. After an agreement was reached, the legitimist reaction was immediate and strong.[28] Because of international opposition, the issue was brought before the International Court at The Hague and declared contrary to the peace provisions forbidding any form of annexation.[29] The influence of monarchist opposition in preventing the realization of the Customs Union is indeterminable, but some considered it significant.[30]

In 1932 Engelbert Dollfuss became the Austrian Federal Chancellor and moved to change Austria to a State based on corporate and fascist principles. He encountered heated opposition from the Social Democrats and Nazis. His attempt to subdue political opposition and create, in effect, a monolithic political party led to civil war in Austria in 1934. Because of his tactics, the Federal Chancellor faced the prospect of ruling Austria with the support of scarcely more than one-third of the population.[31] As a result, he sought to establish closer ties with the legitimists in an effort to enhance the support of his regime.[32] Years later, Kurt von Schuschnigg expressed succinctly the situation that attracted monarchism into the vortex of Austrian politics:

> One thing should be remembered: The form of a state cannot be of supreme importance when its very existence is debatable. Therefore, the new Austria did not demand from any of its representatives a definite acknowledgement concerning its outward constitutional form. But it did demand respect for its great tradition and its historical importance, without which Austria itself would be unthinkable. He who agrees that Austria should be preserved must also find proper and expedient the unhindered cultivation of her great traditions.[33]

The governments of Dollfuss and, later, Schuschnigg found it increasingly difficult to counter internal discontent and external political pressure. Numerous groups within the country desired annexation by Germany. On the other hand, Austria was able to receive foreign monetary assistance from Britain, France, and the United States only if it remained independent and withstood annexation forces. Desperate to garner domestic support, the government estimated that one possibility was to perpetuate Austrian traditions. What Austria needed was "a positive reason for existence, not merely the negative faculty of representing a disassociation from the German political complex that has wrought so much harm to Austria."[34]

Hence, it was natural that the government resurrected traditions and provided an opportunity for monarchists to strengthen their position. The necessity of maintaining the Austrian State made monarchism a respectable political theory, but also led monarchists to overestimate the strength of their position and foreign political observers to wonder whether Austria was contemplating a restoration.

As a result of governmental approbation, a large number and variety of monarchist organizations developed. During its first decade, these organizations were little more than social clubs whose members engaged in armchair political debates and acts of beneficence,[35] but once legitimism became more of a governmental partner in combating the regime's enemies, efforts were made to create an organizational structure broad enough to incorporate all of a monarchist's possible social, political, and economic interests and activities. Legitimists were soon dispersed among an extensive array of organizations. Earlier attempts to unify the legitimists had failed due to personality conflicts and irreconcilable doctrines, but in 1932 there was an amalgamation. Under the leadership of the Austrian Imperial League (*Reichsbund der Österreicher*), over sixty monarchist organizations merged and formed an association entitled the *Iron Ring*.[36]

DOLLFUSS AND HOPES OF RESTORATION

Although the Austrian government catered to the monarchists to gain their support, few legitimists rose to prominent positions in the Austrian State. Most were accorded merely the appearance of their former status. In 1933 the uniform of the imperial army was reintroduced. Two years later the republican banners of the army corps were replaced by the imperial field standards.[37] The civil war of 1934 was followed by a new constitution which dropped the term *Republic* and reinstated the double-headed eagle. Also returned to vogue were the former names of military units, decorations and the imperial anthem *Gott erhalte* (though it was never allowed to supplant the official anthem, *Sei gesegnet ohne Ende*). Even though the primary reason for the return of the imperial trappings was the need of Austrian government to rally support from every possible source, such actions heightened the monarchist belief that the reinstitution of symbols was a prelude to the Habsburg restoration.[38]

Also heightened were monarchist agitation against Nazism and the development of a legitimist political theory stressing the compatability of democracy and monarchy. While believing that a monarch would fill the role of an authoritarian leader, most legitimists recognized that a monarchy needed to be based on a democratic system, as was the case in Great Britain. Monarchy and democracy were not antithetical, it was claimed, because a true democracy was congruent with monarchy. Monarchists believed generally that the throne should not be reestablished because of hereditary rights, but because the Habsburgs were the best possible guarantee for the development and perpetuation of true democracy.[39] By agitating for a Habsburg return solely to Austria, the formula could be applied that, as an independent and sovereign state, the country's choice of a form of government was purely an internal matter.

Legitimists stressed also that a restoration would be a major obstacle to the realization of Nazi plans in Austria. If the Habsburgs were allowed to rule in Austria, it was maintained, the hopes of Germany to annex Austria would be stifled. In addition, internal attempts to develop a subversive movement would fail because the Habsburgs would be too popular.[40] Otto von Habsburg reflected the legitimist conviction that the Austrian situation was a contest between the Nazis and legitimists. When asked what course Austria would take, Otto replied that "there are only two roads which are open: those to monarchism and Nazism. There is no room in my country for a liberal movement."[41] To monarchists, the struggle was a continuation of the contest between the Habsburgs and Hohenzollerns for the control of Central Europe. "Who wishes to save Austria must fight H[itler] with H[absburg]" was a popular monarchist slogan.[42]

In analyzing the legitimist-Nazi antagonism, one foreign correspondent stated that "what is going on in Austria at present is a kind of race between Nazism . . . and the Habsburg legitimacy. . . . Austrian independence depends on the result of the race. If legitimism wins, Nazism is played out in Austria."[43] Although overstated, the statement helps explain the mutual animosity between Nazis and legitimists, and why the Austrian government supported monarchism. As political tension increased in Austria after 1933, thought was given, domestically and on the international scene, to restoring the Habsburgs to counter Nazism and pan-Germanism. As a result of the consideration of a restoration, legitimists increased their agitation, while Nazi circles watched nervously and planned countermeasures.

As a result of the recognition of their heightened political value, however, Habsburg supporters occasionally misinterpreted the words of prominent leaders. Starhemberg, whose political star rose rapidly in 1934, particularly aroused legitimist hopes in attempting to strengthen his own position. In a typical speech, he declared that "from the standpoint of the government there is nothing to be said against legitimist attempts to win adherents for their political program."[44] Like other political leaders, however, Starhemberg always qualified his statements: "It is to be understood that the legitimist efforts, in all cases, are subordinate to the total interests of Austria. Nothing can be allowed to happen that would disturb the unity of those loyal to the Fatherland or make difficulties for the responsible national leadership."[45] There was also a frequent lack of comprehension among legitimists that the movement could be used for purposes other than its own. The creation of the Fatherland Front by Dollfuss in 1934, monarchists claimed, had led the government to authorize an increase in monarchist activities to pave the way for a restoration.[46]

Although it is true that Dollfuss made numerous statements that aroused hope within legitimist ranks, he never considered restoring the dynasty. Dollfuss expressed thoughts calculated to appear as approval of monarchist aims, but he did not take a firm stand on the restoration issue and avoided major decisions relative to the Habsburgs.[47] Rumors regarding Dollfuss' alleged monarchist sympathies became widespread in 1934 when a new constitution was being promulgated which would not contain the Habsburg Exile and Confiscation Laws. In reality, this conciliatory step, which was attributed to the Federal Chancellor, was the work of conservative circles within the Heimwehr.[48] Even if Dollfuss had been the moving force behind the repeal of the banishment and the increased likelihood of a return of the Habsburg fortune, he left little doubt that such actions were not intended to be a path for the dynasty to return to power: "Concerning the Habsburg question we have no secrets. The abrogation of certain measures, which were taken against members of the former dynasty immediately following the dissolution of the monarchy, is from our standpoint exclusively a matter of humanity and has absolutely nothing to do with active politics."[49] So long as the legitimists were willing to support the Dollfuss government, they were tolerated and given minor concessions, but the Federal Chancellor did not encourage increased monarchist activity in order to develop a stronger and more influential legitimist movement. He wanted the existing monarchist groups to expend their energies on behalf of the Dollfuss program.[50] Legitimists were to be used to fill a gap in the Fatherland Front.[51]

When questioned regarding his relations with the monarchists, the Federal Chancellor replied that "the legitimists have enrolled in my league . . . because they are, in the first place, interested in the preservation of Austrian independence. This is for them the only point of contact with my program. It is evident that the Fatherland Front pursues no monarchist plans. Moreover, the issue is not pressing. Inside of the present boundaries of Austria the question of Habsburg restoration cannot be considered."[52] The smaller, and usually more utopian, monarchist groups were disappointed by the stand of the Dollfuss government. The Kaisertreue Volkspartei believed that within the Fatherland Front monarchism should be considered of pressing importance,[53] but the main body of legitimists was not deceived by the friendliness of the Dollfuss government. The Austrian Imperial League declared that it extended its support not as legitimists but as Austrians. Most monarchists recognized that they would not soon see the fulfillment of their wishes "insofar as these exceed the preservation of the independence and autonomy of Austria."[54]

Otto von Habsburg was apprehensive at the route Dollfuss was taking. The ties of the Federal Chancellor with Mussolini and indications that the government was establishing a state based on fascist principles aroused caution among legitimists in their support of the regime. The heir expressed his feelings in a letter that the government would not publish: "I absolutely reject [Nazi] fascism for Austria and see the solution only in a constitutional monarchy along democratic lines similar to that in England. . . but I consider the moment for successful restoration not ripe, because it must be realized by legal means and the contemporary constitution of the Dollfuss government does not insure the necessary guarantee."[55]

Although unable to make the gains they desired by supporting the Dollfuss government, Austria's legitimists believed there was no alternative. Austria needed to follow an authoritarian course and dispose of the Social Democrats and Nazis before there could be serious talk of a restoration. The monarchists admitted that "the Dollfuss course serves a national purpose by ending at the steps of the throne. It is a visionary precaution against Bolshevism, which is universally destructive and will prevail as long as the people refuse to support the sovereign rights of the banished dynasty."[56]

The monarchists' belief that the authoritarian course of Dollfuss would clear the way for the restoration accounts largely for their support of the Federal Chancellor. Discontented with the formerly prevailing system of party politics, they preferred a single authoritarian leader and a National Assembly that would be representative of all classes and not the product of competing parties. Once the new system was in working order and had restored balance to Austrian life, a plebiscite would determine whether the populace "wanted to retain the completed reorganization of public life or return to the chaos of a parliamentary State."[57] Dollfuss was a necessary step toward monarchist goals.

SCHUSCHNIGG AND THE MONARCHISTS

While there was little question where Dollfuss stood on the restoration issue, monarchist hopes rose greatly when Schuschnigg became Federal Chancellor in July 1934. Speaking at a political conference in 1931, he had expressed strong legitimist views when he stated that the monarchy was a better form of State than the one presently in existence and that when the Christian Social Party refused to tolerate monarchists, he would withdraw.[58] Later, as Federal Chancellor, he joined the Iron Ring and the Catholic Nobleman's Association, both legitimist organizations.

After achieving political prominence, however, Schuschnigg's monarchist sentiments never played a role in determining official decisions. In later years he explained that "because Austria's German and European consciousness was most clearly symbolized by the Habsburg concept, I was, according to the vernacular, a legitimist. For the most part, however, this remained a totally insignificant and personal view."[59] Schuschnigg was concerned with reestablishing and strengthening the *pattern* of Habsburg rule, not in restoring the monarchy. His aim was to erect in Austria a single powerful political leadership to combat the forces of extremism.[60] Schuschnigg's support of the monarchists arose out of a desire to obtain their backing. He told a counselor of the German Legation that "the legitimists were a dying class who . . . were impractical men but fundamentally very valuable to the State." Fears of the monarchists gaining control were unfounded, because he did "not concede them any decisive influence whatsoever in the conduct of government."[61]

Despite such statements by the Federal Chancellor, monarchism made significant gains during Schuschnigg's tenure. Berlin's chargé d'affaires in Vienna reported that

> the legitimist movement has gained ground. Although these meetings made a sorry impression two years ago, they are now well attended by all classes

of people. The theme has always been the same: the restoration of the monarchy will bring Austria not only rescue from National Socialism but also economic recovery. There is no doubt that Legitimism enjoys the tacit encouragement of the Federal Chancellor, since he sees in the restoration of the Habsburg dynasty the ultimate goal of his policy. He probably hopes to see the movement in Austria . . . so strengthened that outside influences can no longer impede it. . . . If they [changes in the government] come, they will not be far from the above-mentioned line followed by the Federal Chancellor.[62]

Germany was keenly aware of the increase of legitimist sentiment and recognized its threat. A military officer reported in 1934 that "the legitimist movement is rapidly growing, especially in rural areas. . . . The legitimists are working slowly and systematically. . . . The Government will soon have to choose between National Socialists and legitimists."[63] Berlin feared that public sentiment was turning against the Nazis because several prominent members of the Austrian government were monarchist sympathizers. Prince Alois Schönburg-Hartenstein, the Minister of Defense, for example, was reported to hold pro-clerical views and to be a "convinced legitimist."

In spite of the apparent German opposition to legitimism, there was a contrary and rather curious side to German feelings toward the Habsburg restoration. Aware of the political value of monarchism, Hitler, at one time, was willing to countenance a dynastic return to Austria under German sponsorship. During the winter of 1932–1933, Otto von Habsburg traveled to Berlin to study and conduct research at the Agrarian Institute. While there, he was invited to dinner by Hermann Göring, who presented a plan whereby the claimant would become the leader of the German-nationalist forces in Austria and seize control of the government by utilizing the powers of the Heimwehr and other conservative groups. Of course, it was explained, Otto would be expected to serve as the *Statthalter* for the German government. Without hesitation, the Archduke refused the proposal.[64]

Until 1935 Germany remained secretly in favor of a Habsburg restoration so long as the dynasty would be willing to accept Hitler's conditions. One of the alleged backers of an Austrian monarchy was Franz von Papen, who was appointed ambassador to Austria in an attempt to soothe the feelings aroused by the Nazi putsch of July 1934, which resulted in the assassination of Dollfuss. In reality, Papen had no legitimist sympathies but was willing to propagate Berlin's scheme for a restoration. In his memoirs, Papen explained the solution he presented to Schuschnigg: "In the Reich Emperor Charles and Empress Zita were rejected because of the deceitful role they played at the end of the World War. Against Archduke Otto there was no opposition and I often told Schuschnigg that we could consider the restoration as a domestic matter when the Archduke was prepared to accept a type of union which would confer leadership upon the Reich."[65] Hitler envisioned Austria becoming a kingdom and having the same relationship to the Reich as Bavaria, Württemberg, and Baden. Schuschnigg refused to answer the German proposal, because "he knew that the Archduke would never make such a supreme sacrifice for the unity of the Empire."[66] Following the Federal Chancellor's rebuff, Germany became implacably opposed to a restoration.

The German government agreed with the legitimists that the conflict over Austria would result in a victory for either the monarchists or Nazis. Papen strengthened the German view that the Austrian government was adopting monarchist goals in order to thwart Nazi aims:

> According to reliable information reaching me, the Director of Security for Upper Austria, Count Revertera, Prince Starhemberg's Adjutant Prince Windisch-Graetz, and Count Coreth went to Steenockerzeel on about December 15th in order to deliver a handwritten letter signed by Schuschnigg and Starhemberg. The paper stated that it was regretted that the restoration planned for January 1936 had to be postponed on account of the general situation. After Prince Starhemberg had asked the heir to the throne not to doubt the loyalty of his legitimist sentiments, it was stated that the Austrian government held political remedies to be useless against National Socialism — it must be countered by the principle of legitimism, as this is the only principle likely to succeed.[67]

As a result of their stand against Nazism, the monarchists received support from nonlegitimist, anti-Nazi groups that, for various reasons, including *opposition* to the Austrian regime, desired to help preserve their country's independence, but did not want to operate within the Fatherland Front.[68] Latent legitimism within the Christian Social camp grew considerably, and the circles of liberal Jews in Vienna looked upon monarchism as security against Hitler.[69] The movement received substantial amounts of capital from nonmonarchist groups who feared Nazism and desired an independent Austria.[70]

The Federal Chancellor, however, was caught between two fires. To muster support for his government, he solicited monarchist support, but to avoid foreign hostility, he declared the restoration to be of little consequence. To bow to external pressure and renounce any desire or intent to restore the monarchy would have reduced domestic legitimist support and been a breach of Austria's sovereignty, but supporting the monarchists elicited the wrath of neighboring States. As a result, Schuschnigg played a dual role with the monarchists. He encouraged their propaganda activities but retreated by stating that the restoration question was inconvenient or not of pressing importance.[71] For him, "neither this nor that form of administration but existence or nonexistence, life or hunger, freedom or occupation . . . was the decisive debate for 7 million persons."[72] Schuschnigg was determined not to let the issue of monarchism destroy Austria. According to Guido Schmidt, the Austrian Foreign Minister after 12 February 1938, Schuschnigg, although "leaning towards legitimism sentimentally, always admonished rationality and never played with fire. In a letter he energetically opposed legitimist leaders and in one case threatened imprisonment."[73]

THE AUSTRO-GERMAN CRISIS

As German political pressure intensified and Italy relinquished its influence in Austria in 1935, a change occurred in the relationship between the monarchist movement and the Austrian government. The main concern of monarchist and government officials became not which form of government Austria should have but whether Austria would maintain its independence. Monarchist activity concentrated increasingly on preserving Austria, not restoring the Habsburgs. Papen reported that the Austrian regime was turning more to monarchism as its only way of pursuing an anti-German policy[74] and cautioned that "in spite of the difficulties which this question presents in the fields of foreign and domestic policy, one must in no way underestimate its importance for future development."[75] Speaking before the Iron Ring in February 1934, Friedrich von Wiesner, the head of the Austrian Imperial League, projected the course the monarchist movement would need to take in combating Nazism: "We want to maintain the independence and integrity of Austria. We want the fundamental character of the Austrian national concept to be that of a Christian *Rechtsstaat*. We want to defend the Austrian spirit, essence, and culture against every attempt at political subordination. Most of all, we oppose efforts to coerce us to submit to the philosophy and political dictates of the swastika."[76]

For its part, the Schuschnigg government encouraged legitimism. However, nothing Schuschnigg did stimulated more fear in opponents of the restoration than the partial repeal of the anti-Habsburg laws. Although this action was not intended to be a step toward a restoration, it resulted in a vigorous reaction on the part of Germany and the Little Entente, who feared that the return of any of the Habsburg holdings was a major step toward the restoration of the dynasty.[77]

In its reconsideration of the Habsburg Exile and Confiscation Laws, the Austrian government tried to minimize the significance of its contemplated action. Walter Adam, the Minister of Propaganda, declared that the action was merely an overdue "correction of an injustice with which no political by-play is connected. The question of the restoration is not immediate. Returning the property is of little importance politically."[78] In explaining his government's action, Foreign Minister Egon Berger-Waldenegg noted that in order to preserve European peace, Vienna had contacted every interested State and obtained approval of the contemplated repeal of the anti-Habsburg legislation.[79] The fact that the regime did not rescind the Exile and Confiscation Laws until 1935 indicates that more than a sense of justice was involved. *The* (London) *Times* argued that the most plausible reason was to give the present, or some future, regime another card to use if Austria's independence should be threatened.[80] The prevalent opinion was that Schuschnigg had made the move in order to sooth legitimist feelings and retain their support.[81]

By the fall of 1935, Schuschnigg recognized that to preserve Austria's independence, it was necessary to make an arrangement with Germany. In September he met with Otto von Habsburg to discuss Austro-German relations. While giving rise to rumors of a restoration, the conversations were an attempt by Schuschnigg to defend his intended course of action. The fact that the Federal Chancellor visited the heir and informed him of the reasons for attempting to compromise with Germany indicated that the Austrian government considered the monarchists a political ally that could not be ignored.

In July 1936, Austria signed an agreement (*Abkommen*) with Germany, whereby each party guaranteed not to interfere in the internal affairs of the other. The independence of Austria was recognized by the German government and declared to be a private, domestic matter.[82] Schuschnigg felt such a step was advisable, because the lack of international assistance and the precariousness of Austria's position made it impossible for Vienna to consider a restoration in countering Germany. Schuschnigg knew that his country could not risk certain war with both Germany and Yugoslavia if the Habsburgs returned.[83] The Federal Chancellor was also aware that the Nazis would attempt to increase their influence and undermine his government, but the only way he saw of hindering Germany was in concluding an agreement that gave Austria a firm legal basis that could not be ignored easily.[84] Although the agreement strengthened Austria's legal position, it aided Germany's machinations against the Schuschnigg government. In addition to releasing detained Nazis, two prominent pro-Germans were added to the cabinet. Edmund Glaise-Horstenau became Minister without Portfolio and Guido Schmidt was appointed Secretary of State for Foreign Affairs.[85]

The legitimists opposed the *Abkommen* because it made a restoration impossible for the forseeable future. The monarchist camp feared that a relaxation of political pressure would be a severe blow to the Habsburg cause. Should the July Agreement be successful, the main basis for the recent growth of monarchism would be eliminated. Hence, Austrian legitimists promoted the apprehension that Berlin would not live up to the contract and predicted that the restoration issue would become of increasingly greater importance.[86] Schuschnigg desired the support of the Habsburg claimant but feared that Archduke Otto would take action against the *Abkommen*. So the Director of the Austrian Information Service, Edmund Weber, was dispatched to the imperial residence to explain the government's action and obtain a promise from Otto that he would not attempt to return to Austria.[87] The Federal Chancellor was apprehensive lest the heir speak out against the contemplated agreement, in which case Austria's legitimists would turn against his government. Schuschnigg also requested that the Archduke make it clear in the Parisian political salons where the heir was welcome that the agreement with Germany was not a capitulation but a postponement.[88]

Otto initially refused to countenance the *Abkommen* or create favorable sentiment for it. The agreement, he maintained, was not a barrier against Nazism but a hole in the dam through which a flood of Brown Shirts would engulf Austria. After lengthy conversations, he agreed not to express a negative attitude toward the *Abkommen* and to support Schuschnigg's action in Paris. However, the Archduke remained hostile toward the agreement and expressed his concerns in a letter to the Federal Chancellor. Schuschnigg responded by traveling to Switzerland again to justify his policies to the heir.[89]

Despite the Federal Chancellor's deference for Otto's feelings, Schuschnigg's political acumen made it impossible to consider allowing the young Habsburg to ascend the throne. Monarchism was a card that could be held to oppose Germany and gain legitimist support but could not be played. Only in the event of an extreme emergency would there have been an attempt to use the monarchy in a final effort to save Austria.[90] Schuschnigg calculated that German adherence to the *Abkommen* was highly unlikely, so his efforts to retain the support of the monarchists stressed that proponents of legitimism were free to bring about a restoration so long as it did not endanger Austria. By these tactics, Schuschnigg hoped to avoid creating the impression that the July Agreement had destroyed any chance of a restoration. He wanted dynastic enthusiasts to believe that a Habsburg return had merely been delayed.[91]

In German circles, Schuschnigg's efforts to placate the monarchists were interpreted as moves to restore the monarchy. The Reich's chargé d'affaires in Vienna reported that

> Minister von Glaise-Horstenau called on me today and said confidentially that in the last few days he had obtained a shocking insight into the Federal Chancellor's political mentality. The Federal Chancellor has stated that, from a point of view of foreign as well as domestic policy, National Socialism was the enemy of peaceful development in Austria. The July Agreement had not fulfilled his expectations: the establishment of a relatively close cooperation

with the Reich in foreign affairs, and the maintenance of absolute freedom
to pursue an entirely independent Austrian – meaning clerical and legitimist –
policy in domestic affairs.[92]

Berlin feared that Austrian discontent with the *Abkommen* and the resultant
increase of Nazi influence would move the Schuschnigg government in the
direction of recalling the Habsburgs.

When Guido Schmidt visited Berlin in November 1936, he received
a lecture from Hermann Göring and learned in unequivocal terms that Germany would not countenance a restoration. The reason for the German war
threats, Schmidt reported, was Germany's fear that "the restoration of the
House of Habsburg would result in the creation of a Catholic center of
gravity which would attract the southern German States."[93]

Members of the German diplomatic corps in Vienna noted that the
appeal of a monarchical answer to the "Austrian problem" was not restricted
to sentimentalists but included prominent individuals. In February 1937
Papen commented on an article in the *Wiener Zeitung* calling for a restoration: "the statement in this semiofficial newspaper . . . is significant, for it
for the first time confirms as the official view that the new Austrian Constitution must be crowned with a monarchy."[94] Although overstated, the
ambassador's remarks revealed that Austria was casting about for something
that would guarantee its integrity. As a result of Papen's claims, German
Foreign Minister Neurath visited Vienna. He informed Schuschnigg that,
because of the threat a restoration posed to world peace and the realization
of German goals, Vienna should consult Berlin before taking any action
and pressed for a guarantee that the Austrian Federal Chancellor would
secure the Reich's approval before restoring the monarchy.[95] Neurath refused to accept Schuschnigg's counterargument that the introduction of a
monarchy might be a desirable means of easing tension and settling domestic conflicts and responded that a Habsburg solution for Austria's problems
would be tantamount to committing suicide.[96]

The epitome of the German reaction to the perceived threat of legitimism was the Reich's military contingency plans, which followed upon
Neurath's visit. On June 24, German War Minister Werner von Blomberg
issued a strategic military plan entitled "Case Otto," which outlined the
actions to be taken in the event of a Habsburg restoration in Austria.[97]
Within a week Papen reported that "the restoration of the House of Habsburg has been completely shelved," but by the end of the year he admitted
that "it is not to be misunderstood that legitimism has gained ground.
While these meetings made a miserable impression two years ago, they are
now visited by all classes. The theme is always the same: The resurrection
of the monarchy will not only rescue Austria from National Socialism, but

will also bring economic recovery."[98] Berlin's diplomatic reports from Vienna continued to include messages demonstrating fear of a restoration: "In the immediate future we shall have to expect increased activity by the opponents of the *Anschluss*. We must not underestimate the possibility that someday France and Italy will be convinced that the last remaining means for Austria to escape annexation will be for them to agree, whether they like it or not, on a legitimist solution of the problem."[99]

Years later, Schuschnigg declared that he had intended to use the Habsburgs as his last card in the game against Hitler; but when urged by Archduke Otto, in their final meeting, to appeal to the Western powers, press rearmament, compromise with the Left, and restore the monarchy, the Federal Chancellor stated that the days of the monarchy were past and an attempt to restore the dynasty would plunge Austria into war. As the crisis reached its peak in March 1938, the Austrian monarchists were unable to act. They had overestimated their influence. So had Hitler, who marched into Austria without firing a shot.

NOTES

1. Austria, National War Archives, Härtlein MS, Pt. I, p. 24.

2. Eli Rubin, *Habsburg–Existenzbedingung der Arbeiterschaft Österreichs* (Vienna, 1936), p. 14.

3. Otto Guenther, *Unser Kaiser kehrt Heim. Legitimistische Arbeit in Österreich* (Vienna, 1933), pp. 19–23.

4. *Der Österreicher*, 7 April 1933, p. 1.

5. Friedrich Wagner, "Der österreichische Legitimismus, 1918–1938. Seine Politik und Publizistik" (Ph.D. diss., University of Vienna, 1956), p. 24.

6. Eugen Weber and Hans Rogger (eds.), *The European Right. A Historical Profile* (Berkeley, 1966), p. 330.

7. Julius Braunthal, *The Tragedy of Austria* (London, 1948), p. 23.

8. *Der Österreicher*, 16 October 1936, p. 1.

9. *Staatswehr*, January 1933, p. 3.

10. *Der Österreicher*, 16 October 1936, p. 1.

11. Weber and Rogger, p. 336.

12. *Der Österreicher*, 10 December 1931, p. 4.

13. Interview with Sebastian Blumauer, cited by Wagner, p. 204.

14. *Der Österreicher*, 3 June 1932, p. 1.

15. U.S. Department of State, *Documents of German Foreign Policy* (Washington, 1957–1961), ser. C, vol. III, p. 45.

16. Cited in Härtlein MS, Pt. I, p. 35.

17. *Der Österreicher*, 1 January 1932, p. 1.

18. Cited in Härtlein MS, Pt. I, p. 35.

19. *Neue Zürcher Zeitung*, 28 February 1934, p. 1.

20. Ibid., p. 2.

21. M. W. Fodor, "Traffic in Kings," *Nation* 104 (23 October 1935):463.

22. *Der Österreicher,* 21 June 1935, p. 4.

23. Peter Sugar (ed.), *Native Fascism in the Successor States, 1918–1945* (Santa Barbara, 1979), p. 19.

24. *Neujahrsbote für die Kaisertreuen Österreichs,* 1929, p. 18.

25. *Der Österreicher,* 22 November 1935, p. 2; 26 November 1937, p. 4.

26. M. H. H. Macartney, "Karl's Death and Hungary," *Fortnightly Review* 49 (May 1922):729.

27. *Österreichische Flugblätter,* 1936, p. 2.

28. *Der Österreicher,* March 28, 1931, p. 1; April 15, 1931, p. 1; June 11, 1931, p. 3; July 9, 1931, p. 1.

29. Walter Goldinger, *Geschichte der Republik Österreich* (Vienna, 1962), pp. 158–59.

30. Cited in Härtlein MS, Pt. I, pp. 30–31.

31. C.f. Weber and Rogger, p. 344.

32. *Neue Zürcher Zeitung,* 28 February 1934, p. 1.

33. Kurt von Schuschnigg, *My Austria* (New York, 1938), p. 259.

34. Stanko Guldescu, "Austria and the Archduke Otto," *Dalhousie Review* 41 (Autumn 1961):318–19.

35. Eduard Ludwig, *Österreichs Sendung in Donauraum. Die letzten Dezennien Österreichischer Innen- und Aussenpolitik* (Vienna, 1954), pp. 18–19.

36. Härtlein MS, Pt. I, p. 42.

37. Alfred Kasamas, *Österreichische Chronik,* 2d ed. (Vienna, 1948), p. 471.

38. *Unter dem Doppeladler,* September 1935, p. 1; *Survey of International Affairs* (1936), p. 508.

39. *Die Lupe,* April 1952, p. 1.

40. T. R. Ybarra, "Lost One Empire: Interview with Archduke Otto," *Collier's* 97 (18 April 1936):62.

41. D. Waring, "Interview with Otto," *Current History* 44 (August 1936): 36.

42. Prince Konstantin von Bayern, *Ohne Mache und Herrlichkeit* (Munich, 1961), p. 272.

43. "The Habsburgs," *Contemporary Review* 151 (June 1937):727.

44. *Der Östereicher,* 11 October 1935, p. 1.

45. Ibid.; c.f. *Survey of International Affairs* (1936), p. 408.

46. *Der Österreicher,* 16 October 1936, p. 1.

47. C.f. *Unser Staatsprogramm* (Vienna, 1935), p. 17.

48. Ludwig, p. 151.

49. *Der Österreicher,* 13 July 1934, p. 1.

50. *Linzer Volksblatt,* 10 July 1935, p. 1; Ludwig, p. 208.

51. Hellmut Andics, *Der Fall Otto Habsburg* (Vienna, 1965), pp. 69–70; Anton Rintelen, *Erinnerukngen an Österreichs Weg* (Munich, 1941), p. 249.

52. *Arbeiter-Zeitung,* 1 August 1933, p. 1.

53. Guenther, p. 39.

54. *Der Österreicher,* 6 October 1933, p. 1.

55. *Manchester Guardian,* 29 September 1933, p. 252; John Gunther, "Habsburgs Again?" *Foreign Affairs* 12 (July 1934):581.

56. *Der Österreicher,* 19 February 1937, p. 4.

57. Ibid., 15 May 1930, p. 1; 29 Janaury 1932, p. 1; c.f. 5 February 1937, p. 2.

58. Cited by *Der Österreicher,* 12 February 1932, p. 1.

59. Kurt von Schuschnigg, *Ein Requiem in Rot-Weiss-Rot* (Zürich, 1946), pp. 22–23.

60. *Unser Staatsprogramm,* p. 61.

61. U.S. Department of State, ser. D, vol. 1, pp. 358–59.

62. Ibid., p. 474.

63. Ibid., ser. C, vol. 2, p. 836.

64. Personal correspondence with Count Henry Degenfeld, Secretary to Otto von Habsburg, 22 September 1971; Eric Phipps to John Simon, 23 January 1933, F.O. 371/C975/975/21.

65. Franz von Papen, *Der Wahrheit eine Gasse* (Innsbruck, 1952), p. 400.

66. Ibid.

67. U.S. Department of State, ser. C, vol. 4, p. 936–37.

68. Manfred Schindlbauer, "Der Legitimismus in Östererich während der Regierung des Bundeskanzlers Schuschnigg" (seminar paper, Institute of Contemporary History, University of Vienna), p. 2.

69. Heinrich Benedikt et al., *Geschichte der Republik Östererich* (Vienna, 1954), pp. 26–27.

70. Mitzi Hartmann, *Austria Still Lives* (London, 1938), p. 198.

71. Great Britain, Foreign Office, Minutes, 24 February 1936, F.O. 371/R997/125/67; Schindlbauer, p. 14.

72. Schuschnigg, *Requiem*, p. 176.

73. *Der Hochverratsprozess gegen Dr. Guido Schmidt vor dem Wiener Volksgericht. Die gerichtlichen Protokolle mit den Zeugenaussagen, unveröffentlichen Dokumenten, sämtlichen Geheimbriefen und Geheimakten* (Vienna, 1947), p. 271.

74. U.S. Department of State, ser. C, vol. 4, p. 832.

75. Ibid., 855–56.

76. *Der Österericher*, 2 March 1934, p. 5.

77. Ibid., 5 October 1934, p. 1.

78. Walford Selby to the Foreign Office, 5 July 1935, F.O. 371/R4211/662/3; Sidney B. Fay, "Austria and the Habsburgs," *Current History* 42 (September 1935):651.

79. *Archiv der Gegenwart*, 2134; Fay, p. 651; c.f. Walford Selby to Samuel Hoare, 8 July 1935, F.O. 371/R4634/662/3.

80. Cited by Härtlein MS, Pt. I, p. 74; c.f. Foreign Office Minutes, 29 July 1935, F.O. 371/R4634/66/3.

81. *Neue Zürcher Zeitung*, 5 July 1935, p. 4; U.S. Department of State, ser. D, vol. 1, p. 399.

82. Goldinger, p. 226.

83. *Der Hochverratsprozess gegen Dr. Guido Schmidt*, p. 490.

84. Martin Fuchs, *Showdown in Vienna* (New York, 1939), pp. 24–25.

85. Kasamas, p. 537.

86. Germany, Foreign Office, *Akten zur Deutschen Auswärtigen Politik* (Baden-Baden, 1950 and thereafter), ser. D, vol. 3, p. 241.

87. *Der Hochverratsprozess gegen Dr. Guido Schmidt*, pp. 490.

88. Andics, pp. 82–83.

89. Ibid., p. 83; Ludwig, p. 173.

90. Confidential report of *The* (London) *Times* correspondent to the Foreign Office in Vienna, 29 April 1937, F.O. 371/R2952/989/3.

91. *Der Österreicher*, 26 November 1937, p. 4.

92. U.S. Department of State, ser. D, vol. 1, pp. 474–75.

93. *Der Hochverratsprozess gegen Dr. Guido Schmidt*, p. 43.

94. U.S. Department of State, ser. D, vol. 1, p. 388.

95. Walford Selby to the Foreign Office, 12 March 1937, F.O. 371/R1738/770/67.

96. Papen, pp. 439–40.

97. U.S. Department of State, ser. D, vol 1, pp. 433–34..

98. *Akten zur Deutschen Auswärtigen Politik*, Ser. D, vol. 3, p. 388.

99. U.S. Department of State, ser. C, vol. 1, p. 194.

Social Democracy's Drift toward Nazism before 1938

HELMUT KONRAD

The extent to which Nazism in Austria succeeded in penetrating the ranks of the Social Democrats in the years before 1938 is a question that deeply affected the writing of Austrian history during the mid-1970s. The debate over this currently relevant topic formed the central matter of investigation in, above all, Karl R. Stadler's two great works,[1] as well as in the essays written at that time by Gerhard Botz.[2] Because no conclusive and comprehensive verdict could be reached, research undertaken at that time ceased so that today, regional investigations aside,[3] it is still necessary to draw from the information available a decade ago. This brief interest in the delicate topic of contemporary history was shown during those years, when a special type of historiography ("coalition historiography") seemed to have been overcome at long last.[4] During the first couple of decades after the Second World War, the two major political blocs agreed to accept certain areas of historical and political taboos at a time when it was diplomatically opportune to present Austria as the first victim of German Nazi aggression. Those conditions hardly presented a promising starting point for research into contemporary history, and consequently the first Chair of Contemporary History was not created until the mid-1960s.[5] Not surprisingly, therefore, the independent Austrian contribution to the development of Nazism and the active participation of Austrians in creating structures of both power and downright extermination remained academically underexposed. Not until there emerged a generation of historians who

110

had experienced neither Nazism nor the major turning points of Austrian history (1914, 1918, 1933–1934, 1938, 1945) was there a possibility of approaching those acute questions, beginning merely with systematic investigations of the resistance to Nazism in Austria. These studies, above all, were pioneered by former emigrés.

Feelings of strength within the socialist camp in the 1970s made possible an examination of the dark spots in their own history. In this way, self-criticism was practiced more freely than by conservative historians, who had massive problems of their own to investigate regarding the last decade before the Second World War. However, the shrinking scope for political action during the last decade has once more led to a revival of the *Lager* mentality in Austria, whereby the earlier possibilities of self-criticism in the sphere of historiography were restricted. In this way, progress made through fresh insights within those spheres of research, so important for an appreciation of the contemporary political landscape of Austria, has been lagging.

Today it can be taken for granted that the Nazis made considerable inroads into the Social Democratic camp before the Second World War. At the same time, it is now generally acknowledged that, as a social stratum, the workers were always underrepresented numerically in the Nazi Party, although there was a dramatic influx of members, or at least voters, from other social strata. In any case, taken on their own, general statistical data tend to distort reality. The switch-over by Social Democrats to the Nazis was not by any means a continuous and even process throughout Austria. It went ahead spasmodically, impeded or helped by a multitude of regional peculiarities, connected far more with peculiarities within the workers' movement than within that of the Nazis. While the leading cadres would switch over only in exceptional cases, ordinary Party members were prone to do so in widely varying degrees. An examination of the behavior of the militants, on the other hand, shows clearly recognizable points of time and motives for conversion.

Austrian Social Democracy before 1934 was truly a party of the masses, in which more than 10 percent of Austria's entire adult population was enrolled.[6] Every third voter was a member of the Party, and the Party's self-defense organization, the Republican Defense Corps (Republikanischer Schutzbund) could boast as many as 96,000 members,[7] surpassing the strength of the regular Austrian army (which was no more than 30,000 men) by more than two-thirds.

By way of contrast, before the world economic crisis, the Nazi Party was a splinter party. However, by 1933 it attained a membership the equivalent to about 10 percent of the Social Democratic Party.[8] The Nazi Party managed to increase this percentage during its period of illegality, whereas the Social Democratic Party shrank to just a few centers of organization after being banned in February 1934. This does not mean, however, that the two political movements acted as communicating vessels. Psychologically, the most meaningful reaction on the part of Social Democrats to the events of 1934 was doubtless a paralyzing sense of resignation, resulting in adaptation to the victorious regime of the Corporate State. The dramatic switch to the Nazis, on the one hand, and to the Communists, on the other, do not represent major shifts when seen in purely statistical terms, though in the nature of things they were regarded as spectacular events compared with the norm of resigned behavior and retreat into private life.

The survey that follows examines the basic stipulation of the conversion of Social Democrats to Nazism, as well as some typical forms assumed by it. For a full understanding of those stipulations, it would seem essential to offer a differential treatment, allowing for regional aspects that also possess a great intrinsic explanatory value for the history of the Austrian workers' movement in general and the civil war of February 1934 in particular.[9]

REGIONAL PECULIARITIES OF
AUSTRIAN SOCIAL DEMOCRACY

Research conducted into the history of the Austrian workers' movement hitherto has focused on developments in Vienna, tending to equate these developments with the whole of Austria. For a centrally directed and organized movement, this manner of proceeding might not be entirely without justification, particularly as regards events between the two World Wars, when Austrian Social Democracy recruited over 50 percent of its members in Vienna.[10] Austro-Marxim, Red Vienna, proletarian counterculture—none of these themes took much account of the workers' movement in the provinces. And although works on regional aspects in recent years have corrected that historical image, an interregional comparison is still lacking. Precisely such a comparison, however, can provide answers to the question why a switch from Social Democracy was easier in some areas than in others. Still, some structures are appearing that may be regarded as useful sources of evaluation. Certain factors may be isolated in at least seven spheres of history that, beyond coincidence and purely individual decisions, may offer bases for wider historical explanation.

Courses of Industrialization

Austria contains both old and new industrial areas, which exhibit monoindustrial and mixed industrial structures, respectively. Whereas some industrial areas are rooted in old traditions of local handicraft, others owe their development simply to the existence of infrastructural advantages. The mining sector in most places has the longest tradition.

Differentiated ways of industrialization have created a differentially homogenous working class. The disintegration of the Habsburg monarchy, furthermore, brought about structural imbalances, and the world economic crisis of the 1930s similarly hit the industrial sectors with uneven force. The rule seemed to be that the more stable the working place and the more effectively a counterculture of the workers' movement was able to cushion the impact of unemployment, at least emotionally, the less tempting was a migration to Nazism. Within closed industrial estates one simply would be stigmatized by such a step. Since, however, basic conditions like these had prompted participation in the civil war of February 1934, the workers of those localities regarded the main antagonist to be the Dollfuss-Schuschnigg regime. They consequently regarded alliances against that system as within the realm of possibility, but this did not include desertions to the Nazis.

The Situation in the Industrial Estates

For Austria the industrial enclaves have always been more important structurally than closed industrial areas. Only southern Austria and Upper Styria constitute exceptions. In the case of isolated industries in a rural environment, the commuter share of the working class was always high. Commuters coming from surrounding agrarian areas habitually are exposed to various cultures in the course of their daily and weekly routines, a fact liable to create problems of identity. It was easier for Nazism to penetrate this kind of social milieu than either the resistant sphere of Catholic peasants or that of the well-established industrial workers.

The Political Adversary

It was not everywhere in Austria that Social Democracy was confronted with clearly identifiable political and economic opposition. The scope of action in politics is not determined exclusively by programs and self-images, but in large measure also by the opponents' positions. In this respect Austria's history is striking in the lack of homogeneity of the country's bourgeoisie. Thus, the sociological species of the grand entrepreneur is almost completely lacking since the entire process of industrialization was promoted and fueled by anonymous bank capital. The bourgeoisie of the small cities emerged mainly from commerce, crafts, and the local intelligentsia. Some sections of the latter, such as teachers, were able to play an important part in the workers' movement. Conditions like these sometimes produced tactical alliances between the workers and the national bourgeoisie against the Church. In somewhat smaller industrial communities set in rural surroundings, the adversaries were often large-scale peasant landowners (Grossbauern) imbued with a Catholic cosmology. Where the influence of the educated bourgeoisie was strongest in the workers' movement, and this was noticeably the case furthest away from the metropolis, the change to Nazism was facilitated not least because of the distinctly German-national component in the workers' cultural assets (German cultural heritage). In some areas, this type of workers' movement, often dubbed "teachers' socialism," which operated under the trinity of social, national, and anticlerical slogans, so blurred the dividing line between Socialism and Nazism that the switch to Nazism before 1938, as well as the switch back after 1945, brought no decisive break in the political lives of those concerned.

Organizational and Ideological Developments

Only because the central program of the Austrian workers' movement exhibited a clearly recognizable "Austro-Marxist" profile did its organization convey the impression of being monolithic. However, Marxism was by no means the ideological basis of the provincial sections of the Social Democratic Party, whose political profile was marked by an assembly of creeds including actionism, leftist liberalism, remnants of "classical" anarchism, Lassalleanism, and others. Wherever Party cadres trained in Marxism did exist, the drift toward Nazism was strongly inhibited. Resistance was especially strong where, as in Vienna and the traditional areas of industrial concentration, the movement was impregnated with a solidly shaped counterculture capable of encompassing all aspects of life that intended to mold a "New Mankind."

Religion

Austria has always been regarded as a preponderantly Catholic country. Even the State regarded itself as Catholic between 1934 and 1938. However, side by side with Catholicism there existed a strong Jewish community, as well as a few isolated retreats of Protestantism. There were even some regions in which the Counter-Reformation of the second half of the sixteenth century had been only superficially successful. Here, expecially in the Salzkammergut, the Enns Valley, and in some of the larger regions of Carinthia, criticism of the Catholic central government had deep historical roots, and consequently there was a predisposition not only toward anti-Catholic ideologies, but also a light-hearted switch from Social Democracy into the German-national camp. (Even today's election results tend to bear this out.) That prevalently anti-Semitic sentiments facilitated this process may be regarded as self-evident. Anti-Semitism within the Austrian workers' movement was a phenomenon of the provinces that, in the case of the provincial trade union movement, tended to coincide with criticism voiced against nonpragmatic intellectualism.

The National Question

The national question as it affected the workers' movement had several components. Although, after Hitler's accession to power in Germany, the Austrian Social Democratic Party decided to alter its program of 1926, which advocated an Anschluss with Germany,[11] Austrian patriotism remained a sentiment alien to the rank and file. The Party continued to carry the name *German-Austria* within its title. From the mid-1930s onward, the Communists insisted on a discussion treating Austria as objectively separate from the German nation, but that idea was rejected within Austria's Social Democracy.[12] It is clear, to say the least, that national sentiments did not prevent Austrians from switching to the Nazi Party.

However, it is noteworthy that after St. Germain Austria was never a linguistically homogeneous country and that the areas of mixed nationality created by the borders drawn after the First World War had traumatized the Austrians. Alleged threats from neighboring states (supposedly exploiting the ethnic minorities as Fifth Columns), particularly in Carinthia, tended to color the entire policy of those regions in terms of a defensive struggle. If that were not enough, there were also the German-speaking minorities resident in neighboring countries, South Tyrol and the Sudetenland being cases in point. The more directly such areas of Austria were confronted with national problems like these, the more ready, too, were the Social Democrats in those parts to open their minds to German-nationalist thought.

The Centralist-Authoritarian Party Structure

After overcoming its spontaneous-anarchist tendencies toward the end of the nineteenth century, the Social Democratic Party turned into a centralist party in which policy formation ran from the top to the bottom.

Even though that principle was not followed consistently, local leaders still were in a position to determine decisively the conduct of their followers, so much so that a loss of a leader could bring about the complete paralysis of the regional Schutzbund unit, even a normally very active one, such as that in Wiener Neustadt[13] in the civil war of February 1934. Furthermore, the political defection of some leaders of a militant bent would result in the desertion of entire organizational units, as for instance from the Schutzbund to the Nazi "Austrian Legion" stationed in Bavaria after February 1934. This tendency was particularly marked in Upper Austria, as will be seen subsequently.

Alongside these regional differences in the traditions and politics of Austrian Social Democracy, it is to be noted that Austrian Nazism had different consignees in different regions. The textile industrialists of Vorarlberg, above all in Dornbirn, who had lost their markets as a result of the outcome of the First World War, were especially amenable to Nazi siren songs. The resulting pressures on the workers employed in those industries naturally led to the growth of Nazi influence among them. In both Salzburg and the Tyrol, the tourist trade represented an important target for the Nazis. In Styria and Carinthia the educated petit bourgeoisie, above all the teachers, was a primary target and could be won over by the argument of the supposed German mission in the border regions. The Nazi recruitment target in Upper and Lower Austria was the urban petit bourgeoisie and the self-employed; in Vienna and other university towns it was the students.

THE SWITCH-OVER OF "MILITANTS" AND THE PARAMILITARY

In the late 1920s the paramilitary defense organization of Austrian Social Democracy, the Republican Defense Corps (*Schutzbund*), had 96,000 members, thereby substantially surpassing in numerical strength, though not in equipment, the regular Austrian army of 30,000. Though the Heimwehr units managed to attain a membership of 100,000, they were hampered by their federal structure and contradictory interests. It was not until 1931, however, that a small but combat-ready formation of Nazi stormtroopers (*Sturmabteilungen*, or SA) came into being. The SS (*Schutzstaffeln*) acquired its importance even later than that. Thus, in Innsbruck, the capital of Tyrol, the SA had a mere ninety-six members with the coming of 1932, and it was not until April 1933 that the SS could muster a mere thirty members.[14] It is clear, therefore, that Nazi paramilitary formations had only attracted a fraction of the number of members in the other such groups.

It was not surprising, therefore, that the Schutzbund regarded the Heim-wehr as its prime paramilitary foe.

It is remarkable that Gerhard Botz was able to establish a much younger average age among those in the Nazi paramilitary groups than in either the Schutzbund or the Heimwehr: namely, 23 years as opposed to 27.7 and 27.2, respectively.[15] This indicates that, above all, people in some form of occupational training or those unable to find work on leaving school were precisely the ones who tended toward militant Nazism. Thus, the para-military formations of the Nazis could show no more than 36 percent of their members as of working class origin, against a respectable 36 percent of the Heimwehr and a massive 82 percent of the Schutzbund. Students and, to a lesser extent, white collar employees were the most overrepresented groups among the paramilitary Nazis.[16]

As to strategy, Theodor Körner, then a retired general but later Presi-dent of the Second Republic, suggested that the Schutzbund be anchored in the populace instead of being prepared in conventional war tactics, but his proposal was defeated.[17] The Schutzbund was consequently organized and trained along military lines, and such "playing at soldiers," if anything, facilitated desertions to the Nazis.

In February 1934 Richard Bernaschek, one-time secretary of the re-gional Social Democrats and local commander of the Schutzbund in Upper Austria, took a determined stand against searches of Social Democratic Party premises, thereby setting off brief but intense military operations against the Army, the Heimwehr, and the Police—an undertaking that was doomed from the beginning but nonetheless ought to be seen as the first act of armed resistance against the elimination of democracy anywhere in Europe. However, not even the entire Schutzbund, let alone Social Democracy as a whole, took an active part in those operations, though it is true that there were armed confrontations in Upper Austria, Vienna, Styria, Lower Austria, and to a very small extent also in Salzburg and the Tyrol. According to some estimates only about 20,000 members of the Schutzbund took part in the fighting or were ready for combat, and only members of that fighting group, considering themselves defeated on the battlefield, would subsequently seek opportunities for a renewal of a mili-tant confrontation with the Austrian government. For reasons such as these, an investigation into the readiness and disposition of those in this group to switch political parties after February 1934 is of special interest.

Of these fighters, about 1000 were abroad, in particular in Czechoslo-vakia. Those who fled to Germany (an estimated 200) will be dealt with separately in this paper. Another 1000 fighters found themselves in Aus-trian prisons, while one-third of the remaining 18,000 must be considered as simply having given up. For the other 12,000 there were four political options: work with the illegal "Revolutionary Socialists," a group that emerged from Social Democracy after February 1934; attempt to continue the Schutzbund as an "autonomous" Schutzbund; join the Communists; or join the Nazis.

Historians close to the Communists, such as Garscha and Hautmann, believing that a mass party in the shape of the Austrian Communist Party was evolving after February 1934, interpreted this as a decisive regrouping within the Austrian workers' movement.[18] They are right only in so far as the largest part of the aforementioned 12,000 Schutzbund members, as well as numerous members of the Social Democratic youth sections, swelled the ranks of the KPÖ. The Revolutionary Socialists were the weaker organization, a fact reflected in the struggle over the leadership of the "autonomous" Schutzbund. However, the various regroupings of Schutzbund members never resulted in the creation of a new mass party on the Left.

As regards the social statistics of the illegal Nazi Party, it is remarkable that these new members hardly affected the social profile of the Nazi movement. One would not overestimate much in assuming about 4000 desertions to the Nazis, especially as regards Upper Austria, Styria, and Carinthia, with scarcely any in Vienna. There were, however, active and combative elements among them, so much so that the Director of Public Security of Upper Austria was able to report on 26 February 1934 that "according to agents' reports, a large part of the recently committed bombing attacks attributed to adherents of the NSDAP [Nazis] was carried out by members of the terrorist group Resch [i.e., Republican Defense Corps]."[19] Doubtless these target groups found a kind of emotional fascination in violence. Nonetheless, it must be borne in mind that the Nazis committed five times as many large-scale acts of violence involving bodily harm as those committed by the entire Left during the period 1934–1938.[20] Carsten recently pointed out the wealth of imagination and the spontaneity in Nazi forms of protest, often replete with childish presumption.[21] (In addition to the cases cited by Carsten, this author is aware of an incident in a Carinthian municipality in which paper swastikas were stuffed into the exhaust of the pastor's car. Departing, the pastor left behind a cloud of swastikas in the town square.) In Western Austria, too, the Nazis were banking on the success of a species of "Propaganda of the Deed,"[22] almost in the manner of the anarchists.

All this promoted a feeling among the defeated Social Democrat fighters that only Nazism was actively fighting the hated regime. In Eastern Austria desertions to the Nazis remained rare. Only single instances, such as that of the leader of the Schwechat Schutzbund, Lassnig, can be established.[23] It was in Upper Austria, however, that desertions occurred on a massive scale, with entire closed units switching over to the Nazis. In the normal course of events, desertions did not occur within the framework of illegal activity within Austria but after crossing the frontier into Germany. According to the former Schutzbund leader Hüttl of the coal-mining district of Hausruck, a man who had emerged from the workers' youth section of the Party and who found himself one of the most sought-after members of the Schutzbund after his active fighting in February 1934, he and his comrades took flight into Germany only because the frontier with Czechoslovakia was both farther away and watched more closely. In Nazi Germany the Social Democratic fugitives were welcomed warmly, invited to participate in communal gymnastic exercises, and finally taken to Passau, where allegedly Richard Bernaschek addressed them, calling upon them to join the organizations of the Nazis, even though he himself would not risk taking such a step.[24] Bernaschek was altogether the central character in the drama of desertion to the Nazis. Together with Franz Schlagin and Otto Huschka, two other prominent members of the Schutzbund, and two Nazis, Ignaz Fastner and Karl Strassmayr, he had managed to escape from the Linz County Court of Law during the night of 2–3 April 1934. Karl Dobler, an Austrian prison police officer, organized that flight. These events have been described in some detail by K.R. Stadler and I. Kykal in their book on Bernaschek.[25]

Bernaschek spent two months in Germany, enjoying complete freedom of movement and receiving full honors. Whereas his two friends quickly converted to Nazism, Bernaschek himself never followed their example. In a topical account of those weeks, however, he wrote that the program of the Nazis was closer to the cause of the Austrian workers than that of the Austrian Corporate State and that consequently, in a renewal of the struggle, a Nazi victory in Austria was to be desired. He expressed himself in the matter of Nazism and Communism as follows: "Two powerful socialist experiments are at present capturing the imagination of Europe and the entire world. Which of these will reach its objectives more quickly? Are they proceeding simultaneously? Will they intersect? Or are they going to coalesce somewhere in the still-hazy future?"[26]

To designate the Nazis as Socialists, to wish them victory in Austria – all this was from the undisputed role model of the most activist section of Austrian Social Democracy that, especially in Upper Austria, was commanding a large following! It was not before June 1934 that the illegal Revolutionary Socialists were able to publish a leaflet in Upper Austria that registered Bernaschek's disassociation from Nazism.[27] Meanwhile the Nazis were in a position to exploit his name for purposes of recruitment. A victim of their efforts was Zaribnicky, the sole survivor of the massacre of Holzleithen, one of the most tragic events of February 1934.[28] Josef Redlinger, who was to be SPÖ mayor of that locality in the Second Republic, also fell victim.[29] He joined the Nazi Austrian Legion stationed in Bavaria. Nazi

leaflets–with slogans such as "Socialism is alive–through us National Socialists [Nazis]"; "We are your workers' party"; and "Workers, comrades,
fight on our side! Your dead are calling"[30] –inundated the country and proved quite effective.

After the failure of their putsch of July 1934, the Nazis embarked on
another recruiting drive during which they emphasized that the blood shed
in both February and July of 1934 constituted a unifying bond. Meanwhile, the illegal labor movement had managed to consolidate to an extent
that made possible recruitment in the opposite direction. Stadler quotes
extensively from a leaflet[31] composed with the intention of winning disillusioned Nazis to the side of the Revolutionary Socialists. However, the
results achieved in that direction proved dismal.

A special chapter in the conversion of Social Democrats to the Nazis
concerns the detention camps built by the Corporate State to house its
political opponents, of which Wöllersdorf in Lower Austria was the best
known. Nazis, Social Democrats, and Communists inhabited those camps
together. Apart from benefiting from the camp solidarity that grew naturally among the inmates, the Nazis succeeded in turning those camps into
a cadre-forge by exploiting the common sentiment of being "martyrs in a
'holy' cause."[32] Enjoying ample support from the outside in the form of
both money and basic necessities, they would throw their weight about
noisily on special occasions, such as the Führer's birthday. Numerically the
largest group of inmates, the Nazis supplied most of the room representatives, a function allocated to the politically strongest grouping.[33] All this
had a certain advertising effect on the other inmates of the camp, especially
since, more than any other political group, the Nazis could procure work
for those released from the camp. By way of a footnote to the history of
those camps, it may be noted that in their attempted putsch of July 1934
the Nazis tried to storm one of those camps, Graz Messendorf,[34] in which
Social Democrats had been held since February 1934. Even though this particular attempt was unsuccessful, it provided yet another indication of the
emotional proximity that existed among militant opponents of the Schuschnigg regime.

DRIFT TO THE NAZIS: REGULAR PARTY MEMBERS

Contrary to the militants and members of paramilitary groups, the
drift of regular members of the Social Democratic Party to the Nazis was
not a function of the trauma of February 1934, even though here the outlawing of the Party also acted as a significant catalyst. In this kind of change-
over the incident of regional differentiation, to which attention has been

drawn in this paper, played the decisive part. It is not for nothing that the examples cited in scholarly works, to all intents and purposes, are drawn exclusively from Upper Austria, Carinthia, and Styria. Thus, Carsten refers to a report rendered by a German Consul in June 1933, in which the depth of penetration by the Nazis into Social Democratic circles in the linguistically mixed area of Carinthia is described as "astounding".[35] Above all, in Styria references can be found regarding the ability of Dr. Amin Dadieu, the later Gau chief of the region, to win over some Social Democrats. In February 1934 the Director of Public Security for Upper Austria reported that the Nazi Party was "successfully trying to get hold of the moderate supporters of the dissolved Social Democratic Workers Party for their purposes. To achieve this aim, forms of application are being circulated."[36]

Holtmann mentions a report dated July 1934 according to which only 80 persons appeared in Steyr at a meeting of the Catholic workers association, while on the same day, in spite of pouring rain, over a thousand workers took part in the funeral procession of a German-National gymnast.[37] According to individual interviews, the Nazi Party seemed to many people in the south of Austria to express faithfully their antiecclesiastical, or at least anti-Catholic, feelings.[38] As it happened, the activism of the Nazis, which was primarily turned against the representatives of the Catholic State, pleased more than just the militant supporters of Social Democracy. It was not only on account of the pressures applied by the Alpine-Montan Corporation of Upper Styria that many workers in that area switched from Social Democracy to Nazism. They were prompted by anti-Catholicism as well as other factors listed in this paper. Even at the first postwar Party Congress of the SPÖ in 1945, when it was decidedly inopportune to do so on political grounds, delegate Erwin Linhart professed himself to be a representative of that tradition, explaining that

> we have therefore often worked together with the Nazis against that [Schuschnigg] government. . . . The many idealists who worked with us, our comrades who took part in the rising of February 1934 which was crushed and who subsequently released their rage by participating in the Nazi putsch of July 1934 simply because it was directed against the "black" government and because they believed to be acting against the "blacks" within that movement.[39]

Those successful incursions by the Nazis into the camp of the then Social Democrats did not turn the Nazi Party into a workers' party. Gerhard Botz was able to prove conclusively that working class members remained clearly underrepresented in the membership of the Nazi Party right up to the *Anschluss* of 1938.[40] Above all, in Vienna there were hardly any such incursions. "What we can boast of in the way of proletarian and semiproletarian electors are little white collar workers, chauffeurs, railway workers and streetcar operators" is the way Dr. Walter Riehl, one of the outstanding persons of Austrian Nazism, put it as part of a general analysis.[41] Gerhard Botz was able to confirm those findings by way of quantitative analysis. According to him the Social Democratic camp was able to hold its own during the last free elections of the First Republic,[42] and the Nazis succeeded in making incursions above all in the realm of public transport.[43]

Once in power in Austria, the Nazis were able to change that picture substantially, by founding brand-new industrial enterprises and establishing large new workers' settlements, whose first generation of workers were a new type, aware of owing both their workplace and a dignified existence to the Nazis. These workers were not then Social Democrats but future Socialists. In 1945 the workers in this kind of environment would make the remarkable change from the Nazis to the new Austrian Socialist Party. To illustrate the point, one may cite the completely new Nazi paragon settlement in Steyr-Münichholz. An outright profession of Nazism was a prerequisite for finding an apartment there; yet in the first free elections in 1945, the SPÖ was able to secure close to 70 percent of all votes cast. However, in 1949 when the League of Independents (VdU), a receptacle of former Nazis (Ehemalige), entered the electoral contest, it managed to halve the SPÖ share of the votes by polling 35 percent, almost the same share as the Socialists. Meanwhile, all those who voted VdU in Steyr-Münichholz have returned to the SPÖ, which nowadays manages to receive nearly 80 percent of all votes at all elections, mopping up Communist votes in the process.

It is important to realize that these people of Steyr-Münichholz never performed a double change-over. Unlike some workers in Upper Styria, Carinthia, Salzburg, or Upper Austria, they never switched from Social Democracy to the Nazis in order to find their way back into the Austrian Socialist Party after the war. What the two groups of workers have in common is that both looked upon the Nazis as a party of labor.

NOTES

We gratefully acknowledge the generous technical assistance rendered by the Ludwig Boltzmann Institute for the History of the Labor Movement, Linz.

    1. K. R. Stadler, *Opfer verlorener Zeiten. Geschichte der Schutzbund-Emigration 1934* (1974). I. Kykal and K. R. Stadler, *Richard Bernaschek. Odyssee eines Rebellen* (Vienna, 1976).

    2. G. Botz, "Faschistische Bewegungen und Lohnabhängige in Österreich," in *Internationale Tagung der Historiker der Arbeiterbewegung (X. Linzer Konferenz 1974)* (Vienna, 1976).

    3. H. Walser, *Die illegale NSDAP in Tirol und Vorarlberg 1933–1938* (Vienna, 1983).

    4. G. Botz, 'Die Ausschaltung des Nationalrats und die Anfänge der Diktatur Dollfuss im Urteil der Geschichtsschreibung von 1933 bis 1973' in *Vierzig Jahre danach. Der 4. März 1933 im Urteil von Zeitgenossen und Historikern* (Vienna, 1973), p. 40.

5. H. Konrad, "Zum österreichischen Geschichtsbewusstsein nach 1945," in R. Alt-müller et al. (ed.), *Festschrift/Mélanges Félix Kreissler* (Vienna, 1985), p. 129.

6. J. Weidenholzer, *Auf dem Weg zum "Neuen Menschen"* (Vienna, 1981), p. 19.

7. B. McLoughlin, "Zur Wehrpolitik der SDAPÖ 1923–1934," in E. Fröschl and H. Zoitl (ed.), *Februar 1934. Ursachen, Fakten, Folgen* (Vienna, 1984), p. 288.

8. F. L. Carsten, *Faschismus in Österreich. Von Schönerer zu Hitler* (Munich, 1977), p. 184.

9. H. Konrad, "Zur Geographie der Februarkämpfe," in E. Fröschl and H. Zoitl (eds.), pp. 333–40.

10. Weidenholzer, p. 26.

11. H. Maimann, "Der März 1938 als Wendepunkt im sozialdemokratischen Anschluss-denken," in H. Konrad (ed.), *Sozialdemokratie und "Anschluss"* (Vienna, 1978), p. 63.

12. F. Kreissler, *Der Österreicher und seine Nation. Ein Lernprozess mit Hindernissen* (Vienna, Graz, Cologne, 1984), pp. 174–83.

13. K. Flanner, *Wiener Neustadt im Ständestaat. Arbeiteropposition 1933–1938* (Vienna, 1983), pp. 75–85.

14. Walser, p. 64.

15. G. Botz, "The Changing Patterns of Social Support for Austrian National Social-ism (1918–1945)," in S. U. Larsen et al. (eds.), *Who Were the Fascists? Social Roots of European Fascism* (Bergen, 1980), p. 206.

16. G. Botz, "Introduction," to ibid., p. 196.

17. I. Duczynska, *Der demokratische Bolschewik. Zur Theorie und Praxis der Gewalt* (Munich, 1975), pp. 109–34.

18. F. Garscha and H. Hautmann, *Februar 1934 in Österreich* (Vienna, 1984), pp. 185–87.

19. P. Kammerstätter, *Der Aufstand des Republikanischen Schutzbundes am 12. Februar 1934 in Oberösterreich* (Linz, 1985), p. 1901.

20. G. Botz, *Gewalt in der Politik. Attentate-Zusammenstösse-Putschversuche-Unruhen in Österreich 1918–1938* (Munich, 1983), p. 277.

21. Carsten, p. 230.

22. Walser, pp. 80–104.

23. H. Arnberger, *Die politische Situation im Raum Schwechat von 1930 bis 1945* (Vienna, 1976), p. 179.

24. Interview with H. Hummer.

25. I. Kykal and K. R. Stadler, pp. 101–21.

26. Ibid., p. 138.

27. *Widerstand und Verfolgung in Oberösterreich 1934–1945. Eine Dokumentation* (Vienna, 1982), vol. 1, p. 44.

28. H. Hummer, "Widerstand auf dem Land," in *"Es wird nicht mehr verhandelt . . ."* *Der 12. Februar 1934 in Oberösterreich* (Linz, 1984), pp. 75–80.

29. Kammerstätter, p. 1909.

30. Ibid., pp. 1892–96.

31. Stadler, pp. 97–100.

32. G. Jagschitz, "Die Anhaltelager in Österreich," in *Vom Justizpalast zum Heldenplatz. Studien und Dokumentationen 1927–1938* (Vienna, 1975), p. 130.

33. Ibid., p. 143.

34. Ibid., p. 146.

35. Carsten, p. 193.

36. Kammerstätter, p. 1878.

37. E. Holtmann, *Zwischen Unterdrückung und Befriedung. Sozialistische Arbeiterbewe-gung und autoritäres Regime in Österreich 1933–1938* (Vienna, 1978), p. 173.

38. B. F. Pauley, *Hahnenschwanz und Hakenkreuz. Steirischer Heimatschutz und Nationalsozialismus 1918–1934* (Vienna, 1972), p. 100.

39. Stadler, pp. 94 f.

40. G. Botz, "Changing Patterns of Social Support," p. 211.

41. Carsten, p. 186.

42. G. Botz, "Changing Patterns of Social Support," p. 212.

43. Ibid., p. 208.

Nazi Wooing of
Austrian Social Democracy
between Anschluss and War

ROBERT SCHWARZ

This study was undertaken with a view to determining the nature of the response of the Austrian Social Democratic working class to the *Anschluss*. Though one should be severely mindful that not all Austrian workers were Social Democrats or even left of center, what is meant for the scholarly purposes of this paper is the unquestioned majority who in March 1938 were still sympathetic to Social Democracy in some degree.

As an exclusive source of information this writer elected the editorials of the Viennese edition of the *Völkischer Beobachter*, the press organ of the Nazi Party, between 13 March 1938 and 31 August 1939, the day before the outbreak of war between Germany and Poland. The specific method chosen was the "content analysis" of these editorials.

As well as exhibiting obvious weaknesses inherent to a narrow evidentiary base, this method has its peculiar advantages. Contemporary social science uses content analysis as a statistical device, extracting recurrent words, phrases and other linguistic phenomena with the object of identifying underlying preoccupations and trends, allowing problems both to emerge and crystallize in the process. That indirect method has been rejected as inappropriate here, since it will not allow the evidence to be established in response to leading questions asked initially. The present method is direct, linked as it is to a clear-cut a priori purpose. To that extent it is traditionally historical rather than rigidly scientific. It represents the ap-

125

plication of a kind of content analysis nonetheless. Since it is capable of providing answers to leading questions without the intervention of elaborate
scientific aids, its narrow evidentiary base is, if anything, an advantage.
Thus, it must never be pretended that it is capable of delivering answers
of a near definitive kind in the manner of the rigid axioms of social science.
The answers are approximations, indeed, mere suggestions of the absolute
truth, and to that extent, probabilistic rather than strictly empirical. However, in the present limited context, the method can be of use all the same
in stimulating further thought on its subject. In that sense it is heuristic
rather than scientific.[1]

COURTING THE WORKERS

A concerted attempt by the Nazis to win over the Austrian Social
Democratic workers to the new regime began immediately after the *Anschluss*.
This paper will identify the character and range of those overtures, the subsequent reaction on the part of the workers—muted and unpublicized as
these had to be—and present the reaction of the Nazi regime to those
reactions—all on the basis of the editorials and comments of the *Völkischer
Beobachter* of the period.

It has not been enough to take those writings at their surface value.
One has to go beyond that extrapolating, reading between the lines, specu-
lating from the general tone and manner, and teasing out half-hidden mean-
ings from the finer critical points contained in those editorials and comments. The nuances of temper displayed when replying to letters received
anonymously from discontented workers, for instance, provided some scope
for insight. Criticism of the very workers they wished to attract to the Nazi
cause often had to be veiled in the mild language of pained disappointment
and frustration. Content analysis of this nature was frequently complicated
by the *Völkischer Beobachter's* practice of picking out a so-called minority of
misled workers for criticism, while maintaining the firm pretence that the
majority had already been won over to Nazism.

THE CALL FOR UNITY

The first manifestation of the Nazi propaganda campaign to attract the
workers was its call for unity in the face of the impending plebiscite on the
merger of Austria with Germany due on 10 April 1938, an occasion on
which the Nazis were hoping to produce a landslide in their favor.[2] Within
an overall appeal to all "Aryans" of Greater Germany to cast a "yes" vote,

the part specifically directed toward Social Democratic labor highlighted the poverty-stricken state in which the Schuschnigg regime had left the working masses and more especially, the unemployed. Heavy attacks on the Dollfuss-Schuschnigg regime carried the implication that the Nazis disliked it as much as the Social Democratic workers and that the latter were much closer in their political position to the former than to the Catholic Conservatives. They were also meant to convey the impression that Austria's workers had been misled in the past into believing that the Nazi movement was procapitalist and represented the capitalist system in its last desperate gasp before its final, inevitable demise. From the beginning, no effort was spared in stressing how amicably disposed towards labor the Nazis were, not to speak of the manual working class origin of many of the Nazi leaders and the pro-Socialist leanings shown by the government of Germany since 1933. The serious charges leveled against the *ancien régime* of Austria of being unreceptive to the aspirations of labor, of allowing appalling housing conditions to persist, and all in all, of being the political party closest to the ideology of free market capitalism continued to be made forcefully and were meant to leave no doubt in the Austrian worker's mind that he had no other practical choice but Adolf Hitler's party. This propaganda reached its crescendo by 10 April 1938, after which it tended to weaken somewhat, although certain lines continued unabated until the outbreak of the war.

ANTI-SEMITISM

The overtones were the same as in the original Nazi program of 1919: an appeal to workingmen to vote "Socialist," not the socialism of the "Marxist-Jewish" variety but the "German" kind, by which workers could be good Socialists and good Germans at the same time. In 1938 and 1939 the *Leitmotiv* remained the same: the Jewish leaders of the Austro-Marxist movement had led the German worker down the garden path. Genuine socialism was German socialism, and this was to be found exclusively within the ranks of the Nazi movement. The Jewish leaders of Social Democracy in Austria had talked a great deal about matters of theory, while leading the Aryan workers into a hopeless civil war from which they emerged defeated and disillusioned, impoverished and frustrated.

It seemed, however, that the Nazi press, realizing that it ran the risk of not being believed if it attacked the accomplishments in the social sphere of Red Vienna between 1918 and 1934, prudently abstained from crudely assailing the Social Democratic leadership in these matters. The most common technique employed was the denunciation of the non-German leadership, which supposedly had seduced the German workers of Austria into supporting an international Bolshevik cause.

It is interesting to note that the Dollfuss-Schuschnigg regime had used a not altogether dissimilar technique in its efforts to gain the support of labor after February 1934, without, to be sure, the hysterical anti-Semitic venom characteristic of the Nazis. The failure of the Fatherland Front in that respect is a matter of public record. Whether the Nazis subsequently succeeded where the Fatherland Front had failed miserably will be a matter for closer examination.

ANTICLERICALISM

A tactic to which the journalists on the staff of the *Völkischer Beobachter* were especially partial was to pose as the other great anticlerical party, with the emphasis on the distrust of the Catholic hierarchy that was shared by old-time Social Democrats and Nazis. The anticlerical argument was used extensively and vigorously to impress labor. At first soft-pedalled for fear of unnecessarily offending an already somewhat demoralized Church, the anticlerical line was stepped up immensely after the show-down between Cardinal Theodor Innitzer and Reichskommissar Josef Bürckel in the autumn of 1938, reaching levels of great vehemence. The pages of the *Völkischer Beobachter* held numerous hints and allusions to a "politicizing clergy" (*ein politisierender Klerus*), allegedly as odious to the Nazis as to the Social Democrats. This was a prized Nazi device to curry favor with the Social Democratic workers. Again, the underlying political intention was to drive them into a corner, with no home to go to but Nazism.

The lure of Nazism, as expressed in the constant attempts, by the *Völkischer Beobachter* to convert the Austrian Social Democractic workers, increased during the late summer of 1938, reaching a pitch during the mini-*Kulturkampf* between the regime and the Archdiocese of Vienna during the early fall of that year. The broadside attacks against the Church on that occasion would undoubtedly have been as severe even without the sideshow of winning over Social Democratic sympathies. Nonetheless, in one editorial after another, the *Völkischer Beobachter* pressed home every opportunity to connect its own anticlerical position to the traditional antipathy of the Social Democrats toward the Church. The natural consensus—implicit, and never made explicit, but spontaneously real all the same—between Nazis and Social Democracy in this matter, a factor in Austrian politics long before the period under discussion here, was to be raised to the status of a proffered alliance in the autumn of 1938. Playing up to Social Democratic animosity toward the Church and the latter's supposed collaboration with capitalism, the Nazis sensed a propaganda advantage that they were ready to exploit to the full. By constant allusion to the former partnership between the Church and the regime overthrown by the Nazis, reminders were suggested of the isolated position of the workers from which the Nazis were prepared to rescue them.

SOCIAL ACHIEVEMENTS

Such golden opportunities of winning over the lost sheep of Social Democratic masses were accompanied by less dramatic but almost ceaseless efforts to publicize alleged Nazi achievements in the social sphere. Over and over again, those masses were invited to give Nazism a trial before condemning it, to see for themselves what the Nazis could achieve in social matters. Examples of German social reforms favoring the laboring masses were cited in the columns of the *Völkischer Beobachter*, sometimes on the front page, more often in the special *Ostmark* supplement, or in that adventitious part of the paper especially designed for home consumption. Addresses by Nazi leaders from the rank of Gauleiter downward, many imported for the purpose from Germany, made banner headlines. These were reported as praising German progress in prolabor programs and projects since 1933 and were delivered during visits to Austrian industrial centers heavily populated by working families, such as Floridsdorf in Vienna or the Kapfenberg-Donawitz area in Styria. Needless to say, Nazi leaders who did not carry the stigma of being strongly antilabor, like Josef Bürckel, were put in the forefront of the drive to attract the workers, whereas those known to have no particular love for workingmen's sentiments, like Odilo Globocnik, appeared only rarely at those prolabor rallies.

Added to those propaganda efforts was the important ideological point that "National Socialism," unlike Marxism, knew no classes; that all Germans were of one class, a united nation of workers. Class warfare and conflict in the manner advocated by Marxism had been abolished in Germany without recourse to violent revolution. The Austrian workers were invited to coalesce with the whole German nation, all workers of one kind or another.

One common theme ran through those reported visits and was given special stress: the abolition of unemployment in Nazi Germany. Beyond that, the improvement of housing raised the workers' material standard of living, satisfying both the socioeconomic and patriotic needs of the German workers, and carrying the clear message that, under Nazi leadership, Austria would not lag behind Germany for long.

In particular, soon after the *Anschluss* the *Völkischer Beobachter* initiated the practice of printing regular statistics illustrating the decline in Austrian unemployment, a practice kept up during the entire period under consideration here. To rub in the point—an intention reflected in the reports carried by the *Völkischer Beobachter* during that period, but markedly so during the first six to eight months after the *Anschluss*—a project was launched for the express purpose of alleviating the misery of the Austrian unemployed. Support from Germany was organized for feeding and clothing the poorest part of the proletariat. However, like the Salvation Army's insistence on your listening to a sermon before receiving your soup, the Nazis did likewise. While putting their best foot forward in posing as humanitarians and philantropists, they made their supply of food and clothing conditional on those wretched people being exposed to a "moral" crash program.

On every possible occasion, the Nazis would pose as the saviors of German labor from international Marxism, which had always manipulated them to its own political advantage. Since the Nazis were utterly unable to rival the achievements of Austro-Marxism in housing, provision of kindergartens, playgrounds, protection against landlords (*Mieterschutz*), to mention but a few areas, they placed the stress on the Schuschnigg regime's neglect of these matters. In this way, they were hoping to get the best of all worlds by simultaneously attacking Marxism for choosing the path of ultimate Social Democratic destruction yet refraining from attacking the popular Marxist programs of the 1920s and early 1930s. By carefully apportioning blame for the demoralization of Austrian labor, by defining authentic Socialism as "National Socialism," and by pointing to the putative successes in Germany, the Nazi propaganda mirrored in the pages of the *Völkischer Beobachter* of that period hoped to prove that only the Nazi movement was capable of providing a contented home for Austrian labor.

BIG BUSINESS

Believing correctly that the Social Democrats had been fed on the pabulum that the Nazis were procapitalist, proindustry, and therefore anti-labor, the Nazis now attempted to undo this impression by pointing out that a prolabor point of view had been in evidence in the Nazi movement from the beginning. In trying to capitalize on the workers' dislike of big business, the Nazis attempted to suffuse that dislike with strong doses of anti-Semitism to create the impression that the Nazis were not overly fond of big business, and that the Jews were the worst practitioners of unbridled capitalism. From this presentation of matters, it was to be inferred that the true anticapitalist was bound to be an anti-Semite as well, and hence, for all intents and purposes, a Nazi. The alleged philo-Semitic leanings of the Schuschnigg regime, and more particularly its supposed association with and support for Jewish businessmen, was a favorite bait with which to catch

Social Democratic fish. Much emphasis was given to shady Jewish deals that the Schuschnigg regime had allegedly covered up, to friendship between leaders of the Fatherland Front and Jewish owners of Viennese department stores, as well as to putative financial support granted by wealthy Austrian Jews to the Schuschnigg regime. In all these ways, they hoped to hold up a picture to the Aryan worker of corrupt Jewish capitalists working hand in glove with the hated "blacks" at a time when Austrian labor was languishing in poverty and neglect, while portraying the Jewish leaders of Austro-Marxism as demagogues seeking to destroy the healthy Austrian worker by pulling him into an "un-German," as well as anti-German, international conspiracy. Only within the Nazi ranks, it was insinuated, would there be any hope of a morally regenerated, self-respecting Austrian working class that would march alongside all other Germans toward national goals, while enjoying material standards of living far higher than any they had known.

The Nazis had to walk a tightrope between their attacks on Marxism and their anxiety not to estrange the Social Democratic workers by attacking the tenets of democratic socialism outright. They were compelled to pose as lovers of socialism, or at least of labor, while stressing the difference between Austro-Marxism and the Nazi type of socialism. The Nazi press proved ever sensitive to the charge that Nazism was inherently hostile to labor.

GRUMBLING AS "SILENT RESISTANCE"?

As shown elsewhere, a fair amount of grumbling was evident among the Austrians during the period,[3] and this was reflected in the allusions made in the *Völkischer Beobachter* to the notorious Viennese practice of *raunzen* (whining in a complaining way). It is suggested here, but the suggestion is a controversial one, that in the context of the time the practice of grumbling in the way indicated represented a form of silent resistance. Since the *Völkischer Beobachter* would never loudly proclaim or at any rate do much to publicize the workers' reaction to the ceaseless propaganda aimed at them, its only response to those workers' reactions was to convey the desired conclusions to the readers by innuendo. Let it be admitted at once, however, that going solely by the responses elicited in the *Völkischer Beobachter*, no prima facie case of outright workers' dissatisfaction can be made. This was true especially during the first weeks after the *Anschluss* when, according to that Nazi paper, the workers were prepared, and in some instances eager, to welcome Nazi speakers with enthusiasm, greeting Nazi visitors to their plants with cordiality, and in general behaving like prime candidates for conversion to Nazism.

Even if this were a faithful description of events, it is submitted here that little can be made of this type of feedback. Enthusiastic reception of Nazi functionaires in the first flush of post-*Anschluss* euphoria does not attest to a willingness to go along with Nazism indefinitely. The warm welcome that Hitler was accorded by many thousands of Viennese, many of whom undoubtedly workers and former card-carrying Social Democratic Party members, although perhaps disturbing, would not by itself ensure the success of subsequent prolabor propaganda conducted by the Nazis. Nor should too much be made of the articles in the *Völkischer Beobachter*. In these Viennese workers, speaking in their own dialect, would be encouraged to comment favorably on the positively invigorating times the country was living through, and how after their bitter disillusionment with Austrian Social Democracy they were now placing confidence in the new regime that was making good its promises of positive works for the working class.

Much more significant than those tidbits was the ill-concealed anger displayed against those workers in the pages of the *Völkischer Beobachter*, particularly after the plebiscite of 10 April 1938, which produced the wished-for landslide vote of 99.75 percent of Austrians (as against 99.25 percent of Germans) in favor of a merger between the two countries. The newspaper berated those workers who "still don't understand" what the Nazis were trying to do for them, ingrates who would complain about food prices while overlooking the good works the regime was performing. Having been lifted out of the gutter by Adolf Hitler's strong arm – such was the sentiment expressed by the *Völkischer Beobachter* in its editorials in late spring and early summer of 1938 – certain Viennese grumblers, instead of showing their gratitude, were complaining about the scarcity of fruit and vegetables, spreading rumors about food shipments to Germany and the general increase in the price of groceries, while undermining the regime by generally irresponsible talk.

In reply to those voices of discontent, the *Völkischer Beobachter* was always careful not to deprecate the Social Democratic heritage of the industrial workers to the point of appearing to be antilabor. The thrust of the argument was always that the regime's actions had been misunderstood, and that, in any case, it was far from being hostile to labor. Nonetheless, the discontent can be inferred from the extent and degree of impatience shown by the Nazi press organ. There is also a slight but noticeable shift in the paper's propaganda tactics toward the workers. Signs of frustration could be detected from May and June 1938 onward, when the campaign takes on a practical character. More and more importance is attributed to the facts and figures proving a drop in unemployment, whereas purely theoretical statements making abstract points about the nature of true socialism, the denunciation of heresies, and homilies of that kind are seen to be taking a backseat. The only theme that continued was the use of Goebbels' rhetoric, first employed a decade before the *Anschluss* to convert Berlin's workers from "red" to "brown." Wherever there was a ripple of discontent among the Austrian working class, his type of frontal attack, combined with early statistical returns of a rising employment, would be used as ammunition against the griping of Austria's consumer masses. The latter were not necessarily composed exclusively of members of the working class—the Austrian bourgeois was not altogether unknown to complain—but the phrasing of rejoinders and reminders in the *Völkischer Beobachter* allowed the presumption that the bulk of those complaints was of working-class origin. Occasionally the paper followed in the footsteps of Göring who, on one of his first visits after the *Anschluss*, criticized the Viennese temperament for its innate *Gemütlichkeit*. One cannot at this point help but accuse the Nazi press organ of hiding its antilabor sentiment under a cloak of patriotic fervor in calling all Austrians to their duty in their capacity as nationals of Greater Germany to work harder and complain less. That point in time was also chosen for reviving the old charge that class conscious, instead of State-conscious, Marxism demands for the laboring classes what is plainly inconsistent with national goals.

Frequently the *Völkischer Beobachter* felt obliged to add further clarification to its previously adopted lines of propaganda for the benefit of those who "still do not understand." This is done mostly in the form of elucidating the responsibilities of the laboring classes now that they had been given work and security, incorporated in a vast German labor front, and to cap it all, ensured of the support of a strong country and government. Those who failed to appreciate these blessings had to learn to think "nationally," as well as "socially." With the advent of full employment, they were lectured sternly, they had to accept the responsibility of closing ranks (*sich einreihen in die Gesellschaft*). Those who start whispering campaigns to the effect of new employment opportunities being created for purposes of rearmament should remember that they are first and foremost Germans, expected to defend a strong and proud country and to back the Führer in his efforts on behalf of Germany as a whole.

These and other similar homilies were to be found in the pages of the *Völkischer Beobachter* with increasing frequency before 1938 was over. They were manifestly directed against unfortunate workers who had been overheard complaining. And although some of the paper's paternal thrusts were directed against the Austrian temperament in general, the prime intended target was the working class. As international tension increased toward the end of 1938 and throughout 1939, the prevailing tenor of those journalistic sermons pointed to the need for social unity as an essential prerequisite for the effective righting of the injustices Germany was having to endure. Class divisions could not be afforded at such critical times in the nation's life. German workers had understood this ever since the Saar and Rhineland crises in 1935 and 1936, respectively, so why could not the Austrian workers do likewise?

It matters little for the purposes of this study by how many Austrian workers these lines in the *Völkischer Beobachter* were being read. It is sufficient to show that, when faced with an anonymous mass of industrial workers, the Nazi press organ was compelled as a matter of self-justification to rationalize its way out of a dilemma. On the basis of a fair amount of evidence gathered by some Austrian scholars from Gestapo and Party records, it can be assumed that the spreading discontent among the workers caused the Nazis nervousness about labor and consumer dissatisfaction, especially after the first four or five months after the *Anschluss*.[4] Nearly always, the Nazi Party paper would resort to a policy of divide and conquer by attempting to isolate the eternal grumblers, who were accused of having been brainwashed by the Otto Bauer–Julius Deutsch demagoguery in which everything was seen in terms of material gains and losses on the part of the proletariat. They represented a lost hope for the Nazis. The masses of Austrian workers, according to the scribes of the *Völkischer Beobachter*, were qualitatively different, prepared as they were to value and appreciate full employment, the existence of a regime partial to the dignity of labor and the blessings of life in a strong, rejuvenated country.

If only a handful of grumblers was bothering the Nazi news media in Austria, why unleash a propaganda *Blitzkrieg* against them, instead of relegating them to the lunatic fringe? The evidence emerging from the columns of the *Völkischer Beobachter* would seem to indicate that there were rather more grumblers than was being admitted and that resentment against the regime was on the increase. It should, however, be admitted frankly that on the basis of this narrowly specialized inquiry it is impossible to put precise percentages to the number of discontented Austrian proletarians.

Indications that the theoretical lecturing on true socialism was not going over at all well came when, after a few months, the impetus of these propaganda efforts began to weaken. It would be safe to infer that the growing emphasis on the practical results achieved, especially in relation to employment, pointed to a realization on the part of the Nazi propagandists that those theoretical pontifications were having little effect. Whether on account of the crude nature of Nazi political theory when contrasted with the highly sophisticated body of Marxist knowledge commanded by trained (*geschulte*) officials of the former Social Democratic Party or whether the average Austrian worker simply cared as little about political theory in the then prevailing circumstances as workers in the United States do at any time, is a moot point. Yet, in dealing in oversimplified categories, the Nazis may have underestimated the degree of exposure of the rank-and-file Austrian Social Democrat to Marxist indoctrination, since, of all European socialists, the average card-carrying member of the Austrian Social Democratic Party had probably more background in Marxist theory than the Nazis gave him credit for. These and similar considerations may have induced the Nazi propagandists to switch to a policy of dwelling on their own alleged social achievements and, beyond that, reminding the workers of a common bond of anticlericalism and probing for some of the deeper layers of anti-Semitism that even some Austrian Social Democrats were harboring.

THE "SILENT" RESISTERS?

When the Second World War broke out, Nazi propaganda efforts to capture Social Democratic minds and souls abated. The war effort now commanded the Nazi medias' full attention. During the period between the occupation of Czechoslovakia in March 1939 and the outbreak of the war, the *Völkischer Beobachter* became increasingly perfunctory in its routine exercises of propaganda destined for the Austrian working class. To be sure, employment statistics continued, endless comparisons with the Schuschnigg era became habitual, and the alleged associations of capitalist with Jewish corruption were the staple food of labor-oriented propaganda. However, no new idea enlivened those exercises.

What the Austrian workers really thought of the propaganda barrage aimed at them cannot be divined wholly from an analysis of the pages of the *Völkischer Beobachter* and may consequently never be known in its entirety. That tangible success eluded the Nazis in this particular propaganda exercise cannot be asserted absolutely either, but it may be presumed from the desultory, sometimes almost defeatist, language used as the war was approaching.

It is virtually certain that the well-trained leaders of Social Democracy at most levels were immune to the propaganda emitted by the *Völkischer Beobachter* and that those among them who did become converts had arrived at their new political convictions independently, through their own intellectual reflection or personal experiences. The rank and file may well have flirted with Nazism for a while before their loyalty assumed a nominal rather than real character. Most Nazis were probably aware of that. If the principal Nazi press organ is used as a yardstick for measuring the impact of Nazi propaganda directed at labor, a definite loss of zeal is noticeable after the turn of the year 1938. At that point, the punch and muscle appears to have gone out of the Nazi attempt to dazzle Austria's working masses. Nazi disillusionment, as betrayed in the columns of the *Völkischer*

Beobachter, was most severe regarding those who after at first paying some attention to the Nazi serenades, eventually turned a deaf ear.

To be sure, the editorial admonitions, reminders, and attacks were not aimed exclusively at Social Democratic workers, but the kind of so-called material indolence, which came to be the butt of those ciriticisms during the last ten months of the prewar period, makes plausible the deduction that the Social Democratic workers were the intended target.

In the final analysis, a question ought to be asked whether it is permissible to equate evidence of a spirit of discontent among the Austrian workers during the period under examination with a determination to resist. It is this writer's cautious thesis that in the wholly unfavorable political circumstances prevailing in Austria at that time the answer may well be in the affirmative. Resistance of the kind offered by the Austrian workers—"silent resistance," as this writer prefers to call it—certainly could not be compared with the dramatic resistance offered by Yugoslav or Greek partisans, who by their actions were able to capture the imagination and admiration of the world. However, dispassionately viewed, discontent capable of perennially irritating the Nazis to the extent that their main press organ was reduced to displaying unmistakable symptoms of nervousness could be justifiably termed "silent resistance."[5] In this respect the action, or inaction, of the Austrian working class may have resembled that of Germany far more than that of countries under the Nazi yoke in which resistance was inspired by primarily national rather than social and ideological considerations.

It might be instructive to conduct a comparative analysis between the reactions of the Austrian and the German workers to the Nazi regime in order to ascertain whether specifically local Austrian historical factors were at play. Such an attempt still has to be made.

NOTES

The author wishes to thank Professor Werner Braatz, of the University of Wisconsin at Oshkosh, for his permission to use the materials presented in an oral presentation to a meeting held at that university in 1974. The present version is a structured and edited paper based on that presentation.

1. See B. Berelson, *Content Analysis in Communication Research* (Glencoe, 1952); O. R. Holsti, "An Adaptation of the "General Inquirer" for the Systematic Analysis of Political Documents', *Behavioral Science* 9 (1964):382–88; and A. N. Oppenheim, *Questionnaire Design and Attitude Measurement*, 2d ed. (London, 1988).

2. On this point, see the subtle distinction made between "resistance" and "refusal" in R. Löwenthal, "Widerstand im totalen Staat," in R. Löwenthal and P. von zur Mühlen (eds.), *Widerstand und Verweigerung in Deutschland 1933 bis 1945* (Bonn, 1982), pp. 11–24. See also, generally, K. Stadler, *Austria* (London, 1971).

3. K. Stadler, *Österreich 1938–1945 im Spiegel der NS-Akten* (Vienna and Munich, 1966).

4. Ibid.

5. See references in notes 2 and 3.

Bürckel and Innitzer

ROBERT SCHWARZ

W hen, in future years, the history of the seven-year occupation of Austria is written and rewritten, one of its most intriquing episodes will undoubtedly be the latter-day *Kulturkampf* of 1938. The events constituting this episode can be roughly divided into three periods: the détente between the post-*Anschluss* Church and the Nazi Party, with the Hitler–Innitzer meeting as its nodal point, lasting until after the plebiscite of 10 April; the increasing hostility of the Nazi Party under the leadership of Josef Bürckel, the man in charge of consolidating the so-called *Wiedervereinigung* (reunion), toward the Catholic hierarchy; and the complete collapse of the "honeymoon" of March and April, with the storming of the archdiocesan palace in Vienna's first district.

GENERAL INTRODUCTION

This study is almost totally based on interviews the author undertook fifteen years after the end of the Second World War while on a sabbatical leave in Vienna. At that time, a large number of people were questioned about the Innitzer affair in all its aspects: prelates of the Church, Catholic laymen, eyewitnesses to the defenestration of October 1938, Nazis (rehabilitated and otherwise), and academic men and women, who commented from a scholarly point of view. The author has also read most of the relevant

137

secondary literature as well as newspaper material but relied mostly on his own colloquies with persons of diverse ideology, points of view, and historical interpretations. Some of the people interviewed perferred not to give their names, others, who did not mind, are mentioned in this paper.

The plot of the drama is too well known to informed readers and students of history to be discussed in full: a brief summation should suffice. On 15 March 1938, four days after Hitler's army crossed the Austrian frontier, a meeting took place between Hitler and Theodor Cardinal Innitzer, archbishop of Vienna and head of the Austrian Catholic Church, in which the former successfully persuaded the Cardinal to "depoliticize" the Austrian Church and to pursue a purely ecclesiastical function, in return for being left undisturbed by the new regime. Implied in this promise was also the pledge to treat the German clergy and Catholic laymen more cordially if Innitzer were to cooperate. (One of the anonymous interviewees told the author, in 1961, that on this occasion Hitler is supposed to have told Innitzer that in his youth he himself had wanted to become a cardinal, but no corroboration of this remark could be found.) It was, of course, expected that the Church would call on the faithful to vote "yes" in the plebiscite of 10 April 1938. A few days later a bishops' conference issued a declaration accordingly, expressing its approval of the merger with Germany and appealing to all Catholics "to do their duty to the German fatherland." In addition to these developments, Innitzer triggered a severe controversy when he signed a letter to Josef Bürckel, Hitler's appointed director for the implementation of the fusion between Austria and Germany, with the words "Heil Hitler," a "greeting" he repeated in a letter on 31 March, these gestures of submission being quickly publicized in the Nazi press for domestic consumption. The result of all this was great confusion among loyal Catholics, who were puzzled over Innitzer's overnight switch of fidelity from Schuschnigg to Hitler; shock and disbelief throughout the non-German world; satisfaction in Nazi quarters at the successful maneuver; mistrust of Innitzer and other collaborating Nazi clergy at the Vatican; and despair among those who saw in Innitzer's surrender the end of the last hope of standing up to Hitler internally, after all the external interests had already been content to be mere spectators.[1]

The period of putative good feelings between Church and Party did not survive the late summer of 1938. Shortly after the plebiscite landslide victory of 10 April, it became obvious that the Nazis were rapidly losing interest in a continued détente. Publications like *Das Schwarze Korps*, the press organ of the SS, as early as midsummer began to harass the hierarchy, even though Innitzer kept his word about "staying out of politics." By early October 1938 a showdown between the beleaguered Church and the Nazi masters became a reality.[2]

SOME OPENING QUESTIONS CONCERNING
THE PHENOMENON

The Party rally of September 1938 in Nuremberg attempted to emphasize the supposed unity existing in Greater Germany. But the speeches
could not cover up the serious problem that had developed in Austria since
the early summer and that came to its first harsh crisis in September and
October. Only by diverting the attention of Germans to the Sudeten crisis
of the autumn of 1938 could the Nazi orators hope partly to sweep under
the carpet the truth about the Austrian Catholics. What was the crisis really
about? Many eminent students of Nazi history, as well as scholars in the
field of recent Church history, have given this problem a closer attention
than possibly any other domestic question except the Jewish Holocaust.
The problem of the Church–Party relationship is complex for a number of
reasons, not the least of which is that the hierarchy and the laity were not
always "on the same wave length"; nor did the bishops show any consensus
with reference to the Nazi phenomenon. The bishops ranged from pro-
Nazi and anti-Semitic in the theological sense to outspokenly anti-Nazi (if
not equally outspokenly philo-Semitic) positions. The Catholic laity, too,
included people who perceived themselves as true sons of the Church but
were partial to much of the Nazi program—men of the so-called *Nationale
Lager* like Seyss-Inquart and Borodajkewycz belonged to this camp—as well
as men and women whose Catholicism dictated a sharp rejection of Nazism,
and all the gradations within that parameter. Thus, there was scant unity
among the practicing Catholics, ordained or otherwise. The Nazis, on the
other hand, displayed far more unity, though there were wide differences
here as well between what has been called the neo-pagan group and the
"Catholic Nazis."

In conversation with observant Austrians in the fall of 1961, the author
explored this question at length. Commenting on the greater unity in the
Nazi camp than in the Catholic camp, Professor August Knoll, a member
of the "liberal" Catholic position, anti-Nazi, valiantly pro-Catholic in the
religious sense, pointed out that many "Catholic Nazis" sincerely, if mistakenly, believed in the compatibility of the Nazi Program, as distinguished
from the Nazi mob outrages, with the political side of Catholicism. Dis-
tancing himself uncompromisingly from this group, Professor Knoll opined
that the anti-Bolshevism of the Nazis was a powerful attraction for Catholics who saw in the *Christliches Abendland*, which the Nazis professed to protect against godless Communism, the main reason for siding with the Nazis.
The rift within the Catholic world, inside and outside the Austrian scene,
with regard to the Church's stand vis-á-vis fascism in Italy and Spain and
Nazism in Greater Germany was Professor Knoll's great nemesis. In 1938

he had hoped for a victory of the anti-Nazi forces both in Rome and within the Austrian hierarchy. At the same time he took the view that historically the Church "has to stand wherever God places it," including in the lion's den of persecutors, be they Roman, Russian, or German, to wait there for better days and meanwhile taking up the cross of hardship and saving souls. Thus was Professor Knoll's judgment of the crisis of the besieged Church in 1938 as discussed in 1961.[3]

Other views were held by Austrian Catholics. Professor Borodajkewycz, whose notoriety in the neo-Nazi scene of the 1960s became the subject of much discussion a generation ago, invited the author to his home declaring openly to be "still a National Socialist" and defying him to cancel the interview (a stance that was at once frightening and frighteningly honest). Unlike Professor Knoll, Professor Borodajkewycz considered himself, a person who saw no contradiction between Nazism and Catholicism, although he professed to oppose the neo-pagan hotheads as fanatics and heathens. According to him, Innitzer could have lived in peace with the Nazis if he had only stood up to the Vatican more firmly and remembered his loyalty to the German priesthood. Summoned to Rome, Innitzer told the Papal Secretary of State, as he had told the Papal Nuncio in Vienna, that he was not only a priest but a German priest, with the strong implication that the days of Innocent III and the Middle Ages were over. To Professor Borodajkewycz this was not enough. As a liaison person between the Vatican and the Nazi leadership in Bürckel's office, Borodajkewycz claimed to have had the necessary insight from both sides of the controversy as it unfolded by September 1938. Innitzer's Sudeten German background did lend credence to his early profession of sympathy with the new regime and may even have contibuted to such gestures as the flagging of St. Stephen's Cathedral with the swastika, but he also, Professor Borodajkewycz maintained, gave in far too much to the "anti-Nazi" higher clergy in Austria and the still loyal Schuschnigg partisans among the laity. A certain amount of truthfulness attached to the charge of a "politicizing clergy," as Bürckel and the Nazi press referred to Innitzer's speech "Christ is the King" and his other pronouncements, especially his reminder to Catholic parents not to let the Nazi Party take over the souls of their children, according to Professor Borodajkewycz.[4]

The author's visits to the archdiocesan palace in October and November 1961 resulted in some interesting exchanges. Discussing the Innitzer–Bürckel jousting of July–October 1938, Dr. Richard Barta of the *Kathpress* remarked that one of the tragedies in the affair was the optimism in some Catholic circles with respect to their Nazi adversaries. Some of these persons believed in the possibility of coexistence, "*Wir werden die Nazis schon taufen*," to use Dr. Barta's idiom in characterizing this group. He also mentioned that Bürckel, on the advice of Berlin, was considering the formation of a *Ring deutscher Priester* (Organization of German Priests) in Austria, along the lines of the *Deutsche Christen* in Germany (who, however, were Protestants). Dr. Barta insisted that Innitzer put up a stiff resistance to this idea and, in fact, prevailed on this particular point. But the final victory belonged to the Nazis, at least until they left the stage of history in 1945, for the Austrian Church was without any protection after its *seelsorgende* (sacramental and charitable) infrastructure was destroyed, Dr. Barta contended. The Nazis insisted that the German Concordat was not applicable to Austria, leaving the Austrian Concordat invalid. Thus, the canonical basis for legitimizing any kind of relationship between the Austrian Catholics and the Nazis was removed, a point often overlooked by people considering the Innitzer–Bürckel tug-of-war.[5] Monsignor Lorenz Freiberger, the editor of the *Münchner Kirchenblatt*, commented on the breakdown of the Church–Party association and the subsequent isolation of the Austrian Church in a similar way.[6]

Soon after the October riots in Vienna, the *seelsorgende* aspect of the Austrian Church was curtailed and then dissolved for all intents and purposes. It is interesting, according to several priests the author interviewed, that Hitler's idea in the March meeting with Innitzer (that in getting rid of political action the Church would have more time and energy for *Seelsorge*) was in fact true. The Church devoted itself more than before to what it perceived as its real function, saving souls, dispensing sacraments, and cultivating its role as mentor, healer, and teacher. Many churchmen rejoiced at first in their sense of liberation from the political burden they had had to carry as supporters of Dollfuss and Schuschnigg and propagandists for the Fatherland front, a task never much to their liking and diverting from the sacerdotal part it was meant to play. According to Dr. Barta, and supported by Professor Knoll and others, orally and in print, the Church's early euphoria over this emancipation for political strife of the pre-1938 years had no sustaining power because even that function, vowed by Hitler and Bürckel as a reward for staying out of politics, was taken from the hierarchy before the end of October. The question the author put in this connection was why the publications of the Church throughout 1938, which pointed to the *volksbewusste Tugenden* of the Catholic population, were rejected by the Nazis as insufficient and false. A study of the *Kirchenblatt* of Vienna and elsewhere after March 15 shows frequent professions of loyalty to Greater Germany, the folk character of the Alpine German, and other phrases dear to the heart of dyed-in-the-wool Nazis. None of these declarations made an impression on Bürckel and his confrères.[7] The answer was that the Nazis no longer needed Catholic approval after the plebiscite, in the same way that Schiller made the Moor say in the drama

The Conspiracy of Fiesco in Genoa: "The Moor has done his duty; the Moor can go."

One of the most interesting aspects of the Innitzer–Bürckel struggle was the Cardinal's trip to Rome prior to the showdown in early autumn. According to several interviews, the journey to Rome was to justify his policy since the *Anschluss* rather than the sermon of "Christ is the King" that made Bürckel close down the Catholic shop in Austria. According to Prelate Josef Wagner and substantiated by Himmelreich, the liaison man between Bürckel and Innitzer, Bürckel tried to prevent Innitzer from going to Rome and is said even to have stopped the train. Still, Innitzer went and recanted by signing a mea culpa statement, withdrawing all his pro-Nazi utterances. One official in the archdiocese, whose name was promised to be omitted until his death, said to the author that the recantation of Innitzer was like the second thought of "many Austrian clergy," not because they came to their senses about Nazi crimes and sins but because they themselves got hurt. ("*Viele haben sich im Klerus eines besseren bedacht, nicht aus Überzeugung oder wegen der Untaten der Nazis, sondern weil sie auf die Füsse getreten wurden.*") This is significant and plays a large role in the split between Catholics who were in collusion with the Nazis and those, like Professor Knoll, who stood fast against all the siren calls of the "crusaders against atheism."[8]

How the Nazis in Austria changed their tune toward the Catholic leadership can best be seen by contrasting an appeal in the *Völkischer Beobachter* of 26 March 1938 and Odilo Globocnik's article in the same paper on 13 October. This contrast, discussed by the author and Professor Ludwig Jedlicka, sheds light on the Nazis' exploitation of the Church from the very beginning. In the appeal to all faithful we read of the help priests must give in the plebiscite campaign:

> We want peace, National Socialism opposes the misuse of religion, which is also in our interest. It protects with all its might every genuine faith; it asks of the *Volksgenossen* Christianity in action (*Tatchristentum*) and obligation to God. In dozens of cases one can see that we priests stand by the [German] folk. The invitation goes out to the clergy to cooperate actively in this great movement. We would rather take care of our souls than the lost [political] power which we should never have had in the first place. Whoever is ready to work along with National Socialism should report at once to Dr. Mikolussi, Professor of Theology, Convent of St. Florian. Heil Hitler. [Signed: Dr. Mikolussi][9]

More than half a year later the following statement of Globocnik appeared: "If Cardinal Innitzer," so writes Globocnik, "sidled up to the Führer in March he now demonstrates that it was not joy that made him join the jubilation of a liberated people. He probably attempted to save what could be saved. His bitterness over the latest victory of Nazism over a war-mongering world made Innitzer incautious and tore the mask off his face." Obviously, Globocnik referred to the Sudenten crisis, which he claims resulted in a German victory that embittered Innitzer enough to show his true colors.[10] In a discussion with the author, Professor Jedlicka expressed the view that men like Dr. Mikolussi were naive enough to believe their own words in March and April but that many like him changed their minds by October, not because they saw the error of their ways but because the Nazis "kicked them out." However, those Catholic Nazis, who were more Nazi than Catholic and for whom a compromise never rang true, Professor Jedlicka asserted, turned away from organized Catholicism more and more and remained Catholic in name only.[11] When the author brought up this point with Professor Borodajkewycz, he agreed in principle with his colleague but added that it was the Church that betrayed the covenant with Hitler, not the Nazis.

If the appeal just quoted (translation is the author's) seems moderate, such exclamations as in the *Kirchenblatt* of April 1938, in which the writer asks the faithful to pray for the Reich and Hitler, adding: *"Herrgott! Führe unsern Führer. Herrgott! Segne unsern Führer. Segne unsere Heimat und das grosse deutsche Volk!"* (Lord God, lead our leader, bless our leader, bless our country and the great German nation!) have a strident ring that reminds one of Theodor Körner's patriotic poetry in the Napoleonic wars. One must wonder which way such writers turned when the sobering appeared. One must wonder what such men said when, six months later (2 October 1938), a decree came out stating that pupils as young as fourteen could henceforth quit religious instruction without permission from their parents! Innitzer was especially emphatic about education in the Catholic spirit and admonished parents not to let the Nazis alienate their children. It must seem as if educational decress like the one just quoted were the true death knell of what started as a different chime: the *"Glockengeläute am Vorabend des Wahltages"* (the bells from the church towers on the eve of the plebiscite). One could almost write a short story: Two Kinds of Bells.[12]

SOME REFLECTIONS

In conversations with Catholics and others in 1961–which I like to think was one of the early enterprises of what is today popularly known as oral history–this author was often told that Innitzer was no Nazi but a politically naive young man from the Erzgebirge who made good in the Church, that he was duped by Hitler only because he did not appreciate Nazi duplicity, and that being mortal and fallible, he repented soon enough.

A famous dialogue between Herbert Butterfield and Isaiah Berlin involves the question of whether a historian should involve himself in moral and ethical controversy and take sides. Interestingly enough, the Christian historian Butterfield argues for a moral neutrality when the writer acts in the capacity of historian, whereas Berlin sees nothing wrong with, say, being filled with righteous anger at the deeds of certain political leaders. In the case of Innitzer, can one stay within the Butterfield camp and yet refrain from a shallow neutrality? It is worth a try. It seems to me—it is time to shift to the first person singular in this part of the paper—that Innitzer's naiveté, while practically proven by his actions, does not absolve him from the accusation of helping the dictator. One may agree with Professor Knoll, whose view was shared by Friedrich Heer in the same week, that the Church must take its chance "wherever God had placed it."[13] I see merit in this argument, implying though it does that the Church must tacitly submit to the State, gritting its teeth and trusting to survive as so often before in history. But Innitzer did not just sit still, at least not until he was forced to be quiet. He went out of his way to appease the dictator, making declarations of love all along. His change of heart was forced upon him by the adversary, a great difference from a change of heart from reasons of conscience.

Another reflection came out of my conversations in Vienna. Several times during the interviews, as in the course of research, the notion is mentioned that many Austrians who did not feel close to the Church joined whatever was still permitted to be joined and filled many churches at services. The reason given for this was that this was a protest against Nazism. It is also asserted that, though many of these people were motivated politically rather than religiously, in the process of "filling the churches" they came ever closer to the Church, from which quite a few earlier had become alienated, with the Church gaining in the long run, as these people often came to find a spiritual home. I put this question to the politically progressive Catholic intellectuals I contacted and everywhere found a generally affirmative answer. This is not to say that a religious upsurge of major proportions occurred or that the Austrian resistance to Hitler was visibly enhanced. But the protest inherent in this attraction was seen to be a fact of life. I have no problem believing the assertion of a higher church attendance, for though young in years, I witnessed this increase in local church attendance in parts of Vienna between the fall of 1938 and March of 1939, when I left the country. Whether I still would give the same interpretation to the phenomenon I leave open for the time being, except to say that the sources at my disposal for the period after October 1938 would not bear out that a greater interest in religion or simply church attendance signified a greater respect for Cardinal Innitzer, whose earlier collusion with the Nazis and the distasteful manner of this collusion was not forgotten. It is difficult to decide whether compassion with an errant priest, who allowed himself to be deceived, outweighed a silent contempt for a man who seemed not even to know what the Nazis had done to their adversaries in Germany in the half decade before the *Anschluss*. His Sudeten German patriotism, even if defensible in a Cardinal of the greatest international church in the world, nor his political simple-mindedness (admitted even by archdiocesan personnel fifteen years after the war) can hardly serve as excuses in this context.[14]

The attacks against the Church for collaborating with the Nazis in the early stages of annexation received a strong impetus among the lay public when, in the 1960s, Rolf Hochhuth's *The Deputy* raised questions of moral laxity about the Church and its leadership in Rome. At the time, it was commented that the claims against the Papacy fueled a renewed attack on churches everywhere else for supposed collusion with Nazism or fascism, such as in Spain and Austria. I believe that, in fact, such a contagion is at work. If it were made public that today in a certain country the Church is a partner to a right-wing dictatorship, other accusations of a kindred nature would surely be reactivated, including the Innitzer affair. Thus, it has always been since the days of Dreyfus.

This raised anew the question of whether certain claims of resistance within the Church, such as those of Prelate Jakob Fried and Dr. Karl Rudolf, are fair or extravagent.[15] It would be a mistake to identify Innitzer's own position with that of all 6 million Catholics. But a letter of the Cardinal, published in the *Völkischer Beobachter* on 31 March 1938, when the honeymoon was officially still a recognized fact, may shed some light on the "mind-set" of the Cardinal, who saw fit to do what the Austrians would call a *Fleissaufgabe*, effort beyond the call of duty. In this letter, which was a clearly voluntary move on the part of the Cardinal, according to Himmelreich and Borodojkewycz, but also accepted by anti-Nazis, Innitzer wrote:

> I feel impelled to make some corrective observations concerning a report which I have received, and which Havas of Berlin has spread, in discussing the Manifesto (*Aufruf*) of the Austrian bishops. The Havas representative writes that the Manifesto could be seen as part of a visit by the Papal Nuncio in Berlin to Foreign Minister Ribbentrop. In this regard, [Innitzer's letter continues,] I must state that there is no such connection. The Manifesto [of the Austrian bishops] was issued as a spontaneous statement in this historic hour of reunion [between Austria and Germany]. This should be clear from the preamble to the Manifesto. The Havas representative is also to be refuted when he says that the Manifesto of the bishops was to be seen as a relaxing gesture (*entspannende Geste*), since I regard it beneath my dignity to work with gestures in such a fateful hour."

It is very probable that the Cardinal was sincere with these words and that he believed, as he said in a later passage, that the declaration of the bishops was a turning point in the religious-cultural life of the entire nation. But the whole letter, printed with obvious glee in the Nazi press, was unnecessary because according to all shades of opinion in this matter it was not written under Nazi pressure and therefore constitutes a classic case of *Fleissaufgabe*.[16]

In my interviews in the archdiocesan palace, I came upon an assistant to Bishop Weinbacher, who had personally suffered when the Hitler Youth attacked the building.[17] Recalling my talk with him leads me to a further reflection on the events of March-October 1938. It becomes progressively clear that the Nazis, and in particular Bürckel after his first conversation with Hitler following annexation, meant to play the part they did in fact play during the summer and fall. In other words, the events did not force their hand. As with the treaty between Austria and Germany of 11 July 1936, which, it is now plain, the Nazis saw as a takeover instrument right from the start, so did they view the fraternization game they played in the four weeks between the *Anschluss* and plebiscite. It has been suggested, for instance by Friedrich Heer in our conversation in his Burgtheater office, that the neo-pagans, principally Alfred Rosenberg, gained Hitler's ear after the *Anschluss*. They then pressed for an offensive against all Christianity, especially Catholicism, because the addition of 6 million Austrians to the Reich made that religion more powerful than it should be in their opinion.

I put this question to Professor Jedlicka and Professor Friedrich Engel-Janosi, who wrote probably the first article on persecution and resistance in *Österreich in Geschichte und Literatur*, as well as to Professor Robert Kann.[18] I did not get an unambiguous affirmation from any one of them, but privately I believe that there was such a campaign and that within the Nazi hierarchy the victims were seen to be the "*betont katholisch*" like Seyss-Inquart. But even if such neo-pagan impact can be proved, I still think that the Nazis decided soon after the *Anschluss*, perhaps right after the meeting at the Imperial, to play the game the way they did in fact play it: first using the Church, then ignoring it (after 10 April little was said for weeks about Church–Party relations in the Nazi press), then provoking it, and finally neutralizing it. I came to this conclusion after my interviews with Professors Borodajkewyzc and Jedlicka, whose cautiously positive reply strangely contradicted the neo-pagan thesis, to be sure, and after studying Reimann's book on Innitzer.[19]

Die echte Seelensorge kann jetzt gefördert werden. (The real soul caring work of the Church can now be promoted.) I return as a matter of final conclusion, to a point made earlier. This was the hope of many sincere Catholics, who favored what they considered to be lifting by the Nazis of the onus of nonsacerdotal obligations from the shoulders of the Church. The *Reichspost* of 13 April 1938, in an article called "*Befreite Seelsorge*," lamented the necessity of the Church in the inter-war years to "go to bat" for the conservative-clerical regime. It continues, *jetzt anders* (now the difference): a real separation of church and State, no more *Mauer machen* (playing a supporting role) for a party, now nothing but *Seelsorge*. One can hear the sigh of relief reading the article.[20] Many of my interviewees explained the early approval of the new regime by pointing to the sense of relief at being rid of an unwanted political task. I put this matter before several of my partners in conversation, Professor Weinzierl, Professor Knoll, Professor Hacker,[21] and others. Although there is no doubt that such a sense of relief was real and the underlying reason sincere, it seems to me that the freedom from political chores should not constitute a reason to favor a regime that otherwise is so unworthy of acceptance. If a Latin government tells its Church that is should celebrate its freedom from political burdens and enjoy a return to giving to Caesar what is Caesar's and to God what is God's, will this gladden the hearts of the contemporary liberation theologians in Latin countries? When I discussed this issue in its purely Austrian context with Professor Knoll, he reverted to his conviction that the Church could only do its job by being sacerdotal even on enemy subsoil and that shedding its political work can indeed be seen as a blessing. He admitted, however, as a good democrat, that in such a case the purely temporal issues of public life must revert to the hands of a democratic government not a dictatorship. And this seems to me to be the pivotal point. I think that the Church is entitled to a sigh of relief if political burdens have in large part (not altogether, though) been taken over by the State and if that State is democratic–and not otherwise.

This brings the paper back to Innitzer. When he died in 1950 the obituaries in the North American and European press were mixed. There was bitterness at the collaborator with Hitler, there was contempt for a man with childlike naiveté and trust in the honesty of the dishonest, there was also praise for a priest who did his best and recovered his wits before it was too late. My own evaluation includes parts of all these judgments. I think that when a man makes mistakes in public he may be vindicated if he has a "finest hour." I think Innitzer had such an hour. After all, the Rosenkranz Rally of the Catholics at St. Stephen's that 7 October 1938 was the greatest act of resistance in the whole period of the Nazi occupation of Austria. And that is, in a world where everything is relative, no mean feat.

NOTES

1. Otto Molden, *Der Ruf des Gewissens* (Vienna, 1958), pp. 61–66.
2. *Das Schwarze Korps*, July–October 1938, passim.
3. Conversation with Professor August Knoll, autumn 1961.

4. Conversation with Professor Taras Borodajkewycz, autumn 1961.

5. Conversation with Dr. Richard Barta, autumn 1961.

6. See *Münchner Kirchenblatt*, summer and autumn 1938, passim.

7. See *Wiener Kirchenblatt*, 1938, passim.

8. Conversation with Josef Wagner, autumn 1961. Correspondence with Josef Himmelreich, Munich, autumn 1961.

9. Letter to Dr. Mikolussi in the *Völkischer Beobachter*, 26 March 1938.

10. Letter of Odilo Globocnik in the *Völkischer Beobachter*, 13 October 1938.

11. Conversation with Professor Ludwig Jedlicka, autumn 1961.

12. See Bruce Pauley, *Hitler and the Forgotten Nazis* (Chapel Hill, 1981), p. 217.

13. Conversation with Friedrich Heer, autumn 1961.

14. Conversation with Professor Erika Weinzierl, autumn 1961. See also her book *Kirche in Österreich*, (Vienna, 1966–1967).

15. Dr. Karl Rudolf, cathedral curator, describes these events and analyzes their meaning in his *Aufbau im Widerstand*. See also Prälat Jakob Fried, *Nationalsozialismus und katholische Kirche in Österreich* (Vienna, 1947), passim.

16. Letter of Cardinal Innitzer in the *Völkischer Beobachter*, 31 March 1938.

17. Conversation with Pater Jakob Weinbacher's assistant, autumn 1961.

18. Conversations with Professors Ludwig Jedlicka, Friedrich Engel-Janosi, and Robert Kann, autumn 1961 and at an American Historical Association meeting, respectively.

19. See Viktor Reimann, *Innitzer, Kardinal zwischen Hitler und Rom* (Vienna, 1967), passim, for a comprehensive and sound treatment of the subject.

20. *Reichspost*, April 1938.

21. Conversation with Professor Walter Hacker, autumn 1961.

II

Popular Opinion in Vienna after the Anschluss

EVAN B. BUKEY

In dredging up the unhappy past of one of Europe's most stable democ-
racies, the recent Waldheim affair has invariably raised questions about
popular attitudes in Austria during the Nazi era. Within the Alpine
republic, historians have long acknowledged the mass enthusiasm that
welcomed the *Anschluss*, but by emphasizing the domination of Austrian
society by Reich German officials and by publishing evidence of widespread
suffering, discontent, and even resistance to the Hitler regime, they have
generally evaded the problem of political consent, unwittingly contributing
their own share to the collective amnesia.[1] This paper seeks to address this
particular problem of historical remembrance by examining popular opinion in Vienna after the *Anschluss*, especially during the half decade before
Hitler's defeat at Stalingrad in early 1943 shook public confidence in Nazi
rule. As both the center of Austrian tradition and culture and the second
largest city of the Greater German Reich, the Danubian metropolis merits
investigation for countless reasons though, in the course of the following
analysis, three deserve emphasis: (1) as a target of Hitler's youthful resent-
ments, Vienna experienced discrimination under the Nazi regime; for example, in 1944 to the point of being denied adequate antiaircraft units for
the city's defense; (2) with the largest Jewish population in Central Europe
before World War II, Vienna was the scene of anti-Semitic outbursts that
shocked even the Gestapo and the SS; (3) toward the end of World War II,

Vienna became the strongest center of active resistance to Nazism in Austria and possibly in all Greater Germany.

At the outset, it needs to be made clear that information on the popular mood in Vienna, as in Berlin,[2] is uneven. Compared to Lower and Upper Austria[3] and, above all, to Bavaria,[4] the Nazi opinion surveys that have survived (or been made available) are impressionistic, incomplete, or after 1941, exiguous.[5] For the period between 1938 and 1941 there are a good many SD (Sicherheitsdienst) situation reports, a substantial collection of neighborhood surveys by the NSDAP and the NS *Frauenschaft*,[6] a file of anonymous letters to the Reich Commissioner for the Reunification of Austria with the German Reich,[7] and a number of eyewitness accounts by diplomats, foreign correspondents, and later refugees. For the second half of World War II, only a handful of opinion surveys are available, though for late 1944 and early 1945 judicial accounts and SD reports describing widespread disenchantment are more numerous.[8] Despite these not inconsiderable gaps, it is nevertheless possible to combine contemporary sources with the works of scholars such as Karl Stadler, Radomir Luža, Gerhard Botz, Felix Kreissler, and Erika Weinzierl to reconstruct certain broad trends of opinion.[9] Given the general lack of information in Nazi records on occupation or class, it is not as easy to discern the attitudes of specific social groups, though it may be assumed that regime approval was strongest among those sections of society most overrepresented in the Austrian Nazi party, officials and the aspiring new middle class of employees and managers,[10] and that disapproval was greatest among those groups most overrepresented in active resistance movements, skilled workers and middle-class intellectuals.[11] In this regard, it is also important to recall that reported dissent was usually verbal, consisting of complaints frequently heard in societies under stress and that what the Gestapo, and later Austrian historians,[12] regarded as opposition was often little more than partial dissatisfaction with certain aspects of the regime.

ANSCHLUSS: EUPHORIA AND DISILLUSIONMENT

It is, of course, well known that the *Anschluss* of 1938 unleashed a torrent of enthusiasm for Nazism in Vienna that overwhelmed contemporary observers (including Hitler) and to this day has not been adequately explained. To what extent decades of German Nationalist propaganda, pent-up hatred of the Dollfuss-Schuschnigg dictatorship, or hopes for economic betterment contributed to the psychological hysteria of what Helmut Qualtinger's Herr Karl has called *"ein riesiger Heuriger"* must remain matters of conjecture. What is indisputable is that (1) the *Anschluss* was endorsed by the Austrian episcopate, by the remnants of organized labor, and in the plebiscite of 10 April 1938 by the population as a whole; (2) the "affirmative consensus" behind the *Anschluss* was reinforced by the rapid introduction of measures relieving social distress, the revitalization of the economy, and above all, the elimination of unemployment; (3) support for the regime, although emotional rather than ideological, persisted in Vienna until the battle of Stalingrad early in 1943 and throughout the rest of Austria until much later.[13]

It is also fairly well known, though hardly emphasized in contemporary Austria, that the first real disaffection with the new order developed primarily within the ranks of the Viennese Nazi Party. Whereas Hitler generally favored a native-born leadership in the provinces, he deliberately turned a cold shoulder on his followers in Vienna, resolving to keep the city firmly under Reich German control and entrusting both the reorganization of the Party and the (temporary) administration of the Ostmark to the Gauleiter of the Saarpfalz, Josef Bürckel. As Reich Commissioner for the Reunification of Austria with the German Reich, Bürckel surrounded himself with trusted aides from the Palatinate and awarded posts either to German Nazis or to members of the superradical Carinthian branch of the Austrian NSDAP.[14] The Viennese cadre, receiving only secondary posts or assignments outside the Ostmark, responded with a cascade of bitter complaints about "Prussians" and "Piefkes" that resonated through the Party, not only eliciting sympathy at municipal Gestapo headquarters but shortly before Christmas even leading to a shoot-out in the Café Savoy between an Austrian stormtrooper (SA) and a German SS man.[15]

Although it would be both glib and perverse to credit Viennese Nazis with founding the much-vaunted (and overrated) Austrian resistance movement, there can be no doubt that their disillusionment lay at the root of the anti-German mood coming to prevail in the city during the *Anschluss* years. Fueled by economic grievances, traditional Viennese xenophobia, and the arrogant, often tactless behavior of Reich German officials, resentment of the "Piefkes" spread so rapidly from Hitler's Viennese followers and their families to all classes of society that by 1939, according to the Gestapo, "Germans from the Reich under any pretext are annoyed and heckled."[16] In the months that followed, anti-German sentiment escalated to regular confrontations in taverns, especially in Grinzing, to outbursts in theaters, including catcalls directed at Frau Göring in the opera, and to a series of soccer riots that in November 1940 cost Gauleiter Baldur von Schirach the tires and windows of his limousine.[17] That Hitler came to view Vienna as "a rebellious metropolis at the southeast border of the Reich"[18] was not entirely without cause.

The anti-German sentiment that evolved in Vienna after 1938 clearly contributed in some measure, as has been frequently stressed, to the development of contemporary Austrian nationalism, but until late in World War II, it represented neither an expression of genuine Austrian patriotism nor a manifestation of active resistance to the Nazi regime. As Radomir Luža has correctly emphasized, "the mood reflected opposition to the influx of Germans taking positions of power rather than a rejection of the [*Anschluss*]."[19] Spawned by Austrian Nazis and confined primarily to Vienna, Teutophobia was, as Gestapo records made abundantly clear, particularistic and cultural rather than patriotic or oppositional. To quote the remarks of a Swedish correspondent who reported on Viennese discontent after the battle of Stalingrad, "It was not so much National Socialism they disliked as things German in themselves."[20]

Coinciding with the disgruntlement of Hitler's Viennese retainers with Bürckel's heavy-handed administration was an awakening of ideological discontent among large numbers of Roman Catholics. Although Cardinal Theodor Innitzer had endorsed the *Anschluss* and sought to come to terms with the regime, Hitler responded with an anticlerical campaign marked by the abrogation of the Austrian Concordat of 1933, the introduction of compulsory civil marriage, the secularization of education, the dissolution of Catholic associations, and even the deportation of individual clergymen to Dachau. In reaction, a massive protest demonstration erupted on 7 October 1938 in St. Stephen's Square as 8000 youngsters emerged from mass, chanting *"Erzbischof befiehl, wir folgen dir!" "Wir wollen unseren Bischof sehen!" "Wir danken unserem Bischof!"* and *"Christus ist unser Führer!"*[21] The Catholic youth clearly expressed the outraged feelings of many devout Viennese Christians, but just how pervasive or, for that matter, political anti-Nazi sentiment was among the city's Catholics is not revealed in the records—at least to the extent that it is for the provinces, where religious dissent was closely linked to agricultural grievances and hence regarded as more dangerous to the regime.[22]

In coming years, it is certainly true that Viennese Catholics, both clergy and laity, reacted to Nazi persecution with acts of protest, defiance, and active resistance in the case of Roman Karl Scholz's *Österreichische Freiheitsbewegung*.[23] On the other hand, so long as Innitzer and the Austrian episcopate continued to seek an accommodation with Hitler and after 1939 supported his war, especially after it spread to Soviet Russia, acts of Christian opposition were usually narrow, isolated, and ineffective. Although we may assume that ordinary parishioners shared the ambivalent, contradictory feelings of Church leaders, the absence of opinion surveys makes it risky to generalize further. All the same, there is little reason or evidence to conclude that Catholic opinion in Vienna, any more than in Austria or

Greater Germany as a whole, actually broke with the Nazi regime as such until the end of World War II.

The waning of *Anschluss* enthusiasm that began in the Viennese Nazi Party and, for completely different reasons, spread to sections of the Catholic population gave way in the autumn of 1938 to a more general mood of uneasiness in society at large. Although the Munich crisis dampened public euphoria in Vienna, it was primarily bread and butter issues that produced the first real wave of discontent, especially among blue collar workers.

In contrast to the Altreich, the Nazis did not regard the labor movement in Austria as their principal adversary. Though suspicious and fearful of Marxist ideology, they believed that blue collar workers could be won to their cause through propaganda and dramatic improvements in living conditions. The extent that they succeeded remains controversial, rooted in local conditions, and systematically unexplored. In Vienna, the Nazis at first bedazzled the hard-pressed workers by reappointing Social Democrats to municipal office (*Neubacher Action*), by extending German social security benefits, by creating jobs for the city's 170,000 unemployed (though often in the Altreich), and by improving conditions in the workplace. Promising to alleviate the housing shortage through "Aryanization," they also elimi-nated the unpopular bicycle tax, slashed electricity rates and bus fares, and reduced the prices of poultry, eggs, milk, sugar, and bread.[24] Although many of these measures met with only limited success, the astonishing re-duction of unemployment by 60 percent within less than a year engendered such working-class confidence that even two left-wing historians have ad-mitted "for many employment became the measure of all things; lost rights were tolerated and compensated by the feeling of having at last found work again."[25]

On the other hand, Nazi promises did not always keep pace with reality. By late autumn 1938, rural flight, currency revaluation, and both equalization and austerity measures designed to align the Austrian economy with that of the Altreich all combined to produce occasional food short-ages, rising prices, and lower real wages. With the introduction of the Ger-man income tax on 1 January 1939, moreover, Viennese wage earners found the contents of their pay envelopes cut by as much as 30 percent.[26]

The malaise that gripped the Viennese public after the Munich crisis, especially in working-class districts, has been both amply documented and widely publicized by Austrian politicians and scholars. Although there can be no doubt that the discontent represented a general sobering of opinion, examination of Gestapo surveys and other contemporary evidence reveals an attitudinal climate not altogether different from that prevailing else-where in the Reich. Nazi officials thus characterized the local mood as "good," "satisfactory," or "enthusiastic and uncritical," while reporting bitter complaints about rising consumer prices and shortages of eggs, butter, oranges, apples, and other staples. As in Bavaria, there was trust in Hitler, especially among younger women, coupled with widespread fear of war and growing Catholic resentment of Nazi interference in Church affairs. True to the spirit of the times, there was also little concern with infringements of personal liberties. What distinguished Viennese opinion from that in the Altreich in 1939 were three additional features: (1) well-founded grievances over frozen wages and skyrocketing living costs that found expression in work stoppages, absenteeism, and sporadic industrial sabotage; (2) a rising tide of resentment of German officials and tourists, especially from North Germany; (3) general approval and acclamation of the regime's anti-Semitic barbarities.[27]

CRYSTAL NIGHT: ACCLAMATION AND CONSENT

In retrospect, it is all too clear that, while large numbers of Viennese resented discrimination as second-class citizens, suffered religious persecution, or felt increasingly alienated by losses of real income, Judeophobia was so deeply ingrained in the collective psyche that it generally neutralized antagonisms, providing for the Nazi dictatorship what the British historian Ian Kershaw has called a "transcending consensus of support."[28] In the city where Hitler had acquired the "granite foundation" of his thought, foreign observers and even German officials were shocked by the enormous crowds of shrieking men and women that welcomed the *Anschluss* by joining Nazi gangs in orgies of violence against thousands of Jews, attacking them in the streets, indiscriminately robbing them of personal possessions, and forcing them to scrub walls and pavements with lye or hydrochloric acid. Although Bürckel's office and the SS gradually put an end to incidents of "wild Aryanization," brutally establishing procedures for forced emigration, anti-Semitic outbursts continued throughout the summer of 1938, accelerated rapidly in October, and culminated in the massive devastation of Crystal Night in early November. On that evening in Vienna alone 42 synagogues were burned, 4038 Jewish shops were looted, and 7800 people were taken into custody, of whom at least 27 were murdered, 88 were severely injured and 680 committed suicide.[29]

Although Hitler's persecution of the Jews was planned and executed by the Nazi Party, the general reaction of the Viennese public was approval, encouragement, and in some cases, active participation. There is no way of identifying the mobs of jeering bystanders who surrounded Jewish victims or chased them from parks and public places in the months after the

Anschluss, but surviving testimony suggests involvement of broad strata of society ranging from well-tailored young women and prosperous business-men to petty bourgeois shopkeepers, domestics, workers, and prostitutes.[30] There were Viennese who were appalled by the atrocities, especially by the November pogrom that according to one SS report, met with "condemnation and shock" or to another "had a depressing effect on the general mood whereby the initially favorable reception of the entire operation turned to sympathy."[31] However, those who rejected the violence often did so because of the unnecessary destruction of property. Indeed, most Gestapo records indicate "great satisfaction" with Crystal Night, reporting a crowd prompted "to take active part in the action"[32] or that "there was hardly a sign of sympathy with the fate of the Jews, and where it awkwardly came to the surface, it was immediately and energetically rejected by the crowds; some over-obvious philo-Semites were arrested."[33]

There is, of course, no accurate way of measuring Viennese Judeophobia under Nazi rule, but its pervasiveness and lethal quality, often not unlike that of Hitler himself, is all too apparent in surviving records, especially in a collection of anonymous letters addressed to the Reich Commissioner for the Reunification of Austria with the German Reich. Examination of the letters reveals complaints about random violence, "excesses" damaging to the NSDAP, or difficulties caused by Aryanization, such as a frozen bank account or the temporary loss of a job; there are also protests against the maltreatment of Jewish war veterans or of individuals such as the neighborhood grocer. Nevertheless, few of the protest letters question the Nazi goal of removing the Jews from the people's community, and many of the others make accusations against specific Jews (usually for "masquerading" as Aryans), object to legal exemptions for Jewish-Gentile *Mischlinge* under the Nuremberg Laws, or call for harsher measures ranging from immediate expulsion to outright extermination of what one writer called the "bloodsuckers of the German people."[34] In short, although large segments of Viennese public opinion clearly objected to acts of random violence, a strong consensus existed for ridding the metropolis of Jews in a legal and orderly manner. As a former Social Democrat shop steward explained after Crystal Night, "National Socialism doesn't need this sort of thing. If the Jews are to be done away with, then it should be done officially and legally, not by individuals who make a witch-hunt (*Hetze*) out of it."[35]

WAR: AMBIVALENCE AND DISAFFECTION

The major trends of opinion identified here generally intensified after the outbreak of World War II. As in most parts of Greater Germany, the public greeted the war with little enthusiasm and considerable unrest. There was widespread confusion during blackouts, discontent with the official ration of milk, potatoes, cooking fat, and flour, and a general sense of foreboding. As in the Altreich, the SD reported renewed religious dissatisfaction and an upsurge in activity by Communist groups including intensified circulation of pamphlets calling for an overthow of the regime. After the conquest of Poland, the mood became optimistic, as hopes spread for a quick end to hostilities, and an extension of bonuses to wage earners enabled the SD to contrast the "good" and "positive" mood of blue-collar Floridsdorf with the pessimistic climate of working-class areas of Bavaria. The Gestapo also registered a groundswell of demands to tighten anti-Semitic restrictions and to settle accounts with the Jews once and for all.[36]

During the first winter of the war a massive shortage of coal in the Reich seems to have hit Vienna especially hard. Accompanied by bottlenecks in food rationing, a war surtax, cuts in social security benefits, and a sharp rise in the cost of living, the coal crisis unleashed a new wave of anti-German feeling.[37] Ironically, Reich planners had long been trying to meet economic grievances by awarding defense contracts to Viennese industry but were finding that obsolete equipment, high transportation costs, and outmoded production techniques limited orders for advanced military weapons. Instead of opening up jobs, the war had the reverse effect of producing an exodus of skilled labor to better-paying positions in the Altreich, a trend that not only retarded modernization but aggravated tensions by separating large numbers of families.[38] What gave the deteriorating public mood its distinctive anti-German tone, however, was the continued resentment of the Viennese Nazis. Still excluded from top party offices, their anger came to a boil in early 1940 when Reich Commissioner Bürckel dismissed one of their own (Josef Fitzthum) as metropolitan Vice Police President and, on 1 April, announced the final dissolution of Austria as an entity.[39]

Hitler's spectacular victories in the West in the spring of 1940 temporarily eased tensions in Vienna, leaving most of the public "breathless" and brimming with admiration for the Führer.[40] As most Austrians had not fully shared the German thirst for revenge over France, the enthusiasm did not last very long. By autumn, the SD was reporting bitter complaints about high prices and low wages that were still out of line with those in the Reich, quarrels in markets over scarcities of food, clothing, and shoes, and apprehension of another winter of war. The dissatisfaction, as usual, focused on the German element in Vienna, especially after it was announced that Hitler had replaced Bürckel, whom he dismissed on 8 August, not with an Austrian Gauleiter, as in the provinces, but with Reich Youth Leader (Reichsjugendführer) Baldur von Schirach, born in Berlin.[41] At the end of October, a foreign correspondent described the city as "gray and listless, the people weary and threadbare,"[42] a characterization hardly different from that of the Gestapo which registered "an alarming deterioration of the mood." "On every possible occasion," the SD continued,

> the Viennese population, among them a great many Party members, give unmistakable expression to their disdain. Germans from the Reich need only open their mouths to be heckled and insulted. . . . It is a daily occurrence that Germans who ask information . . . receive wrong directions. Women from Germany are often refused what Viennese can buy. No sporting events . . . between *Ostmärker* and German teams take place without friction and unpleasantness.[43]

From the Nazi perspective, it is to Schirach's credit that, despite Hitler's later disapproval, he was able to shore up the *Anschluss* consensus in Vienna for at least a year. After taking up residence in the Ballhausplatz, the Gauleiter made a number of public statements reassuring the workers. He openly acknowledged the insensitivity of many "repugnant and ill-mannered" Germans, promised to make the opera the leading stage of Greater Germany, and ceremoniously awarded government posts to a number of veteran militants such as Alfred Proksch, who had headed the Austrian NSDAP between 1926 and 1931. In February 1941, Schirach traveled to Obersalzberg, where he persuaded Hitler to consider a carefully drawn-up package for economic development, including subsidies of 150 million reichsmarks, allocations of machinery, special import-export agreements, freight reductions, and tax relief. Due to the invasion of Russia four months later, the plan was scarcely implemented, but it did result in the return of some 80,000 skilled workers from the Reich. In October, Schirach again met with Hitler, this time pressing him to undertake the construction of new housing units. The dictator responded with anger, however, communicating through Bormann

> that you should see your task in Vienna not in the construction of new residential areas but in the elimination of present conditions. To begin with . . . all Jews to be deported as soon as possible, next the Czechs, and then all other foreigners who have made the political indoctrination and education of the Viennese extremely difficult. Once you have reduced the population of Vienna to 1.5 or 1.4 million, the housing crisis will be solved in the best, easiest, and quickest way.[44]

Always a faithful lackey, Schirach sheepishly complied; instead of undertaking new construction projects, he cooperated fully and enthusiastically with the SS (despite later disclaimers) in deporting the city's remaining 60,000 Jews to the ghettos and gas chambers of Poland.[45]

Although evidence on Viennese opinion in the two years before the battle of Stalingrad is exceptionally scanty, Schirach seems to have made some headway mollifying the municipal Nazis, flattering the cultural elite, dampening clerical unrest, and appeasing some blue-collar elements. Due to Hitler's animosities and to the pressures of war, the Gauleiter did not succeed in closing the economic gap between Vienna and the Altreich, in improving food supplies, or in solving the critical housing crisis.[46] So far as can be ascertained, the Viennese public reacted, not surprisingly, with considerable ambivalence. On the one hand, there was widespread ridicule of Schirach for his pompous and pretentious ways, continued grumbling about wartime scarcities and "Piefkes," and growing anxiety about the war, especially after the beginning of the Russian campaign, in which substantial numbers of Viennese troops participated. According to the Gestapo, there were also many more acts of sabotage and arrests for political offenses than in the Altreich. On the other hand, the public still supported the regime, contributing more to the winter relief campaign (*Winterhilfswerk*) in 1941 than any other city in Greater Germany, appreciating Vienna's not inconsiderable cultural revival, and turning out in great numbers to cheer speeches by Hitler, Goebbels, and other Reich dignitaries.[47]

Above all, there was heartfelt approval and deep-seated satisfaction with the final removal of the Jews. Although no opinion surveys have been found on the matter, abundant evidence exists of Jews being denounced to the Gestapo, beaten in trolley cars, or kicked in the street by passers by. Once Schirach's deportations got under way, moreover, the streets of the city were regularly lined by jeering crowds, yelling catcalls and obscenities as SS trucks rumbled by to the Aspang depot with their fearful cargoes bound for Theresienstadt, Treblinka, or Auschwitz.[48] As a Swedish pastor who had headed a mission in Vienna between September 1939 and May 1941 confided to his diary, Judeophobia was not the "hatred of a small clique," but a genuine "popular hatred" (*Volkshass*). Everywhere in the city of music he had heard, "The Jews must be exterminated. They must be smoked out the way lice are smoked out of a house." Most of all, he recorded, cultivated, affluent, and otherwise reasonable people could not grasp his concern for the Jews: "You are helping the Jews! That is not true! That is simply not possible!"[49]

SOME CONCLUDING REFLECTIONS

In reviewing this survey of public opinion in Vienna under Nazi rule, at least two conclusions come to mind. One is that, although the scholarly search for a usable past based on evidence of "resistance and persecution" has been of enormous benefit in molding a positive identity in contemporary Austria, it has also concealed an important dimension of historical reality whose sudden appearance in 1986 most Austrians found difficult to grasp, let alone to accept. The hundreds of acts of political dissent, defiance, and resistance that have been so meticulously documented for Vienna[50] must be viewed from now on within the larger context of collaboration in which by 1942 over 172,000 Viennese had joined the Nazi Party and over 200,000 had left the Church.[51] Until greater attention is paid to the issue of political consent and to the attitudes of authoritarianism and anti-Semitism that made Nazism attractive to so many people after 1938, Austria cannot hope to recover from the collective amnesia for which the term *Waldheimer's disease* is not altogether inappropriate.

A second conclusion of this essay is an affirmation of the deepening awareness of the diffuse, complex, and multifaceted nature of Nazism. The greatest mass party (*Sammlungspartei*) of the twentieth century, Hitler's movement attracted such diverse and conflicting elements that even in Vienna, the capital city of a conquered province, it had a magnetic appeal for most of the population at one time or another. As the German-American historian Johnpeter Horst Grill has recently written, "National Socialism and the Third Reich were held together not only by the enormous popularity Hitler and his 'conservative policies' enjoyed among the Germans as a whole, but also by the support of long-term populist (*völkisch*) true believers who followed Hitler's policies to their logical conclusions—war and extermination."[52] In the case of Vienna and the Ostmark, there was little support for the Führer's "conservative policies" or his war, but the popular enthusiasm that greeted his anti-Semitic program provided a key ingredient in keeping the metropolis under his spell—at least until that point in 1943 when the Jews had been expelled, the war was clearly lost, and the Allies' Moscow Declaration of October 1943 offered the tantalizing prospect of a resurrected Austrian state in which neither Jews nor Germans would play a role.

NOTES

1. Although the Austrian literature taking this approach is endless, two important exceptions are the outstanding work by E. Hanisch, *Nationalsozialistische Herrschaft in der Provinz: Salzburg im Dritten Reich* (Salzburg, 1983) and the more recent study by S. Karner, *Die Steiermark im Dritten Reich 1938–1945: Aspekte ihrer politischen wirtschaftlich-sozialen und kulturellen Entwicklung* (Graz and Vienna, 1985). On Austrian views of the Nazi past, see Evan B. Bukey, *Hitler's Hometown: Linz, Austria, 1908–1945* (Bloomington and Indianapolis, 1985), pp. xiii–xv, 260; and the remarkably astute column by R. Knight, "The Waldheim Context: Austria and Nazism," *The Times Literary Supplement*, 3 October 1986, pp. 1083–84.

2. M. G. Steinert, *Hitler's War and the Germans: Public Mood and Attitude During the Second World War* (Athens, 1977), p. 19 n.

162   EVAN B. BUKEY

3. A fairly complete collection of *Landrat* situation reports for Lower Austria is available at the Niederösterreichisches Landesarchiv under the signature NÖLA/ZR Ia-10. For Upper Austria, see H. Slapnicka, *Oberösterreich – als es "Oberdonau" hiess* (Linz, 1978), pp. 279–94; and Dokumentationsarchiv des österreichischen Widerstandes (DÖW), *Widerstand und Verfolgung in Oberösterreich 1934–1945: Eine Dokumentation*, (Vienna, 1982), vol. 1, pp. 195–99, 364–68; vol. 2, pp. 260–65, 293–99, 321–30.

4. I. Kershaw, *Popular Opinion and Political Dissent in the Third Reich: Bavaria 1933–1945* (Oxford, 1983).

5. The Allgemeines Verwaltungsarchiv (AVA), Vienna, contains incomplete files of SD situation reports for 1939–1940 in its collection of the Reichskommissar für die Wiedervereinigung Österreichs mit dem Deutschen Reich (Rk), Ordner 312–14, 322. These same files have long been available from the National Archives, Washington, D.C., Microcopy T 84, Rolls 13–14. For the period 1940–1944, it is reasonable to assume that the AVA's vast, uncatalogued Schirach collection may also hold SD opinion surveys, but my own sample probes over a period of many months in 1985 yielded no results.

6. For example, at DÖW, Vienna, docs: 201–12, Stimmungsberichte von Ortsgruppen der NSDAP an das Kreispropagandaamt IX; 1179, 1189, Situationsberichte der NSDAP–Ortsgruppe Wien Kettenbrücke; 2054, Lageberichte der NSDAP, Wien II (1940); 4207, Stimmungsbericht des Blockwartes der NSDAP–Wien 9, 13 January 1939; 12,225, 12,557, Verschiedene Unterlagen, Stimmungsberichte, Standesliste der SA der NSDAP, Ortsgruppe Erdberglande, Wien III.

7. AVA, Rk, Ordner 338–350.

8. For example, in L. Jedlicka, *Der 20. Juli 1944 in Österreich* (Vienna and Munich, 1966), pp. 90–105.

9. K. Stadler, *Österreich 1938–1945 im Spiegel der NS Akten* (Vienna and Munich, 1966); R. Luža, *Austro-German Relations in the Anschluss Era* (Princeton, 1975); idem., *The Resistance in Austria, 1938–1945* (Minneapolis, 1984); G. Botz, *Die Eingliederung Österreiches in das Deutsche Reich: Planung und Verwirklichung des politisch-administrativen Anschlusses (1938–1940)* (Vienna, 1976); idem., *Wohnungspolitik und Judendeportationen in Wien: Zur Funktion des Antisemitsmus als Ersatz nationalsozialistischer Sozialpolitik* (Vienna and Salzburg, 1975); idem., *Wien vom "Anschluss" zum Krieg: Nationalsozialistische Machtübernahme und politschsoziale Umgestaltung am Beispiel der Stadt Wien 1938/39* (Vienna and Munich, 1978); F. Kreissler, *Der Österreicher und seine Nation: Ein Lernprozess mit Hindernissen* (Vienna, Cologne, and Graz, 1984); and E. Weinzierl, *Zu wenig Gerechte: Österreicher und Judenverfolgung 1938–1945* (Graz, Vienna, and Cologne, 1985).

10. Botz, *Wien*, p. 220.

11. Luža, *Resistance*, p. 315.

12. Most flagrantly perhaps by Stadler, p. 12: "In view of the demand for total obedience by those in power and the sanctions threatened in the event of its violation, all opposition in the Third Reich must be rated as an act of resistance even where it was merely a case on the part of individuals to 'remain decent'."

13. For exceptionally vivid accounts of the *Anschluss* in Vienna, see the dispatches by G. E. R. Gedye in *The New York Times*, 14–16, 22, and 25 March and 3 April 1938, as well as his memoir, *Betrayel in Central Europe: Austria and Czechoslovakia: The Fallen Bastions* (New York and London, 1939), pp. 270–353. Also see D. Wagner and G. Tomkawitz, *Anschluss: The Week Hitler Seized Austria* (New York, 1971); Botz, *Wien*, pp. 35–189; and Luža, *Austro-German Relations*, pp. 57–227.

14. B. F. Pauley, *Hitler and the Forgotten Nazis: A History of Austrian National Socialism* (Chapel Hill, 1981); Kreissler, pp. 145–50; Botz, *Wien*, pp. 195–231; and Luža, *Austro-German Relations*, pp. 57–125. On Hitler's ambivalent but hostile attitude toward Vienna, see

K. R. Stadler, "Provinzstadt im Dritten Reich," in Botz, *Wien*, pp. 15–21; Norbert Schausberger, "Hitler und Österreich: Einige Anmerkungen zur Hitler-Interpretation," *Österreich in Geschichte und Literatur* 18, no. 6 (1984):363–77; and above all, the dictator's own angry testimony on 24 June 1943, as recorded by Goebbels in M. Wortmann, *Baldur von Schirach: Hitler's Jugendführer* (Cologne, 1982), pp. 216–20.

15. Luža, *Austro-German Relations*, pp. 63 passim, especially p. 164 n; Austria, *Justice for Austria: Red-White-Red Book: Descriptions, Documents and Proofs to the Antecedents and History of the Occupation of Austria (From Official Sources)* (Vienna, 1947), p. 89; and Stadler, p. 50.

16. *Justice for Austria*, p. 91.

17. Ibid., pp. 91, 105–106; Luža, *Austro-German Relations*, pp. 164–68, 264–311, passim; DÖW, docs: 9627, NSDAP Gauwien, Kreisleitung VII, 23 February 1939; 1445, Bericht der Urlauber aus der Spinnerei Kulmbach Baiern, die in Wien ihren Urlaub verbracht haben über die Stimmung in Wien, 16 June 1939; 7506, Report of the British Consul General in Vienna, 15 June 1939; 209, Ober-Döbling, 29 March 1940, 1940; AVA, RK, Ordner 322: SD-Leitabschnitt Wien, Stimmungsbericht, 10 May 1940; *The New York Times*, 12 March 1939, 8 December 1940.

18. Quoted in Luža, *Austro-German Relations*, p. 297.

19. Ibid, p. 288.

20. Quoted in ibid, p. 231.

21. Ibid., pp. 182–91; Botz, *Wien*, pp. 383–96; and Kreissler, pp. 140–45. On Church–State relations in the Ostmark, see R. V. Luža, "Nazi Control of the Austrian Catholic Church, 1939–1941," *The Catholic Historical Review* 40, no. 4 (October 1977):537–72.

22. See, for example, DÖW, *Widerstand und Verfolgung in Oberösterreich* II, pp. 293–317 for Upper Austria; and Hanisch, pp. 98–104, 166–73, 269–73 for Salzburg.

23. Luža, *Resistance*, pp. 49–59.

24. Luža, *Austro-German Relations*, pp. 152–69; and Botz, *Wien*, pp. 129–51, 215–328.

25. H. Hautmann and R. Kropf, *Die österreichische Arbeiterbewegung vom Vormärz bis 1945* (Vienna, 1974), p. 106.

26. Botz, *Wien*, p. 313.

27. Steinert, pp. 25–43; Kershaw, pp. 283 ff.; F. M. Rebhann, *Das braune Glück in Wien* (Vienna, 1973), pp. 14–15; Stadler, pp. 116–23, and DÖW, docs: 201–12, Stimmungsberichte von Ortsgruppen der NSDAP and Kreispropagandaamt IX.

28. Kershaw, ibid., p. 385.

29. On the tidal wave of anti-Semitic terror in Vienna, see Gedye, *Betrayal*, pp. 282–328; and his *New York Times* articles, 14, 15, and 25, March, 3 April, 1938; Botz, *Wien*, pp. 93–105, 248–54; J. Moser, *Der gelbe Stern in Österreich* (Eisenstadt, 1977); pp. 109–22 ff.; H. Rosenkranz, *Verfolgung und Selbstbehauptung: Die Juden in Österreich 1938–1945* (Vienna and Munich, 1978), pp. 20–168 ff.; idem., "The Anschluss and the Tragedy of Austrian Jewry 1938–1945," in J. Fraenkel (ed.), *The Jews of Austria: Essays on their Life, History, and Destruction* (London, 1967), pp. 479–546; and N. Bentwich, "The Destruction of the Jewish Community in Austria 1938–1942," in Fraenkel, pp. 467–98. For extraordinarily gripping memoirs of two survivors, see C. Zuckmayer, *Als war's ein Stück von mir* (Vienna, 1968), pp. 70–81 ff.; and G. Clare, *Last Waltz in Vienna: The Rise and Destruction of a Family 1842–1942* (New York, 1982).

30. Information provided by R. John Rath. Also see *New York Times*, 22 March, 23 May 1938; and Gedye, *Betrayal*, pp. 283–302.

31. Weinzierl, p. 65.

32. DÖW, doc. 1780, SD Unterabschnitt Wien II/112 an den SD Führer des SS-Oberabschnittes Donau, 10 November 1938.

33. Rosenkranz, "Anschluss," p. 497. Also see idem., *Reichskristallnacht 9. November in Österreich* (Vienna, 1968).

34. AVA, Rk, Ordner 338–51.

35. AVA, Rk, Ordner 387, "Stimmen der Arbeiterschaft Dezember 1938."

36. Steinert, pp. 50–65; DÖW, docs. 201–12; AVA, Rk, Ordner 387, Täglicher Inlands-bericht, 9, 15, 16, 20, and 27 September, 2 and 5 October, 4, 5 and 25 November 1939; and H. Boberach (ed.), *Meldungen aus dem Reich: Die Geheimen Lageberichte des Sicherheits-dienstes der SS 1938–1945*, vol. 2, pp. 366, 382, 391, 400, 422, and especially vol. 3, p. 634 (18 December 1939).

37. Stadler, pp. 123–38; DÖW, docs: 201–12 and AVA, Rk, Ordner 322, SD-Leitabschnitt Wien, Stimmungsbericht, 10 May 1940.

38. H. Freudenberger and R. Luža, "National Socialist Germany and the Austrian In-dustry, 1938–1945," in William Wright (ed.), *Austria Since 1945* (Minneapolis, 1982), pp. 73–75 ff.

39. Luža, *Austro-German Relations*, pp. 264–77.

40. AVA, Rk, Ordner 322, SD-Leitabschnitt Wien, Stimmungsberichte, 20, 22, 27 and 29 May 1940.

41. *Justice for Austria*, pp. 103–106.

42. *New York Times*, 28 November 1940.

43. DÖW, doc. 7508, SD-Leitabschnitt Wien, Stimmungsberichte, 23 October 1940; and *Justice for Austria*, pp. 105–106.

44. Luža, *Austro-German Relations*, pp. 297–352; and Wortmann, pp. 187–229.

45. Wortmann, ibid., pp. 205–206.

46. Ibid., pp. 187–215; and Luža, *Austro-German Relations*, pp. 311–30.

47. Luža, ibid., pp. 304–30, and *Resistance*, p. 129.

48. Rosenkranz, *Verfolgung und Selbstbehauptung*, pp. 297–301 ff.

49. Weinzierl, pp. 114–15.

50. H. Steiner (ed.), *Widerstand und Verfolgung in Wien 1934–1945: Eine Dokumenta-tion*, 3 vols. (Vienna, 1975).

51. Luža, *Austro-German Relations*, pp. 372–73; and Botz, *Wien*, pp. 390–91.

52. J. H. Grill, "Local and Regional Studies on National Socialism: A Review," *Journal of Contemporary History* 31, no. 2 (April 1986):282.

Austrian Catholicism

Between Accommodation and Resistance

ERNST HANISCH

In 1938 the Austrian Catholic Church had to face a completely new situation. The State, which had been its protector, partner, and financier for centuries, had changed its position radically. Formerly the Church's close ally, with which it was prepared to share power, the State was now both its ideological and political adversary.

THE CATHOLIC CHURCH: A SUBSYSTEM OF NAZI POWER

Initially, the Church attempted to purchase as much power as feasible by performing an unprecedentedly humiliating gesture of accommodation to the new Nazi regime. However, conflict between the Church and Nazism was already inherent to both ideological systems. Both made well nigh unlimited demands on the individual, with the Church holding historical primacy, compelling the Nazi movement to assert itself against both the traditional ideological control and material power of the Church. Because of the unusually dominating position of the Church in Austria, the strife between it and the secular State assumed more intense form than it had in pre-1938 Germany (the so-called Altreich). The ensuing conflict was all the more intense because of the absence of the formal barrier of a Concordat. And if that were not enough, there was also the motive of Nazi revenge for the close bond maintained between the Church and the Dollfuss-

Schuschnigg regime, which had resulted in a good deal of political persecution of Nazis between 1934 and 1938. The crucial question was whether the Church would be able to maintain and strengthen her previous political and ideological sway over Austria's rural population. This was a matter the Nazis could ill afford to ignore.

Any critical historical analysis must treat the Church in the Third Reich in terms of a system of power, as an organized social macrocosm capable of maintaining an articulated political interest and commanding the means of conveying that interest to at least parts of the population.[1] And although the Church represented a system of power ready to implement its interests through a process of socialization and the exertion of its influence on norms and values, at the same time it found itself in the position of being the sole macrocosm of non-Nazi and nonmilitary provenance able to keep intact its organizational structure throughout the period of Nazi rule in Austria. This very fact made it possible for partly oppositional groups to grow around the village church and parsonage. Thus, the realm of the Church was turned into an area of freedom that was to remain relatively unaffected by Nazi ideology.

However, the position of the Church viewed as a system of power under the Nazi regime in Austria was exceptionally ambivalent. For the duration of the Third Reich, the Church acted as a partial ally of the Nazi State, thereby contributing to the stabilization of the Nazi order. Ideologically, that partial alliance was prompted by a conviction that Nazism was the pillar of governmental authority and that consequently the Epistle to the Romans, Chapter 13 was applicable. Authority, even where many of its acts were seen to be unjust, had to be obeyed. There was the additional factor that the Nazi system of control proved fully capable of mobilizing the basic patriotism of Catholics and exploiting that sentiment in aid of the war effort. In a joint pastoral letter, the German episcopate after all had stated at the outbreak of war: "In this decisive hour, we encourage and urge our Catholic soldiers to fulfill their duty by sacrificing their entire person in obedience to the Führer."[2]

An absurd situation was to arise from this, whereby in Austria (the Ostmark) Austrian Catholics were praying for the victory of Greater Germany, whereas in exile Austrian Catholics were praying for an Allied triumph.[3] The war waged by Germany against the Soviet Union from 1941 onwards, which could be portrayed as a Holy War against atheistic Bolshevism, was particularly fitted to facilitate the sharing of a common objective between the Church and Nazism. This is well borne out by the proclamation issued by Austria's bishops against Bolshevism on 27 November 1941.[4] Some humble commoners showed a better appreciation of the situation. A gravedigger commented tersely on the anti-Soviet campaign: "He who travels far, has a long way home."[5]

The Nazi regime in Austria succeeded in partially neutralizing and obfuscating the moral-ethical role of guardian in the past performed by the Church, at least in dealing with "the others," the non-Christians, especially the Jews. Aryanization, the orgy of terror and theft known as *Reichskristallnacht*, ostracism of the Jews first from the public then from the private economic sector, and finally deportation – all those outrages were accepted by the official Church in silence. On the other hand, in isolated cases some priests and other individual Catholics asserted themselves bravely on behalf of the Jews. Both officially and semiofficially, Cardinal Theodor Innitzer made courageous efforts at least to help Catholic converts among the Jews. He also pleaded unswervingly for money and exit visas for "non-Aryan" Christians. Yet, the Austrian Catholic Church declined to read a special mass for Jewish Christians on the grounds that "no differences shall be made in the inner sphere of the Church."[6]

In spite of its hierarchical and authoritarian structure, the Catholic Church proved to be a multifarious organization. At least three segments in its structure can be distinguished analytically: the bishops, the clerics, and the laity. The attitude of the clerics and laity toward Nazism in the spring of 1938 was different from what it would be in the autumn of 1944. To obtain a true historical picture, it is not enough to proceed chronologically. Account must also be taken of developments on various hierarchical levels to round off the picture.

MODERNIZATION IMPOSED

The central concern of the bishops after 1938 was to guarantee pastoral care, and in order to achieve that, they proved willing to compromise by cooperating with the Nazi regime in certain areas. All considered, that action can be pronounced successful, as the moral and social stature of the Church grew considerably during the period of Nazi rule. This proved the rule that the stronger the social and political status of the Church – during the Dollfuss-Schuschnigg regime, for instance – the weaker its moral and intellectual prestige. The moment the politcal stature of the Church was sharply reduced, its moral prestige would tend to soar.

Nazism imposed a process of modernization on the Church, from which the latter was to emerge strengthened and rejuvenated. Modernization, in the present context, signifies process of social separation between State and Church. Three examples may be cited to illustrate that point.

First, over many decades the Church in Austria had done its utmost, politically through the Christian Social Party, to prevent the enactment of a marriage law that was in conformity with contemporary social reality. On 6 July 1938, however, the Nazis implemented legislation by which divorcees were granted the legal right to remarry, an overdue adaptation to social change relieving many families from emotional strain. This marriage law was accepted by the Church without resort to fervent public protest. Nonetheless, not an iota of ecclesiastical dogma was abandoned, for so far as the Church was concerned a civil marriage continued to be incapable of replacing the sacrament of marriage in Church. Those married only by civil ceremony were banned from all sacraments and denied a Catholic burial. However, the Church subsequently had to manage without the support of the State in the enforcement of the canonic law of marriage.

Second, a further step toward modernization was taken with the introduction of a Church tax in 1939. It can be taken for granted that the Nazis intended to harm the church through this piece of legislation by causing its parishioners to give up their membership. Indeed, the number of withdrawals increased sharply between 1938 and 1943. What was even more significant, however, was that for the first time the Church was made financially independent of the State, thereby rendering itself less vulnerable to Nazi blackmail.[7]

Third, Nazism did away with the chaotic growth of associations in which religion and politics had been inseparately enmeshed. In this way, the Church was able to wash its hands of everyday political affairs. Many priests found this to be a relief, as it gave them more time to devote to their basic religious duties.

In the autumn of 1938, the strife between Church and State recommenced,[8] resulting in a widened gap in access to the public. Catholic newspapers either had to toe the political line or suffer closure; Catholic schools and most theological educational establishments were shut down; religious education in State schools similarly was reduced or at the most confined to the immediate sphere of the Church. Clearly out for booty, the Nazi State seized Church buildings. Hundreds of ecclesiastical houses, monasteries, and even churches were confiscated for use as Nazi offices.

Wherever the property of the Church was in danger, measures like these were fiercely opposed by the bishops, who submitted memoranda, petitions, and protests to Hitler and other officers of the Third Reich. These proved mostly in vain. Only in isolated cases were the bishops successful in taking advantage of the existing polyocracy by playing off one Nazi sector against another, and only on rare occasions would episcopal protests cover anything besides purely Catholic affairs. One such rare occasion was when suffragan bishop Andreas Rohracher of Gurk, Carinthia, lodged his protests against the compulsory transfer of Carinthian Slovenes. His energetic opposition to euthanasia should also be recorded.[9]

In theory, the borderline between conformity and resistance was laid down with precision by Prince-Archbishop Sigismund Waitz in a pastoral letter of 15 October 1941. This act provoked yet another crisis in the strife between Church and State to which nearly all monastic buildings in Austria fell victim. The basic import of his pastoral letter may be gathered from the vigor of its introductory passage, by which each priest who failed to sum up sufficient courage to read the letter to his parishioners was to be "suspended *ipso facto a Divinis.*"[10] In a dramatic manner, the pastoral letter appealed to Austria's Catholics in these terms:

> Dear, cherished Catholic people! I am an old man and do not know when I will be called before God's seat of judgment. I do not want to approach Him with a guilty conscience. The Book of Gospels was placed upon my shoulders at my ordination as bishop as God's burden. This I preach and let preach. Today, we Catholics must often give in to an external power. Wherever secular matters are concerned, we can endure and be silent. *However, when it comes to our faith, we cannot give way. We must either stand tall or die.* (Author's italics.)[11]

In practice, each bishop, as well as each individual Austrian Catholic, had personally to define the theoretical line separating secular matters and matters of faith. It is a matter of public record that not one of Austria's bishops was sentenced to long-term imprisonment. By way of contrast, priests were to be found among those groups of professional people suffering most severe persecution. In the Gau Oberdonau (Upper Danube), for example, out of 1125 clerics, 300 were reprimanded and 99 were sentenced to terms of imprisonment longer than one month.[12] Strikingly, not even 1 percent of all Catholic priests were anywhere near being closely affiliated to Nazism. The lower down the hierarchical scale of the Church one descended, the more severely were those individual priests affected by the repressive measures taken by the Nazi regime.

In his New Year's Eve sermon of 1943, Bishop Fliesser of Linz accurately characterized the intentions of Nazism thus: "First they deal with Bolshevism, then they will deal with the Church."[13] During the war, the Nazi Party had to err on the cautious side, contenting itself by threatening the Church with pinpricks, instead of following its natural inclination of clubbing it on the head. This is well borne out in an internal Party memorandum summarized at a conference held in Vienna, as follows: "It is the [Party's] intention to drive the Church from the public sphere back into the private sphere. Ostmark and Sudetenland could serve as test cases . . . as they, just like the most recently occupied territories, are without a Concordat. Basically, we should avoid a course of aggravation, but instead proceed step-by-step and wherever possible, imperceptibly."[14] The slow process of attrition thus envisaged was to prove more dangerous to the Church than large measures against which it could protest effectively.

THE RURAL ENVIRONMENT

Adaptation, nonconformity, social protest, and acts of resistance were all conditioned by the existence of a particular social-cultural environment, which was the product of a number of ingredients, such as prevailing economic conditions, specific class attitudes, cultural outlook, and religious fermentation. Nonconformity has to be seen in relation to the concretely existing totalitarian challenge. Conformity to the Nazi regime in a particular village could be interpreted as nonconformity to its Catholic environment and vice versa: conformity to the Catholic environment could signal nonconformity to Nazism.[15] The totalitarian demands made by the Nazis were frequently less insistent in remote rural areas—the result not only of the mode of settlement but also of the usually solid traditional social structure of villages, their religious attitudes, and patterns of internal communication. Two types may be singled out here for further discussion. In one typical instance, a rather unproblematic relationship would exist between the Nazis and the Church. Even Party members would attend church on Sundays, sing in the church choir, and take part in church processions, much to the annoyance of the Gestapo. Other villages might experience a deep rift between the Party and the Church, resulting in a small but bitter daily warfare between the village Party leader and the village priest.

The Catholic rural environment that would give rise to these relationships exhibited the following characteristics: the close adherence to the institution of private ownership, which called for strong emotional ties to one's birthplace (the village); a dense system of social control through the ties of local culture based on typical parochial piety, which might be transgressed by neither the wealthy nor the poor. In conditions like these, the basic rural experience of Nazi rule occurred on various levels. On the one hand, there was the time-honored tradition of external rule paired with a hard-headed spirit of insubordination. On the other hand, Nazism was virtually experienced as a kind of elemental force, like floods or avalanches: to survive, one had to protect oneself as best one could until the disaster had passed.

In all this, however, a distinction ought to be made between the local dignitaries in the village (the village bourgeoisie) and the native rural traditional elite.[16] The local dignitaries—doctor, solicitor, judge, and teacher—

constituted a relatively mobile category who would normally barely hold its own in the village. Since the nineteenth century, notables of that sort would have been either liberal or pan-German in political outlook. It was they, as a rule, who would speedily embrace Nazism. The indigenous rural elites, on the other hand, were mostly conservative-Catholic in outlook and "patriotically" (in the pro-Austrian sense) inclined.

Nazi penetration of the traditional village would proceed according to the following social pattern. The village Party leader in most cases would be drawn from the local dignitary class (especially from the teachers) and the mayor would come from the local rural or trade class. Gathering around their parson for comfort, the traditional rural elite would remain predominantly resistant to Nazism. In 1941, a Nazi security officer had to report to a Gauleiter that the Church had succeeded in creating a network of sympathizers within the parish church councils, who were acting as a vanguard of political propaganda and vehicle of communication on behalf of the Catholic Church.[17] Party officials kept up a stream of complaints about the religious obstinacy of the rural population. That, however, must not be seen as either resistance in the strictly political sense or a direct criticism of Nazi rule. Obstinacy of that sort was merely tenacious adherence to what was seen as traditional and customary. As it always has been, so shall it remain.

The social system of the closed village was broken down in various ways. One way was through the influence exercised by the Nazi State, another was through Nazi adaptation to a traditional pattern of behavior, which was interpreted in a new ideological way with its symbols accentuated differently. The Nazi promotion of love for the "homeland" not only tended to facilitate the emotional mobilization for the war effort but also managed to play off folk culture against elite culture. Both the Party and the Church fought to obtain a hold over local traditions, but where the Party attempted to resurrect Wotan, the pre-Christian Germanic god, the parsons and members of the Catholic community held on tenaciously to Christian doctrine. Catholic youths would therefore make a point of lighting fires in celebration of the "Heart of Jesus" by way of a deliberate demonstration against the practice of the "pagan" solstice fires.[18]

The traditional literature of the peasants, the peasants' calendar, continued in use, and although Christian names continued to appear in the register of names, they were supplemented by "Germanic" ones, such as Farhilde, Rigobert, Wolfhold, or Dietlinde. Christian religious holidays continued to be celebrated but were surrounded by Nazi festivals such as Heroes' Memorial Day in March, the Führer's birthday in April, Labor Day on 1 May, and Harvest Thanksgiving Day. During the war, Church holidays were the subject of acrimonious debates and consequently were reduced to a minimum. Every single Church procession would be defended by the parsons, while the Party would use petty oppressive measures (like street traffic regulations), threats, prohibitions, denunciations, and arrests in order to obstruct them. Priest and parishioners would in turn respond with a tactic in which cleverness was used side by side with airs of assumed naiveté but also, let it be said, with resignation. This kind of Josephinian "patriotism," which was typical of Austria, proved an obstacle to the pursuit of outright opposition to the Nazi State. Much to the annoyance of the Gestapo, the peasants continued to celebrate their own holidays, even giving "foreign workers" the day off for the occasion. When the State attempted to shift the date of the traditional village petitionary procession from a workday to the following Saturday, it was noticeable that many more people than usual would participate, thereby leaving the Gestapo duped. The Corpus Christi procession, always an occasion for demonstrating the political power of Catholicism, was obstructed by the Nazis whenever possible to a point at which even some Party members began to show solidarity with the embittered parishioners, threatening to quit the Party. In the Tyrol, whole orchestras would refuse to play at Party events unless allowed to participate in those Catholic processions.[19]

Yet, direct action was the exception. In several towns in the Tyrol, church bells were removed by the public lest they be melted down for armament. Or, for example, on the arrest of a parson, an alarm bell was rung in the time-honored symbolic tradition as a signal for rural resistance.[20] The removal of crucifixes from schools nearly produced outright rebellion. In the Tyrol, parents responded to these acts by a school strike. In a letter addressed to the Gauleiter of Salzburg by men serving at the front, a dramatically accentuated message was delivered: "Those of us at the front are planting crosses on the graves of our dead, while at home those crosses are thrown out."[21] A letter of protest from nine mothers in a rural village close to Salzburg is similarly revealing. On the one hand, the traditional loyalty to the State was reaffirmed by reiterating the undoubted right of the State to risk their sons' lives in defense of the Fatherland, as well as calling for a supposed crusade against Bolshevism. Those claims were not contested. On the other hand, a crusade without a cross was considered meaningless. Those women's thoughts were expressed as follows: "We the undersigned mothers who have already lost some of our sons in this crusade while others are still under arms, herewith ask—also on behalf of the remaining mothers in our village, all of whom have at least one son at the front, as well as some children at school—from the bottom of our hearts that the crucifixes to which our children pray for the blessing of Fatherland and Führer, be returned."[22]

The Church would never be prepared to relinquish its authority over anything connected with death. The Party leaders in the villages, initially responsible for reporting deaths to the families concerned—"death birds," as they were called—found increasing difficulty in discharging their task as casualties mounted. Their appearance in front of houses was an occasion of deep dread. In Upper Austria, a village Party leader delivering one such death notice had his face slapped by a peasant wife.[23] Not surprisingly, therefore, the Party did not much mind hiding behind the mourning cloak of the village Church.

One instrument of influence the Church knew exactly how to handle was its regular Sunday sermon. The Gestapo was nearly driven to despair by the ambiguity of those sermons, metaphorically inspired by the biblical motto enjoining the Church to be as clever as the snakes, but meant to depict the concrete state of affairs in which the Third Reich found itself. The well known Christ-the-King metaphor in particular was employed in those sermons as a frequent point of departure, implying that Christ and not Hitler was the true ruler of the world.

Since the Party lacked a centrally located means of social communication in the villages that could equal those of the Church and church square, in 1941 the Nazi Party planned to build community centers to counter the social power of the Church in the villages. The power trinity of those villages, composed of mayor, Party chief, and peasant leader, was to reside in those community centers. Homes for Hitler Youth, kindergartens, and not unnaturally public houses were also envisaged in this connection. Even soldiers killed in the course of duty were to find a final resting place in a heroes' grove, which was to compete with the Church cemetery. In spite of strenuous efforts, all attempts to establish a Nazi cult in rural areas failed. Attendance at Nazi hero memorial services turned out to be much smaller than at services for fallen soldiers celebrated at the local Church.

Nazi fortunes were not any better in areas in which they were able to infiltrate the traditional channels of social communication, such as the "Heimgart" and the "Spinning Room." In the case of the former, the peasants of the neighborhood would congregate at the farmstead in the evenings in order to chat, drink, and make merry. The Party, on the other hand, would use the "Heimgart" as a forum for political indoctrination. The "Spinning Room" gatherings served the same social purpose for the women. Here, too, women would meet at a farmstead to engage in a spot of communal spinning, in the course of which they would sing, chat, and dance, and the leader of the Federation of German Girls (Bund deutscher Mädchen), an official Nazi organization for young women, would read entertaining stories and similarly make merry. Because peasant girls, wives, and daughters enjoyed attending such meetings, the Party saw in those spinning evenings "a tremendous opportunity to indoctrinate those people with Nazi ideas."[24]

In sum, although the peasants were willing to welcome certain measures of modernization taken by the Nazi regime, they would stubbornly
reject wider ideological demands. Aside from the usual strife between the
Church and the State, the peasants were liable to be irritated by all efforts
to carry politics into their homes. The damage caused to the rural sense
of self-reliance by Nazi efforts at gaining permanent control over the farms
by far outweighed the reassuring effects of Nazi propaganda regarding "blood
and soil."

COLLABORATION AND RESISTANCE

The Catholic Church in Austria emerged from Nazi rule both purified
and rejuvenated. After 1945 attempts were made by the Church to portray
itself in retrospect as a Church of Resistance. The number of victims suffered by it is indeed impressive: 15 priests were executed, 724 were arrested,
110 were sent to concentration camps where 20 of them would die.[25]
However, this kind of "resistance" concealed the facts of actual collaboration with the Nazi regime by that same Church throughout the duration of Nazi rule in Austria. It was true that, although there was no Catholic
resistance movement, individual Catholics participated in the resistance
movements.[26] One of the many paradoxes of recent Austrian history is that
Cardinal Theodor Innitzer, who had encouraged Austria's Catholics to vote
in favor of an *Anschluss* in the plebiscite of 10 April 1938, remained in office
after 1945, even though he had personally undergone no suffering under
the Nazi regime; whereas lower-grade civil servants who for some reason
or another had joined the Nazi Party were dismissed from their positions.
In the end, the Catholic environment was to remain intact, even though
some differences in density in its texture were noticeable. Historical traditions dating back to the Counter-Reformation in Austria no doubt acted
as underpinnings of this environment. The stronger the anticlerical tradition, the weaker would be those underpinnings. Percentage withdrawals
from religious instruction in elementary schools may serve as an indicator:[27]

State	Percent
Carinthia	44.17
Vienna	43.28
Styria	27.04
Salzburg	13.77
Tyrol	11.55
Lower Austria	6.35
Vorarlberg	5.21
Upper Austria	0.57

Pan-German anticlericalism was strongest in Carinthia; Social Democratic anticlericalism, in Vienna. The Catholic environment was most coherent in Lower Austria, Vorarlberg, and Upper Austria.

Reinhold Schneider, a Catholic author who wielded some influence over Austria's Catholic intelligentsia during the war, used to quote Jakob Böhme, the mystic, in his well-known book *Power and Grace*, published in Leipzig in 1941, as follows: "The devil holds power, honor, lust and pleasure in the palm of his hand. . . . Similarly, God holds the cross, persecution, misery, poverty, shame and affliction in His hand."[28] Again and again, the Catholic Church in Austria has succumbed to the temptations of power; most recently, in the years between 1934 and 1938. Evidently, the Church dislikes having to carry the burden of the cross on its back but would rather display it as a sign of dignity on its chest. However, during the period of Nazi rule, the Church was again compelled to carry the cross on its back. It was to experience, to paraphrase Reinhold Schneider, the invincibility of the defeated.[29]

NOTES

1. Peter Hüttenberger, "Nationalsozialistische Polykratie," *Geschichte und Gesellschaft* 2 (1976):477 ff.

2. Guenter Lewy, *The Catholic Church and Nazi Germany* (New York and Toronto, 1964), p. 249.

3. Johannes Oesterreicher, *Wider die Tyrannei des Rassenwahns. Rundfunkansprachen aus dem ersten Jahr von Hitlers Krieg* (Vienna and Salzburg, 1986).

4. Ferdinand Klostermann, "Katholische Jugend im Untergrund," in Rudolf Zinnhobler (ed.), *Das Bistum Linz im Dritten Reich* (Linz, 1979), p. 212.

5. Erika Weinzierl, *Ecclesia semper reformanda* (Vienna and Salzburg, 1985), p. 354.

6. Ibid., p. 363.

7. Ernst Hanisch, "Die Katholische Kirche im Dritten Reich," in Erika Weinzierl (ed.), *Kirche und Gesellschaft* (Vienna and Salzburg, 1979), pp. 21–41.

8. Viktor Reimann, *Innitzer. Kardinal zwischen Hitler und Rom* (Vienna, 1967).

9. *In Memoriam Andreas Rohracher* (Salzburg, 1977), p. 27.

10. Konsistorialarchiv Salzburg, 12/21.

11. Ibid.

12. *Widerstand und Verfolgung in Oberösterreich 1934–1945*, vol. 2, ed. by Dokumentationsarchiv des österreichischen Widerstandes (Vienna and Linz, 1982), p. 14.

13. Zinnhobler (ed.), p. 123.

14. Konsistorialarchiv, 12/21. Radomir Luža, "Nazi Control of the Austrian Catholic Church, 1939–1941," *Catholic Historical Review* 63 (1977):537–72.

15. Klaus Tenfelde, "Soziale Grundlagen von Resistenz und Widerstand," in Jürgen Schmädeke and Peter Steinbach (eds.), *Widerstand gegen den Nationalsozialismus* (Munich, 1986), pp. 799–812.

16. Ernst Hanisch, "Nationalsozialismus im Dorf. Salzburger Beobachtungen," in

Helmut Konrad and Wolfgang Neugebauer (ed.), *Arbeiterbewegung, Faschismus, Nationalbewusstsein* (Vienna, Munich, and Zurich, 1983), pp. 69–81.

17. Konsistorialarchiv 12/21.

18. Dokumentationsarchiv des österreichischen Widerstandes (ed.), *Widerstand und Verfolgung in Tirol 1934–1945*, vol. 2 (Vienna and Munich, 1984), p. 97.

19. Ibid. p. 110.

20. Ibid. pp. 256, 267.

21. Konsistorialarchiv, 12/21.

22. Ibid.

23. Dokumentationsarchiv des österreichischen Widerstandes (ed.), vol. 2, p. 298.

24. Hanisch, pp. 270–73.

25. Radomir Luža, *The Resistance in Austria, 1938–1945* (Minneapolis, 1984), p. 71.

26. Klaus Scholder, "Politischer Widerstand oder Selbstbehauptung als Problem der Kirchenleitungen," in Schmädeke and Steinbach (eds.), p. 255.

27. Oskar Veselsky, *Bischof und Klerus der Diözese Seckau unter nationalsozialistischer Herrschaft,* (Graz, 1979), p. 240.

28. Reinhold Schneider, *Macht und Gnade* (Leipzig, 1941), p. 321.

29. Reinhold Schneider, *Philipp der Zweite oder Religion und Macht* (Frankfurt, 1987), p. 302.

Franz Jägerstätter

ANDREAS MAISLINGER

The story of the Austrian peasant Franz Jägerstätter seems to be brief and uncomplicated. United States sociologist Gordon C. Zahn, Jägerstätter's first biographer, summarized the Austrian peasant's life as follows:

Franz Jägerstätter was born on May 20, 1907, in St. Radegund, a small village in Upper Austria. His natural father was killed in World War I when he was still a child, and when his mother married, her child was adopted by her husband. In his youth, Franz had gained a reputation for being a wild fellow, but, in general, his daily life was like that of most Austrian peasants.

In 1936, he married a girl from a nearby village, and they went to Rome on their honeymoon. A Catholic by birth, he experienced a religious awakening—apparently about the time of his marriage—and later served as sexton of his parish church.

When Hitler's troops moved into Austria in 1938, Jägerstätter was the only man in the village to vote against the *Anschluss*. Although he was not involved with any political organization, he did undergo one brief period of military training, he remained openly anti-Nazi, and publicly declared he would not fight in Hitler's war.

After many delays, Jägerstätter was called to active duty in February 1943; by this time he had three daughters, the eldest not quite six. He maintained his position against fighting for the Third Reich, and was imprisoned, first at Linz, then at Berlin. After a military trial, he was beheaded on August 9, 1943.[1]

The reader might ask why the editor of this book on Austrian Nazism decided to devote an entire article to Franz Jägerstätter? After all, Jägerstätter was but one of millions who perished at the hands of the Nazis. As a student of Austrian Nazism and Jägerstätter, this author discovered at least part of an answer to the question. In the United States and Great Britain, Franz Jägerstätter is the most well-known Austrian dissident and victim of the Hitler era. Jägerstätter first surfaced as a public figure in the United States and the United Kingdom following the release of Gordon C. Zahn's book about him. Subsequently, Jägerstätter has emerged as the only Austrian dissident of the Nazi era to be the subject of books and brochures published in the United States and Great Britain. However, the developments just mentioned do not themselves fully justify the editor's decision to include a separate article on Franz Jägerstätter. He is also an important religious figure to many in the United States and Great Britain. Dwight Macdonald has refered to Jägerstätter as one of the twentieth century's "few moral heroes."[2]

Interest in Franz Jägerstätter extends beyond the Catholic intellectual milieu. Scholars have devoted dozens of articles and book reviews on the exploits of this simple Austrian peasant. Israeli and Jewish–North American publications have included works on him. Prominent West German and Austrian newspapers, such as the *Frankfurter Allegemeine Zeitung*, have carried pieces on him. No other Austrian victim of Nazi tyranny has attracted attention of this magnitude on an international level.

Although not as well known as Father Maximilian Kolbe, Claus von Stauffenberg, and Anne Frank, Jägerstätter occupies a special place among the victims of Nazi terror. Unlike the others, Jägerstätter had relatively little formal education and acted alone as an opponent of the Hitler regime. On the other hand, Kolbe had the support of the Catholic church in Poland, and Stauffenberg had the support of a resistance group based in the German military staff. Within the ranks of the most well-known Nazi victims, Jägerstätter is distinguished because of his simple peasant background and his willingness to resist Hitler on his own.

Before the publication of Zahn's book, Jägerstätter was completely unknown in Austria. He is not mentioned in the early works on the Austrian resistance movement. Historian Karl Stadler compiled two documentations on Austrian victims of Nazism.[3] Stadler's first publication does not contain even a single reference to Jägerstätter. Only the second documentation mentions Jägerstätter by way of a quotation taken from Zahn's *German Catholics and Hitler's Wars*.[4] Prior to the Zahn publication, references to Jägerstätter could be found in only a few Catholic publications.

Shortly after the war the Catholic Church authorized Prelate Jakob Fried of Vienna[5] to compose a documentation on *National Socialism and the Catholic Church in Austria.* Fried's report was written with the intention of justifying the behavior of the Austrian Catholic church during World War II. In this report, Fried examined in detail the life and death of Jägerstätter. At one point, the report concludes that Jägerstätter is *"das heldenhafte Beispiel einer grossen Märtyrergesinnung eines braven katholischen Bauern."*[6] Fried contended that Jägerstätter was merely a typical example of a member of the Austrian resistance. Yet he does not give another example of a resistance figure from the Austrian peasantry. Nor does Fried's report include references to any outside sources of information pertaining to Jägerstätter.[7]

Even though this book was widely distributed, Jägerstätter remained a relatively obscure figure until the mid-1950s. The first article actually devoted to Franz Jägerstätter appeared in Heinrich Kreutzberg's book on Father Franz Reinisch, an Austrian priest who refused to take the German military oath.[8] The appendix to Kreutzberg's book included a four-page account of Jägerstätter's resistance toward Hitler's drive to war. This chapter stimulated Gordon Zahn's imagination. Kreutzberg had been a chaplain of the prison that held Father Franz Reinisch, and a year after that priest's execution would hold Franz Jägerstätter.

Since the appearance of Father Kreutzberg's chapter on Franz Jägerstätter, publishers have released three books on the Austrian peasant. Zahn's book has been published in four languages (German, Italian, Greek, and French) and, as recently as 1986, Templegate Publishers produced a new edition of Zahn's original text. In 1980, a German priest by the name of Georg Bergmann wrote the second book on the life of Franz Jägerstätter from a strictly religious perspective.[9] The dissertation by Erna Putz, an Austrian Catholic journalist, is the most recently published work on Jägerstätter.[10] Putz' dissertation contains many previously unreleased details.

THE UNITED STATES: AN EARLY RECOGNITION

The recognition of Jägerstätter in the United States began in the 1960s. In 1968 an American from Missoula, Montana, commemorated the twenty-fifth anniversary of his death by placing a bronze plaque next to the grave of Franz Jägerstätter on the village church of St. Radegund. The statement inscribed on the memorial plaque reads: "Thank God for Jägerstätter: he knew that we are all brothers and that the command of Christ is essential for everyone. He has not died in vain."[11] The same year, Thomas Merton included a chapter on Jägerstätter in his book, *Faith and Violence. Christian Teaching and Christian practice.*[12] In the introduction of this book Merton noted: "In the case of Franz Jägerstätter we have a faith that stood up against an unjust but established power and refused to practice violence in the service of that power. On the other side, we have Simone Weil who was a French pacifist before World War II and who later joined the French resistance against the Nazis."[13] Merton also compares Jägerstätter with Father Alfred Delp, a well-known martyr of the German resistance.

Jägerstätter's legacy had a clear influence on the thinking of prominent members of the North American anti-Vietnam War movement. On a number of occasions, Daniel Ellsberg acknowledged that his decision to release the Pentagon Papers was influenced by Jägerstätter's "moral resistance."[14] Merton also was an opponent of the United States participation in the Vietnam war. In a general sense, Jägerstätter has become a Christian hero. Father Boniface Hanley, cited Jägerstätter as one of eight "models of behavior and guides for mature Christian living."[15] The others are Charles de Foucauld, Thomas Dooley, Edith Stein, Vincent Lebbe, Miguel Pro, Eva Lavallière and Titus Brandsma. To most of his admirers in the United States, Jägerstätter is a symbol of moral conscience. For example, Hanley's chapter on Jägerstätter concludes with the following quotation from a speech by Martin Luther King, Jr.: "Cowardice asks the question, 'Is it safe?' Expediency asks the question, 'Is it politic?' Vanity asks the question, 'Is it popular?' But conscience asks the question, 'Is it right?'"[16] Hanley maintains Jägerstätter's refusal was right.

THE CATHOLIC CHURCH: A LONG LEARNING PROCESS

On 20 May 1987 the Diocese of Linz held a ceremony commemorating Jägerstätter's eightieth birthday. Never before had the Diocese of Linz bestowed such a prestigious honor in memory of its former parishioner Franz Jägerstätter. Members of the peace movement in the United States were present at the ceremony, including Bishop Thomas J. Gumbleton from Detroit. Bishop Maximilian Aichern from Linz and Bishop Gumbleton jointly conducted a memorial service. In his sermon, Gumbleton stated that the United States peace group Swords Into Ploughshares drew a great deal of inspiration from Jägerstätter for their nonviolent actions against the US–Soviet arms build up.

Before the Linz ceremony, opinion within the Catholic church about Jägerstätter was divided. Critics within the Catholic church have come primarily from Austria herself. Until 1963 the Bishop of Linz did not allow the publication of articles about Jägerstätter in the Diocese's weekly paper. In 1946 Bishop Joseph Fliesser gave the following explanation of his negative attitude:

> I consider the greater heroes to be those exemplary young Catholic men, seminarians, priests, and heads of families who fought and died in heroic fulfill-

ment of duty and in the firm conviction that they were fulfilling the will of God at their post, just as the Christian soldiers in the armies of the heathen emperor had done. Or are the greater heroes Jehovah's Witnesses and Adventists who, in their "consistency," preferred to die in concentration camps rather than bear arms? All respect is due the innocently erronous conscience; it will have its reward from God. For the instruction of men, the better models are to be found in the example set by the heroes who conducted themselves "consistently" in the light of a clear and correct conscience.[17]

To this day, the Austrian church hierarchy remains ambivalent about Jägerstätter. The Archbishop of Vienna, Hans Hermann Groer, refused to support Jägerstätter's action unconditionally. Groer claims his reluctance to pass judgment on this matter stems from a lack of information.[18] Compared with Cardinal Franz König's statements on Jägerstätter, this pronouncement represents a step away from recognizing the true nature of this affair.

Within the Austrian church, Cardinal König is Jägerstätter's most well-known supporter. König is of the opinion that Jägerstätter performed his duty as a Christian. Needless to say, König supports the various actions by the Diocese of Linz. Of course, this identification of some members of the Austrian Church with the Nazi victims has irritated his critics. Some residents of St. Radegund and the surrounding area have threatened to leave the Catholic Church if Jägerstätter should be declared a saint. However, all the priests who came into contact with Jägerstätter counted themselves among his most ardent admirers. It seems that Jägerstätter at long last has made a favorable impression on the Catholic sextons of Upper Austria. In July 1984, 100 sextons from the Linz Diocese, many of whom were from the Innviertel area, held a memorial service for their martyred colleague. Jägerstätter's widow, St. Radegund's sexton, participated in the event. This affair indicates that support for Jägerstätter within the Catholic Church is strongest in its lower ranks. The virtual silence of Austria's Conference of Bishops regarding the Jägerstätter issue reinforces the view that rank-and-file Catholics are more interested in publicizing the matter than the Church hierarchy. Of course, some members of the Church hierarchy outside of Austria have shown a strong interest in Jägerstätter. A Vatican II intervention by Archbishop Thomas D. Roberts praised Jägerstätter: "I plead with the Fathers to consider this man and his sacrifice in a spirit of gratitude. May his example inspire our deliberations."[19]

Some Catholics have advocated Jägerstätter's canonization. The first calls for this surfaced after the publication of Zahn's book. But even earlier, Jägerstätter had been compared to Sir Thomas More, the former chancellor of England, who was executed in 1535. Henry VIII ordered More's execution on the grounds that the latter was a Catholic loyalist. As early as 1952,

Father Kreutzberg noted the similarities surrounding the executions of More and Jägerstätter. In both cases, the victim was forced to choose between a duty to family and a duty to God. Furthermore, the victims placed their alliance to God above their loyalty to the State. More recently, Father Bruce Kent of Great Britain noted that "the parallels with Sir Thomas More are obvious except that Thomas was an international figure whom the world of his day watched. Franz was a nobody who clearly expected to be soon forgotten."[20]

AUSTRIA: FACING THE TRUTH

Austria's dual status as victim and perpetrator of Nazism often makes the process of coming to terms with Jägerstätter's protest very difficult for his fellow Austrians. The official viewpoint of the Republic of Austria emphasizes the fact that the German-speaking country was the first State victimized by Nazi Germany. Despite the emphasis on Austria's status as the victim of German imperialism, most Austrians still believe that during World War II they fought to defend their fatherland. Nearly every Austrian village has erected a memorial in honor of its citizens who died in battle during both world wars. The names of the soldiers who perished during the First World War are listed along with the names of the soldiers who perished during the Second World War. All the fallen soldiers listed on the memorial plaques are said to have died while fighting in defense of their homeland. The memorials ignore any mention of Austria's status as a conquered nation after the *Anschluss*. More than half of the Austrian war memorials refer to the fallen soldiers of the Second World War as heroes. In St. Georgen, a small village located near St. Radegund, the following words are inscribed on the local memorial: HEIMAT GEDENKE: FÜR DICH GABEN WIR UNSER LEBEN. This quotation calls on the people of Austria to honor their fellow citizens who died while defending the homeland. It is typical of the messages found on memorials throughout Austria.[21]

The inability of Austrian authorities to define clearly the nature of the relationship between Austria and Nazi Germany hampered attempts made by Franziska Jägerstätter to receive a widow's pension. In 1946 Frau Jägerstätter was given an "Amtsbescheinigung." This document recognized Frau Jägerstätter as the surviving dependant of a victim of Nazi terror. However, two years later the Austrian authorities claimed that the "Opferfürsorgegesetz" does not apply to Franz Jägerstätter. The Austrian authorities gave the following reason for their decision to revoke Frau Jägerstätter's "Amtsbescheinigung." Although Jägerstätter was a victim of Nazism, he did not fight for a free and democratic Austria as mentioned in paragraph 1 of the

"Opferfürsorgegesetz 1947." According to a 1948 report by the Gendar-meriepostenkommando Ostermiething, Franz Jägerstätter refused to serve in Hitler's army on account of mental depression and religious convictions. These factors, so the Austrian authorities claimed, had nothing to do with the struggle for democracy and Austria. In a letter written to Father Kreutz-berg, Franziska Jägerstätter maintained that hostile public opinion in the Braunau area, Hitler's birthplace, was the primary cause of the report. Normally war widows had little or no problem obtaining pensions. Jäger-stätter's widow, however, was forced to wait for two years before receiving her first pension payment. Clearly Austria's authorities withheld pension payments from Frau Jägerstätter because of the controversial nature of her husband's action.[22]

As already mentioned, Jägerstätter emerged as an Austrian national figure only after the German translation of Zahn's book. Styria, a Catholic publishing house, released a German translation of Zahn's book in 1967. About a hundred Austrian and other German-language newspapers have carried book reviews of the Styria publication. Even publications not sym-pathetic or even hostile to the doctrine of Catholicism carried book reviews praising Jägerstätter. A book review appearing the the Social Democratic *Arbeiter-Zeitung* contended that Jägerstätter was a martyr for the struggle against totalitarianism. The same article accused the Catholic Church of capitulating to pressure from the Nazi State by failing to support Jägerstät-ter. Surprisingly enough, the Communist *Volksstimme* also included a book review praising Jägerstätter. Like the *Arbeiter-Zeitung*'s review, the *Volks-stimme* article bitterly criticized the Austrian Catholic Church's handling of the Jägerstätter affair. Only the *Linzer Kirchenblatt*, the official publication of the Diocese of Linz, reproved Zahn.[23]

The showing of the movie *Der Fall Jägerstätter* (*The Refusal*) in prime time on Austrian television was a national event that elevated public con-sciousness regarding this incident. *The Refusal* was broadcast on 26 October 1971, the Austrian national holiday commemorating the 1955 Austrian declaration of permanent neutrality. Public response to the film was over-whelming. Catholic adult learning centers organized hundreds of discus-sions about the contents of the drama documentary.

NAZISM: THREE TYPES OF VICTIMS

Individual victims of Nazi persecution belong to one of the following three categories: (1) genetic victims; (2) political victims; and (3) victims of conscience. In the context of this study, genetic victims include those who suffered repression because of "what they were in terms of genetic or, to a lesser extent, cultural origins."[24] Jews and gypsies were genetic victims and, to a lesser extent, so were the Slavic peoples. The category of political victims is made up of individuals persecuted by the Nazis because of participation in an organized resistance movement. The most frequent political victims were activists from the Communist, Social Democratic, and conservative parties. Victims of conscience are persons who suffered persecution because of their refusal to cooperate with the Nazi regime. Jägerstätter was a victim of conscience. His decision was not simply based on his commitment to Christian ideals. As an Austrian patriot, he rejected the idea of serving in a foreign army dominated by the Nazi dictatorship. Both of these factors must be taken into account if the context within which Jägerstätter made his decision is to be truly appreciated. On the other hand, it should be emphasized that Jägerstätter had no contact whatever with the anti-Nazi resistance.

Austria's political atmosphere after 1938, similar in nature to that of Germany, made opposition more difficult than in other occupied countries, such as France and Poland. Klemens von Klemperer has examined the motivations behind the decision of Julius Leber, Johann Georg Elser, Ludwig Beck, Carl Friedrich Goerdeler, Count von der Schulenburg, Count von Moltke, Dietrich Bonhoeffer, Count von Stauffenberg, and Franz Jägerstätter to resist Nazism. With regard to Jägerstätter, Klemperer concluded that this victim of Nazi terror worked political as well as moral elements into justifying his act of defiance. A strictly moral decision would, according to Klemperer, have prevented Jägerstätter from abandoning his family by committing political suicide.[25]

The near-total absence of resistance groups in Austria, especially in rural areas, isolated people like Jägerstätter. Unlike the anti-Nazis of France and Poland, Jägerstätter had almost no possibility of leading like-minded Austrians. Jägerstätter's isolation is exemplified by the total absence of the word resistance from his personal notes. It was only while awaiting execution that Jägerstätter learned that another Austrian had refused to serve in Hitler's army. Shortly before his execution he was told by Father Kreutzberg that "this priest's name was Franz, like yours. He was Austrian, like you. And if you want to die, then step bravely into eternity as he did."[26] Father Kreutzberg noted that Jägerstätter experienced a moral uplifting upon learning of Father Reinisch's willingness to sacrifice his life rather than take the German military oath. Jägerstätter responded to this comparison of himself with Father Reinisch by expressing a deep sense of satisfaction: "I have said this to myself before that I am not following the wrong path. If a priest has made the decision to go to his death, then I am allowed to do the same."[27]

CHURCH AND CONSCIENTIOUS OBJECTION:
AN AMBIGUOUS STAND

Over the years, the Catholic Church has taken an ambiguous stand regarding conscientious objection to war. Within it, there seem to be three different positions concerning war and peace. Some Christian teachings take a pacifist approach to the resolution of conflict. Two of the Catholic Church's most well-known proponents of nonviolence are Daniel and Phillip Barrigan. The just war doctrine, a theoretical concept developed by Saints Augustine and Thomas Aquinas, represents a second approach adopted by Catholic theorists in answering the question whether or not Catholics should participate in a war: (1) it must be waged by a public authority for the common good; (2) a just cause must be stated; (3) it must be fought with just intentions; and (4) the harm done by war must not exceed the good that comes from it. Applying those criteria, an objective decision maker would have been compelled to declare Nazi Germany's aggression the cause of an unjust war. Pope Pius XII did not pass any official judgment concerning the nature of World War II. "In Germany, in 1939, the Roman Catholic hierarchy urged soldiers to support their country and 'to do their duty in obedience to the Führer, ready for sacrifice and with commitment of the whole being.'" A third position within the Catholic Church regarding the issue of warfare is the crusader doctrine, the main idea of which is that the end justifies the means.[28]

Through his actions Jägerstätter showed an implicit commitment to the doctrine of just war. He did not oppose all wars. Rather, Jägerstätter objected to the motivation behind Germany's aggression under Hitler. Nazi Germany's imperialist ambitions clearly repelled Jägerstätter. Furthermore, he objected to the atrocities being committed by the German armed forces. However, above all else, he had no desire to serve a government that had put an end to Austria's independence. In his commentaries he avowed his willingness to fight for his homeland, especially against the menace of Nazism. Although his act of disobedience set him apart from most of his religious peers, Jägerstätter was preceded by other Catholic conscientious objectors. Until the fourth century A.D., Christians rarely served in the military. Officially, the Church recognizes St. Martin of Tours as Catholicism's first conscientious objector. When asked to fight for the Romans, St. Martin replied: "I am a soldier of Christ, I cannot fight." With the rise of conscripted armies during the French Revolution, conscientious objection became an issue within Catholic circles. Father St. Jean Vianney is generally considered the first Catholic conscientious objector of modern times. Jean Vianney refused conscription into Napoleon's army and eventually entered the priesthood. Father Kreutzberg mentioned Jägerstätter's express desire to be executed on the feast day of St. Jean Vianney, and the Nazis complied by beheading him on Vianney's feast day in 1943.[29]

THE MASS MEDIA: PUBLICIZING THE INCIDENT

In recent years the mass media of Austria, West Germany, and Great Britain have publicized the Jägerstätter incident by way of films and radio broadcasts. As already mentioned, Axel Corti's *Der Fall Jägerstätter* (*The Refusal*) had a marked impact on the Austrian public. Only five months after its initial broadcast, the film was broadcast a second time. This unusual development occurred as a consequence of the general interest and controversy generated by its first broadcast.

The Refusal's controversial subject matter and the skilled craftsmanship that went into making the film obviously appealed to broad sections of Austria's population. After *The Refusal's* second showing Austrian television (ORF) carried a discussion of the contents and the implications of the film. The discussion group included Austria's Minister of Defence, Karl Lütgendorf, a former Wehrmacht officer. To the public's surprise, General Lütgendorf sympathized with Jägerstätter and expressed his support for the enactment of an Austrian conscientious objector's law. In addition to its political and religious ramifications, *The Refusal* received several film awards, among them an award as the best religious film at the Baden Baden Film Festival in 1971.

After the release of *The Refusal*, the West German public broadcasting system produced a documentary on the Austrian response to the Jägerstätter incident that contained interviews with some of Jägerstätter's associates, as well as with his wife and Father Karobath. In addition to broadcasting the documentary, West German television also showed Corti's film. As a result of their close proximity to West Germany, many East Germans had the opportunity to view the films. Four years after its production, *The Refusal* (with English subtitles) made its British debut at London's Academy Three cinema. The film drew the attention of London's movie critics. The *New Statesman's* John Coleman, the *Daily Telegraph's* Patrick Gibbs, the *Financial Times's* Nigel Andrews, and other reviewed *The Refusal*. In the April 3, 1975, edition of *The Listener*, Gavin Millar wrote:

> The pitfalls of such a film are obvious. It attempts the most difficult of tasks, to make a great act of sacrifice appear admirable and without priggishness or bigotry. Jägerstätter is played by Kurt Weinzierl, and it is a performance beyond praise, chiefly by virtue of what you might call its absent flaws. Had there been a moment at which the actor showed through, a moment of calcu-

lation, technique or "style," a moment at which an eyebrow or the corner of the mouth had registered self-consciousness in any degree – the willingness, even to impress would have lost its extraordinary touch. Weinzierl is perfect because it is impossible, having seen the film, not to believe that he has, himself, some of the personal qualities of Jägerstätter. How else could he be sober without joylessness, resolute without complacency, intelligent without conceit? He has a perfect tact towards the near superhuman feelings he is called upon to represent. They never take him by surprise, but neither does he play them like trumps.

However, some criticisms were directed at the film. Sylvia Millar contended that

> Corti is not always as dispassionate and judicious as the weight and intelligence of his material demands. A grave seen from the corpse's point of view, the wife and priest in prison divided by the enormous foreground helmet of a guard, the garish underlit glimpse of the commandant as sentence of death is read outside the guillotine chamber: the narrative needs no such metaphorical buttressing, which only devalues the simplicity and frankness of the real interviews."

It should, however, be noted that virtually all of Britain's film critics praised Jägerstätter's courage and moral integrity.

In the United States, the Pax Christi Center on Conscience and War has been the sole distributor of *The Refusal*. The national director of the Pax Christi Center is Gordon Zahn. The film has been shown primarily at meetings of peace groups and religious organizations. The Pax Christi USA has placed a high priority on informing its public about Jägerstätter. The pamphlet *Peace, War, and the Christian Conscience*, distributed by The Christophers and Pax Christi, cites only two conscientious objectors from the Second World War: Jägerstätter and Dietrich Bonhoeffer. Over 800,000 copies of this pamphlet have been issued to churches, peace groups, and other organizations in the United States.

THE EIGHTIETH BIRTHDAY CELEBRATIONS

Austria celebrated the commemoration of Jägerstätter's eightieth birthday on 20 May 1987. The honesty and seriousness of the vespers celebrated by Bishops Maximilian Aichern and Thomas Gumbleton on 20 May were impressive even for less religious people. They had an attitude of religious support without zealotry, a reflection of Jägerstätter's own conviction.

The example of Jägerstätter strengthens others in their political and religious points of view, both in supporting one's own ideas and in not decrying those of others. A result of the increasing interest in Franz Jägerstätter is the foundation of a Pax Christi group in the Tyrol. Its first activities were the translation of Gordon Zahn's brochure, *Martyr for Conscience*, and a Franz Jägerstätter seminar.

Though Jägerstätter has been criticized since his death and though many angry calls and letters were sent to the organizers of the commemoration, one should bear in mind Reverend Johann Bergsmann's words on Jägerstätter: "*Viele wollten es damals nicht sehen; viele haben es nicht gesehen und von den Sehenden haben nur wenige die Kraft gefunden, dem Druck zu widerstehen.*" (Many did not want to see it at that time; many did not see it, and of those who could see it only a few found the strength to resist the pressure.) Franz Jägerstätter had resisted.

NOTES

I wish to express my thanks to my research assistant at the University of New Orleans, Mike Howells.

1. Gordon Zahn, *In Solidary Witness. The Life and Death of Franz Jägerstätter* (Springfield, 1986), p. 3. This book was first published in 1964.

2. Ibid., backcover.

3. Karl Stadler, *Die NS-Justiz in Österreich und ihre Opfer* (Vienna, 1962); and *Österreich 1938–1945 im Spiegel der NS-Akten* (Vienna, 1966).

4. Gordon Zahn, *German Catholics and Hilter's Wars. A Study in Social Control* (New York, 1962).

5. Jakob Fried, *Nationalsozialismus und katholische Kirche in Österreich* (Vienna, 1947).

6. Ibid., p. 82.

7. There is at least one other Catholic Austrian peasant who publicly declared he would not fight in Hitler's war, Vinzenz Schaller of Kalkstein in East Tyrol; see Andreas Maislinger, "Bauern gegen Hitler," *Österreichische Monatshefte* 7 (1985); Vinzenz Schaller, "Einsamer Weg," *Thurntaler* 11 (December 1984).

8. Heinrich Kreutzberg, *Franz Reinisch. Ein Märtyrer unserer Zeit* (Limburg, 1953), pp. 182–85.

9. Georg Bergmann, *Franz Jägerstätter. Ein Leben vom Gewissen entschieden* (Stein am Rhein, 1980).

10. Erna Putz, *Franz Jägerstätter . . . besser die Hände als der Wille gefesselt . . .* (Linz, 1985).

11. Gordon Zahn, *Franz Jägerstätter. Martyr for Conscience* (Erie, 1986), p. 14.

12. Thomas Merton, *Faith and Violence. Christian Teaching and Christian Practice* (Notre Dame, 1968), pp. 69–75.

13. Ibid., p. 11.

14. Gordon Zahn, *Franz Jägerstätter*, p. 2.

15. Boniface Hanley, O.F.M., *Twentieth Century Christian Heroes: No Strangers to Violence – No Strangers to Love* (Notre Dame, 1983), pp. 120–46.

16. Ibid., p. 146.

17. Gordon Zahn, *In Solidary Witness*, pp. 165–66.

18. Letter of 11 March 1987.

19. Information from Gordon Zahn.

20. Bruce Kent, *Franz Jägerstätter* (London, 1986), pp. 1–2.

21. This is the result of my research project "Kriegerdenkmäler in Österreich."

22. Erna Putz, pp. 276–81.

23. The collection of articles about Franz Jägerstätter will be continued and is available from the author.

24. Gordon Zahn, "Pacifists as Holocaust Victims," paper presented at the conference "The Other Victims: Non-Jews Persecuted and Murdered by the Nazis," United States Holocaust Memorial Council, 23–25 February 1987.

25. Klemens von Klemperer, "Sie gingen ihren Weg . . .," in Jürgen Schmädeke and Peter Steinbach (eds.), *Der Widerstand gegen Nationalsozialismus* (Munich and Zurich, 1985), pp. 1097–1106.

26. Franz Kreutzberg, p. 183.

27. Ibid., p. 183.

28. C.f. James H. Forest, *Catholics and Conscientious Objection*, (New York, 1980).

29. The book *Kriegsdienstverweigerung im Dritten Reich* by Albrecht Hartmann and Heidi Hartmann (Frankfurt, 1986) mentions, besides Franz Jägerstätter, four other Catholics: Michael Lerpscher, Franz Reinisch, Josef Ruf, and Ernst Volkmann.

Nazism, the Austrians, and the Military

KARL STUHLPFARRER

The period of Nazi rule in Austria from 1938 to 1945 poses a question that, on the face of it, appears simple but that in reality touches on the much deeper problem of identity, namely, what could have been regarded as Austria and who could have been called an Austrian. Austria as a country–the Nazi name, Ostmark, means Eastern Marches–was dissolved shortly after its incorporation into Germany and into its constituent *Länder*. The name *Austria* (Österreich) was obliterated after the plebiscite on 10 April 1938, and even the Nazi term *Ostmark* was replaced by the name *Alpen- und Donaureichsgaue*, which, moreover, was devoid of symbolism. Those who continued to be Austrians and wanted to fight for Austria's resurrection were sent to concentration camps by the thousands or, convicted of high treason, sent to prison. Many were sentenced to death and executed.

THE AUSTRIAN IDENTITY

However, it would be dishonest to rest content with restricting the qualification of Austrian to those who were persecuted, to the resistance fighters, and perhaps in addition to those groups of emigrants who were recognized by some Allied Powers as Austrians during the war and who fought in exile for the resurrection of an independent and free Austria. To adopt this attitude means upholding those cheap ideologies of justification which claim there could not have been any Austrian participation in the Nazi regime and its crimes, since Austria never existed as a State during the period 1938–1945. There cannot be any dispute about the two outstanding facts that (1) Austria was invaded by the German armed forces, and (2) Austrians were implicated in leading positions, not only in the Nazi seizure of power in Austria itself but also in her subsequent incorporation into the German Reich. Although not always rewarded according to their expectations and usually subordinated to Reich Germans, Austrian Nazis were able to play a leading part in the machinery of repression in Germany and her occupied territories. Not a few Austrians participated substantially in the deportation of Jews and in their genocide.

It is true that, as a country, Austria had ceased to exist, but its former federal Länder continued unaltered by and large. Only the Burgenland was partitioned and Vorarlberg was annexed to the Tyrol. Within the regional context was an evident continuity between the Austrian federal Länder and the Nazi Reichsgaue of Germany, on the one hand, and between the Reichsgaue and the Second Austrian Republic after 1945, on the other. Far from being disputed, this state of affairs was taken for granted.[1]

PROBLEMS OF RESEARCH

Austria's Declaration of Independence of 27 April 1945 legally re-embraced all those persons who had been Austrian subjects prior to the legal extinction of the State of Austria by the Nazi regime. Some persons who acquired Austrian nationality only after the war, had nonetheless been instrumental in the formation of Austria's historical image. Their testimony is relevant and ought to be included in all critical investigations of Austrian participation and coresponsibility in the Nazi regime and its crimes.

For all practical purposes, therefore, focusing on persons rather than institutions, a workable definition of the subject must dispense with unduly formal-legalistic hindsights and insist on adumbrating all those who (1) were Austrians before the so-called *Anschluss* in March 1938, including Austrian Nazis in Germany whose Austrian nationality was annulled by the Dollfuss-Schuschnigg regime of 1934–1938; (2) persons born in Austria who experienced only their primary socialization and subsequent adolescence in the country; and (3) those who became and remained Austrians after 1945 in their capacity as resettlers, refugees, or displaced persons.

It is of no operational consequence whether persons of this sort lived in Austria during the period 1938–1945 or were active members of the German apparatus of repression within Germany or her occupied territories as part of the German armed forces, police, and the judiciary, administration, and so on. Nor should the "other" Austrians be excluded, those who fell victim to Nazi repression (Jews, gypsies, members of national minorities, and the physically and psychologically disabled). Neither should one over-look those active in the Austrian resistance, at home or abroad, or those emigrants who fought within the ranks of the Allied armed forces. Finally there are the children born to Austrian women during the Nazi rule in that country. It is these, even those who never suffered persecution or repres-sion but, in so far as they survived, suffered from the ill-effects of the Nazi regime in having sustained more than negligible injury. It is precisely those children whom the Nazi regime treated with contempt, contrary to its ostensible ideological professions. Leaving aside the exceptional case of Anne Frank, these children have not been made the subject of historical research, as if some sort of phobia inhibits contact with the fate of those children and their history.

From what has been said, it is evident that the institutional definition of the subject under investigation is only of minor importance in the pre-sent context. The same is not true as regards the determination of sources. The search for suitable sources is basically a European–one would almost be tempted to say worldwide–problem. And over those two dimensions, it can be claimed without exaggeration, the search is being promoted far more widely than in Austria herself. There is a practical problem, too. The dissolution of Austria into seven Reichsgaue by the Nazi regime produced a situation in which considerable documentary resources essential for the analysis of governmental conditions, as well as the distribution and location of power, have been locked away within the archives of Austria's federal Länder. Apart from a few exceptions, the governments of those Länder rigorously restrict access to these documents, so much so that those en-gaged in research are compelled to seek their material from sources located abroad. This lack of support in Austria makes historical research more dif-ficult, and restricts the possibility of answering numerous questions.

Austria is a country whose public is broadly democratic in outlook and displays a great interest in the clarification of all details of Nazi policy, not only on the part of the general public but also the socially prominent groups and leading politicians. It is a country that, according to the official version, regards the Nazi regime as responsible for raping Austria–its "first victim"–and dragging it into war against its will. Moreover, it is a country involved in a major controversy concerning the person of the Federal Presi-dent. For all these compelling reasons, one might have expected a clamor for the opening of the 1938–1945 archives in order to enable a broadly based debate on all essential aspects of the relationship of the Austrians with Nazism, making available all source materials relevant to answering those basic questions.[2] Instead, the opposite has been the case, and as a result, the chances of historians gaining access to Austrian, as well as some foreign, archives to obtain data essential to the study of the period of Nazi rule in Austria appear to be slimmer today than ever before.

Three elements would seem to account for the relatively low level of concern, shown by both research workers and the public, about Austria's past on a level that goes beyond mere nostalgic reminiscing. The first element is Austria's State doctrine, harping on Austria's historical status as the "first victim" of German Nazism. For a long time this attitude prevented asking the questions that might have separated the Austrians in their capacity as perpetrators from those who were victims, rather than treating those two categories in mutual relationship. The formal-legal fixation characteristic of that State doctrine ruled out all attempts at treating those themes in conjunction as impermissible or even impossible.

The second element consists in the tendency to be hostile toward historical research in favor of encouraging the formation of legends. As a result, while the relevant sources of historical research are kept in the archives behind firmly closed doors so as to make them inaccessible to historians, obeisance is being rendered to the opinions of those who regard research in this area as both too difficult and insufficiently justifiable. As if that were not obstacle enough, there is also the fact that analysis of the controversial chapters in the history of the First Austrian Republic and the Dollfuss-Schuschnigg regime started rather late and never was properly completed. It is not surprising therefore that, when a new set of prophets appeared clamoring for the existing emphasis of contemporary historical research to be shifted to the period after 1945, they encountered little opposition. For if they had had their way, the Nazi period in Austria's history would continue to remain unexplored, left in the hands of the hero-worshippers and makers of legends.

This does not mean that no research has been done on the Nazi rule in Austria. Researchers have expended great personal effort and produced excellent and well-founded work.[3] These results have not, however, been diffused sufficiently among the Austrian public to bring about a transformation in the collective historical consciousness of the Austrians at large. It is precisely the arguments concerning the personal history of Federal President Waldheim—above all as they are reflected in readers' letters in the major Austrian daily newspapers—that show conclusively that efforts at enlightenment conducted on the purely intellectual plane are incapable of overcoming the efforts at repression of memory by those who claim to have been present but nonetheless never noticed anything.

AUSTRIA'S FEDERAL ARMY AND NAZISM IN AUSTRIA

The Nazi movement had its origins in the German-Slav border areas of the Habsburg monarchy but failed to maintain its relative strength in Austria until the late 1920s. Undermined by the German Nazi Party under Hitler's leadership–and ultimately absorbed by the it–the Austrian Nazi Party never succeeded in achieving substantial inroads into the Austrian electorate, even after the onset of the world crisis. This was confirmed by the outcome of the parliamentary elections of 1930. Only during the various Länder elections, two years later, did the Nazis succeed in invading the former positions of the German-Nationalist parties at the regional level and also in seriously embarrassing the Christian-Social Party in Vienna. After that the Christian-Social Party never dared to call for general elections, even when it was allied with the Fascist Heimwehr, preferring–in accord with with the interests of some sectors of Austria's industry, on the one hand, and those of Fascist Italy, on the other–to establish a Fascist dictatorship in the country. While primarily directed against the workers' movement, as attested by the latter's crushing defeat in February 1934, this dictatorship at the same time had to maintain itself against its Fascist rival, the Nazi movement in Austria. The Nazi movement made strenuous efforts to replace the Austro-Fascist regime with its own brand of dictatorship by engaging in propaganda and sending financial aid, as well as by dynamite and arms from Germany.[4] As is the case in studying the genesis of Fascist dictatorships anywhere, much attention has to be paid to the attitudes adopted by the armed forces–in Austria, the police and gendarmerie and, above all, the Austrian military.

The Austrian Federal Army was originally designed, according to the will of the Great Powers, as a small inadequately equipped professional army. From the 1920s onward, that instrument was consistently adapted by a Christian-Social Minister of War in accord with the political interests of his Party, the influence formerly exerted on the Federal Army by the Social Democrats being gradually reduced. It may safely be said that its most frequent use consisted neither in the active defence of Austria's frontiers, which never happened, nor in rendering of aid during natural disasters, as provided in Austria's Defense Act, but in its use as an instrument against the working class during labor disputes or strikes. This one-sided attitude, which even today is presented as both nonpolitical and impartial, was reflected in the restrained use of the Federal Army during the putsch of 1931 attempted by the Styrian Heimwehr, a paramilitary organization financed mainly by some sections of Austrian industry and Italy's fascist government.

The purely domestic uses of the Federal Army meant that, in accord with the state of government coalitions, German-Nationalist soldiers and officers organizations were gaining a foothold alongside those of a Christian-Social nature, once the equivalent Social-Democratic organizations had been widely eliminated. Those German-Nationalist army organizations constituted the core of the Nazi organizations within the Federal Army in the 1930s. The official tolerance of them was, however, cut short by the foundering of the negotiations for a rapprochement between Christian Socials and Nazis, as well as by the outlawing of the Austrian Nazi Party. The purge of Nazis in the Austrian Federal Army was still incomplete when Austria's Federal Chancellor was assassinated during an attempted putsch by the Austrian Nazis on 25 July 1934.[5] That attempted Nazi putsch taught both the government in Austria and Hitler in Germany that Austria's armed forces, even when ideologically unsympathetic toward the government, were able to act in support of the State's power in a positive way; they had patently failed to act in support of the Nazi putschists of July, whose core had been recruited from among veterans of the Federal Army. The victory scored by the Austro-Fascist regime over the Austrian Nazi putschists, which led to the former's brief flowering and the climax of its power, caused Nazi Germany to alter its policy toward Austria. Quite possibly, it also seduced the Austrian regime into relying on a near-permanent consensus of support in the Federal Army for the regime in Vienna.

It is not easy to assess the success of the strategy of penetration practiced by the illegal Nazi "Soldatenring" within the Federal Army during the four crucial years between the failure of the July putsch of 1934 and the Nazi seizure of power in Austria in 1938 and the simultaneous defeat of the Austro-Fascist regime. Who can say whether the membership of the Nazi "Soldatenring" within the Federal Army at that time was tantamount to nonconformity in action or, in the case of contemplated action against the German army, tantamount to a refusal to fight or fight effectively?[6]

In passing judgment on the state of power, one has to take into consideration the gradual formation of a quasi-Austrian counterarmy in Nazi Germany, the "Austrian Legion." This represented a permanent threat of invasion to the regime in Vienna. In addition, that regime—and especially its two diplomatic partners, Fascist Italy and Horthy's Hungary—began a progressive rapprochement with Nazi Germany itself. In July 1936, Austria's Federal Chancellor had agreed to conduct the country's foreign policy only in consultation with Nazi Germany. The Austro-German agreements, subsequently reached at Berchtesgaden in February 1938, led to the significant Austrian concession to dismiss the Austrian Chief-of-Staff, who had been prepared to defend the country against Germany, as well as an Austrian declaration of intent by which the Federal Army was to be assimilated, if not annexed outright, through an intensive exchange of officers.

Some members of the Austrian Federal Army, above all some of those in strategic positions within the Federal Ministry of National Defence, had already quite evidently furthered such collaboration and had been passing on information to the German military attaché on a regular and highly treasonable basis concerning the situation within the Army and the current state of defensive measures against Nazi Germany.[7]

To assess the attitude of the Austrian Federal Army during the critical days of February and March 1938 is even more difficult without detailed investigation than to provide an answer to the same question in respect to July 1934, for on the strict order of resigning Federal Chancellor Schuschnigg in the late afternoon of 11 March 1938, the Federal Army was to take no action against the invading German forces. The situation within the Federal Army at that moment was far more difficult than in 1934 in that— in contrast to 1934—and as a direct consequence of the introduction of general conscription decreed in 1936—a proportion of those under the colors were no longer professional soldiers but conscripts called up in the autumn of 1937.[8]

According to one hypothesis, the Federal Army would have been prepared to fight; according to another there would have been a mutiny. Good reasons can be adduced for either hypothesis. Far more convincing, however, is a third hypothesis, according to which, judging exclusively by the morale prevailing within the officer corps, part of it would have fought for Austria, while another part would have sabotaged such efforts with all means at its disposal.[9] Which side the majority would have favored in such an event would have ultimately depended on the extent to which a government other than that in power in Vienna at the time could have swayed the majority and united it with that part of the working class also willing to fight.

However, none of this actually happened. Instead Schuschnigg stood by, almost idly, while the Nazis of Styria, and not only of Styria, determined to take over regional power with the help of the new Minister of the Interior, Seyss-Inquart, yielding altogether in face of the threats delivered by Nazi Germany and the Austrian Nazis. The invasion by Germany's armed forces proceeded without Austrian countermeasures, and the seizure of power by the Nazis developed more smoothly and rapidly than even imagined by Hitler. In view of all this, it would seem rather rash to draw any conclusions from the conduct of the commanding officers and other officers in the Federal Army after the capitulation of the Vienna regime and to their possible attitude when confronted with an order to fight. One would not, however, be far wrong in assuming that the traitors within the Ministry of Defence at the Stubenring in Vienna would have continued to collaborate with Nazi Germany, and that the willingness to fight Nazi Germany on the part of those officers and commanders who on their own free will joyfully welcomed the German troops in Austria would not have been particularly resolute.[10]

INCORPORATION

Both the immobility without resistance on the part of the Austrian Federal Army and the occasionally joyful welcome of the German invasion of Austria by members of that Federal Army provided signals to the German Nazi leaders about the lack of danger emanating from the Austrian military. The rapid incorporation of the latter into the German armed forces, therefore, represented the first step toward securing the Nazi regime in Austria. On 13 March 1938, Austria's soldiers and officers had to take the oath of loyalty to Hitler, and units of the Federal Army were allowed to march together with German troops in front of him.[11]

The smoothness of the takeover of the Austrian army conceals to some little degree the fact that not all members of the Federal Army had gone over joyfully to Hitler. Jewish Austrians within the Army, whether declared religious Jews or not, were eventually to be subject to discrimination, robbery, and persecution; and unless they preferred, like so many, to commit suicide, they were eliminated from the Army at the beginning of May 1938. Other Austrians refused to take the oath of loyalty to Hitler and, for that reason or some other, were not taken over into the German armed forces, but were dismissed instead. Others, like the former Secretary of State for Defence, General Zehner, died under mysterious circumstances, allegedly by suicide.[12]

There were two waves of purges, affecting about 55 percent of the generals, 40 percent of the colonels, and 14 percent of other officer ranks from lieutenant-colonels right down to lieutenants.[13] However, the vast majority of former members of the Federal Army preferred to take the easy way out, by coming to terms with the new regime or by eagerly seeking the fulfillment of their long-standing wishes with regard to their career within the new type of society, which was far more efficiently militarized than that under the old Austro-Fascist regime. Here, they found themselves in agreement with the attitudes adopted by a majority of the Austrian population.

Just as the country of Austria was dissolved as a politically organized unit, so the Austrian Federal Army was not incorporated into the German armed forces as a closed group but, on the contrary, was penetrated by the latter. Two German regional defence commands (Wehrkreiskommandos), centered in Salzburg and Vienna, were created to carry out the functions of replenishment of military personnel and territorial security. In spite of that, throughout the Nazi period, a number of military units within the German armed forces were recruited in large measure, but never exclusively, from Austrian stock. This was particularly true of special mountain units, and the 44th Infantry Division, in large part was composed of Viennese, Lower Austrians, and Burgenlanders, which was subsequently almost totally annihilated at Stalingrad.[14]

A nostalgic book of historical reminiscence published in Vienna in 1969 attempted to trace a line of tradition from the Vienna regiment of the Hoch- und Deutschmeister of the Habsburg monarchy via the 44th Infantry Division in Nazi Germany to the light infantry battalion (Jägerbatallion 4) in today's Federal Army, without being aware, or wishing to be aware, that a historical image was thereby being promoted that rested on the disappearance of Austria and the glorification of Nazi Germany's war of aggression.[15]

COLLABORATION AND RESISTANCE

Active collaboration with the Nazi regime and military resistance to it are the two poles of a broad spectrum of behavioral modes within which the Austrians attempted several courses of action. One was to profit from the Nazi regime, its terrorist and repressive policies as well as its seductive gifts offered at the cost of the persecuted or the outcast. Other courses pursued were simply to survive the Nazi regime or to fight it as effectively as possible. This was true in the civilian sphere as much as in the military one throughout the Nazi period. Many who, during the early days of the Nazi regime in Austria, had considered themselves its starry-eyed supporters opened their eyes after witnessing the terror or perhaps experiencing it themselves. However, there were also those who had turned themselves into accomplices of Nazi crimes and who, on the collapse of the regime, were preparing their escape, submergence, or the systematic trivialization of their deeds. To resort to the claim of having acted under higher orders and by doing so fulfilled one's duty is not by any means a standard excuse of very recent vintage but a justification regularly put forward in Austria for some time past.[16]

Austrians were to be found on both sides. Austrian members of the armed forces of Nazi Germany at all hierarchical levels were active participants in a war of robbery pursued by Nazi Germany within almost the whole of Europe and North Africa. Austrians were simple soldiers as well as Supreme Commanding Generals of an Army Group; Austrians were officers in the German air force, as well as ordinary sailors in the German navy. Regional military commands, Wehrkreise XVII and XVIII–that much has been established–served to feed such a large number of German military units, estimated at roughly 3500–4500 units in the field, that it is impossible to enumerate them all.[17]

The claim, most likely exaggerated, has been made that Nazi Germany could not have started its war or at least could not have waged it so successfully in its initial stages without the active support, or at least benevolent tolerance, of the Austrians. Even a raw laymen in military matters can easily figure out that the German thrust into Czechoslovakia, and above all the savage assault on Yugoslavia, could hardly have taken place without the Austrian hinterland as military base. Although it has been contended that few Austrians were among the German military units that attacked Yugoslavia in April 1941, the immense responsibility of the former Commander-in-Chief of Austria's air force, Alexander Löhr, for bombing Belgrade cannot be disputed, only trivialized.[18] Löhr, commander of Army Group 'E', headquarters in Salonika, but subordinate to Army Group 'F' in Belgrade, had to share the dock with other German colonel-generals of Austrian origin – Rendulic, De Angelis, and Böhme – who after Germany's final defeat were accused of having committed massacres against Yugoslavia's civilian population. Without having completed its investigations, the Yugoslav War Crimes Commission was able to ascertain as early as 1947 that, out of 4433 German war criminals, 2062 were of Austrian origin.[19]

The active use of Austrians in the machinery deployed in the course of the German war of aggression is also manifested in the great number of high and very high war decorations, which were intended not only for the purpose of tying its recipients more closely to the Nazi regime, but also to act as an example for the young who were to be induced into actively supporting the war.[20] It has furthermore to be borne in mind that the maintenance of the German war machine required more than the availability of fighting units. The disciplining of those soldiers who expected neither fame nor honors nor, even less so, death for the sake of the fatherland, demanded the presence of a comprehensive set of judicial institutions. It is undeniable that Austrians acted as military judges pronouncing in court martials in all three branches of the German armed forces; they acted as guards in military prisons; they were represented in the ranks of the military police (Feldgendarmerie); and, in the military search service (Fahndung), they sought out Austrian deserters. This particular chapter in the Austrian participation in the German war of aggression and in the maintenance of the effectiveness of the German military machinery has been investigated much less than the Austrian participation in various German fighting units. The latter type of investigation, if anything, fell victim to the temptation to foster nostalgic reminiscences and to indulge in true or pretended deeds of heroism. At least some evidence can be found in the columns of Austria's newspapers immediately after the end of the war about those cases in which members of the German military authorities who were of Austrian origin were being traced by the newly established authorities of the Second Austrian Republic for alleged maltreatment of prisoners, the use of inhuman methods during interrogation, and the passing of sentences of death.[21]

The encroachment of the Nazi regime on the Austrians, but by no means exclusively on them, was intensified as the war dragged on and the chances of a Nazi victory became more and more remote. Men who were physically unfit for fighting service in the field were now needed for combating the partisan movement and guarding strategically important points, such as centers of armament production. One of their duties was the guarding of prisoner of war camps.[22]

Youths and women were used in particular as aids in the supporting services of the German air force. It is estimated that several thousand such young air force auxilaries originating from Austria must have been employed in the radio message and telecommunications services; 13,000 women supported the maintenance of the air force's technical services in their capacity as members of the radio and metereological complex.[23]

It is not easy to establish whether all those persons are included in the overall figures published relating to the numerical participation of Austrians in the German armed forces and the Waffen-SS (literally, arms-carrying SS, the fully militarized branch of the SS forming an integral part of the German army). Estimates based on the average number of Austrian men called up in the appropriate drafting year support the conclusion that there were about 1.2 million Austrian members of the German armed forces and Waffen-SS,[24] unless it is assumed that the figure of 1.2 million Austrian prisoners of war, given during a budget debate in the Austrian Parliament at the beginning of 1946 by the then Minister of the Interior, Oskar Helmer, is to be regarded as more precise.[25]

In view of the fact, however, that twelve months later Helmer mentioned a much lower figure, which included all those Austrian prisoners of war who had been informally released after the end of the war, he might have been referring in his previous statement to the total number of Austrians having served in the German armed forces.[26]

What is decisive, however, is not the absolute number of those Austrians but their position, function, and use in the German war machine and, even more so, their awareness of being part of one of the most important instruments for the maintenance and expansion of Nazi rule. Some appear to have acknowledged this but are reluctant to accept the full implications. Typical of those is the writer of a letter addressed to the Austrian weekly *profil* of 11 May 1987, who resentfully constructed the following chain of reasoning:

It was only after a country had been conquered by the German armed forces that it was possible to establish authorities in it that issued orders for deportation or carried out the shooting of hostages. Seen from that angle, all the German armed forces, including the air force and navy, were involved in the criminal activities of the Third Reich . . ."[27]

Even today some are incapable of perceiving or unwilling to imagine that, devoid of an effective fighting machine, the Nazi regime would have been unable to start its war of aggression and to pursue policies that depended on the systematic plundering of the peoples of Europe. That recognition had come to a number of Austrians, at different times and for varying reasons, during the war and induced them to act accordingly. Their number was far smaller than that of those who acted in accordance with what was expected of them by the Nazi regime. The small band of Austrians who resisted nonetheless must remain for us monuments of a probity which is proof enough of a scope for conduct for Austrians under the Nazi regime wider than the one produced for purposes of self-justification, namely the lack of alternatives to acting in compliance with Nazi standards or at least their explicit or implicit toleration. A report issued in January 1946 mentioning the number of Austrians serving in German penitentiary military units during the war as constituting one-third of their strength may quite possibly be exaggerating the share,[28] but some individual reports about members of those penitentiary companies persistently demonstrate their unbroken resistance to the Nazi regime that led them, wherever feasible, to desert or join partisan fighting units.[29] It has not been possible so far to determine the exact number of those Austrians who—for reasons of conscience, because of religious conviction, or for other reasons—refused to honor the draft summons, failed to swear the oath of loyalty to Hitler, refused to take orders, or deserted. As regards refusal to be called up, none ranked ahead of the Jehovah's Witnesses. However, individual cases, like that of the Upper Austrian Catholic Franz Jägerstätter, who refused to serve and was promptly executed in 1943, cover up the ambivalent attitude of the Catholic Church hierarchy vis-à-vis the Nazi regime.[30]

There were Austrians who fought as partisans in the Styrian-Carinthian frontier area,[31] and other Austrians who took up the fight against the German armed forces, as well as against SS and police troops, sometimes as in the case of Yugoslavia organized in their own Austrian battalions within national liberation movements. Some Austrians took up the fight against Nazi Germany within the ranks of the Allied armies,[32] even if not all of them regarded themselves as Austrians any longer.

The objective assessment of the importance of all those individual or group actions and the weight attributable to them was made more difficult by the efforts of the Austrian authorities after 1945 to live up to the promise

held out to them in the Moscow Delaration of 1943, to underline the
Austrian contribution to its own liberation and to play down the participation of Austrians in Nazi Germany's war, if not to trivialize it altogether.[33]

All this could lead to such grotesque judgments as that passed by the
Socialist deputy and pre-1934 mayor of Vienna, Karl Seitz, in Austria's Parliament on 20 March 1946, in which he claimed, in emphasizing the innocence of the Austrians in the war: "In front was the enemy and behind
them were the Gestapo agents (Gestapospitzel) [loud cheers on the Left],
who drove the men on with revolvers and light arms."[34] However, it is precisely the events of 20 July 1944 in Vienna and the attempts made by
Austrians in the German armed forces in the final days of military operation to hand over Vienna to the Red Army without a fight that tend to
strengthen the claim that the Austrians, far from being the helpless victims
who were forced to act against their own will, were to be found on both
sides of the divide right to the end – that of resistances and struggle against
Nazi Germany, on the one hand, and that of unconditional support and
fanatical defence of it, on the other.[35] Besides, the events of 20 July 1944
offer, in the person of Lt.-Colonel Robert Bernardis, an officer of the former
Austrian Federal Army who had joined the illegal NS-Soldatenring in 1937
and subsequently made quite a career in the German armed forces but who,
by 1944, had become a declared foe of the Nazi regime.[36] The history of
the action of 20 July 1944 also proves clearly that in cases of conspiracies
of this sort and magnitude, success depends not only on the personality
of the conspirators but also on a well functioning system of command and
a plan of transformation capable of being operated by nonconspirators. For
reasons like these, the man at the center of the conspiracy, Major Szokoll,
a Viennese, remained undetected and unmolested by Nazi security, ready
to spring into action jointly with other Austrians, primarily officers and
noncommissioned officers, in the spring of 1945 and prepared to deliver
Vienna to the Red Army, as already indicated. The vision of making contact between then Sergeant-Major Käs and officers of the Red Army succeeded, but the plan for an uprising within Vienna failed through treason
committed by an Austrian. Three of the leading Austrian officers involved
in the conspiracy – Biedermann, Huth, and Raschke – were executed by the
retreating SS troops.[37]

POSTWAR JUDGMENTS

Resurrected Austria concentrated her attention on regaining her full
sovereignty as quickly as possible. The Austrian government therefore emphasized anything capable of corroborating the thesis of a raped Austria

that attempted everything possible to participate in its own liberation, as well as mitigating anything that was plainly imcompatible with this thesis, such as the participation by Austrians in the crimes committed by the Nazi regime. In addition, Austria, seen by its government to have been weakened by war losses, strained every muscle to bring about the speedy return of Austrian prisoners of war, who were referred to euphemistically as "homecomers" (Heimkehrer).[38]

Everywhere in Austria arose war memorials in honor of those killed during the war and already existing war memorials from the First World War were added to, without drawing any special distinction between those two World Wars. Without discrimination of any sort the "Fatherland" or the "Homeland" for which those killed had allegedly given their lives could then be either the Habsburg monarchy or Nazi Germany.[39]

This faith in the legitimacy of all actions performed by the German armed forces was also in evidence when a petition, signed by 600 former Austrian officers who had served in the armed forces of the Habsburg monarchy, in the Austrian Federal Army, as well as in the German armed forces, was addressed to the President of the United States in favor of the former colonel-general of Austrian origin, Lothar Rendulic, who served in the German armed forces and was sentenced at Nuremberg to twenty years imprisonment for the murder of hostages. Indeed, Rendulic was freed in December of the same year, only three years after his conviction.[40] Far from showing any remorse, Rendulic gave his support from Austria to a consistent justification of the German armed forces during the Second World War. This work attempted to free members of those forces of all responsibility for their defeat and tried to remove them from the proximity of the Nazi regime, preaching the example of the unpolitical soldier whose credit was compromised due to mistakes committed by the political leadership. The virtue of "fulfillment of duty," "performance and sacrifice of the German armed forces," comradeship and "innate discipline" were all to be upheld for the benefit of young people who, even in 1954 after the end of the Korean war, were failing to embrace those military virtues.[41] What is not quite clear is whether Rendulic's utterances wre directed to the West German or the Austrian public. During this time a debate was going on in respect of the entry of West Germany into NATO, and it was a time when, at least in the Western zones of Allied occupation in Austria, the militarized police forces (Gendarmerie) provided the core of what was subsequently to be turned into the Austrian Federal Army. In any case, perennial efforts were undertaken by far right-wing organizations in Austria, even after the conclusion of the State Treaty on 15 May 1955, to raise officers of the German armed forces during the Second World War who were of Austrian origin, like the late fighter-pilot Walter Nowotny, into symbols of heroism for the benefit of young people steeped in the traditions of Nazi Germany–however, with little success.[42]

More important are those far-right-wing organizations in Austria that idolize militarism in general, deny the Nazi crimes, and glorify the Nazi war of aggression, thereby trivializing its horrors. Cause for misgivings in that connection is provided by the presence of political party representatives of the region at meetings that inter alia foster the traditions of the SS, and whose attendance renders such meetings socially worthy and generally respectable. Another cause for anxiety is the tie established in some respects between the tradition of the late German armed forces of the Second World War and the present post-1955 Austrian Federal Army by their attendance.[43] The Federal Army, legitimized by the State treaty of 1955, was designed in accordance with the spirit that decisively ruled out any possibility of participating in a war of aggression. This, in turn, must mean that any tendency toward the glorification of the Nazi regime is to be excluded emphatically.[44] That is one reason why Article 12 of the State Treaty provides that officers of the former German armed forces during the Second World War, at the level of colonel or above, must not be members of the Austrian Federal Army. The same applies to former members of the Nazi Party or any of its former associated units.[45] At present no monograph can inform us accurately to what extent those provisions have been honored.

The existence of more unanswered questions than conclusive answers to questions asked need not always be a sign of uncertainty. We know for certain that the majority of Austrians allowed themselves to be corrupted during the Nazi period and to be seduced into participating in the program of Nazi conquest. But we also know for certain that a strong minority of Austrians took up the struggle against the Nazi regime on the military plane by refusal and active resistance. For Austrians today, it is necessary to decide whether to embrace the traditions of the corrupt or the traditions of those Austrians who frequently laid down their lives in the hope of crushing the inhuman racism of the Nazi regime and in the expectation of a democratic social system founded on human dignity and the legal and moral equality for all people willing to live in peace.

NOTES

The author of this paper wishes to express his thanks to Dr. F. Parkinson for having translated it from German into English.

1. On the subject of Austrian identity, see G. Botz, "Eine deutsche Geschichte, 1938–1945?" *Zeitgeschichte* 14 (1986):19–38. As to the development of an Austrian national consciousness, see F. Kreissler, *Der Österreicher und seine Nation* (Graz and Vienna, 1984).

2. See *Pflichterfüllung. Ein Bericht über Waldheim* (Vienna, 1986).

3. See literature cited in Botz, pp. 35 and 38.

4. On the setting up of a dictatorship in Austria, see the symposium edited by E. Fröschl and Helge Zoitl, *Februar 1934. Ursachen, Fakten, Folgen* (Vienna, 1984).

5. G. Jagschitz, *Der Putsch* (Graz, Vienna, and Cologne, 1955).

6. See the pessimistic assessment of Nazi prospects in Austria's Federal Army in a Nazi Party report of 15 December 1937, which sees monarchists in control everywhere. "Von Zehner angefangen über Jansa steht alles für Otto, den Legitimismus und radikal contra Reich!" See J. Mende, *Dr. Carl Freiherr von Bardolff* (Diss., University of Vienna, 1984), p. 223.

7. L. Jedlicka, "Heer und Staat in der ersten und zweiten Republik," in *1918–1968. Die Streitkräfte der Republik Österreich* (Vienna, 1968), pp. 28–35.

8. O. Tuider, *Die Wehrkreise XVII und XVIII. 1938–1945* (Vienna, 1975), p. 10.

9. P. Gschaider, *Das österreichische Bundesheer und seine Überführung in die deutsche Wehrmacht* (Diss., University of Vienna, 1967), pp. 70–79.

10. As to the situations in Salzburg and Styria, see E. Hanisch, *Nationalsozialistische Herrschaft in der Provinz, Salzburg im Dritten Reich* (Salzburg, 1983), pp. 30–32; S. Karner, *Die Steiermark im Dritten Reich. 1938–1945* (Graz and Vienna, 1986), p. 54.

11. Tuider, p. 9.

12. Jedlicka, p. 28.

13. Johann C. Allmayer-Beck, "Die Österreicher im zweiten Weltkrieg," in *Unser Heer. 300 Jahre österreichisches Soldatentum in Krieg und Frieden* (Vienna, Munich, and Zurich, 1963), pp. 342–375.

14. Tuider, pp. 6–16; Allmayer-Beck, ibid., pp. 344–50, 356.

15. A. Schimak, K. Lamprecht, and F. Dettmer, *Die 44. Infanterie-Division. Tagebuch der Hoch- und Deutschmeister* (Vienna, 1969), p. 14.

16. On the highly controversial problem of the Austrian resistance against the Nazi regime, compare R. Luža, *Österreich und die grossdeutsche Idee in der NS-Zeit* (Vienna, 1977); and K. Stadler (ed.), *Österreich 1938–1945 im Spiegel der NS-Akten* (Vienna and Munich, 1966).

17. Tuider, p. 29.

18. Ibid., pp. 25, 112 ff.

19. Federal People's Republic of Yugoslavia, *Report on the Crimes of Austria and the Austrians against Yugoslavia and her Peoples* (Belgrade, 1947), pp. 29–45.

20. Allmayer-Beck, p. 358 ff.; but compare the affirmative publication by G. Fraschka, *. . . . mit Schwertern und Brillanten. Aus dem Leben der siebenundzwanzig Träger der höchsten deutschen Tapferkeitsauszeichnung* (Rastatt, 1958), pp. 34–44, 75–84.

21. See the reports published in the *Wiener Zeitung* of 16 June 1946, 18 June 1946, 19 June 1946, 27 June 1946, and 3 July 1946.

22. Tuider, p. 31 ff.

23. O. Tuider, *Die Luftwaffe in Österreich 1938–1945* (Vienna, 1985), pp. 18, 52–64.

24. Tuider, *Wehrkreise*, pp. 31 ff.

25. *Wiener Zeitung*, 6 April 1946.

26. Federal Ministry of the Interior (Vienna), *Das Buch des österreichischen Heimkehrers* (Vienna, 1949), p. 111. Compare the data provided in the catalog of the Heeresgeschichtliche Museum of 1968, which mentions 494,939 Austrian prisoners of war and civilian internees returned between 1945 and 1968.

27. Reader's letter composed by Franz Ehm (Graz) in *profil*, 19 (11 May 1987).

28. *Wiener Zeitung*, 4 January 1946.

29. See also F. Vogl (ed.), *Österreichs Eisenbahner im Widerstand* (Vienna, 1968), pp. 94, 226.

30. The hitherto most comprehensive investigation and documentation on this sub-

ject is F. Vogl, *Widerstand im Waffenrock. Österreichs Freiheitskämpfer in der Deutschen Wehrmacht, 1938–1945* (Vienna, 1977).

31. On this point, see an analysis based on interviews conducted with surviving partisans who were active in the Koralpen area: C. Fleck, *Koralmpartisanen Über abweichende Karrieren politisch motivierter Widerstandskämpfer* (Vienna and Cologne, 1986).

32. See F. Reitlinger, 'Als Tiroler in der britischen Armee', in Anton Pelinka and R. Steininger (eds.), *Österreich und die Sieger* (Vienna, 1986), pp. 53–56. On the collaboration between Austrian resistance fighters and deserters from the German armed forces on the one hand, and the Friulan partisan division 'Osoppo Friuli' in 1944, see a paper shortly to be published in *Zeitgeschichte*. See *Wiener Zeitung* of 1 December 1945 on Lieutenant Francis Perry of the United States Army, an Austrian emigrant active in the Czechoslovak liberation movement.

33. Above all, Austrian Federal Government, *Red-White-Red Book* (in German) (Vienna, 1946), pp. 94–118.

34. *Wiener Zeitung,* 21 March 1946.

35. Vogl, p. 14 ff.; Tuider, *Wehrkreise*, p. 36 ff.; and Hanisch, p. 233 ff.

36. L. Jedlicka, *Der 20. Juli in Österreich* (Vienna and Munich, 1965), pp. 141–48.

37. Vogl, pp. 60–73.

38. *Das Buch des österreichischen Heimkehrers* (Vienna, 1949).

39. A. Maislinger, "Mit zwei Wahrheiten leben?" *Die Furche* (11 August 1982); also idem, "Tirol in der NS-Zeit"; *Vierzehn Kriegerdenkmäler,* n.d.

40. Lothar Rendulic, *Glasenbach, Nürnberg, Landsberg. Ein Soldatenschicksal nach dem Krieg,* 2d ed. (Graz and Göttingen, 1953), p. 222.

41. *Wie das Gesetz es befahl. Das Volksbuch vom Zweiten Weltkrieg. Den Gefallenen zur Ehre und den Lebenden zur Erinnerung* (Wels, Starnberg, 1954).

42. For instance, *Der Trommler* 4 (1958):1.

43. Dokumentationsarchiv des österreichischen Widerstandes, *Rechtsextremismus in Österreich nach 1945* 8th ed., (Vienna, 1981), especially pp. 73, 118–125, 164–71.

44. J. Ellinger, "Österreichische Wehrverfassung," in *Unser Heer.* pp. 458, 461.

45. G. Stourzh, *Geschichte des Staatsvertrages* (Graz, Vienna, and Cologne, 1980), pp. 255 ff.

The Austrians and Slovenia during the Second World War

TONE FERENC

Slovenia occupies a special place in the relations between the Austria and Yugoslavia during the Second World War. With the exception of Prekmurje in the northeast and the Slovenian Veneto in the northwest, almost all the Slovenian territory belonged to Austria in the Austro-Hungarian monarchy. Slovenia, one of the smallest European nations, bore the heaviest brunt of the German imperialism in its drive towards the Adriatic Sea, the target it had set itself in the mid-nineteenth century. Efforts to achieve this target found their most painful expression in the Germanization of the Slovenian territory, especially in Carinthia. Before the fifteenth century, chiefly on account of language assimilation, the people of Slovenia, neighbors of the larger German nation, had lost two-thirds of the territory settled by it during the sixth century.

NORTHERN SLOVENIA

The establishment of Yugoslavia as a State stopped the thrust of German imperialism toward the Adriatic Sea, since the major part of the Slovenian territory was incorporated into the new State. The border between Austria and Yugoslavia was fixed by the Treaty of St. Germain of 1919 and the plebiscite in Carinthia of 1920, which did not favor Yugoslavia. This left some all-Slovenian territory in Austria (Carinthia, villages near Radgona).

On the other hand, some parts of territory with a German-speaking majority (Apaška, Kotlina, Kočevsko) came under Yugoslavia, while other primarily German areas remained in Austria, especially in Lower Styria.

With the new border the Germans did not lose so much of their territory as the Slovenes. Yet, between the two world wars, they demanded with the utmost aggressiveness that the border be altered and based their claims on a variety of arguments, mostly pseudoscientific ones. Several German and Austrian writers of pseudoscientific literature demanded the return of some regions to Austria, especially on the strength of the claims put forward by two professors at Graz University: geographer Robert Sieger and the historian Hans Pirchegger. The moderates claimed from Lower Styria all Podravje (that is, the land along the Drava river), whereas the extremists went for the entire territory down to the river Sava. They based their claims especially on the so-called German national soil (*deutscher Volksboden*), on the German cultural soil (*deutscher Kulturboden*), and even on the German living space (*deutscher Lebensraum*). Most active in this was Helmut Carstanjen, who wrote articles and treatises under the pseudonym of Gerhard Werner and a book, *Die Sprache und das Volkstum in der Untersteiermark* (*Language and Nationality in Lower Styria*). He "found" that 32, 578 Germans lived in Lower Styria and, since it would have been absurd to demand that 400,000 Slovenians be annexed to Austria with these Germans, Dr. Carstanjen resorted to the so-called Windisch theory. According to the theory, in addition to the Germans and a small number of nationally conscious Slovenes were the so-called Wenden or Windisch people who spoke a dialect similar to the Slovenian language but were German-oriented. For this reason Lower Styria ought to be considered a "German border march" (*deutsche Grenzmark*). Likewise, the German and Austrian authors began to lay claims to the northern part of Prekmurje.

German-Austrians were also active among the Germans in Slovenia in propagating the Nazi movement, which began to spread after the Nazis had seized power in Germany. Among those who brought Nazi literature, who visited Nazi groups, and lectured at their courses, were to be found Dr. Carstanjen, Anton Dorfmeister, and others, later officials in Lower Styria.

After the *Anschluss* the Germans in Slovenia came under the influence of new Nazi institutes in Graz and Klagenfurt (Celovec). Among the most important of these were the Südostdeutsches Institut, founded in May 1938 under Dr. Carstanjen's leadership in Graz, and the two provincial border offices (Gaugrenzamt) of the Nazi Party (NSDAP) in Graz and Klagenfurt (Celovec) established by decree on 2 February 1939 through the main NSDAP office. The Graz office was headed by Dorfmeister and the one at Klagenfurt by Alois Maier-Kaibitsch, a prominent participant in the so-called defensive battles in Carinthia after the First World War, leader of the

Kärtner Heimatbund and the provincial organs of two other associations (*Deutscher Schulverein Südmark* and *Volksbund für das Deutschtum im Ausland*), all directed against the nationally conscious Slovenes residing in Carinthia. During 1934–1938 Maier-Kaibitsch, as a member of the Carinthian provincial government, supported the Nazi underground, especially Odilo Globocnik and Friedrich Rainer, so that by 1942 he rose to the rank of colonel of the SS. The Austrians (Carstanjen, Maier-Kaibitsch, and Dorfmeister) were the principal officials in Graz and Klagenfurt laying the foundation for the subsequent Nazi occupation of northern Slovenia.

In summer 1940, Germany and Italy divided their spheres of influence in Europe and Hitler expected that Great Britain, after the defeat of France, Belgium, the Netherlands, and Luxembourg, would be willing to enter into negotiations with Germany about its supremacy over the oceans. (Germany was supposed to exercise its supremacy over Europe.) Some memoranda were drafted in July and early in August in Graz and Klagenfurt claiming the annexation of certain parts of Slovenia to the German Reich. In Klagenfurt, Maier-Kaibitsch drew up three memoranda concerning the Mežiška Dolina valley (Miesstal), the so-called Jesenice Triangle (Dreieck von Assling), and the former Austrian political districts of Radovljica, Kranj, and Kamnik (Radmannsdorf, Krainburg, and Stein) in the Gorenjsko region bordering on Carinthia. The fourth memorandum in Klagenfurt, known only in its draft form, was written by the deputy of the provincial leader of the Nazi Party in Carinthia, Franz Kutschera, demanding the annexation to the German Reich of the entire Kranjska region, Carniola, (with the exception of the region of Krško), and the western part of Lower Styria. He based his claim that Carinthia "could assimilate and lead territories speaking at present mostly another language" (*jetzt zum Grossteil andersprachige Gebiete zu assimilieren und zu führen*) on the enormous national power of its population. He explained that (1) in the First World War the Carinthians of all the German tribes suffered the severest losses; (2) after the First World War they fought to preserve the integrity of their country; (3) among the Carinthians the Nazi movement began as early as 1921, before 1938 when Carinthia "was known as the most National Socialist province," and was the first Austrian province to proclaim the seizure of power by the Nazis; (4) of the heroes of Narvik in 1940, two-thirds came from Carinthia. The draft of this memorandum had two appendixes presenting geographical and economic arguments in favor of the annexation of the aforementioned Yugoslav territories to the German Reich. In Graz, Dr. Carstanjen drew up the memorandum "The Southern Border of Styria" (*Die Südgrenze der Steiermark*), in which he suggested three possibilities for the alteration of the German-Yugoslav border. The first possibility envisaged a border running along the so-called Vitanje Line, which during 1918–1920 represented the minimal

Austrian claim concerning the delimitation between Austria and Yugoslavia. The second proposal advocated a border along the hills south of the
town of Celje; and the third solution placed the border along the course
of the Sava and Sotla Rivers. The explanation of the map that was added
somewhat later to the Graz memorandum also claimed the northern region
of Prekmurje as part of the German Reich. In 1945, another memorandum
was found in the archives of the Graz Südostdeutsches Institute on the Territorial Division and National and Political Settlement in Lower Styria
(*Gebietliche Gliederung und volkspolitische Gestaltung der Untersteiermark*). It
also envisaged the annexation of entire Lower Styria to Germany, as well
as several measures taken by the German authorities of occupation after the
invasion of this province in the spring of 1941. These memoranda were
discussed in the German ministries of Interior and Foreign Affairs in Berlin,
and as far as we know, at least one of them was handed over to Hitler by
the Gauleiter of Styria, Siegfried Uiberreither. The manner in which the
Graz Nazis then understood the need for altering the German-Yugoslav
state frontier is also borne out by a confidential tract *Des Reiches Südgrenze
in der Steiermark* by Hermann Ibler, a university don, as well as by the preparation of various handbooks published by the Südostdeutsches Institute.

   At that time, the offices of the Nazi intelligence services in Graz and
Klagenfurt also expanded the scope of their work. Thus, the bureaus of
military intelligence (Abwehr), under the name of Military Archives (Wehr-
machtsarchiv), and the SS Security Service (Sicherheitsdienst) gathered not
only information of a military nature, but increasingly also that concerning
Yugoslav institutions and personnel, all of which was then used by the occupation authorities in northern Slovenia. To gather information they used
members of the German national minority, which was organized in the
Swabian-German Cultural Association (Schwäbisch-Deutscher Kulturbund)
and increasingly was Nazified for use as an instrument of Nazi occupation
policy.

   Even before Germany and Italy attacked Yugoslavia, on 3 April 1941
Hitler had divided the Yugoslav territory among four occupation countries
and annexed northern Slovenia to Germany. After a brief military administration this territory, on the strength of two decrees issued by Hitler as early
as 14 April 1941, the area came under the German civilian administration
and was divided into two provisional administrative units: Lower Styria
and the Gorenjsko region, including the Mežiška Dolina Valley (officially,
the Occupied Territories of Carinthia and Carniola, and according to the
sources, Southern Carinthia). Then Hitler decreed that the entire territory
should be annexed to the neighboring Austrian provinces, Styria and Carinthia, in order to be quickly and thoroughly Germanized. Until the formal
and legal annexation, the two units were administered by the highest Nazi

party officials in Styria and Carinthia, Uiberreither (born in Upper Styria) and Kutschera (born in the Sudetenland) in their capacity as heads of the civilian administration. They set up quarters at Maribor and at Bled, returning to Graz and Klagenfurt in November 1941 and January 1942, respectively. Within the scope of Hitler's instructions they wielded unlimited powers in their administrative areas. The decrees and instructions issued by Berlin ministries and other central institutions were followed only if the two officials had published them in their respective locales. As appointed heads of the civil administration, they became Himmler's plenipotentiaries in charge of strengthening the "Germanity" (*Deutschtum*) of the area. Their work was coordinated by the German Ministry of Interior through its special Southeastern Department, headed by Secretary of State, Wilhelm Stuckart. For a few months, the department delegated liaison officials to each of the heads of the civilian administration, Hans Müller Scholtes and Kurt Sierp.

In the staff of each head of the civilian administration were more than twenty commissioners for various administrative provinces. As this system of the civilian administration was supposed to be provisional, that is, to last until the formal annexation of the two provinces to the German Reich, the commissioners were selected from among the civil servants occupying posts in the bureaus of State deputies for Styria and Carinthia with their respective seats in Graz and Klagenfurt. With a single exception of a German from Maribor, they were all Austrians. Some commissioners were heads of identical departments, others were their assistants. Some held the ranks of higher officers of the SS; for example, SS-Standartenführer (colonel) Alfred Fleischmann for the economy in Lower Styria; SS-Sturmbannführer (major) Ernst Dlaska for education in Gorenjska; SS-Sturmbannführer Albert von Gayl for food and agriculture in Gorenjska; SS-Obersturmbannführer (lt. colonel) Karl Lapper for propaganda in Gorenjska. Others were officers in the SA; for example, SA-Oberführer (colonel) Franz Steindl, chief of staff for Lower Styria; and SA-Sturmbannführer Karl Uragg for education in Lower Styria. Members of the staff included Carstanjen and Maier-Kaibitsch, who were responsible for Nazi political matters.

The heads of the civilian administration abolished all the Yugoslav administrative departments, replacing them with German political commissars, later renaming them district counsellors (Landrat). Out of twenty commissars only one or two were Germans from Lower Styria, all the others were Austrians. Some of them were very prominent Nazis who had asserted themselves in the Nazi civilian administration in Upper Styria, like Fritz Knaus, former provincial organizational head of NSDAP for Styria and SA-Standartenführer, who had left the post of provincial counsellor for the Graz countryside to become chief burgomaster (Oberbürgermeister) in

Maribor. Another was Erich Seitz, former mayor in Graz, who was appointed political commissar in the town of Ptuj. Dorfmeister, from the provincial leadership NSDAP in Graz, had became political commissar in the
town of Celje, and so on. Also a great majority of civil servants from department or district bureaux came from Austria, only occasionally were a few
Germans from Lower Styria appointed. The reason that in spite of a lack
of personnel in war conditions, so few Germans from Lower Styria were
used as civil servants, probably lies in their social background; most were
private businessmen who continued to devote their energies to economic
matters. Only a few were bureaucrats.

In the case of mayors and municipal officials it was a little different.
Although the heads of both civilian administrations had abolished all municipal councils elected before the German invasion, the municipalities remained the lowest rung in the administrative ladder and they authorized
the district political commissars to appoint mayors. The native Germans
were selected for this purpose, but where these were lacking (as for instance
in the Gorenjska region), Slovenians loyal to the German occupying authorities, especially those who spoke German, were chosen. But as early
as the spring of 1941 some 100 officials were sent for this purpose from Upper to Lower Styria. Indeed, the Nazis tried to appoint as mayors as many
Germans as possible. If they did not succeed, it was not for want of trying,
but due to war shortages, to the lack of suitable German bureaucrats, who
had to be mobilized for military service.

In May 1941, in the execution of their main task set by Hitler himself
in his famous instruction, "*Machen Sie mir dieses Land wieder deutsch!*" (Make
for me this land German again!), both heads of the civilian administration
founded two mass denationalizing organizations, or "societies." One was
Steirischer Heimatbund, for Lower Styria, and the other was Kärntner
Volksbund, for Gorenjska region and the Mežiška Dolina Valley. These two
organizations were supposed to be active only for a few years, until the Nazi
Party could be established in these provinces. The majority of the population from both occupied territories joined the organization voluntarily or
under political pressure (fear of deportation). The federal and the district
leaders of both organizations were mostly Austrian Germans. Only in Lower
Styria were there some native Germans represented. In Lower Styria, the
organization was headed by the former headmaster from Upper Styria and
SA Oberführer (colonel) Franz Steindl. Federal leaders were also from the
Nazi political authorities, Carstanjen and Maier-Kaibitsch. In two districts,
the political and administrative functions were headed by one person (district head, the Landrat or provincial counsellor). Because of a lack of Germans in the Gorenjska region, who were supposed to form the backbone
of the Carinthian Heimatbund, the new head of civilian administration for

Gorenjska was the Carinthian Nazi and SS-Obergruppenführer (full general) Friedrich Rainer, heading the Nazi Party organization in Gorenjska and in the Mežiška Valley as well, from 1 January 1942. Its district heads were naturally all Nazis from Carinthia. Local Nazi leaders were civil servants, teachers, gendarmes, and the like, mostly drawn from Carinthia.

Within these Germanizing organizations was a paramilitary unit (Wehrmannschaft), a variant of the SA charged with the task of military training, Germanization, and Nazification of adult men. At the provincial and district levels, this organization, too, was led by SA officers from Austrian provinces. A similar role was played by the leaders of the Nazi youth organizations (Deutsche Jugend in Lower Styria and Hitlerjugend in the Görenjska region and in the Mežiška Dolina Valley). Both Wehrmannschaft and the youth organizations were, of course, professionally linked with higher echelons of SA and youth offices in Graz and Klagenfurt, respectively.

In accordance with the program of Germanization, the heads of the civilian administration abolished all Slovenian instruction in the schools and replaced it with instruction in the German language. As early as April 1941, the Nazis founded three "action groups" with a view to taking over the schools after the occupation. The first group included fifteen district school commissioners who had been briefed for a week at Wetzelsdorf near Graz, and then, in mid-April, brought to Lower Styria. In the second group were 150 teachers, who were brought to Lower Styria on 23 April to organize German schools at the municipal level. In the third group came teachers for individual schools. Within a few weeks there no less than 860 schoolmasters and school-mistresses came from Upper Styria, joined by 80 Germans from Lower Styria and 153 graduates from teachers' colleges in Austria. Later, the number of German schoolmasters and schoolmistresses reached 1235. In Gorenjska the elementary schools, with instruction in German, were opened as late as in autumn 1941, but until then more than 600 German instructors from Carinthia and Salzburg, in two or three shifts, taught three-week courses in German language for children and adults. In September 1941, 260 teachers came from Austria to Gorenjska and remained there. The Nazis considered kindergartens and elementary schools to be the basic institutions for Germanization. The Slovenian children, of whom only 0.5 per cent understood German, according to German statistics, were Germanized, chiefly by Austrian teachers.

The heads of the civilian administration organized their bureaux in Maribor and Bled as Himmler's plenipotentiaries for the strengthening of Germanity (*Deutschtum*). The Maribor bureau was headed by the old Austrian Nazi and SA Standartenführer Erwin Seftschnig, and the Bled bureau, after September 1941, by Maier-Kaibitsch. These two bureaus were staffed mostly by SS and SA officers, including several Austrian Nazis. Let us mention only those with the highest ranks: SA Brigadeführer (major general) Alfred Persche, SS Sturmbannführer (major) Ernst Feichtinger, and Werner Delpin.

The central commands of the armed forces of the German regime of occupation–police, gendarmerie, and the regular amed forces–were located in Wehrkreis XVIII at Salzburg. Of the three higher officials Police and SS generals (Alfred Rodenbucher, Gustav Adolf Scheel, and Erwin Rösener), only Rodenbucher was an Austrian. Two Austrians, Erwin Schultz and Karl Brunner, were inspectors of the ordinary police (Schutzpolizei) and security service (Sicherheitsdienst) respectively, both holding the rank of SS-Brigadeführer (major generals). No Austrians were among the three inspectors and commandants of constabulary (Colonel Helmut Moscus and Major Generals Karl Brenner and Hans Knofe).

For persecution of antifascists and opponents of the German Reich in general and the mass deportation of Slovenes, the Main State Security Office (Reichssicherheits-Hauptamt) in Berlin set up administrative offices in Maribor and Bled and an office of commandants of the ordinary police (Schutzpolizei) and security service (Sicherheitsdienst). As early as the summer of 1941, these were to become the driving forces in the fight against the national liberation movement. Throughout the period of the occupation of Slovenia, the commandants headed the secret state police (Gestapo), the criminal police, the security service (Sicherheitsdienst), and from 1941 onward, its own resettlement staff (Umsiedlungsstab) for the mass deportation of Slovenes. Both key commandants–SS Standartenführer Otto Lurker, ironically Hitler's former jailer at Landsberg, for Lower Styria, and SS Obersturmbannführer Fritz Volkenborn both came from Austria, as did most of their staff, especially from Graz and Klagenfurt. Of the three commandants at Maribor, none was an Austrian, but of the four commandants at Bled, two were Austrians, Volkenborn and SS Obersturbannführer Alois Persterer. In the offices of both commandants, as well as in some branch offices, were several lower and noncommissioned officers of the SS of Austrian provenance. The head of the Gestapo at Bled, SS-Sturmbannführer Hans Bauer of Vienna, emerged as a fanatical opponent of the national liberation movement and the Slovenes in general. At the resettlement staff at Bled, all officials (SS officers) were Austrain Nazis, but only a few in Maribor.

As in the ordinary police, state security, and secret service, the majority of gendarmes that joined the two civil administrations came from Austria. As early as mid-April 1941, 643 gendarmes arrived, assisted by 2390 men from the SA, and 255 men from the NSKK (the paramilitary Nazi motorized corps). The gendarmes remained at some 160 stations, but the men of the SA and NSKK returned to Upper Styria and Carinthia in April and May

1941. Of the Austrian gendarmes serving in Slovenia the highest rank of major was held by Rudolf Sager (also an SS-Sturmbannführer) in Maribor and Ludwig Berger in Kranj. Among the police units arriving in Slovenia in 1941 was the police reserve company "Wien," commanded by Captain Mechels and made up mainly of Viennese. Its platoons were used for shooting hostages. From the sources now available, it is not possible to establish precisely the percentage of Austrians in other units of the ordinary police and the regular armed forces. It is, however, to be noted that some larger units arriving in Slovenia during the period 1941–1945 – the 188th reserve mountain division and the regiments of Division 438 and 418 for special assignment – had been formed on Austrian territory and were probably composed of Austrians of older classes, as were most of the frontier guard units.

Annexation

The German regime of occupation in northern Slovenia, set up during the spring of 1941, discharged its basic tasks of occupation with vigor. Those tasks exhibited certain fundamental characteristics. One of them was annexationism, the striving for speedy annexation of the occupied Slovenian territories to the German Reich, which meant the annexation to the neighboring provinces of Styria and Carinthia. This should have been effected after a thorough "cleansing" of the undesirables in the occupied territories by 1 October 1941. However, due to the unsolved problem of who was going to be the new Gauleiter of Carinthia (they were looking for a new Gauleiter NSDAP and the State Governor for Carinthia), the formal annexation was postponed for three months. This problem was solved when the Carinthian Nazi Friedrich Rainer was appointed Gauleiter for Carinthia and head of the civilian administration for Gorenjska. After the partisans successfully attacked a German police patrol on 12 December 1941, he suggested that the annexation of both provinces should be postponed for another six months. Hitler agreed, and as the conditions in spring 1942 worsened, the problem of annexation was probably no longer discussed. Nevertheless, many parts of the occupied Slovenian provinces were placed on the same level as those in the neighboring provinces.

Denationalization

The other basic characteristic of the German occupation was denationalization. The most direct and painful measures included mass deportations of Slovenians. The original plans envisaged the deportation to Serbia or elsewhere of 220,000 to 260,000 Slovenians from the German occupied territory, which meant one Slovenian in three. However, owing to war conditions and the armed uprising of the Yugoslav peoples, only 80,000 Slovenians were actually deported, mostly to Germany. In order to "cleanse" both provinces, the Nazis examined the entire population in the occupied Slovenian territories politically and racially–a unique case in Nazi-occupied countries. The racial examination was conducted by the head of the main racial and colonization bureau of the SS, Obergruppenführer (general) SS Otto Hofmann, and the head of the racial department in this bureau, SS Standartenführer (colonel) Bruno Kurt Schultz, both Austrian Nazis. Those who had received a negative racial mark were deported. After the war, they were to be sterilized. The second measure consisted in a mass colonization of Germans on the homesteads of expelled Slovenians. Settled there were mostly Germans from Kočevsko, South Tyrol, Bessarabia, Bukovina, and some from Upper Styria. However, the fact that Slovenians were not deported in the numbers envisaged, as well as the impact of the national liberation struggle, prevented the Nazis from settling the planned 70,000 Germans. Only 17,000 were actually settled. The third measure consisted in destroying everything that might have inspired, maintained, or strengthened Slovenian national consciousness (Slovenian societies and organizations, Slovenian literature, Slovenian schools, Slovenian capital) and introducing the German language in all fields (German kindergartens and schools, German youth organizations, German libraries, compulsory learning of the German language, and German as the only official language). In Lower Styria, they openly proclaimed that within three to five years the population would have to speak only German. In the drive for Germanization, especially in Lower Styria, an important role was played by the Styrian Country Union (Heimatbund), in which the leading positions were occupied by Austrians and Germans from Lower Styria.

Mobilization of Human and Material Resources

The third basic characteristic of the German occupation was the mobilization of human and material resources for the needs of the Nazi Reich. In contravention of the relevant rules of public international law, in 1942, the heads of the civil administration introduced compulsory military service for the Slovene population, gradually drafting men into both the German labor service (Reichsarbeitsdienst) and the military. In addition to bringing about increases in their military strength by a few divisions, the Nazis endeavored by this move to speed the process of Germanization and Nazification in order to prevent the population from joining the partisans. In

1943 and 1944, the mobilization of recruits for the partisans was spreading rapidly, snatching from the grasp of the occupying authorities some tens of thousands of men.

In the mobilization of material resources, the Germans were able to make good use of the industrial capacities of the Gorenjska and Mežiška Valleys above all, as well as the coalmines, wine, agriculture, and so on of Lower Styria. Since northern Slovenia was annexed to the German Reich in the economic sense, too, the German occupying authorities tried to raise the standard of living and improve the technology of industrial and agricultural production. Unemployment was ended.

Repression

The fourth basic characteristic of the German occupation was repression. Nazism, which oppressed its own nation, was even less considerate with an occupied people. In northern Slovenia, their repression found its most painful expression in the persecution of antifascists and nationally conscious Slovenes, in mass deportation, and in the suppression of the national liberation movement. No single method of terrible repression was not used by the German occupying authorities in occupied Slovenia – merciless torture of imprisoned people, mass deportations to concentration camps, mass shootings of hostages (more than 194 groups including more than 2860 hostages), burning down of entire villages (twelve villages in 1942 in Gorenjska alone) – which met the same fate as the Czech Lidice, and others. In this, there was absolutely no difference between the Nazis from Germany and those from Austria. The terrible repression reached its climax in 1942 when even some of the Nazis, such as Rösener, described the occupation policy as bloodthirsty (blutdürstig). It must be borne in mind that before 1943 every single punishable offence, political or non-political, was dealt with by the Gestapo. At Bled, political offenses were treated by a three-member police commission, including the so-called "special court" on which sat two Austrian Nazis. In Maribor (in 1942 for some time in Celje), "punishments" were decreed by the head of the Gestapo department and death "punishments" by the commandant of the security police and secret service. For common criminal offences, a criminal department headed by the Austrian Karl Swoboda, was responsible.

SOUTHERN SLOVENIA

After the surrender of Italy, the Germans extended their domination over southern Slovenia. On 10 September 1943, Hitler established the operational zone of the "Adriatic Littoral" (Operationszone Adriatisches Küstenland, henceforth referred to as the Zone) over a large territory including southern Slovenia, the Croatian Littoral, Istria, and Friuli. This Zone had nothing to do with operations since the front line was still far away in southern Italy. The name was merely a pretext for annexation, expressed especially by Nazi officials from Austrian provinces and attested to by Rainer's letter of 9 September 1943 to the German Minister of Foreign Affairs, Joachim Ribbentrop, as well as by some fragments of Goebbels' diary. Hitler, however, was somewhat restrained by Mussolini's Little State in northern Italy, the so-called Italian Social Republic at Salò, so he could not just annex outright the newly occupied territories to the German Reich. The Zone of the Adriatic Littoral, which contained a multinational population of 2 million, included the Ljubljana, Trieste, Gorica, Pula, Rijeka, and Udine provinces, and the Croatian Littoral.

On 10 September 1943, Hitler appointed Dr. Rainer supreme commissar of the Zone with headquarters in Trieste. His bureau consisted of ten administrative departments, all headed by Austrians, to the effect that some of these found themselves acting as officials of three offices, the State Governor of Carinthia, of the head of civil administration in Gorenjska, and the supreme commissar of the Zone. As provincial administrators (prefects), Dr. Rainer appointed Italians who had never occupied such posts but were natives of the Zone. In Ljubljana, it was General Leon Rupnik, a Slovene, until the mayor of that town was appointed head of the provincial administration. In the offices of the head of the provincial administration were a number of Italian officials and, in Ljubljana, Slovene officials. Because the administrators of the provinces were not German, on 22 October 1943 Dr. Rainer assigned them German advisers and district officials (three of them recalled from Gorenjska) who were all Austrians and had their offices, organized on lines similar to those of the supreme commissar in Trieste, staffed by Austrians. It must be recalled, however, that the municipal administration functioned only in towns and large townships when aided by German or traitor garrisons, whereas the countryside was generally run by administrative departments of the partisans.

It is almost certain that it was Rainer's wish that Hitler and Himmler select as Leader of the SS and Police in the Zone the notorious SS-Gruppenführer and Lieutenant-General of Police, Odilo Globocnik, an Austrian of ill-repute who, after his recall from the Lublin district of Poland, had been appointed by Himmler as Higher Leader of the SS and Police for the central section of the German front in the Soviet Union. Hitler and Himmler complied with Rainer's wish, and Globocnik set up his office in Trieste on 13 September, a day after Rainer had seen Hitler and Himmler in East Prussia. His personal assistant in Lublin and Trieste SS-Sturmbannführer (major) Ernst Lerch of Klagenfurt, and for a period of time Globocnik's adjutant was SS-Obersturmführer (first Lieutenant) Peter Count von Czernin of Vienna.

The propaganda department in Globocnik's office was headed by the Carinthian Hradetzky, until the autumn of 1943 a district official in Gorenjska. This department included two Austrian SS officers, Franz Stanglica and Hermann Pirich and worked in collaboration with the propaganda section of Ranier's office under Dr. Lapper. With the exception of Ljubljana, Hradetzky's department maintained branch offices in the main towns of the provinces. In Klagenfurt, Globocnik established a special liaison office headed by an SS officer, Reinhold Mohrenschildt, who was succeeded by another SS officer, Peter Feistritzer, an Austrian.

Except in the province of Ljubljana, which in matters of police was subordinate to Rösener, Globocnik had deputies in the provinces of the Zone. Among these were some higher officers of the SS of Austrian provenance, such as Lerch in Rijeka, SS-Brigadeführer (Major General) Karl Tauss in Gorica, and SS-Oberführer (Colonel) Hans Feil in Udine. Some Austrian Nazis were also to be found in the bureau of the commandant of the ordinary police and security service of the Zone in Trieste, which was first put in the charge of SS-Obersturmbannführer Ernst Weimann (between 1938 and 1943 head of the Gestapo office for Carinthia in Klagenfurt). During the last few months of the war the highest ranking official from Austria in the Trieste bureau was SS Sturmbannführer (major) Hans Rexeisen. The same patterns prevailed in the branch offices in the main towns of the provinces. Special mention should be made of SS Sturmbannführer Helmut Prasch, head of the branch office in Pula, the first in the Zone and perhaps in all the occupied territories to be awarded the Golden Badge, (goldenes Bandenkampfabzeichen) for his merits in fighting the partisans.

Globocnik also acted as head of the so-called economic police (Wirtschaftspolizei), which fought the black market and smuggling, together with SS Sturmbannführer (major) Fritz Wölbing, an Austrian who had been Rainer's commissioner in charge of the suppression of the black market.

Together with Globocnik, or soon after his arrival, a few score of members of the so-called Action Group Reinhard (Einsatzkommando Reinhard) descended on the Zone, especially on Trieste. They came from Lublin, where they had exterminated Jews in the camps of Treblinka, Sobibor, Bezec, all situated in eastern Poland. Until his death in June 1944, the unit was commanded in Trieste by SS-Sturmbannführer (major) Christian Wirth, to be succeeded by Dietrich August Allers, one of the leading protagonists of pseudo-euthanasia in the German Reich and some occupied territories. That unit had its prison and a camp in the former Trieste rice mill San Sabba, where Jews were kept and robbed of their possessions before being sent to Auschwitz. That unit was also employed in killing members of the national liberation movement, guarding fortifications, and so on. Among its officers were two Austrian Nazis, SS-Hauptsturmführer (captain) Franz Stangl and Franz Reichsleitner.

After the summer of 1944 Rainer and Globocnik supervised the fortifications in the Zone and outside it in northern Italy. For this task they employed some 4300 political officials from Carinthia and Tyrol and daily employed about 120,000 people of various nationalities as a kind of forced labor. In January 1945, Globocnik was decorated with the German silver cross by Hitler, mainly upon Rainer's recommendation.

Because of the adverse military situation of Germany (including a strong partisan movement in the Zone) and because of the presence of Mussolini's State in northern Italy, the Germans pursued a policy of occupation in the Zone that was less ambitious than that in northern Slovenia. In addition to seeking purely *military objectives*, such as the protection of the Istrian coast and the Gulf of Trieste to prevent the landing of British and United States forces and the suppression of the partisan movement, German policy was aimed especially at exploiting the *human and material resources* of the area. With this in mind, there was continuous recruitment of the local population into various collaborationist units to be deployed against the partisans, into the Organisation Todt (a Nazi construction enterprise), for industrial work, and the like. The German occupation authorities also used the Zone as a staging area for various fighting units that, in case of a conflict between "East" and "West" could offer their services to the latter. Before the war ended, therefore, Rainer and Globocnik concentrated in the area a fairly large number of collaborationist units drawn from other provinces of Yugoslavia as well and Cossacks from the Soviet Union.

The brutal repression practiced by the occupation authorities in the Zone was no less severe than in other Slovenian provinces. In Trieste and in other capitals of the provinces, except in Ljubljana, members of the national liberation movement were tried by special courts among whom were to be found judges from Carinthia. The judicial department within the office of the supreme commissar was headed by Paul Messiner of Klagenfurt. However, many suspects were killed without trial. (On 2 April 1944 seventy-two persons were hanged at Opčine; on 21 April 1944 fifty-two persons were hanged in the Via Ghega prison, Trieste, for instance.)

AUSTRIANS IN THE RESISTANCE IN SLOVENIA

It would be unjust if, in view of the rather substantial contribution made by numerous Austrians to the German occupation regime in Slovenia, no account were taken of the active participation by a certain number of Austrians in the national liberation struggle in Slovenia. Unfortunately, the number of Austrians in the latter was incomparably less numerous than in that of the former, reason enough for their deliberate anti-Nazi decision to be fully acknowledged.

Before 1944 only a few Austrians in the Slovenian territory chose to fight againt fascism or went so far as to join the partisans. Of those who relatively early had stood up to Nazi occupation policy in Slovenia, the case of Oskar vom Kaltenegger of Vienna must be mentioned. A member of Kut-schera's action staff at Bled, as early as July 1941, he openly contradicted his superior and, in a letter sent to the highest offices of the German Reich, openly opposed the mass deportations of Slovenes. For this reason, he was drafted into the military. When, in September 1943, Dr. Rainer invited him to accept the post of the German adviser in Ljubljana or Pula, he immediately refused the job. He stated that he did not want to cooperate with people who had ordered hundreds of hostages to be shot and deported thousands of innocent Slovenes. Thus, already the second of Kaltenegger's memoranda addressed to the Supreme Command of the German Army that is known to us eventually found its way into the archives of the Ministry of Interior.

Though nothing too definite can be said about this matter at the moment, owing to insufficient empirical evidence, it would nonetheless seem that in the spring and summer of 1942 a certain amount of dissatisfaction began to be felt among some members of the staff of the Nazi regime of occupation in Lower Styria and among some Lower Styrian Germans about the harsh measures taken in pursuit of occupation policy. This can be inferred from the uncompromising speech made by the head of the civil administration, the Austrian Dr. Uiberreither, who stated in August 1942: "For more than a year there have been men and women in Lower Styria doing nothing else but criticise. . . . There are even people who are not afraid to claim that what has happened should be described as foolish. Criticism is wrong and its breaches discipline." Carstanjen, in a similar vein, stated in his instructions to speakers at public meetings in summer 1942 that, particularly in connection with mass deportations of Slovenes, "wild rumours were rife not only in Styria, but also in other parts of Austria."

Only from 1944 onward did more information become available regarding individuals and small groups of Austrians joining the Slovenian Partisan Army. Most of these were drawn from industrial localities in Upper Styria (Leoben, Kapfenberg). Of the Austrians who joined the partisans in Lower Styria, the then official Fritz Matzner, later to be a member of the Styrian provincial government in Graz under the Second Republic, deserves being singled out, as does Dr. Wilhelm Hess, a judge. Mention must also be made of Karl Rosner, manager of the Senovo coalmine in Lower Styria, who cooperated with the partisans.

Later in the summer of 1944, Franz Honner, a member of the Central Committee of the Austrian Communist Party, arrived in the liberated partisan territory from Moscow. An agreement was reached between him and Edvard Kardelj, a member of the Central Committee of the Communist Party of Yugoslavia on increased assistance to the Austrian liberation movement, then in its infancy, as well as on the establishment of Austrian Partisan units in Slovenia. The most palpable outcome of that agreement was the formation of the first Austrian Partisan battalion in Bela Krajina on 24 November 1944. This was the largest Austrian unit, though during the last weeks of the war, two or three more Austrian battalions were established in other parts of Yugoslavia. Members of the First Austrian Partisan battalion, which fought within the Slovenian Partisan Army until the end of the war, were Austrians who had come from the Soviet Union and Austria, as well as deserters or prisoners from the German armed forces, police, or gendarme units. Later, during the last weeks of the war, a few small Austrian partisan units came into being together with the somewhat larger unit Kampfgruppe Steiermark, which operated along the border between Upper and Lower Styria within or in close support of the Slovenian partisan unit, Lackov odred. In the vicinity of this border, in the Upper Savinja Valley, a small group of Austrian antifascists was active. They acted as the Styrian and Carinthian provincial leaders of the Austrian Liberation Front (Österreichische Freiheitsfront). They distributed some leaflets calling upon the Austrians to join the partisans, but there was no mass response.

Undoubtedly, the archives of the heads of the civilian administrations, probably now stored in the provincial archives in Graz and Klagenfurt, would provide more information on various forms of antifascist resistance of the Austrians in Slovenia. But the materials there are still inaccessible and will probably remain so for decades to come. This is decidedly odd from a country that considers itself to have been the first victim of the German Nazi conquest, yet it is going to be the very last of such victims to open to the public the archives covering the period of the Second World War.

BIBLIOGRAPHY

Documents

From the archives of the Institute of the History of the Working Class Movement (Ljubljana):
    Archive Holdings of the German Authorities of Occupation in Slovenia; and Archive
    Holdings of the Commission Enquiry into Crimes of the Occupants and Their Assist-
    ants in Slovenia.

From the Berlin Document Center, in West Germany: Personalhauptamt SS, *Personalmappen der SS-Führer, die in Slowenien und im Adriatischen Küstenlande eingesetzt wurden;* Oberste SA-Führung: *Personalmappen der SA-Führer, die in der Untersteiermark und in Oberkrain eingesetzt wurden.*

T. Ferenc, *Viri o Nacistični Raznarodovalni Politiki v Sloveniji, 1941–1945* (Maribor, 1980).

Government of Yugoslavia, *Saopštenje o Zločinima Austrije i Austrianaca protive Jugoslavije i njenih Naroda* (Belgrade, 1947).

Secondary Works

E. Collotti, *Il Litorale Adriatico nel Nuovo Ordine Europeo, 1943–1945* (Milan, 1974).

T. Ferenc, "Le système d'occupation des nazis en Slovenie," in Institute of Contemporay History (Belgrade), *Les Systèmes d'occupation en Yougoslavie, 1941–1945* (Belgrade, 1963).

————, *Nacistična Raznarodovalna Politika v Sloveniji v letinh 1941–1945* (Maribor, 1968).

————, "Spomenice o nemških ozemeljskih zahtavah v Sloveniji leta 1940," *Zgodovinski časopis,* Nos. 3–4 (Ljubljana, 1975), pp. 219–46.

S. Karner, *Die Steiermark im Dritten Reich, 1938–1945* (Graz and Vienna, 1986).

K. Stuhlpfarrer, *Operationszonen "Alpenvorland" und "Adriatisches Küstenland," 1943–1945* (Vienna, 1969).

Institute of Contemporary History (Belgrade), *The Third Reich and Yugoslavia, 1933–1945* (Belgrade, 1977).

Austria Abandoned

Anglo-American Propaganda and Planning for Austria, 1938–1945

ROBERT H. KEYSERLINGK

In 1938, the march of Nazi troops into Austria seemed to symbolize all that was evil and reprehensible in the Nazi dictatorship. Yet, subsequent Anglo-American statements and actions lent themselves to varying interpretations. In the view of the British and Americans, was post-*Anschluss* Austria an occupied country or an integral part of the Nazi Third Reich? Did they continue to look upon Austrians as nationals of an occupied country or did Austrians become Germans and enemy aliens as a result of the *Anschluss*?

To resolve these questions, it is necessary to refer back to the primary Anglo-American historical record of the 1938–1945 period. A great deal has been written about Austria up to the 1938 *Anschluss*, and again after 1945, but historians have investigated only fleetingly the Great Powers' wartime plans regarding that country's postwar future. Jurists and political scientists employing published official statements until now have made most of the running. Austrian historian Fritz Fellner judged the present historical record to be so full of lacunae that it was a matter for speculation whether an independent United States policy really existed at all and whether it differed from the British position.[1] The topic is still so lacking documentary investigation that Gerald Stourzh, author of the most recent and lucid history of Austria's postwar march toward national independence, utilized a passing remark uttered by New York's Cardinal Spellman as a major source of information regarding President Roosevelt's alleged postwar intentions for Austria.[2] Concentrating largely, but not exclusively, on the United States record, this paper will attempt to demonstrate that the "occupationist" position does not represent a true view of Anglo-American attitudes towards Austria between 1938 and 1945. It was spawned by military propaganda and domestic political considerations rather than wartime political planning. In fact, the Britons and Americans upheld annexationist attitudes about Austria after 1938 and continued similarily pessimistic about Austria's postwar future as a viable, independent political state.

OCCUPATION OR ANNEXATION?

Upon being informed of the Nazis' March 1938 military action against Austria, the British promptly handed the German government an angry note briskly rejecting the use of military force to invade a small neighbor in defiance of international treaties.[3] However, the British conceded publicly that they would act as though Austria had disappeared as a State.[4] So they transformed their Vienna Legation into a Consulate-General under their Berlin Embassy and informed the Germans that henceforth German–British treaties would cover Austrian matters.[5] United States Secretary of State Cordell Hull's official statements after the *Anschluss* also stressed the Administration's dislike of the use of force in international relations.[6] The country's diplomatic notes in response to the *Anschluss* spoke of "technical" or "practical" steps regarding the status of the United States representation in Vienna and the matter of Austrian debts, which seemed to parallel those of the British.[7] Did these and subsequent wartime actions, planning, and declarations represent clear rejection of the *Anschluss* and support for an occupied Austria to be reconstituted at the conclusion of hostilities?

The problem of Austria's legal position following the *Anschluss* became a fascinating conundrum for international jurists, who frequently consulted obscure political statements and international agreements, public records, and legal judgments, only to arrive at contradictory conclusions. An "occupationist" or Stimsonian position has remained the majority view among most Western, including Austrian, experts.[8] According to this school, which based itself largely on American statements and actions, after 1938 Austria was an occupied, friendly country rather than an integral part of the enemy Third Reich. The 1943 three-power Moscow Declaration on Austria called the *Anschluss* null and void, promised postwar Austrian independence, and called for the Austrians to revolt against their Nazi occupiers. In 1945, as a result, Austria was freed by the Allies, and eventually regained its rightful independence.[9]

This "occupationist" position was reflected in an important public state-

ment on Austria issued in late 1946 by the United States government. Eighteen months earlier, Socialist Karl Renner had established a provisional coalition government in Austria with Soviet support. At first, the British and
Americans distrusted his capabilities and Soviet connections, but by the fall
of 1945, they also decided to recognize the new government. In October
1946, Austria's postwar Foreign Minister, Dr. Karl Gruber, arrived for a first
State visit to the United States. Following a long session with President
Truman, who expressed warm support for the reborn democratic Austrian
republic, Gruber was handed a State Department note, which purported
to outline American policy toward post-*Anschluss* Austria, and the Administration's support for the fledgling Second Austrian Republic. The State
Department's note advised Gruber that already in 1938 the United States
had considered the *Anschluss* null and void and that the country had never
granted the Austrian annexation by Nazi Germany de jure recognition:

> The attitude of the United States to the military occupation of Austria by
> Germany and its formal incorporation in the German Reich in 1938 was
> always guided by this consideration [strong disapproval of Nazi attempts to
> force Austria into the Reich] and by the well-established policy of the United
> States towards the acquisition of territory by force. While, as a practical mea-
> sure, the United States was obligated to take certain administrative measures
> based upon the situation created by the Anschluss, this Government con-
> sistently avoided any steps which might be considered *de jure* recognition of
> the annexation of Austria by Germany.[10]

This American "occupationist" position melded smoothly with the legal
and political doctrine which the Second Austrian Republic adopted in 1946.[11]

Adherents of a small "annexationist" school of legal positivists including Hans Kelsen, father of the 1919 republican Austrian Constitution,
disagreed with the occupationists. They conceded that the *Anschluss* had
entailed a forcible transfer of territory. But they referred to the Nuremberg
trials, which deemed the *Anschluss* the result of a belligerent act rather than
one of war.[12] This meant that technically the *Anschluss* was not a war-related
act, despite Austria's occupation for the duration of the war. The *Anschluss*
was undoubtedly illegal, agreed the annexationists. But complete de facto
Nazi control in Austria and the abolishment of Austrian State institutions
meant logically the disappearance of Austria and de jure Nazi rule. As Nazi
institutions were substituted there, Austria was de jure absorbed and annexed into the Third Reich.[13]

Yet, if the Allied and Austrian positions were officially occupationist,
why was the United States Department of State's official record of American
diplomatic rulings, *The Digest of International Law*, so ambiguous about
Austria? This authoritative multivolume *Digest* was published in several suc-

cessive series since the beginning of the century. The 1940s series adopted a surprisingly veiled phraseology and inexplicable silence concerning Austria.[14] It refused to celebrate negative United States' reaction to the *Anschluss* as a sterling example of the Stimsonian doctrine, or the sanctity of international law, merely reproducing the ambiguous 1938 diplomatic notes regarding Austria without analysis or comment. Many relevant sections of the *Digest*, as those on de facto and de jure governments, failed to mention Austria at all. After the war and the 1946 note to Gruber, one might have expected that a new edition of the *Digest of International Law* would now reflect an unmistakably Stimsonian position on Austria. However, when the State Department issued its revised *Digest* in the 1960s, the outlines of the Austrian picture emerged even more indistinct than two decades earlier. Both occupationists and annexationists were quoted at length without editorial comment.[15] What then was the true position on this tragic event?

UNITED STATES' REACTIONS TO THE *ANSCHLUSS*

Even before the *Anschluss* took place in March 1938, the Anglo-Americans had shifted toward a more positive view of Hitler's ambitions. If the British followed an appeasing strategy toward Hitler, the new American diplomatic style of isolationism resulted in a "hands off" posture toward Europe's difficulties.[16] It seemed hardly likely that these two countries would stand up strongly for Austrian independence. A reluctance to irritate Hitler unnecessarily prevailed in both countries. In both instances, new men in influential positions heralded a milder course vis-à-vis Hitler and the Nazis, whatever personal revulsion they might have shared regarding the Nazi style of international politics.[17]

The 1937 internal reorganization in the American State Department's European divisions markedly resembled the better-known concurrent shift in Great Britain's Foreign Office. At that time, the State Department was deeply divided over policy and in a stage of transition. Led by Under-Secretary of State Sumner Welles, a Roosevelt appointee and crony, its directors attempted simultaneously to mute anti-Nazi and anti-Soviet policies of the past by dissolving into two independent West and East European Affairs divisions into a new unit under new personnel. George Kennan, then a member of the East European Affairs Division, bitterly attacked this divisional unification plan as a purge instigated directly by the White House and expedited by the President's men in the Department under Sumner Welles.[18] Jay Pierrepont Moffat, a "realist" about international affairs who since Roosevelt's election had played a growing role in the department, was named chief of the new Division of European Affairs. Moffat had decided that the wisest policy for the United States to adopt would be to placate Hitler or at least remain neutral and not to anger him with useless symbolic gestures.[19] Now, Moffat saw his task in preserving the United States from entanglements in European problems. "My personal perception," he wrote in November 1937, "is to prevent at any costs the involvement of the United States in hostilities anywhere, and to that end to discourage any formation of a common front of the democratic powers."[20]

When the tragedy of the *Anschluss* took place, pressure on Moffat and his fellow realists came from department "idealists" such as Assistant Under-Secretary of State George Messersmith not to recognize the *Anschluss*. But the State Department realists managed to procure a three-week delay before putting out an American note.[21] They argued that Americans should wait to see how Great Britain would react to the *Anschluss* and its results before officially committing themselves. The realists released a few rhetorical generalities to the public in order to preempt the anticipated storm of indignation from idealists both inside and outside the department but refrained from reacting directly to the *Anschluss*.[22]

In the course of these departmental discussions, it seemed a sound idea to solicit the opinion of ex-Secretary of State Henry Stimson, creator of the so-called Stimson Doctrine of nonrecognition of acts of international aggression. Should Stimson publicly support nonrecognition of the *Anschluss*, the Administration would find it very difficult to resist such a pressure. Many people approached Stimson to speak out against the *Anschluss*, but to their consternation, he reufsed.[23] Hull consulted him, too, and was surprised to hear that Stimson firmly opposed nonrecognition of the *Anschluss*.[24] Rehearsing the origins of the doctrine attached to his name, Stimson denied that it held any legal character. The nonrecognition option should be exercized only to galvanize domestic public opinion by appealing to its better nature in support of specific policies the administration enthusiastically supported. In the *Anschluss* question, however, Stimson could discern no adequate reason for rallying public opinion. He had never been convinced that the Austrian Republic was viable. It seemed to him that the United States should not undertake any practical or even moral measures to save the country. He also certified that he would have nothing to do with any public protest movements against the Administration if it refused to follow the path of nonrecognition. Stimson frankly advised Hull against nonrecognition of the *Anschluss*. "I could hardly see how it [nonrecognition] fits," he concluded.[25]

Eventually, departmental realists and idealists worked out a compromise of sorts, which in fact represented a victory for recognition and the realists. Moffat prepared the final text of the United States, diplomatic notes of 5 April 1938 as well as the press statement covering their public issuance. He stressed the United States' noninvolvement in European affairs and underlined this opinion by lunching publicly on that day with a member of the German embassy. His personal record of that meal indicated a friendly meeting, without any sign of friction over Austria. Moffat noted that his German counterpart was in "fine fettle," because he had just been asked to return to accompany Hitler on his upcoming visit to Mussolini.[26] When the United States government spoke officially on Austria through Moffat's State Department diplomatic notes, three weeks after the *Anschluss*, its position closely resembled that of the British.[27] With smug satisfaction, the British noted that the American notes did not differ substantially from their own. In fact, the British maintained, they themselves had at least issued an immediate protest about the *Anschluss*, whereas the Americans remained silent, and then engaged in empty rhetoric to disguise their real sentiments. "The United States are usually behind us in these matters. . . . But they usually contrive to persuade the public that they are in fact doing much better than we are!"[28]

Despite the American notes' calculated ambiguities, they repesented de jure recognition of the *Anschluss* similar to that of the British. Hull confidentially admitted as much to the Attorney-General, when he later wrote him: "The Government of the United States recognizes that Austria ceased to exist as an independent state and has been incorporated into the German Reich and that Germany exercises *de jure* sovereignty over the territory of the former Republic of Austria."[29] However, the State Department was careful not to say so openly in public, preferring to leave the impression that indeed it had rejected the *Anschluss*.

ENEMY ALIENS

Both Great Britian and the United States treated Austrians throughout the war in a similar fashion as well. Although they enacted administrative rulings that purportedly distinguished between German and Austrian exiles, in fact, Austrians remained classified as German citizens and enemy aliens until after the war.[30] This rigid wartime legal classification of Austrians stemmed in part from British and American recognition of the *Anschluss*, but the emigrés' own bitter in-fighting did nothing to convince their Allied hosts to change their minds on this issue. British and American authorities formally categorized Austrians as German nationals, and therefore as enemy aliens, because the German nationality law of July 1938 declared Austrians to be German citizens. In the interval before the war, the British applied administrative restraints or concessions equally to German and Austrian refugees and, once war started, interned some Austrians for being danger- ous enemy aliens of German nationality.[31] In 1944, a leading Foreign Office legal adviser, acting as the principal government expert before the court, successfully argued for the retention of all Austrians in the German national and enemy alien category and the continued internment of dangerous Austrians. As a result, until 1945, Austrians in Great Britain could legally be interned without a trial if they were considered a danger to the war effort.[32]

Neither government cared to get involved too deeply with the splin- tered and quarreling Austrian emigré groups, especially in the wake of a few ineffectual attempts to unite them or to cooperate with them. As the Foreign Office wrote to its overseas representatives in 1941: "Generally speaking, although there can be no question of official recognition for any group, HMG has no objection to the formation of such associations among the anti-Nazi Austrians and welcome any tendency to closer unity among Ger- man and Austrian emigrés."[33] Emulating the British, the Americans at first adopted a benevolent public stance toward Austrian emigrés, convinced that they would rally around the Allied war effort as a group. All too soon, they learned about the disappointing British experiences with the feuding Austrian groups and gained their own in this regard.[34] Following their own attempt to set up an Austrian battalion within the United States Army, which failed because of faulty American execution as well as bitter disputes within the Austrian emigré community, the Americans, too, gave up on the Austrian emigrés as useful tools in the war effort. Two full-scale investi- gations of these emigrés reached the conclusion that they were hopelessly riven according to prewar political divisions and that no useful anti-Nazi Austrian front or representative committee could be formed in the United States.[35]

As a result, the United States adopted a similar policy regarding the status of Austrian refugees in the United States. Once the United States entered the war, the American authorities interned several hundred Ger- mans and Austrians, including some of Jewish background, as dangerous enemy aliens. They also interned in the United States groups of Austrian refugee Jews, who were sent from American protectorates such as Panama for safe-keeping.[36] In 1942, a few interned Austrians sought to have the courts release them from internment as enemy aliens. In each case, the State Department contested these legal challenges, thereby demonstrating its de- termination to uphold the Austrians' status as enemy aliens. Although in both cases the government did not appeal negative court decisions, they did so in order not to loose the principle that Austrians were enemy aliens and could be interned as such if dangerous.[37]

POSTWAR PLANNING

The Western Allies initiated the postwar planning process with surprising speed. Postwar planning was taken very seriously, and the main lines for Austria's postwar future were drawn quite early in the war, long before the Allies began work on the German problem. Wartime planning for the postwar era took place as a series of historical seminars that considered the repercussions of the peace of 1919.[38] The West did not fight World War II in order to engender radical social or political change but to rescue prewar Europe and rebuild it on a sounder basis.[39] As a result of their inter-war and World War II studies, these planners sharply repudiated some of the basic principles that had guided the adoption of the 1919 peace formula, especially the assumption that nationalism was the historically based legitimate organizing factor to guide political life in Central and Southeast Europe. Instead, they formulated regional or federative solutions, which would neutralize the evil effects of nationalism. Many planners were specialists in Southeast Europe who viewed Austria with special concern as a key to the solution of Southeast European or Danubian problems of nationalism.[40]

The 1941 Foreign Office paper on Austria and Southeast Europe established British policy. It decreed that the region's countries including Austria form a multinational Danubian State after the war. The proposal, if adopted, might counter not only a possible German threat but resist eventual Soviet pressures as well.[41] By the time the War Cabinet adopted the document almost unchanged as official policy two years later in 1943, the Soviets' military situation had improved dramatically, but British Austrian policy remained firm.[42] By mid-1943, separately evolved American and British policies regarding the formation of federated Southeast European units to include Austria mirrored each other remarkably. "The policies of the American and British governments in respect to the Austrian question," a State Department memorandum comparing both countries' Austrian policies asserted, "appear to be generally in agreement."[43] Seen against this background, the October 1943 Moscow Declaration on Austria must be seen not as a political but as a propaganda document.

THE 1943 MOSCOW DECLARATION ON AUSTRIA

Since the beginning of World War II, propaganda and political warfare, morale busting of the enemy, had enjoyed a much larger role than in World War I. Hitler and the West had learned the wrong lessons from that war,

namely that modern mass-based conflicts were lost or won by the strength
of morale behind and at the front. Both sides believed almost mystically
that military action, coupled with appropriate propaganda campaigns and
economic blockade, could fatally injure an enemy's morale and lead to internal collapse. It was a commonly held view in 1939 that the Germans and
Austrians had collapsed in 1918 because of broken morale, that Hitler had
risen to power through his and his henchman Goebbels' mastery of political
and rhetorical symbols, and that Hitler's military victories were the result
mainly of exceedingly clever propaganda aimed at undermining his opponents' self-confidence. Thanks to the 1943 Allied military victories in Italy
and the Soviet Union, Anglo-American political warriors and the Combined Chiefs of Staff (CCS) believed that the hoped-for breakdown in German morale could now be realistically envisaged. The United States Joint
Chiefs of Staff (JCS) and CCS spent more time discussing the military effectiveness of political warfare in 1943 than ever before. Each CCS meeting
that year discussed the topic in some detail. The year 1943 may be seen
as the high point in the Allies' faith in psychological warfare.[44]

The Western military believed that the Germans would retreat in Italy
to behind the Alps and attempt to hold fast on the Eastern front. Breaching
Hitler's Fortress Europe would not be possible by purely military means.
Further German defeats coupled with crumbling morale in Germany and
the satellites were mandatory. Given this background, effective German
military resistance would melt away.[45] During the summer of 1943, reports
began to circulate regarding shrinking German morale, mutinies in German
ranks, and growing despair on the home front.[46] The British suggested that
it was high time to exploit the enemy's deteriorating morale.[47] For the first
time, British and American political warriors agreed that now German morale teetered on the edge.[48] Among all the links in the German strategic
chain, Austria had long been identified as one of the weakest. Austria appeared to be the ideal target for Allied political warfare.[49]

By the beginning of 1943, the British political warfare organizations,
Special Operations and Political Warfare Executives, concurred that political
warfare activity ought to focus on Austria. Without seeking Foreign Office
assistance, they cooperated in January 1943 in devising a propaganda declaration regarding Austria. This document served as the first draft of the
Moscow Declaration on Austria, issued later that year.[50] In view of the hid-
den running battle between political "regulars" at the Foreign Office and the
political warfare "irregulars," two conflicting papers on Austria were published in early 1943. Most accounts have tended to blur these two papers
into each other, because they were formulated at about the same time. As
a result, their respective divergent political and propaganda purposes were
not fully understood.[51] Foreign Office officials were crystal clear in their

own minds that one paper represented official political planning, whereas the other dealt with the more occult world of political warfare. One was accepted by Cabinet as the official British political line in June 1943, the other was merely as a draft propaganda declaration still to be completed and designed for maximum military effectiveness. The political paper on Austria soberly recommended against the re-establishment of an independent postwar Austria, the draft propaganda paper promised as much as possible to the Austrians, including independence. The latter's real purpose was to foment a revolt against the Nazis in Austria. It represented a psychological attack on the enemy.[52]

United States diplomats and military officers immediately understood the difference between the British policy paper and the draft propaganda declaration on Austria. They realized that one reflected the official long-term political line and that the other was a political warfare-military exercise. On the political question, they agreed wholeheartedly with the British estimate of Austria's political future.[53] At the same time, they also approved of a ringing public Austrian declaration for purposes of pursuing political warfare. The British suggestion that such a declaration be formulated during the upcoming Foreign Ministers' conference in Moscow was accepted as sound. Finally, the Americans suggested a few minor changes on the latter draft, and this amended version was what the British submitted to the Moscow conference.[54]

That the Austrian declaration had military rather than political intentions may be seen in the various countries' draft agendas for the October 1943 Moscow meeting. If indeed the Austrian declaration had been meant as one of the Allies' first political war pronouncements, it would have loomed much larger than it did in these agendas and would have been raised under the heading of the Danubian rather than the German question. The fact was that Austria appeared on the agendas under the German rubric, leading later scholars to the incorrect conclusion that Austria was discussed as part of the German, presumably political, question.[55] In fact, the Moscow conference debates concerning Germany were not political but military in nature, about how best to defeat and occupy Germany.[56]

It was still too early in the war, most participants held, to discuss postwar territorial matters. At the conference itself, the British tried in vain to broach this vital and touchy area. In line with Foreign Office planning and War Cabinet policy, Eden informed his opposite members that the disappearance of the Austro-Hungarian Empire had left the small successor states abandoned in a virtual limbo, which could only be cured by a postwar pooling of their resources.[57] However, in view of Hull's reticence, and Molotov's solitary driving concern that the western Allies open a second front, this initiative failed. Roosevelt would not have permitted his weak Secretary of

State to decide such important matters, whereas Molotov for his own reasons appeared lukewarm to the initiative. Molotov expressed reservations
about Eden's federative proposals, without completely turning them down.[58]
The Foreign Ministers tentatively recommended that Austria's postwar
borders be those of 1937; but in the same breath, they declared that this
did not represent a political decision, because Austria's postwar status was
"a matter which should come within the purview of the general settlement."[59]

The Anglo-American draft for a powerful Big Three statement declaring the *Anschluss* null and void, promising Austrian independence, and calling for an Austrian uprising was given to the conference's drafting committee even before Austria arose for discussion at the conference.[60] The United
States delegate on this committee was State Department legal adviser Green
Hackworth, who was certainly no supporter of an independent postwar
Austria.[61] Only toward the end of the conference did the topic of Austria
arise in connection with deliberations on the defeat and occupation of Germany, under item 7 of the agenda, "Treatment of Germany and Other
Enemy Countries in Europe." A final version of the declaration on Austria
was then presented to the conference during discussions on winning the
war against Germany. The Foreign Ministers accepted it quickly and without discussion. The declaration was considered so unimportant in any
meaningful political sense that it was not even mentioned in the reports
filed to Washington by the United States ambassador in Moscow, Averell
Harriman, concerning the talks carried on under this agenda item.[62] Nor
did his final report, which included the text of the Austrian declaration,
contain any comment about it.[63]

American Cabinet members understood that the declaration on Austria had only military rather than political value. While Hull was in Moscow, his deputy Stettinius briefed Cabinet members that the Foreign Ministers would not make any political decisions in Moscow.[64] Stimson agreed
that any such exercise would be both foolish and premature. Conditions
now demanded military decisions and cooperation, and it was far too early
for political negotiations. Before political matters relating to the postwar
period could be taken up, the war had to be won and the economic future
studied. He was sure that the current talks about Austria had nothing to
do with politics. On 28 October he wrote in his diary, "They are all thinking of cutting Austria away from Germany. Well, if they restored Austria
to her position in which she was left by the Versailles arrangements twenty-
five years ago, why [sic] they would reduce her again to a non-sustaining
state, *and they don't seem to have that in mind at all* [author's emphasis]."[65]
Hull revealed as much confidentially to the press upon his return to Washington. He admitted "off the record" that the declaration had been published solely for propaganda purposes. It was certainly not official adminis-

tration policy. Hull continued that [off the record] there were definite manifestations in Austria against the German Nazis which might prove very embarrassing for them, and that some of his associates had felt that some way of intimidation could be helpful in a practical way."[66]

The Moscow Declaration on Austria did not, however, as hoped, spark an Austrian revolt and a quick end to the war. In fact, in 1944 the war moved away from Austria, and Austria's importance fell dramatically in allied military and political priorities. Allan Dulles' Bern Office of Strategic Services (OSS) office judged in January 1944 that the declaration had had "no profound effect within the country." Austrians were discouraged by the apparent lack of clarity and detail that plagued Allied postwar policy for Austria. They were also bewildered as to what was expected of them, despite tight Nazi control, and wondered how to extricate themselves from the trap in which they found themselves.[67] The United States government agreed with the British that the Moscow Declaration on Austria possessed no legal or political character. Austria had not become an ally of the West like other occupied countries as a result of the declaration. It remained in fact and in law an integral part of the Nazi German empire. Austrians remained Germans cooperating in Nazi Germany's war against the United States.[68]

FROM PROPAGANDA TO POLICY

However, during 1944, mainly for domestic electoral reasons, Roosevelt wished to be seen as taking greater interest in a continued United States presence in postwar Europe. In May, he accepted limited American participation in the occupation of Vienna, a decision that led at the end of the year to Roosevelt agreeing to a United States zone of occupation in Austria. These actions formed part of Roosevelt's successful campaign to create a bipartisan foreign policy and remove the threat of foreign policy as a tool in the Republicans' hands. Roosevelt prodded Hull to convince Republican Congressional leaders of his determination to act quickly and decisively to guarantee the peace after the war, by force if necessary.[69] Thus, in August 1944, Senator Arthur H. Vandenberg, leading Republican member of the Senate Foreign Relations Committee, was informed that the United States had, of course, always rejected the *Anschluss* and supported a free and independent Austria. "This position was never considered to constitute *de jure* recognition of the *Anschluss* however. The attitude of the United States was constantly guided by its policy of refusing to recognize acquisitions of territory by force in violation of treaty obligations."[70] For the first time as well, Hull applied the 1941 Atlantic Charter provisions to Austria, a sover-

eign State that the Germans had occupied illegally and that would be liberated and re-established as a State by the victorious Allies. Clearly, the vague-
ness of previous Administration statements concerning Austria now stood
Hull in good stead.

Subsequent American political planning for an occupied Austria adapted
itself to this policy reversal but, at the same time, continued to demonstrate
little faith in Austria's viability as an independent country.[71] A major September 1944 State Department planning report asked, What had the Moscow Declaration really meant? It complained that "The Moscow Declaration poses the Austrian question without specifying a clear-cut solution."
Nothing in it prohibited a federative union between Austria and other
neighboring States, or even a future *Anschluss* with Germany.[72] Austrians
were also disappointed with the Allies, who had not clarified any of the
burning issues since the Moscow declaration "to point the way more clearly
to a constructive solution of the Austrian problem." The idea of Austrian
independence, as formulated in the Moscow Declaration and interpreted
in Hull's letter to Vandenberg, did not appeal to the planners.[73] A January
1945 OSS document, based upon State Department opinions and com-
missioned by the War Department, still insisted that the Allies were free
of any firm commitments regarding Austria's future.[74]

United States officials were aware that they were adapting past events
to current concerns when the government claimed nonrecognition of the
Anschluss and faithful American support for an independent Austria. By
late 1946, as experience with the Soviets in Germany and Austria accumu-
lated, they admitted confidentially that this historical revisionism regarding
Austria was also useful in countering Soviet intransigence over Austria.[75] This
new view was adopted for contemporary political ends, not from any deep
faith in Austria's viability. Regarding American recognition of the new
Austrian government, the State Department conceded that the decision was
purely a political exercise, devoid of long-term commitments, and could
be reversed at a later stage: "The expession 'recognizes' is a word of art with a
technical legal connotation, but here also the act of recognition is determined
by the political decision."[76] The practicality of this position became increasingly evident in time, as the wartime Allies quarreled concerning Austrian
reparations and other occupation questions. If Austria was indeed a liberated,
independent State with its own constitutional laws, reparations could not
be legally demanded of such an Allied-approved sovereignty and Soviet
demands for veto power over new constitutional laws could be bypassed.[77]
As well, Austrians could hope to be absolved of any responsibility for the
Nazi era. As a 1948 Washington military government directive stated, "Your
Government, therefore, does not consider the Austrian Government re-

sponsible for the acts of the Nazi regime or its representatives during the effective period of the *Anschluss*."[78]

Although for practical reasons in public the British toned down their Austrian plans at the end of the war, they remained less forgiving toward the Austrians than the Americans, refusing to adopt the exculpatory "occupationist" approach. As a legal expert in the Foreign Office wrote in late 1944: "There is no doubt that from a legal point of view, Austria is enemy territory."[79] The British did not deviate from this position even after the war. In fact, Great Britain and most of the Dominions remained legally at war with Austria until 1948.[80]

AUSTRIA AT LOOSE ENDS?

Before 1943, Anglo-American policy toward Austria, if somewhat ambiguous, appeared positive. In that year, the Allies seemed to express the view that Austria was an occupied country to be liberated at the end of the war and to promise Austrian independence. Despite some ambiguity on the issue of war guilt in the Declaration, if Austria was an occupied country the expectation could be that Austria would not be associated with the crimes of the occupying Third Reich. But the truth was that British and American officals remained deeply skeptical throughout the war that any distinction could be made between Austrians and Germans. Austrians had shown themselves unable to administer their own affairs before 1938, appeared to accept the *Anschluss*, and became Germans as a result of it. Ausrians were found, like Germans, in the Nazi Party and the German army. Throughout the war, "dangerous" Austrian exiles were interned in Great Britain and the United States on the same basis as Germans. The same surrender applied to both, even though the terms were to be administered more lightly in Austria. Both Germans and Austrians were to be subjected to Denazification.

The 1943 Moscow Declaration emerged not as political policy but as part of a wartime propaganda campaign. Anglo-American postwar planning denied Austria's right to obtain preferential treatment on the basis of the past Austrian record and indicated a consensus that in the long run an Austrian State would be precarious and dangerous to European security. Therefore, the Western Allies insisted, even past the end of the war, on a federative long-term solution for Austria. They saw the need for some temporary postwar Austrian administrative structure, but Austria's future lay within a southeastern or Danubian federation, or perhaps even as part of a democratic Germany.[81] As the Americans laid down in January 1945, "independence alone, however, would not be an adequate basis for Austria's future."[82] In July 1945, the British still advocated a Daunbian federation into which Austrians should be placed. Only such an organization would ensure political and economic stability in the area and therefore protect Great Britain's vital communication routes to the eastern Mediterranean.[83]

That the propagandistic 1943 Moscow Declaration on Austria came to be interpreted in a political sense had to do with domestic American politics and the subsequent unexpected falling-out of the wartime Big Three. The year following the issuance of the Declaration, its favorable view of Austria's past and future prospects was publicly advocated by the Roosevelt Administration for domestic purposes and became frozen into place in the ensuing Cold War period. The British appeared to adopt this same policy after the war, whereas Austrians understandably employed the Western occupationist interpretation to legitimize and underpin their new State.

NOTES

1. Fritz Fellner, "Die aussenpolitische und völkerrechtliche Stellung Österreichs 1938 bis 1945. Österreichs Wiederherstellung als Kriegsziel der Alliierten," in E. Weinzierl and K. Skalnik (eds.), Österreich. Die Zweite Republik, vol. 1 (Graz, 1972), especially pp. 53–79. One of the best recent accounts is Manfred Rauchensteiner's Der Sonderfall. Die Besatzungszeit in Österreich 1945 bis 1955 (Graz, Vienna, and Cologne, 1979), pp. 15–32.

2. Gerald Stourzh, Geschichte des Staatsvertrages 1945–1955. Österreichs Weg zur Neutralität (Graz, Vienna, and Cologne, 1980), p. 4.

3. Great Britain, Foreign Office, Documents on British Foreign Policy 1919–1939, 3d series (London, 1949), pp. 21–23, Viscount Halifax to Neville Chamberlain, 11 March 1938. Robert E. Clute, The International Legal Status of Austria 1938–1955 (The Hague, 1962); and Stephan Verosta, Die internationale Stellung Österreichs. Eine Sammlung von Erklärungen und Verträgen aus den Jahren 1938–1947 (Vienna, 1947).

4. Great Britain, The Parliamentary Debates. The House of Lords, vol. 108, 16 March 1938.

5. Clute, pp. 97, 98.

6. United States Department of State, Press Releases, vol. 1, no. 133, 19 March 1938.

7. Secretary of State Cordell Hull to the German Ambassador, Washington, 5 April 1938, United States Department of State, Foreign Relations of the United States (hereafter referred to as FRUS), Diplomatic Papers 1938, vol. 2, pp. 483–84; also quoted in Robert Langer, Seizure of Territory: The Stimson Doctrine and Related Principles in Legal Theory and Diplomatic Practice (Princeton, 1969), p. 162.

8. Quincy Wright, "The Denunciation of Treaty Violators," American Journal of International Law 32 (1938):526; Herbert Wright (with the exiled Austrian Professor Wilibald Plöchl), The Attitude of the United States Towards Austria, Congress, House documents 10845 and 477, (Washington, 1943); H. Wright, "The Legality of the Annexation of Austria by Germany," American Journal of International Law 38(1944):621. Note the interchangeability of the two words occupation and annexation at this early stage of the discussion. The distinction between the two terms only arose later; see Clute; and Langer.

9. Langer, ibid.; K. Marek, Identity and Continuity of States in International Public Law (Geneva, 1969); S. Verosta. For an indication of a recent shift away from this principle, see

L. T. Galloway, *Recognition of Foreign Governments. The Practice of the United States* (Washington, 1978).

10. Quoted in United States Department of State, *Digest of International Law*, Marjorie M. Whitman, (ed.), (Washington, 1960–), vol. 5, pp. 900–901; Karl Gruber, *Between Liberation and Liberty. Austria in the Postwar World* (New York, 1962), pp. 80–83.

11. Austrian Federal Ministry for External Affairs (*Bundesministerium für Auswärtige Angelegenheiten*), letter to the author of 30 March 1981, Nr. 517.0017/1–11, 1/81. This letter also referred the author for more information to Stephan Verosta's *Die internationale Stellung Österreichs 1938–1945*; Karl R. Stadler, *Austria* (New York, 1971), p. 256; Felix Ermacora, *Österreichische Verfassungslehre* (Vienna and Stuttgart, 1970), pp. 63–69; Ludwig Jedlicka, "Verfassungs- und Verwaltungsprobleme," Institut für Österreichkunde, *Die Entwicklung der Verfassung Österreichs vom Mittelalter bis zur Gegenwart* (Wien, 1970), p. 136; Gerhard Stourzh, "Die Regierung Renner, die Anfänge der Regierung Figl und die Alliierte Kommission für Österreich, September 1945 bis April 1946," *Archiv für österreichische Geschichte* 125(1966):339–41.

12. International Military Tribunal, *Trial of the Major War Criminals Before the International Military Tribunal, Nuremberg, 14 November 1945–1 October 1946*, vol. 1, pp. 291, 309, and 318–19.

13. H. Lauterpacht, *Recognition in International Law* (Cambridge, 1947), pp. 87–97; Hans Kelsen, *Principles of International Law* (New York, 1952), pp. 260–64; M. M. Whiteman, *Digest of International Law*, vol. 2, 60 ff, 754–65, 785–86.

14. United States Department of State, *Digest of International Law* (Washington, 1940–), Green H. Hackworth (ed.), vol. 1, pp. 127–28.

15. Whiteman, vol. 1., 327 ff.

16. Arnold A. Offner, *American Appeasement. United States Foreign Policy and Germany, 1933–1938 (New York, 1976), pp.* 234–38; Martin Gilbert, *Britain and Germany Between the Wars* (London, 1966), pp. 70–71; Donald C. Watt, "Appeasement: The Rise of a Revisionist School?" *The Political Quarterly* 35(1965):191–213, and "Roosevelt and Neville Chamberlain: Two Appeasers," *International Journal* 28(1973):185–204.

17. Robert Dallek, "Beyond Tradition: The Careers of William E. Dodd and George S. Messersmith," *South Atlantic Quarterly* 66(1967):233 ff.; and Kenneth Moss, "George S. Messersmith: An American Diplomat in Nazi Germany," *Delaware History*, 54:236–49.

18. George F. Kennan, *Memoirs, 1925–1950* (Boston, 1967), pp. 66, 83–84; and Frederic L. Propas, "Creating a Hard Line Towards Russia: The Training of State Department Soviet Experts, 1927–1937," *Diplomatic History* 8(1984):225–26.

19. Nancy H. Hooker (ed.), *The Moffat Papers. Selections from the Diplomatic Journals of Jay Pierrepont Moffat, 1919–1943* (Cambridge, 1956), pp. 97 f., 146; diary entry of 31 January 1938, *Diplomatic Journal*, J. Pierrepont Moffat Papers, Harvard University.

20. Hooker, p. 183.

21. Diary entry of 14 March 1938, Moffat Papers.

22. Hull's press statement of 15 March 1938, United States, Department of State, *Press Releases*, vol. 1, no. 133; diary entries of 15 and 17 March 1938, Moffat Papers.

23. J. H. Holmes, C. H. Strong, G. Macdonald, and R. M. Schwartz to Stimson, telegram of 21 March 1938 and Stimson's reply, *Stimson Papers,* Box 27, file 9, Yale University.

24. Ibid, vol. 28, diary entries of 24 March and 4 April 1938.

25. Ibid., diary entry of 24 March 1938.

26. Diary entry of 5 April 1938, Moffat Papers.

27. Beatrice and Travis B. Berle (eds.), *Navigating the Rapids, 1918–1971. From the Papers of Adolf A. Berle* (New York, 1973), p. 169; and diary entry of 18–24 April 1938, Moffat papers.

28. R minute, 27 July 1942, "Attitude of the United States to Austria," Public Records Office, London, England (PRO), Foreign Office (FO) 371, 30942.

29. Hull to Attorney General, 27 April 1939, National Archives, Washington (NA), RG 59, United States Department of State, 763.72113/2838.

30. There were 10,000 Austrian refugees in Great Britain and about 40,000 in the United States. Helene Maimann, *Politik im Wartesaal* (Vienna, 1975); F. Goldner, *Das einsame Gewissen. Die österreichische Emigration 1938 bis 1945* (Vienna and Munich, 1972).

31. Lord Halifax, Washington, to Foreign Office, London, 1 March 1942, PRO, FO 371, C2281/1304/18.

32. Ibid., C10210/30/3, Bennett minute, 16 October 1944, and a long file on this question before the High Court in 1944.

33. Ibid., C4523/2951/18, C11816/321/18, Anthony Eden, secret Foreign Office print, "Free Austrian and Free German Movements," 18 June 1941.

34. Berle, memorandum of 1 January 1942, copy in Berle Papers, Franklin D. Roosevelt Library, Hyde Park (FDR), Berle Diary, 213.

35. Federal Bureau of Investigation, "Austrian Activities in the United States," May 1943, FDR, Official Files (OF), p. 23; OSS report, 16 June 1943, NA, RG 59, 863.01/782; ibid., 863.01/822, Berle memorandum, 6 January 1944.

36. Ibid., 740.00115EW39/4158, Rabbi Yasipol, Nashville, to Hull, 9 October 1942.

37. Ibid., 740.00115EW39/7423, Solicitor-General Fahy to Hull, 29 September 1943; ibid., 740.00115EW39/7960, Flournoy memorandum, 27 August 1943.

38. G. Stanley, "Great Britain and the Austrian Question," (unpublished Ph.D. diss., University of London, 1973), pp. 85 ff.; R. Wagnleitner, "Grossbritainnien und die Wiedererrichtung der Republik Österreich," (unpublished Ph.D. diss., University of Salzburg, 1975), pp. iv ff.

39. D. Stafford, *Britain and European Resistance, 1940–1945* (London, 1980), p. 34.

40. In the United States, the Council on Foreign Relations began postwar planning in 1939. Regarding the similar role in Great Britain of the Royal Institute of International Affairs (RIIA), see A. J. Toynbee to Geoffrey Gathorne-Hardy, 31 March 1938, and Gathorne-Hardy's reply of 1 April 1938, Toynbee Papers, Box 39, Bodleian Library, Oxford University; and for his wartime Foreign Research and Press Service (FRPS) see FRPS Committee, 1st meeting, 7 May 1941, annex 1, and Toynbee, "Why FRPS Has Been Set Up," RIIA Council, meeting of 13 May 1942, appendix A, RIIA, 2/1/6b and 2/1/7b, RIIA Archives, St. James's Sq., London; also R. H. Keyserlingk, "Arnold Toynbee's Foreign Research and Press Service, 1939–1943, and Its Post-War Plans for South-east Europe," *Journal of Contemporary History* 21 (1986):539–58.

41. Toynbee to R. Makins, enclosing Laffan's draft FRPS memorandum on Austria, one copy for Eden, 2 October 1941, PRO, FO 371, 26538.

42. The 1943 War Cabinet decision read: "There was general agreement that we should aim at a Central European or Danubian Group centered in Vienna . . ." PRO, CAB 65/34, WM 86(43), 92–93, 218 of 25 May 1943.

43. Memo of 10 March 1943, NA, RG 59, General Records, Office of European Affairs, p. 11.

44. Minutes of CCS for 1943, FDR, Map Room (MR), 27.

45. CCS, "Defeat of the Axis Powers in Europe," 17 May 1943; Joint Staff Planners, "Comparison of Various Post-Huskey Operations in Relation to Allied Air Capabilities," JCS, no. 223, 3 July 1943; Joint Staff Planners, no. 438, "Estimate of the European Situation, 1943–1944. European-Mediterranean Area," 4 August 1943: United States Joint Chiefs of Staff (JCS) Records, European Theatre, University Microfilms, reel 1.

46. For instance, "Germans Are Deserting," *New York Times,* 20 September 1943; "U-Boat Mutinies Reported Growing," ibid., 4 October 1943.

47. J. Wheeler-Bennett's 54-page paper, "On What To Do With Germany," 30 June

1943; and "The Dismemberment of Germany," 13 October 1943, PRO. FO 371, 34459, C6683 and C12101.

48. Joint Intelligence Committee, "Morale in Germany," 22 September 1943, pp. 18–23, FDR, *Hopkins Papers*, 227.

49. OSS report, "Austria: Violent Anti-Nazi Sentiment Developing," 11 December 1943, FDR, MR, 72.

50. Political Warfare Executive's proposed Austrian propaganda statement and Foreign Office negative reactions, January 1943, PRO, FO 371, 34464, C321, especially 13 and 20 January 1943.

51. For instance, Stourzh, pp. 2–3.

52. O. G. Sargent to Lord Cranborne, Dominions Office, 9 October 1943, PRO, FO 371, 34466/C11389, C14085; Harrison memorandum, 28 November 1943.

53. Secret memorandum of October 1943 with draft declaration, and Cannon memorandum "Evaluation of the British Foreign Office Secret Paper 'The Future of Austria,'" 23 September 1943, NA, RG 59, 863.014/29.

54. State Department draft of the declaration and comments, 9 October 1943, initialled by eight divisions, NA, RG 59, 863.014/29.

55. Fritz Fellner, p. 70; Stourzh, p. 4. "The idea of an Austrian declaration, which was in reality a middle- and southeast European declaration . . ." Rauchensteiner, p. 19.

56. For the President: Tri-Partite Conference Moscow 1943; Minutes and Conversations, NA, RG 59, *Notter Papers*, 18.

57. W. Averell Harriman, and Elie Abel, *Special Envoy to Churchill and Stalin, 1941–1946*(New York, 1975), pp. 236, 244.

58. Minutes of 25 October 1943, Minutes and Conversations, Moscow 1943, NA, RG 59, European Advisory Commission; Harriman to Under-Secretary of State, 25(?) October 1943, FDR, MR, 35.

59. Protocol of 1 November 1943 meeting, item no. 7, FDR, Hopkins Papers, p. 7.

60. Clark Kerr, Moscow, 28 October 1943, PRO, FO 371, C12794/321/18; Stanley, p. 121.

61. 25 October minutes, Tri-Partite Conference of Foreign Secretaries, Moscow, NA, RG 59, European Advisory Commission, p. 29.

62. Harriman to State Department, 25 October 1943, FDR, MR, p. 32.

63. Harriman to State Department, 31 October 1943, FDR, Special Files, 32; also FRUS, 1943, pp. 65, 152–54.

64. Diary entry of 13 October 1943, Stimson Diary, 44/192.

65. Diary entry of 28 October 1943, ibid., 44/231.

66. Department of State, Memorandum of Press and Radio Conferences no. 105, 15 November 1943, NA, RG 43, World War Two Conferences, 1A.

67. OSS report from Bern, 19 January 1944, FDR, MR 73.

68. Hackworth memorandum for Hull, 23 November 1943, NA, RG 59, 863.01/814.

69. Dallek, *Franklin D. Roosevelt and American Foreign Policy,* pp. 487–488.

70. Hull to Senator Vandenberg, 26 August 1944, NA, RG 59, 863.01/8–1844.

71. Ibid., RG 59, OSS, Research and Analysis #2111.1, 6 January 1944, "The Revival of Austrian Political and Constitutional Life Under Military Government."

72. H194, "The Future Status of Austria," NA, RG 59, Notter Papers, 155, and FDR, PSF, 32A.

73. Ibid.

74. Office of European Affairs, no. 10, "Treatment of Austria," 11 January 1945, NA, RG 59.

75. R. W. Flournoy, legal division, to Hackworth, 17 April 1945, NA, RG 59, 711.63/4–

1745; 863.00/5–145, L. A. Merchant memorandum, 12 January 1945; secret telegram from Dean Acheson to the Americal legation in Vienna, 19 November 1946.

76. Ibid., 863.00/10–1846, Coburn Kidd memorandum to Hickerson and Riddelberger, 10 August 1946.

77. Ibid., 711.63/7–2148; R. T. Yingling, legal division, to A. Gould, 9 August 1948.

78. F. T. Williamson memorandum to OE, ADO, DRE, "Policy and Information Statement–Austria," 18 June 1948, State Department Archives, Austrian desk, 1945–1949.

79. P. Deen minute, October 1944, PRO, FO 371, 39003/13387.

80. For instance, the New Zealand opinion in June 1946 was: "In our view, Austria has not deserved, nor can she legally claim, a treaty more favorable than that applied to other active supporters of Germany and even Italy. She will, in any case, fare better than Germany herself because settlement will be earlier and more lenient." New Zealand Minister of External Affairs to the Canadian Acting Secretary of State for External Affairs, 12 June 1946, DEA, 7-D(s); see Robert H. Keyserlingk, "Policy or Practice: Canada and Austria, 1938–1949," in Martin Kovacs (ed.), *Roots and Realities Among Eastern and Central Europeans* (Edmonton, 1983), pp. 25–30.

81. OSS, R&A, no. 2111.1, "The Revival of Austria's Political and Constitutional Life Under Military Government," 6 January 1944, and OSS, R&A Branch, "Implementation Under Military Government of the Moscow Declaration on Austria," 14 August 1944; OSS, R&A Branch, "A Civil Affairs Guide for Austria and the Applicability of the German Guides." NA, RG 59, OSS, R&A Branch.

82. Ibid., Office of European Affairs, 10, "Treatment of Austria," 11 January 1945.

83. Overseas Reconstruction Committee report, 11 July 1945, PRO, FO 371, C3940/134/3.

III

SPÖ, ÖVP, and the "Ehemaligen":

Isolation or Integration?

ANTON PELINKA

The two major Austrian parties, the Sozialistische Partei Österreiches (SPÖ) and the Österreichische Volkspartei (ÖVP), literally Austrian People's Party, have both been hostile to Nazism from their inception in 1945.[1] Both parties were organized by men and women who had been persecuted by the Nazis and whose political views, formed while resisting Nazism, were based on Socialist and Christian democratic values that contrasted sharply with the antihumanist, vulgar Darwinist roots of Nazism. They were moreover imbued with a will to reconstruct Austria and, in the process, to turn the German occupation, euphemistically called the *Anschluss*, into a never-to-be repeated episode of the past.

Those political foundations must be analyzed in the light of their regrouping process, defined explicitly in the ÖVP as the "remake," which took place immediately before, during, and shortly after the liberation of eastern Austria in the wake of hastily concluded agreements.[2] The desire to form a government of political unity that would include the Communists, primarily in order to comply with the conditions imposed by the Moscow Declaration of October 1943, implied cogently both the substance and the organization of the political parties. To present a credibly anti-Nazi Cabinet, likewise, the creation of credible parties was necessary.

This starting position, which must be seen alongside the starting positions of the Second Republic, has remained basically unaltered during the subsequent four decades. The changing attitudes of the parties toward

245

ANTON PELINKA

Nazism, similarly, has to be interpreted alongside the development of the Second Republic and its political system. A kind of neutralization and partial integration of Nazi elements began to assume shape in place of an unalterably rigid, diplomatically motivated retreat from Nazism and in place of an unconditional opposition to Nazism and its phenotypes. Whereas these two major parties never turned Nazi, they proved ready to modify their attitudes in that respect for a variety of reasons, in the course of which their initial attitude of principle was transformed into an attitude of pragmatism.

THE INTEGRATION OF NAZI ELEMENTS

The thesis just outlined will be verified on several levels with respect to the integration of prejudices, institutions, styles, and targets of Nazism. In that sense, it will be possible to see Nazism in the present context as a general political attitude, as well as an authoritarian personality structure impregnated with specifically Austrian peculiarities.[3] This paper will take as the main theme underlying the analysis of the elements of Nazism the phenomenon of authoritarian personality structure in its concrete Austrian form.

The partial integration of Nazi elements into the two major parties, noticeable also on the level of political institutions, applies especially to some organizations having explicitly nonpartisan objectives yet infiltrated by clearly identifiable Nazi ideas.[4] Both the Kärtner Heimatdienst (Carinthian Home Service) and the Österreichischer Kameradsschaftsbund (Austrian Veterans Association) are cases in point. Yet, not only members of the rank and file, but also representatives, and in some provinces even leading politicians, of SPÖ and ÖVP have taken an active part within those two organizations. Though the latter cannot be labeled Nazi on that account, in terms of their entire range of activities, they may be regarded as partially Nazi. Thus, the former organization is acting within the tradition of the Austrian brand of German nationalism by emphasizing "Germanity" (*Deutschtum*). By opposing the demands of the Slovene ethnic group under the State Treaty of 1955, the Kärtner Heimatdienst goes along with the tradition that ranges from a German-nationally interpreted ideology of Abwehrkampf (defensive struggle against Yugoslavia), a pro-Nazi policy in Carinthia, and demands for the evacuation of Slovenes, to the outright denunciation of Carinthian Slovenes as "alien" and "communist."[5] The Österreichischer Kameradsschaftsbund, whose primary objective is the creation of an umbrella organization for former soldiers, similarly cannot be classified as Nazi in the first instance. However, the political engagement of some of its members, in playing down the nature of aggressive Nazi war while putting forward military ideas, renders that organization partially Nazi, too.[6]

The participation of respectable politicians from the two major parties in organizations like these may be justified on grounds of the moderating influence they claim to exert toward a democratic consolidation. However, the secondary effect of such acts is to enhance the presentability and deepen the impact that those mass organizations may produce. The dilemma of the two major parties in regard to Nazism is brought out into the open. Since Nazi attitudes, Nazi objectives, and Nazi organizations exist, the two parties have the choice of either isolating those independently existing phenomena by firm objection or integrating them by a policy of neutralization. Both major parties have opted for a strategy of integration from 1949 onward at the latest. Beyond that, Nazi elements have been partially integrated also in terms of political style. Politicians of the major parties have tended to refer to Nazism by way of utterances, gestures, or actions. Various anti-Semitic utterances made by ÖVP politicians have taken the form of this type of partial integration.[7] Yet, behavior of this type, following the specifically Christian Social kind of anti-Semitism clearly conflicts with the ÖVP's party platform. In spite of this, no known case exists where any of the individual politicians concerned had to suffer disadvantages of any kind in their party. Anti-Semitic messages of this nature evidently were not visited by any adverse consequences in the case of those politicians. Public statements that were interpreted, at least by observers and commentators, as beckoning gestures toward Ehemalige and as substantial concessions to Nazism occasionally affected SPÖ politicians, too.[8] Like the general tolerance of the ÖVP in connection with the anti-Semitic utterances of some of its officials, the behavior of the Socialists, as evidenced in their conduct concerning the controversy in respect of the SS background of former FPÖ chairman Friedrich Peter, could be construed as a policy aiming at the partial integration of Nazi patterns.

By evading pragmatically distinct and rigid limits bearing on this question recognizable by any voter, the two major parties see a chance of expanding, of winning over groups and attracting ideas normally beyond their traditional orbit. To be sure, partial integration of Nazism in those repects is not to be seen as the straightforward adoption of Nazism—that would be quite inconceivable—but merely as attempts to neutralize it by such tolerant behavior signifying a partial acceptance designed to attract additional voting groups.

THE TURNING POINT

The turning point between the policy of the consistent isolation from Nazism, pursued by the two major parties since 1945, and the policy of partial integration occurred somewhere betwen 1945 and 1949 and came in two stages, exemplified by (1) the outbreak of the Cold War, and (2) the voting enfranchisement of formerly disenfranchised Nazis.

The policy of isolating Nazi interests and conceptions was closely linked to the overall policy of uniting all antifascist forces. This antifascist alliance formed the foundation of the Declaration of Independence signed on 27 April 1945 by the three founding parties. It forms the basis of the tripartite coalition within Renner's provisional Cabinet, as well as of the continued coalition after the transition to constitutional normality in Figl's Cabinet after the autumn election of 1945. This coalition also reflected the then prevailing international situation and the interest of the new Austrian Republic in adapting to it. Although the Austrian Communist party was reputed to be the Soviet instrument for the manipulation of Austrian domestic policy, the alliance of the two major parties—"Western" oriented in a general sense with regard to their conception of democracy—with the Communists must be seen as the domestic political sequel to the Allied fight against Nazi Germany. The termination of that specific international situation with the advent of the Cold War was again reflected in Austria's domestic policy, reaching its climax in the withdrawal of the Communists from the cabinet in 1947, and in the allegedly Communist-inspired general strike attempted in September and October 1950.[9] From now on, the Communists were, if anything, seen as the primary political foe by the two major parties, a fact that manifested itself inter alia in a lessening of open hostility toward Nazism. At that point, the latter had clearly lost its function as the overall adversary uniting all other political forces. From then onward, both international and domestic political considerations combined to produce a "purged" type of Nazism, which would not be too inconsistent with the new constellation of external and internal political forces.

In 1949 tendencies of that sort were, if anything, reinforced, when the two major parties had to take into account the voting potential of the 600,000 formerly disenfranchised Ehemaligen in connection with the forthcoming parliamentary elections. A situation was arising where, in view of the small margins that separated them, the two parties were compelled to court the votes of the Ehemaligen (see Table 1). At that juncture, the ÖVP began to apply a policy of partial integration. Their "Junge Front" was to attract Ehemalige to the ÖVP by extolling "war heroes," while various more or less discreet talks with former Nazi representatives were motivated by a desire of seeing their followers integrated into the ÖVP. The so-called Oberweis talks with its protagonists Julius Raab, Alfred Maleta, and Taras Borodajkewycz turned out to be the most publicly debated contacts of this type.[10]

In pursuing a subtle policy of abandoning its formerly firm stand in favor of the isolation of the Nazis, the SPÖ began backing an independent party for the new voters of that type, its aim being to prevent the strengthening of the ÖVP through the votes of the Ehemaligen. Oskar Helmer, Minister of the Interior and representative of the right wing within the SPÖ, indirectly became the promoter of the Verband der Unabhängigen (League of Independents) capable of absorbing the votes of the majority of the Ehemaligen in 1949.

Yet, neither the VdU nor its successor, the Freiheitliche Partei Österreichs (Austrian Freedom Party) succeeded in turning itself into the natural political home of the vast majority of Ehemalige. In the event, the bulk of the Ehemaligen was absorbed by both ÖVP and SPÖ in the name of the healthy desire, which must at all times underly the vital constituents of a democratic multiparty system to compete for the votes of all those entitled to cast one.

THE POLICY OF INTEGRATION

Having absorbed portions of the Nazi electoral reserve army in their voting bases, the two major parties continued their policies of integration by concentrating on the VdU and its successor, the FPÖ. In the course of several phases of policy connected with the two parties' shifting interests, the latter have been trying again and again to attract the VdU and FPÖ to the centers of the decision-making processes. The general idea of these efforts was to excel the rival party in gaining the benevolence of the Party of the "German-national" camp to obtain the votes of most floating Ehemalige. Several stages in the development of the new policy can be discerned. First of all, there was an ÖVP attempt in 1953 to form a coalition in conjunction with the VdU, which failed on account of general Socialist opposition as well as fierce resistance by Theodor Körner, Austria's President. Second, there was an electoral alliance of ÖVP and FPÖ, when they supported the identical nominee for President. Third, the SPÖ thought fit to pressure the ÖVP by considering, or pretending to consider, a "small coalition" with the FPÖ in the wake of the Habsburg crisis of 1963, an attempt, which miscarried due to the weakening position of Franz Olah, the main exponent of this tactic, within the councils of the SPÖ. Finally, there emerged the well-known formation of a "small coalition" between SPÖ and FPÖ between 1983 and 1987, which witnessed the Reder-Frischenschlager incident. To this list must be added a number of local coalitions between either of the two major parties and the FPÖ against the third, as occurred in Bregenz (Vorarlberg), where it was directed against the ÖVP, and in Graz and Klagenfurt, where the SPÖ was the target.

TABLE 1
VOTING BEHAVIOR OF THE EHEMALIGEN
Comparison of the Numbers of *Minderbelastete* National Socialists Admitted to the 1949
Nationalrat Elections with the Number of Votes Cast for the Various Parties

Province		Valid Ballots 1. 1949 2. 1945 3. difference	Number of Votes per 100 Votes cast for the various parties 1. 1949 2. 1945 3. gain or loss				Number of Votes divided according to party 1. 1949 2. 1945 3. gain or loss			
			OeVP	SPOe	KPOe	VdU	OeVP	SPOe	KPOe	VdU
Vienna 1–7 Bezirk	1. 2. 3.	1,142,160 889,324 252,836	35 35 0	49 57 -8	8 8 0	7 7 +7	401,854 310,803 91,051	565,440 508,214 56,226	89,710 70,307 19,403	79,149 – +79,149
Lower Austria 8–11	1. 2. 3.	886,095 704,878 181,217	53 55 -2	37 40 -3	6 5 +1	4 – +4	464,854 384,214 80,640	330,631 284,430 46,201	48,459 36,234 12,225	39,385 – +39,385
Upper Austria 12–16	1. 2. 3.	597,523 469,027 128,496	45 59 -14	31 38 -7	3 3 0	21 – +21	268,578 276,676 -8,098	184,042 179,975 4,067	18,574 12,376 6,198	124,520 – +124,520
Salzburg 17	1. 2. 3.	172,060 126,390 45,670	44 57 -13	34 39 -5	3 4 -1	18 – +18	75,212 71,631 3,581	57,752 49,965 7,787	5,759 4,794 965	31,919 – +31,919
Tyrol 18	1. 2. 3.	226,497 153,571 72,926	56 71 -15	24 27 -3	2 2 0	17 – +17	127,728 109,360 18,168	53,820 40,857 12,963	3,705 3,354 351	39,377 – +39,377
Vorarlberg 19 Bzk.	1. 2. 3.	101,837 69,707 32,130	56 70 -14	19 28 -9	2 2 0	22 – +22	57,402 48,812 8,590	19,262 19,189 93	2,435 1,706 729	22,287 – +22,287
Styria 20–23	1. 2. 3.	653,755 493,861 159,894	43 53 -10	37 42 -5	5 5 0	14 – +14	280,719 261,358 19,361	244,482 205,779 38,703	29,617 26,724 2,893	94,991 – +94,991
Carinthia 24	1. 2. 3.	248,834 179,260 69,574	34 40 -6	41 49 -8	4 8 -4	20 – +20	83,801 71,265 12,536	101,356 87,572 13,782	10,002 14,451 -4,449	51,247 – +51,247
Burgenland 25	1. 2. 3.	164,972 131,336 33,636	53 52 +1	40 45 -5	3 3 0	4 – +4	86,700 68,108 18,592	66,739 58,917 7,822	4,805 4,311 494	6,398 – 6,398
All Austria	1. 2.	4,193,733	44 5	39	5	12	1,846,581	1,623,524	213,066	489,273

Province	New Voters 1. Total 2. Minderbelastete 3. Non-NS		Percent NS in total electorate	New Voters 1. percent NS 2. percent non-Nazi	1. Ballots of new voters per party 2. Percent of new voters per party			
					OeVP	SPOe	KPOe	VdU
Vienna 1-7 Bezirk	1.	252,836	9.9	44.7	91,051	56,226	19,403	79,149
	2.	112,945		55.3	36.0	22.2	7.7	31.1
	3.	139,891						
Lower Austria 8-11	1.	181,217	8.7	42.6	80,640	46,201	12,225	39,385
	2.	77,196		57.4	44.4	25.5	6.7	21.7
	3.	104,021						
Upper Austria 12-16	1.	128,496	12.8	59.3	-8,098	4,067	6,198	124,520
	2.	76,225		40.7	-6.5	.3	.5	96.9
	3.	52,271						
Salzburg 17	1.	45,670	17.0	63.9	3,581	7,787	965	31,919
	2.	29,190		36.1	7.8	17.1	2.1	69.9
	3.	16,480						
Tyrol 18	1.	72,926	18.9	58.6	18,168	12,963	351	39,377
	2.	42,762		41.4	24.9	17.8	.5	54.0
	3.	30,164						
Vorarlberg 19 Bzk.	1.	32,130	15.9	50.5	8,590	93	729	22,287
	2.	16,225		49.5	26.7	.3	2.7	69.4
	3.	15,905						
Styria 20-23	1.	159,894	13.7	55.9	19,361	38,703	2,893	94,991
	2.	89,441		44.1	12.11	24.2	1.8	59.4
	3.	70,453						
Carinthia 24	1.	69,574	15.8	56.5	12,536	13,782	-4,449	51,247
	2.	39,326		43.5	18.0	19.8	-6.4	73.7
	3.	30,248						
Burgenland 25	1.	33,636	8.7	42.6	18,592	7,822	494	6,398
	2.	14,343		57.4	55.3	23.3	1.5	19.0
	3.	19,293						
All Austria 1-25	1.	976,379	11.7	51.0	244,354	188,626	38,809	489,273
	2.	497,653		49.0	25.0	19.3	4.0	50.1
	3.	478,726						

Source: Max E. Riedlsperger, *The Lingering Shadow of Nazism: The Austrian Independent Party Movement since 1945.* (New York, 1978). The term *Minderbelastete* refers to the large majority of former members of the NSDAP who were reinstated in their political rights before the 1949 election.

THE STRUGGLE FOR VOTES

The first actions against the Nazis were decided on and carried out jointly by all parties. After the Declaration of Independence, the Nazi Party was banned and a war crimes law put in the statute books. In 1947, the Denazification Act was passed unanimously in Parliament, after its preparation had provoked some internal discussions, both between and within the two major parties. Yet, by all appearances, ÖVP and SPÖ were willing to act jointly in this matter. A common political front existed against the Nazis both in the provisional government of State Chancellor Renner and within Figl's "grand" coalition, even after the withdrawal of the Communists from the government in 1947.[11] The policy of integration, which became a noticeable reality after 1949 at the latest, destroyed that anti-Nazi unity, giving way to a policy of competing for the votes of the Ehemaligen. This was exemplified in the attitude of the Socialist Party, which in 1945 had still been canvasing for the idea of exchanging Austrian prisoners of war detained in the Soviet Union for Austrian Nazis at liberty at home. For this, the Socialists were reproached by the ÖVP during the 1949 electoral campaign, with the result that the former desisted from the pursuit of that tactic, contenting itself instead with competing for their votes.[12] This type of competition, never advertised during the following decades, was brought out into the open only by chance in some spectacular cases connected with the persons of Borodajkewycz, Peter, and Reder.

Borodajkewycz

This ehemaliger historian was a member of the Catholic Cartellverband (CV) which used to act as a major recruiting instrument of politicians for the Christian Social Party (predecessor of today's ÖVP) before 1932, for the Patriotic Front, roof-organization of the Dollfuss-Schuschnigg regime between 1934 and 1938, as well as for the ÖVP during the postwar period. Borodajkewycz, expelled from the latter for his Nazi past, remained on good terms with leading politicians of that Party, a contact of which the ÖVP was to use during the Parliamentary electoral campaign of 1949. Borodajkewycz turned out to be one of the most important participants in the Oberweis talks convened by prominent representatives of the ÖVP, among them Julius Raab and Alfred Maleta, which were intended to prevent the formation of the League of Independents (VdU) by making timely concessions to the Nazis in order to obtain the majority of their votes for the ÖVP. Borodajkewycz was rewarded for his part in the affair by being given the Chair of Economics at the Hochschule für Welthandel (later named the Economic University), a branch of the University of Vienna. In 1965 he made some anti-Semitic remarks that provoked a protest march, which in turn resulted in a neo-Nazi counter demonstration. In the course of the latter, a former inmate of a Nazi concentration camp was killed by a neo-Nazi in Vienna. Borodajkewycz was subsequently suspended as a university professor and ultimately compelled to take early retirement.[13]

Peter

Friedrich Peter was a former Waffen-SS officer who became a leading member of the FPÖ on its foundation in 1956, succeeding Anton Reinthaller as its chairman in 1958. Peter's official biography stated that he had discharged his "duty" "at the front" during the Second World War. In 1975, Simon Wiesenthal showed that the SS unit in which Peter served was mainly concerned with the large-scale slaughter mostly of Jewish civilians behind the front. Yet, Peter continued to be Party chairman. His most prominent defender at that time was SPÖ chairman Bruno Kreisky who, while protecting Peter, launched harsh and personal attacks against Wiesenthal.[14]

Reder

Walter Reder had joined the fighting Nazi Austrian Legion, based in Bavaria, before 1938, for which he was stripped of his Austrian nationality. In 1944 he was the Waffen-SS officer responsible for the mass murder of the civilian population of the Italian village Mazzabotto, for which he was sentenced to death by an Italian court. That penalty was later commuted into a life-sentence. Despite the fact that Reder was stateless, the costs for his defence counsels were paid by the Republic of Austria, and without being able to lay a valid claim to it, he was granted Austrian nationality in 1956. Also without any legal basis to a claim, he obtained further financial aid from Austria, even from official institutions. On returning to Austria after his premature release from prison in 1985, Reder was officially welcomed by Minister of Defense, Friedhelm Frischenschlager.[15]

These three cases, not unrepresentative of many more of the kind, show up the methods as well as the consequences of the policy of integrating the Nazis into the major parties. Borodajkewycz' background marked him as middleman between the Christian-conservative camp and Nazism. Reder obtained the support of both major parties, as well as that of the Catholic Church, but the events surrounding his return produced an outcry both at home and abroad, considerably affecting the political health of the "small coalition" government composed of SPÖ and FPÖ. Peter had been one of the architects of the "small coalition." Having opened the FPÖ for such a coalition with the SPÖ, he was defended in public by Kreisky. The case was typical of the length to which the two major parties were prepared to go in search of political favors extended by the FPÖ.

All three cases resulted in injury to Austria's international reputation and adversely affected her further democratic development. The case of Borodajkewycz resulted in the first civilian death springing from domestic conflict since 1945. The case of Peter ruined the credibility of the honorable anti-Nazi tradition of the SPÖ. That of Reder moved Austria into the center of international criticism.

Ehemalige were promoted by both parties into prominent positions from 1949 onward. Reinhard Kamitz, ÖVP Minister of Finance between 1951 and 1960, was an Ehemaliger. The first all-Socialist Cabinet of 1970 was joined by five Ehemalige.[16] Although it must be said that neither Kamitz nor the Ehemalige in the first Kreisky Cabinet owed their appointment to the mere fact of their former Nazi status, they were appointed in spite of it. Their appointments must be seen as simply the logical consequence of a policy of "normalization" by way of "integration."

INTEGRATION

Any political force opposed to democracy calls for response on the part of existing democratic parties. Basically there are two strategies by which Nazism could be conquered, at least in theory. There was first the strategy of isolation, pursued by all parties after 1945, and there was the strategy of integration, chosen by both major parties since 1949. The clear ascendance of the latter strategy over the former one can be explained in terms of the sheer size of the reservoir of Nazi votes, membership of the former Nazi Party at 700,000 being roughly comparable to that of each of the two major parties of the Second Republic. The NSDAP (Nazis) of Austria was a large organization, well rooted in Austria's political culture. Though barred from overt political activity qua a Nazi Party as a consequence of Nazi Germany's military defeat in the Second World War, the members of that camp survived the war to re-emerge after a brief period of repression.

Notwithstanding the possibilities of a principled policy of enlightenment, a political party focusing on the next election day and straining every nerve to win tends to prefer the gain of nondemocratic voters (who may be covered by a wafer-thin film of conversion) to an arduous process of transforming radical antidemocrats into reliable democrats.[17] The major Austrian parties chose to succumb to the former temptation in the main

TABLE 2
ANTI-SEMITISM AND PARTY PREFERENCE, 1982

Note: The question asked of a representative sample of people was, "It is not by pure chance that the Jews have been persecuted so many times in history. At least to a certain extent, are they responsible for that themselves?"

Political Preference	Stark Anti-Semitism	Not Anti-Semitic
SPÖ	16%	24%
Keine	20%	22%
ÖVP	25%	19%
KPÖ	27%	22%
FPÖ	42%	12%

Changes between 1969 and 1982: Stark Anti-Semitism

Political Preference	1969	1982
SPÖ	18%	16%
Keine	27%	20%
ÖVP	30%	25%
KPÖ	22%	27%
FPÖ	55%	42%

Source: John Bunzl and Bernd Marin, Antisemitismus in Österreich (Innsbruck, 1983), appendix. Number of people questioned: 1969, N=1712, N=2142.

and inter alia to deny electoral victory to the rival party–all according to the good rule book of democracy. In this way, both ÖVP and SPÖ were willing to absorb any potential voters regardless of the several dangers of seeing their own ideas and interests adversely affected in the long run.

SPECIFICALLY AUSTRIAN FACTORS

The tendency toward integration resulting from the functional requirements of the democratic system has been strengthened by the presence of factors having specifically Austrian roots. As an indicator of the presence of Nazi attitudes, anti-Semitism still exists within the major parties–not as a result of any Nazi intellectual influence but as a consequence of conceptions that existed, and especially within the Christian Social conservative camp, long before the rise of Nazism to prominence (Table 2). The events occurring in the course of the presidential electoral campaign of 1986 merely confirm this.

By way of a summary, it ought to be noted that, far from being Nazi, the two major political parties of Austria do not display any immanent tendencies toward Nazi ideology. Shallow judgment motivated by current events that make use of superficial criteria such as "fascist" or "neo-Nazi" are missing out on the far more complex political realities. SPÖ and ÖVP are both major democratic parties that, to be sure, have developed a foggy relationship towards Nazism in their political practice.

This is why the attitude of the major parties toward Nazism represents a real problem for democracy in Austria. The ill-defined position adopted in those matters by the two prominent parties—parties that play important roles in the decisions in all the major political areas of the State, the provinces, and the municipalities—has the effect of rendering racist, anti-Semitic, and other Nazi attitudes fairly harmless and trivial. The failure of those parties to set their face firmly against "commonplace fascism" for the sake of serving their short-sighted self-interest, endows that same "commonplace fascism" with a prestige that, in a democracy, should not be enjoyed by an enemy of that same democracy.

NOTES

1. M. A. Sully, *Political Parties and Elections in Austria. The Search for Stability* (London, 1981).

2. W. B. Bader, *Austria Between East and West, 1945–1955* (Stanford, 1966), especially pp. 11–25.

3. P. Aycoberry, *The Nazi Question. An essay on the interpretations of National Socialism (1922–1975)* (New York, 1981).

4. See especially John Bunzl and B. Marin, *Antisemitismus in Österreich* (Innsbruck, 1983).

5. H. Haas and K. Stuhlpfarrer, *Österreich und seine Slowenen* (Vienna, 1977); L. Flaschberger and A. F. Reiterer, *Der tägliche Abwehrkampf. Kärntens Slowenen* (Vienna, 1980).

6. For further details concerning the various organizations cited, including Österreichischer Kameradschaftsbund and Kärtner Heimatdienst, see H. Exenberger's entry, "Organisationen," in Dokumentationsarchiv des Österreichischen Widerstandes, *Rechtsextremismus in Österreich nach 1945* (Vienna, 1979), pp. 132–72.

7. Bunzl and Marin, pp. 67–69.

8. See especially M. van Amerongen, *Kreisky und seine unbewältigte Gegenwart* (Graz, 1977).

9. Bader, pp. 155–83.

10. L. Reichhold, *Geschichte der ÖVP* (Graz, 1975).

11. For the whole process of Denazification in Austria, see D. Stiefel, *Entnazifizierung in Österreich* (Vienna, 1981); S. Meissel, K.-D. Mulley, and O. Rathkolb (eds.), *Verdrängte Schuld, verfehlte Sühne. Entnazifizierung in Österreich, 1945–1955* (Vienna, 1986).

12. N. Hölzel, *Propagandaschlachten. Die österreichischen Wahlkämpfe, 1945–1971* (Vienna, 1974).

13. H. Fischer (ed.), *Einer im Vordergrund: Taras Borodajkewycz. Eine Dokumentation* (Vienna, 1966).

14. Van Amerongen, pp. 96–107.

15. W. Hacker, "Die Einbürgerer sind unter uns," in W. Hacker (ed.), *Warnung an Österreich. Neonazismus: Die Vergangenheit bedroht die Zukunft* (Vienna, 1966), pp. 141–46.

16. Van Amerongen, pp. 48–56.

17. This mechanism is extensively described by A. Downs, *An Economic Theory of Democracy* (New York, 1957). For the mechanism used by the erstwhile "grand coalition," see H. P. Secher, "Coalition Government: The Case of the Second Austrian Republic," *American Political Science Review* 27 (1958):791–808.

FPÖ

Liberal or Nazi?

MAX E. RIEDLSPERGER

I n September, 1986 a prominent Austrian news magazine carried a caricature of the newly elected chairman of the Freiheitliche Partei Österreichs (FPÖ), Jörg Haider, in Carinthian folk dress, standing before a painting showing another, brown-shirted, Haider wearing a red armband with a partially obscured black insignia on a circular white field.[1] Brown-shirt Haider is shown strangling his liberal predecessor, Norbert Steger, representing at least the caricaturist's answer to the question posed by this essay. Two months later, on November 23, Austrian voters handed both major political parties stunning losses in parliamentary elections and increased the parliamentary representation of Haider's party by one-half. This election was triggered by the success of the German-nationalist wing of the Party in capturing leadership from the group that, for the first time had brought the Party into a government coalition and that recently promulgated the Party's first ideological and decidedly liberal program. In a year when the election of Kurt Waldheim to the Presidency reawakened the world to memories of Austrian Nazism, the long dormant question posed in this paper becomes a matter of current concern.

THE HISTORICAL BACKGROUND
OF THE "NATIONAL-LIBERAL" CAMP

To the casual reader, unfamiliar with the historiography of Austrian politics, the juxtaposition of liberal and Nazi in reference to the same party might appear ludicrous. Liberalism and Nazism after all hold anti-thetical views of the place and role of the individual in the State. The question is legitimate, however, because there are sufficient indications of both political inclinations in the history and current political stance of the FPÖ to warrant an interpretative answer to the question, FPÖ: liberal or Nazi?

Attempts to place this party and its predecessors on a linear political spec-trum have always been confounded by the fact that the so-called national-liberal camp embraces a broad political span and is, or has been, home for liberals, ex-Nazis, undoubtedly some neo-Nazis, and conservative as well as liberal German nationalists. The historical reasons for this unlikely jux-taposition were explained by the Austrain historian Adam Wandruszka as part of his now traditional division of Austrian political, social, intellectual, and cultural life into three *Lager*, or camps: the Christian-Social-conservative, the Socialist, and the German-national-liberal.[2] The militant flavor of the *Lager* concept was entirely justified by the hostility among the camps dur-ing the inter-war period. In 1945, however, only two of the traditional camps were viable. Socialists created the Socialist Party of Austria (SPÖ) and the former Christian Socials formed the new Austrian Peoples Party (ÖVP). Recognizing that the *Lager* mentality of the inter-war years had been largely responsible for the failure of the First Republic, both parties agreed to share responsibility for government and formed the first in a series of coalition governments that ruled Austria until 1966. The German-national-liberal camp was so discredited by its complicity in Nazi terrorism and its enthusiasm for the *Anschluss* that no immediate attempt was made to revive its legacy. Vestigial remains of *Lager* politics remained in elections when party politi-cians could revert to old-style electioneering tactics to mobilize their voters, but once the electoral game was over, a return to cooperation was guaran-teed. By 1966, however, party lines were blurring as Austria moved from *consociational democracy*, in which political élites cooperate in a fragmented political environment, to a *centripetal democracy*, in which the government could be entrusted to whichever set of élites was elected by the people.[3] Ab-solute commitment to a particular party has declined, and increasingly vot-ers are influenced by political personalities, immediate economic problems, scandals, and other current events that attract the attention of the tele-vision cameras and the tabloids. Increasingly there is a relatively large reser-voir of voters that can be tapped by either major party or by a third party capable of mobilizing them for opposition to "business as usual." This volatility reached a new high in the 23 November 1986 election, when the FPÖ almost doubled its number of voters, with half of those deciding only in the last two weeks of the campaign.[4]

1945: THE END OF NAZI AUSTRIA AND THE
RE-CREATION OF THE "NATIONAL-LIBERAL CAMP"

If the *Lager* concept is no longer descriptive of the political climate of the major parties, the question (FPÖ: liberal or Nazi?) still requires knowing whether a "national" *Lager* exists. Given the general disillusionment within the camp in 1945, it was quite possible that its former constituents might have been successfully assimilated by the two major parties; indeed, many were. The major impediment to the process that might have settled the question was the clumsy handling of Denazification by the government coalition. In an obsequious attempt to encourage the Allies to return sovereignty to Austria at an early date, the provisional government passed the so-called *Verbot* (prohibition) Law that arbitrarily imposed a collective guilt on all former Nazi Party members and too severely punished individuals whose only crime was loyalty to a party in which membership became illegal retroactively. The result was the exclusion of more than 500,000 Austrians from their normal, middle-class existence and the creation of a deeply embittered body of second-class citizens.[5]

In addition many unincriminated, German-nationally minded, anticlerical *Bürger* and peasants from the old German-national-liberal camp could not forgt the *Lager* heritage of the major parties. To these can be added politically dissatisfied *volksdeutsch* refugees and veterans embittered that their military service was now considered near-criminal by a government eager to please the Allied occupiers.

From this diverse raw material of opposition, a political movement developed under the leadership of two Salzburg journalists, whose liberal sensitivities were offended by the callous treatment of innocent people and by the arrogance of the coalition government. Herbert Kraus, whose *Berichte und Informationen* polls revealed widespread dissatisfaction with the *Verbot* Law and the presence of significant numbers of voters with no commitment to either of the coalition parties, joined with Viktor Reimann, assistant editor of the *Salzburger Nachrichten*, to create a "Third Force" to represent the alienated and dissatisfied and "lead them into the liberal camp."[6] When almost half-a-million "less-incriminated" ex-Nazis were given the right to vote in 1949, Kraus and Reimann formed the League of Independents (Verband der Unabhängigen, or VdU) and ran a slate of candidates for election to the parliament. From the beginning, liberals and German-nationalists were unable to agree on an ideological statement for the new party. Instead a vague campaign program was worked out, emphasizing the necessity of a free market economy and condemning the coalition's nationalization policies, excessive bureaucracy, inefficiency, and inflation.

Only passing mention was made of Austria as part of German *Volkstum*. The impasse that prevented either the words *liberal* or *national* from appearing in the first VdU program also kept the programs of its successor, the FPÖ, deliberately vague and of little importance for the integration and development of the Party. This deadlock presaged the ultimate splintering of the VdU and the subsequent inability of the FPÖ to this day to find a program that could unite the Party.

The Independents won 11.87 percent of the vote in the 1949 elections and moved into the new parliament with sixteen representatives. Neither major party had achieved a majority and the VdU hoped to play a balancing role between the two parties or enter a small coalition. At this point, however, the self-interests of the major parties dictated that the VdU not be invited to share in government. The ÖVP could not seriously consider coalition with a party it had reviled in the campaign as neo-Nazi as a means of defending against inroads into its own middle-class constituency. The SPÖ, although delighted to have another party to divide the middle-class vote, was unwilling to invite the VdU into the coalition and give a majority to ministers generally dubious about the expansion of democratic socialism.

At the time of its initial electoral victory, the VdU was not a *Lager* party. Had it been integrated into the circles of government, its élites could have been drawn into *consociational* behavior with the élites from the other parties and, like them, would have been permitted "to depart periodically . . . in order to maintain the membership of their *Lager* and to mobilize their 'ghetto' vote to the fullest possible extent."[7] Instead, the VdU delegation was shunted into the extreme right bank of benches in the parliament and vilified as Nazis. With no need to develop coalescent élite behavior, the VdU's only raison d'être was the exercize of a vocal but futile opposition. The liberals who dreamed that the league could become an above-party "Third Force" were shouldered aside by the German-nationalists. Ultimately, the VdU joined with a new party forming around Anton Reinthaller, former Nazi Minister of Agriculture in the *Anschluss* Cabinet of 1938, and formed the Freiheitliche Partei Österreichs (Austrian Freedom Party, or FPÖ) in the fall of 1955.

THE FORMATION OF THE FPÖ AND "THE GHETTO YEARS"

The essential difference between the new FPÖ and its predecessor was in emphasis rather than substance. Most VdU adherents shifted their support to the new Party, although cofounder Kraus resigned, issuing a bitter statement accusing the new Party of trying "to create a new political platform for the once tumbled greats of the National Socialist regime."[8] The

FPÖ also lost the younger generation of non-Marxist workers, who had been a strong source of support for the VdU in Upper Austria and in the high Alpine hydroelectric construction sites. Thus, the FPÖ, much more than the VdU, had a traditional, middle-class structure with most of its membership drawn from the ranks of self-employed professionals, craftsmen, independent shopkeepers, tradesmen, and to a degree public, officials.[9] In addition, a number of former Nazis and German-nationalists joined, causing the center of gravity of the FPÖ to shift to the Right.

In 1956 parliamentary elections took place in the warm afterglow of the Austrian State Treaty, which had been negotiated by the coalition government and ended a decade of Allied occupation. The barely organized FPÖ chose to run its campaign on a note of vigorous German nationalism but found to its dismay that the question whether Austria was a separate nation or a second German State was immaterial to most Austrians. Although the FPÖ lost eight of the VdU's seats, the remaining six delegates were able to take their seats in the center of the parliament due to skillful negotiation by the unquestioned liberal, Willfried Gredler, with Federal Chancellor Julius Raab. Within the FPÖ, the election disaster unleashed a vigorous programmatic debate. The right-wing wanted to adopt a more strongly German-nationalist stance but was successfully opposed by Gredler, who argued that there were no more votes to win on the Right. Some of the ex-Nazis chafed under the emerging leadership of liberals and moderates and hoped that Reinthaller would provide leadership for a strong Pan-German movement. Reinthaller disappointed them, recognizing that "neo-Nazism is a danger for the fatherland and a threat of death for our Party."[10] Many other ex-Nazis agreed. Whereas the extremists were not driven out of the Party, a fact that many critics have used to challenge the democratic integrity of the FPÖ,[11] they were unable to lead it to their own ends. Perhaps the major reason why the FPÖ was able to survive, while the VdU splintered itself out of existence, was precisely that the FPÖ was led by many reformed ex-Nazis who wanted to create a viable opposition to the major Party coalition. They had no desire to recreate a new Nazi movement but nevertheless had credibility with ex-Nazi voters. With few exceptions, the Freiheitliche were German-nationalists. Most accepted Austrian independence and the perpetual neutrality required by the State Treaty but were committed to the preservation of the German character of society. In its program the FPÖ did not shrink from calling itself a national Party with responsibility for protecting the German *Volk* and cultural community. It rejected the idea of an Austrian nation as a postwar invention but attached no political consequences to its contention that Austria was a second German State. Instead, it envisaged identity and equality for all nationalities within a United States of Europe and supported the earliest possible entry into the European community. The German-nationalist influence is also evident in the FPÖ's emphasis on German values in educational and family policy. The fundamental ideal reiterated throughout the program is freedom of the individual in all matters of public and private life. The program demanded free trade and supported the creation of a social market economy in which the State is to ensure free economic competition while enforcing anticartel legislation for the good of society as a whole.[12]

For a while in 1957, it appeared that the FPÖ would be allowed an early exit from its political isolation, when the ÖVP courted the FPÖ into supporting a joint, above-party candidacy for the Presidency. The ÖVP in return promised to introduce an electoral reform advantageous to the FPÖ. After the election, which resulted in a loss for the ÖVP-FPÖ candidate, acrimonious accusations about who lost the election destroyed any opportunity for future cooperation. The ÖVP reneged on its promise and attached itself more firmly to the coalition than ever before, while the FPÖ experienced its "ghetto" years.

While the FPÖ had succeeded in consolidating itself, it lacked the character of a modern democratic party. With the death of chairman Reinthaller in 1958, the choice of ex-SS man Friedrich Peter as his successor only strengthened the stereotype of the FPÖ as the party of the Nazis and undercut its potential as a coalition partner. Peter subscribed fully to the Party program and appealed strongly to the middle-aged "front generation" with his refusals to admit any shame over having done his duty during the war. However, Peter was also a realist (his critics prefer the term *opportunist*). When the 1959 election produced a slight gain of two seats in parliament, he began to see the potential for his Party in the role of democratic opposition to the rigidity and unpopular policies of the coalition and possibly as a partner in a small coalition, should the major party coalition ever collapse. Also, German-nationalists began to accept the ideal of a United Europe as an acceptable contemporary interpretation of their ideals, thus finding common ground with liberals who wanted European integration for economic reasons.

This convergence was recognized by the *Salzburg Bekenntnis* (Confession) of 1964. While it made the requisite bow to the German-nationlists with a strong statement on the importance of loyalty to the *Volk*, it also laid claim to the more than one-hundred-year-old tradition of freiheitlich democrats who had fought for economic, political, and intellectual freedom. Chairman Peter even looked beyond the *Lager* when, at the Salzburg convention, he pleaded for a reorientation of the Party so that young voters, women, and Catholics could just as easily vote freiheitlich as German-nationalists and liberals and so build the basis for a party of constructive opposition. The *Bekenntnis* criticized the system as a caricature of democracy and committed the FPÖ to a struggle against the absolutism of the coalitions, just as freiheitlich predecessors had fought the Kaiser on behalf of a constitutional State. Once the coalition was broken, the FPÖ would be willing to retreat from its persistent opposition and share responsibility in a truly democratic government.[13] According to an FPÖ liberal of the next generation:"With this convention, the FPÖ changed its self-image. The problems ensuing from the war, which until then had stood in the foreground, were conquered."[14] Chairman Peter had returned to Kraus's idea at the time of the founding of the VdU, that of either becoming the "balance on the political scale" in a coalition-free democracy or a partner in a small coalition government.

Until the 1960s these goals were hopeless. The FPÖ was treated by the major parties as if it were the Nazi Party incarnate, although each had secretly undertaken negotiations in case a small coalition were to become advantageous. In some of the States, however, a real, three-party system operated, with VdU and later FPÖ delegates playing important roles in government. Before the 1962 election, the two-party coalition at the federal level was showing severe signs of old age and Peter's strategy of making the FPÖ attractive as a potential coalition partner began to pay off. Both parties made contact with the FPÖ to probe the possibility of a "small" coalition, but internal politics within each major party ultimately made a return to the "large" coalition the only acceptable option. The SPÖ did, however, keep its door open by arranging for several FPÖ people to be appointed to prestige positions in the bureaucracy. The new coalition pact was not very comfortable, however, and the ÖVP was constantly confronted with the implicit threat that the SPÖ would withdraw and form a "small" coalition with the FPÖ–a possibility that the SPÖ-FPÖ 1963 vote against the return of Otto Habsburg made seem eminently realistic. A change in the leadership of the ÖVP brought Josef Klaus to the position of Party chairman and Federal Chancellor along with a new generation of politicians who preferred opposition to further coalition with the Socialists. Although the FPÖ had just experienced its first successful vote in coalition with the SPÖ on the Habsburg affair, Klaus also began to investigate the possibility of cooperation.[15] The 1966 election, however, gave the ÖVP a majority and Klaus was able to construct Austria's first single-party government in the Second Republic.

RIGHT-LIBERALISM IN ASCENDANCE

For the FPÖ, there were two immediate consequences to the events of the past several years. First, the liberal trend caused a number of right-wing German-nationalists, whom critics point to as proof of the neo-Nazi character of the FPÖ,[16] to defect behind Norbert Burger into his new Nationaldemokratische Partei (NDP). Second, the end of the government coalition meant that much of the FPÖ program criticizing the tyranny of coalition government was obsolete. To this end, a program committee developed a draft on the basis of widespread discussion in the Party that was adopted at the Bad Ischl convention in 1968. The freiheitlich, German-national, and social elements of previous programs were retained, but the European integration theme was refined to mean the "creation of a European Federal State." A new element was concern for the environment and the call for planning to protect the quality of life.[17] With its emphasis on the maximum freedom of the individual, the importance of freedom of economic competition, and the right to work, it is understandable how the program could be seen from the Left as "paltry sloganeering," and "élitist, liberal, egalitarian, social and scurrilous."[18] The scurrilous charge relates to the stated task of maintainig and developing German and Western cultural values that, according to Reiter, was read by critics as disguised anti-Semitism.[19] Although the FPÖ would not accept the word *paltry* to describe the *Ischler Programm,* it continued program development, which ultimately resulted in the *Freiheitliche Manifest* of 1973.

Although the election of 1970 brought no significant improvement to the FPÖ in the parliament, the relative majority achieved by Bruno Kreisky and the SPÖ created a situation that promoted and accelerated the nascent liberal trend among the Freiheitlichen. To many in the SPÖ, the only possibility seemed to be a return to the major-party coalition, but Kreisky dared to dream of a minority government. Before the election, chairman Friedrich Peter had declared, under conservative German-nationalist pressure in the FPÖ and against his own predilection, that his Party would enter into coalition only with the ÖVP.[20] As Kreisky was struggling to reach agreement with the ÖVP on the shape of a new government, Peter announced that he could envisage a minority SPÖ government and speculated that it could sustain the support of his Party at least until the budget debate in the fall. Kreisky shrewdly made demands upon the ÖVP that he knew it could not accept. The FPÖ's price for supporting an SPÖ minority government was an electoral reform law that would approximately equalize the number of votes necessary for each party to win a seat in parliament.[21] The FPÖ in return would oppose any vote of no confidence against the Kreisky government and would support the SPÖ budget for 1971. A bonus to the FPÖ from this silent partnership with the SPÖ accrued as a consequence of the ÖVP refusal even to be a party to negotiation on a Socialist budget. As a result, the FPÖ became the conduit for a non-Socialist Austria in the budget debate, winning considerable prestige in the process.[22] The SPÖ minority government for its part was guaranteed temporary stability in a time of economic recovery and was able to choose the time for new elections, which in October 1971 produced an SPÖ majority and the beginning of a twelve-year reign as the sole governing party.

The years 1970–1971 marked a major turning point in the history of the FPÖ. Although its share of the total vote had flattened out to about 5.5 percent, the change in the relationship among the major parties created the possibility for a functioning three-party system. Young, reform-minded Party members emerging in leadership positions began to argue that the key to future success at the polls and to attractiveness as a coalition partner depended on a new definition of freiheitlich ideals. The example of the recent adoption by the West German Freie Demokratische Partei (FDP) of the liberal Freiburger Thesen and cooperation in a socialist-liberal coalition provided additional incentive.[23]

Simultaneously, the so-called Atterseer Circle was forming as a liberal, academic, intellectual support group for the FPÖ. Virtually all of its members, who later emerged as the "neo-liberal" leaders of the FPÖ, came from families that at the very least were grossdeutsch if not outright ex-Nazi. Although they were content with the social aspects of SPÖ policy and with the free market aspects of ÖVP rhetoric, remnants of *Lager* mentality precluded their political activity in parties still bearing traces of either Marxist or Catholic Church domination. For them, German-nationalism was obsolete as a basis upon which to develop the FPÖ and liberalism – even if long suppressed – was an element of continuity in the *Lager* that could be used to build an ideological basis for a Party to transcend the German-nationalist and ex-Nazi basis upon which it had been built. Certainly, liberalism also provided a convenient psychological means by which they could emancipate themselves from feelings of collective guilt about the Nazi era. But many of the basic values of these new liberals were shaped in homes where Nazi crimes were not discussed and industriousness, family and social obligations, efficiency, and so on were stressed as German virtues. Thus, although these young "neo-liberals" were genuinely committed to escaping the shadow that Nazism had always cast on the FPÖ, their subconscious language and actions frequently gave occasion for critics to see them as neo-Nazis clothed in the trendy liberal jargon of the 1970s and 1980s. Friedhelm Frischenschlager, later a controversial FPÖ Defense Minister, fits this description precisely. He had founded the Atterseer Circle and made it into a powerful brain trust that interacted with reform-minded members of the FPÖ itself.[24] Out of this activity emerged the support for the *Freiheitliches Manifest*, which became the de facto program for the liberalizing FPÖ from 1973 until 1985, when a new program incorporating most of the *Manifest* was adopted.[25]

After the incorporation of amendments made from the floor of a Federal Party Leadership convention 5–6 September 1973, the *Manifest* was unanimously adopted. Its goal was to provide a liberal definition of the Party's freiheitlich and national policies appropriate to a democratic, pluralistic democracy. For the liberals who determined the main ingredients of the *Manifest*, freedom of the individual had to be at the center of one's consciousness, but that freedom was not to be absolute. Society is organic and the individual has obligations emanating from such institutions as marriage, family, *Volk*. There is an emphasis on promoting the "active-element," which is the "motor of society" and rises on the strength of its competitive drive. Educational opportunity, tax policy, and the social market economy should promote the individual's achievement of affluence as the best assurance of social security. Although there was no German-nationalist statement in the draft submitted for approval, a successful resolution from the floor added a statement recognizing the *Volk* as a natural community created by common descent, language, and culture. But, the *Manifesto* continues, nation-states have been proven obsolete. In their place, the specific values, rights, and cultures of all peoples must be tolerated and can be protected only at the higher level of European community. A disharmonious element in this regard is a clause that warned of the excessive expense in social welfare measures for foreign "guest workers." Those whose presence was necessary should be encouraged to retain their cultural identity and ultimately return home. Assimilation was to be discouraged. Finally, a number of paragraphs dealt with ecological issues anticipating the Green movement that attracted a following in the 1980s.[26]

Whether the *Manifest* succeeded in giving the FPÖ a liberal program is largely a matter of opinion. There are probably as many definitions of *liberal* as people and parties supporting or opposing liberalism. According to Frischenschlager, the center of the FPÖ concept of liberalism is individual freedom, and in this sense the *Manifest* can claim to be liberal. In contrast with the West German FDP, which wants "to achieve 'social liberalism' and strives for equalizing social relations, the FPÖ remains the prisoner of conservative liberal principles in the economic and social-political areas." He concedes the label *Right-liberal* but insists "that it is within the liberal spectrum."[27] Political scientist Anton Pelinka has characterized the FPÖ as a far Right party, but not in the sense usually understood in Austrian politics. "The phenomenon is much more complex," he writes:

> The FPÖ is no neo-Nazi Party. . . . The old generation, most of whom experienced their decisive political imprint via National Socialism, is stepping down. The new generation does not think much of Teutonic sayings or of anti-Semitism. Old style German-nationalism is, of course, a long way from being dead. . . . Carinthia proves this. But for the young politicians at the

head of the FPÖ, the decisive problems lie elsewhere. . . . The transition could make the FPÖ into a liberal party, but a Right-liberal, not a Left-liberal party.[28]

The programmatic development of the FPÖ, by 1973, could be said to have brought the Party to a point that could be called liberal in the historic European sense. It shares many of the ideals of the Libertarian movement in the United States or the prevailing elements of the Republican Party, but little of what is understood as liberal in the United States or for that matter by the FDP, whose model the FPÖ professed to admire. The 1986 demand for tax incentives for the single-income family in order to encourage women to return to the role of wife and mother is not liberal by today's standards,[29] but critics would be hard put to call it right-wing extremism in any Western country except Austria or the Federal Republic of Germany. Certainly, the German-nationalist emphasis in the program was strongly muted, and liberal predominance was reflected in a drastic transformation of the Party leadership as young people replaced the generation that had founded the Party.

NAZISM OR POPULAR DEMAGOGUERY?

If the emerging Party leadership was straining to revitalize the long-dormant element of liberalism, many of the Party's voters remained mired in a more recent nostalgia. In 1970, when a poll showed 66 percent support for the idea that Austria was a nation,[30] only 36 percent of the FPÖ voters agreed.[31] Similarly, 50 percent of those who were identified as being strongly anti-Semitic were inclined toward the FPÖ, and the remainder split fairly evenly between the SPÖ and the ÖVP. It should be noted however, that this same poll showed 24 percent of all Austrians to be strongly anti-Semitic and 46 percent to be somewhat anti-Semitic.[32] When FPÖ chairman Peter was forced by public pressure to withdraw his candidacy for the position as the third president of the parliament because of publicity about his SS past, 39 percent of the FPÖ supporters polled felt that after forty years, past Nazi activity should not be used to bar a person from any public office.[33] None of these questions has been relevent for recent FPÖ program development and policy, but they do give a profile of the sentiments of many Party members that are obscured by the liberalism of the program and the federal leadership. The successful 1986 revolt against liberal chairman Norbert Steger was rooted at least in part in the hostility of the Western provinces where Austro-German *völkisch* nationalism remains strong.

Unlike the other Austrian parties, the FPÖ is not a membership party but rather an electoral party with a relatively small number of functionaries

to hold it together. The center of gravity is the States, which have their own
statutes subject to federal Party approval. Party fractions in the State
legislatures and other State groups are basically independent and can, to a
large degree, determine their own actions.[34] Thus, the State organizations
can preserve their own character and pursue actions that can contradict and
embarrass the federal Party. Most embarrassing to the FPÖ in trying to
maintain its carefully cultivated liberal image are remarks and actions from
leaders that perpetuate the perception of the FPÖ as a right-wing extremist
party. If one analyzes the names cited by Neugebauer as evidence for his
skepticism regarding the FPÖ claim to liberalism, it becomes evident that
most have left the Party. However, the Carinthian Party is an exception.
It remains tolerant, if not supportive of right-wing sentiment and constitutes
the power base for enfant terrible and new FPÖ chairman, Jörg Haider. In
Carinthia, with its sizeable Slovenian minority, the opportunist Haider
abandoned the liberalism he had affected in his native Upper Austria and
later as an FPÖ functionary in Vienna, in order to don the Carinthian folk
costume and strident *völkisch* nationalism that frequently accompanies it.
He became a popular figure by exculpating ex-Nazi military figures on the
grounds that they had just done their military duty. His 1984 Carinthian
election campaign presaged the successful 1986 assault on the eastern,
liberal Viennese establishment, attacking not only the major parties for corruption in handing out political appointments but his own Party as well.
Particularly effective was Haider's demagogic use of widespread antipathy
for bilingual education for Slovenian children. Ex-liberal Haider played the
German "national card" and the polls illustrated that this was significant
in his Party's success.[35] Although Carinthia represents the extreme in both
its right-wing German-nationalist stance and rebellion against the federal
Party leadership, the State organizations in general maintain their own
unique character, which in many cases has meant a persistent emphasis on
German-nationalism over liberalism.

THE RISE TO RESPONSIBILITY

Despite the efforts of the young liberals to create a new image for
the FPÖ, its results at the polls had not varied more than 0.6 percent from
the 5.6 percent average received in parliamentary elections from 1966 until
the stunning success of 1986. Nevertheless, the overall balance between the
major parties brought coalitions and cooperative efforts between the FPÖ
and both of the major parties and, along with this, a less negative evaluation of the Party in general.

Friedrich Peter's commitment to liberalizing the Party so as to permit it to leave the political ghetto to become either a coalition partner or a balance on the scale between the parties in an environment free of coalitions had been realized. It is ironic that Peter's success ultimately led to his demise as Party Chairman. The "silent FPÖ coalition" with the SPÖ in 1970 permitted Kreisky to break down the taboos against a "Red" government and build the basis for an astonishingly durable single-party government lasting from 1970 to 1983. Election analyses throughout the 1970s indicate the *Lager* had largely broken down and that, at least for the time being, the independent and youth vote was being captured by Bruno Kreisky and his SPÖ. Although the FPÖ had finally positioned itself to exert the balancing weight on the political scale in a situation of political equilibrium, SPÖ dominance of the Kreisky years meant relative insignificance at the federal level. What remained of Peter's policies was liberalization and constructive opposition. The liberalization policy had already alienated many of the right-wing German-nationalists in the Party who were incensed at the "left liberals in the current leadership clique" who cooperate with the Marxists "just so they can become ministers."[36] For the young liberals whom Peter had brought into the Party, his service in a Waffen-SS unit proved in the end acutely embarrassing. Moreover, failure of the FPÖ to increase its share of the vote in three parliamentary elections caused many to look for a change in leaders. Peter was reelected Chairman at the Party convention in 1976, but with only 74 percent of the vote against no opposition. He drew the unmistakable conclusion that his time as head of the FPÖ was passing and announced that he would not be a candidate for re-election as chairman in 1978.

In 1978, the Party united behind the popular mayor of Graz, Alexander Götz. But Götz resigned after scarcely more than a year under many pressures, not the least of which was that of "neo-liberals" led by Norbert Steger, formerly of the Atterseer Circle and chairman of the Vienna FPÖ. The new decade began with the election of the thirty-six-year-old Steger as Chairman with 55.29 percent of the extraordinary convention for him against 44.61 percent for his opponent, Harald Ofner, who is commonly described as "German-national" and a rightist.[37] In his acceptance speech, Steger reiterated the centrist principles of the *Freiheitliches Manifest*, reminding the delegates that "the first real democrats in Austria were the National-Liberals. We can be the reincarnation of this movement if we have the courage to adopt political policy oriented toward the furture."[38] The FPÖ showing in the parliamentary election of the previous year seemed to sustain Steger's optimism. The Party received over 6 percent of the vote for the first time since 1962 and had done well among first-time voters, white collar and public employees and their managers, skilled and unskilled workers, and many retirees.[39] A seeming confirmation of this optimism was the 1979 acceptance of the FPÖ into the Liberal International, albeit as a Right-liberal party. The election of Norbert Steger as Vice-President of the international body the next year further promoted the liberal image of the Party.[40] As environmental issues began to attract the attention of liberals all over the industrialized world, the FPÖ was able to call attention to its early concern about these matters in the 1968 *Ischler Programm*, whereas both major parties had to remain equivocal for fear of offending major constituencies. The FPÖ also was able to take advantage of major party embarrassment in the enormous scandal over the building of the General Hospital in Vienna. Steger became chairman of the parliamentary committee investigating the scandal, winning widespread respect for his diligence and thoroughness.

At this high point in Steger's popularity, the seeds of the 1986 revolt were sown. Encouraged by polls at the end of 1982 that showed the SPÖ unlikely to maintain its absolute majority in the coming spring elections, Steger, without consulting the Party leaders, publicly indicated his hopes for a "Red-Blue" coalition.[41] This violated usual FPÖ policy of not committing itself to any party before an election. Steger was chastized and, in a closed party meeting in which Haider demanded the Party take a strong stand against politicians' privileges, some uncharitably wondered why Steger was so eager for an FPÖ place in government.[42] As expected, the SPÖ lost its majority and rather then fight for posts and privileges with the ÖVP in a major-party coalition, the Socialists turned to the FPÖ to strike a coalition pact.[43] Polls indicated the public had little faith in either the success or the durability of the coalition,[44] and *profil* predicted that if the coalition were to collapse, only Haider would benefit.[45]

The price of respectability for the FPÖ in a coalition government came high. Despite its rhetoric and a new Party program in 1985, which praised individualism and a free market economy, the FPÖ was tied to the continuing Socialist program of subsidies for inefficient nationalized industries and generous social welfare benefits, while annual budgets grew more unbalanced and the public debt spiraled.

THE HAIDER PUTSCH

Steger's decline in credibility outpaced even that of his Party as he quickly became known as *Der Unfaller*, an Austrian equivalent of a political Mrs. Malaprop. FPÖ Defense Minister Frischenschlager was every bit as accident prone. His well-meaning but misguided attempt at politically educating Austrian recruits about the horrors of the Holocaust at the former death camp at Mauthausen[46] outraged both the Right and the Left and his public welcome for pardoned Austrian war criminal, Walter Reder, brought accusations of neo-Nazism against the innocent but historically naive FPÖ liberals.[47] Paradoxically, just as the Reder scandal was making unpleasant headlines for the FPÖ in January 1985, the Party was in the midst of debating its new program developed by liberals, including Frischenschlager among others,[48] which for the first time rejected "national arrogance" and condemned misuse of German-nationalist feelings for totalitarian or imperialistic goals.[49] Even on environmental issues, where the frequently conflicting German-national and liberal horns were missing, Steger became caught in a dilemma. In the debate that climaxed in December 1984 over the SPÖ plan to build a hydroelectric dam across the River Danube at Hainburg, Steger proved loyal to his coalition partner by reneging on his earlier support for the FPÖ's "green agenda." Murmurs of mutiny were to be heard from Vorlarlberg, Upper Austria, Styria, Salzburg, and Carinthia.[50]

By the spring of 1986, dissatisfaction with Steger's leadership of the Party had reached the point of open revolt. Polls showed Steger having dropped from a high point of public sympathy for any FPÖ leader in 1981 to an absolute low by June 1986. Correspondingly, only 2 percent of those polled indicated an inclination to vote FPÖ.[51] Fearing that Steger was leading their Party into oblivion, party functionaries began to look actively for new leadership. Jörg Haider, who had been a constant critic of Steger, was the most frequently mentioned candidate and appeared willing, but when the SPÖ indicated that a Haider chairmanship would mean an end to the coalition, Haider pulled out and the FPÖ leaders agreed to support Steger for another term as Chairman. Despite the armistice at the top, civil war raged within every State Party organization except Steger's liberal bastions in the East. The center of the revolt was Carinthia, where in the spring the State organization had broken off relations with Vienna and declared federal party officials unwelcome. By late August, the Carinthian Party was urging its chairman, Haider, to challenge Steger for the leadership of the federal Party and had found support from elements in Styria, Tyrol, and Upper Austria.[52] German-nationals, long disgusted with the recent direction of the Party, were able to cover their ideological opposition to the liberal Steger by joining with the pragmatists who simply wanted a more attractive candidate to lead the FPÖ ticket. Haider was the ideal candidate. At age thirty-six, he was free of any Nazi stigma, but his carefully groomed image as supporter of German values and reputation as an outspoken "doer" had won him popularity in German-national circles, particularly in Carinthia and in Styria. But the revolt burst into the open in Salzburg. On 3 September, Haider came to Salzburg to deliver a strong attack on Vienna, which for over a century has symbolized big city corruption, socialism, and the powerful Catholic political establishment; this time Vienna also meant the eastern liberal establishment of the FPÖ. In response to enormous applause, Haider offered himself as a "future architect" for the FPÖ declaring that he would run for the chairmanship if asked. Salzburg FPÖ Chairman and Steger-supporter Frischenschlager tried to defuse the issue by arguing for politics built on issues not personalities and urged support for Steger because Haider was not much different on programmatic issues.[53] But for most Austrians, politics has become more a matter of personality than ideological purity and the maladroit image of Steger was very much at issue. As most of the FPÖ State organizations divided on the Haider challenge, FPÖ peacemakers were scouting for possible compromise candidates.

In an attempt to ward off a divisive floor battle at the convention, Steger warned that a Haider victory would spell the end to the coalition, and the press predicted chaos and a splintering of the Party into oblivion. On 14 September, chaos reigned in the Innsbruck *Kongresshaus*. Catcalls, footstamping, and whistles met the pleas of Friedrich Peter and FPÖ government members for solidarity. One delegate used Frankfurt School "authoritarian typology" to describe some of the pro-Haider delegations" as blindly predisposed to their idol and closed to any rational argument."[54] The journalistic "Waldheim hunters" of the spring again swarmed to the scent of Nazism and gave broad coverage to the inebriated barroom euphoria of long-frustrated German-nationalists who brayed that Steger and his liberal gang deserved a gas chamber or shooting, or pulled Hitler medallions out of their pockets at the least provocation.[55] In a last-gasp effort to salvage some semblance of unity, Steger took the stage and offered to step down as chairman in favor of Defense Minister Helmut Krünes if Haider would likewise withdraw and "end his murderous attack on the Party." With this, he held out his hand and in a dramatic gesture exclaimed "Jörg! Take this hand. Don't slap it away."[56] But "Jörg" remained in the darkness of the auditorium surrounded by his jeering sycophants. As Haider supporters then paraded to the speaker's podium, the tumult grew. Shortly before midnight, the vote for Chairman was taken and Haider emerged the victor with 57.7 as against 39.2 percent for Steger.[57] Afterward, an embittered Steger provided one of the themes for the coming election and grist for the press as he worried aloud about "Nazistic tendencies." A few Steger loyalists resigned but most of the "new guard" liberals such as Frischenschlager, Krünes, Partik-Pablé shed the political deadweight of Steger, making their peace with their new Chairman, while FPÖ headquarters, now headed by German-national-liberal pragmatist Norbert Guggerbauer reported hundreds of new members.[58] Even Haider's enemies did not tar him with the right-wing German-nationalist brush but contented themselves with worrying about "Nazistic tendencies" that had again been unleashed. To be sure, Haider had pandered to the German-nationalist Right as a means of building his regional power base in Carinthia. But for those willing to look beyond the anecdotes of "Nazistic behavior" by the Right-nationalist lunatic fringe from which the press, particularly the foreign press, seemed to derive an almost perverse delight, the reasons for Haider's capture of the Party and his subsequent electoral victory are much more a reflection of contemporary political problems than the consequence of the lingering shadow of Nazism. For many Austrians, the chance in Party leadership was immediately positive.[59]

PARLIAMENTARY ELECTIONS 1986: FPÖ, THE SOLE VICTOR

Even before Haider's victory at Innsbruck, *Die Presse* speculated that early elections would be propitious for the ruling SPÖ vis-à-vis the ÖVP and would leave the FPÖ and various Green and Alternative parties in total disarray.[60] The change in leadership by its governmental partner gave the SPÖ the excuse to end the coalition pact, and elections were scheduled for November 23.[61] In the Liberal International, the election of Haider enabled the long-time skeptics of the liberal character of the FPÖ to question its membership in the organization. An investigating commission was established to monitor the election process and report to the executive committee after the election.[62]

At the beginning of the campaign, polls by both major parties showed a close race, with neither party likely to win a majority. Thus, both elephantine parties campaigned as if preparing for a final Viennese coalition waltz after the election, an analogy that the political cartoonists loved to sketch. The turn of events in the FPÖ provided the only political excitement of the season. *Die Presse* accurately predicted that the SPÖ would opportunistically rouse the Nazi issue against the FPÖ, just as it had against Waldheim in the spring.[63] Both major parties attempted to use the demise of the liberal Steger as FPÖ Chairman as the sign of a shift to the Right, with all of the attendant implications.

The campaign was a lackluster affair. The SPÖ uncharacteristically ran on a program to restore efficiency to nationalized industry. The ÖVP tried to make political capital out of Vranitzky's proposal to terminate 10,000 employees at the enormous, State-owned VOEST concern but was severely hampered by its own complicity in the creation of the nationalized monster, as well as by the fact that Vranitzky had applied the business management techniques that they, themselves, had demanded. Led by its colorless chairman, Alois Mock, the ÖVP basically campaigned against ex-Federal chancellors Kreisky and Sinowatz and contented itself with a vague proposal for tax reform.

Although, by European standards, Austria is relatively well off, a general, critical uneasiness and even combativeness is abroad in the land. A large and growing State deficit, repeated, unrelated scandals in both the public and private sectors, and growing environmental concerns have created a protest-minded electorate. The youthful, telegenic, combative Haider became a media star in the otherwise pallid campaign. Haider held true to the campaign platform adopted before his succession to the chairmanship, built strongly on the liberal Party program adopted in 1985. It demanded the reduction of government control over the economy and incentives for individual iniative, an end to privileges for party members, more direct democracy, and an active environmental program.[64] To these ends, in October, the FPÖ floated a tax plan that included a drastic reduction in the progressivity of the income tax to be paid for by reducing loopholes in the law and by cutting State expenditures.[65] While campaigns of the major parties virtually assumed the realization of a great coalition, Haider proposed to form a coalition with the people to oppose what he called the "Black-Red Unity Party" through a vigorous use of citizens' initiatives.[66] As a *Salzburger Nachrichten* editorial saw it, it was this image of the courageous mouse biting the elephants in the calves that made Haider such a popular figure in the election.[67] For the *Salzburger Volksblatt*, Haider's uncompromising demand for honesty and openness in government and an end to privilege, even for members of his own Party, won him the hearts of the voters.[68] Although Haider virtually ignored the traditional German-national element of the Party, his image was enough to bring the German-nationalists back to the FPÖ fold without alienating the Party's liberals. For the first time in the Second Republic, the "third camp" was able to find a balance between its two wings.

The SPÖ retained only a slim relative majority with 43.12 percent of the vote and eighty seats, whereas the ÖVP suffered the worst defeat of its history with 41.30 percent and seventy-seven seats. The big winner was Jörg Haider and his FPÖ, which won 9.73 percent of the vote, almost double its 1983 total, and eighteen seats in the new parliament. Ernst Gehmacher of the SPÖ-oriented IFES polling institute estimated that the FPÖ votes came approximately 20 percent from each of the major parties, as well as substantially from the Greens.[69] A *Presse* analysis estimated that 25 percent of the FPÖ vote came from the SPÖ and speculated that this might even force the foreign media to think twice, because no rational person could believe that good comrades would become unreconcilable Nazis overnight."[70] Political scientist Anton Pelinka interpreted the election as further evidence of the decline of *Lager* mentality that has produced a substantial reservoir of independent voters.[71] Evidently, in the parliamentary

elections of 1986, these voters were attracted by the belligerent, oppositional style of Haider, with the FPÖ emerging the beneficiary.

FINAL THOUGHTS

To return to the question initially posed for this essay, it is generally
accepted that Jörg Haider is no neo-Nazi but rather a flexible, opportunistic,
and extremely ambitious political chameleon with a strong populist appeal,
who has been able to achieve extraordinary political success by telling many
Austrians what they want to hear. Whereas ex-Nazi voters, as is frequently
noted, are increasingly to be found in the municipal cemeteries, extreme,
right-wing nationalism, which is present throughout Europe and North
America, is also prevalent in Austria. Although Haider publicly distanced
himself from such groups, he has pandered to their emotions and benefited
from their votes. In Austria, there is little concern about Haider's ideological principles but rather with the lack of them. Whether he has a legitimate
freiheitlich agenda or is just an ambitious demagogue riding the political
winds remains to be seen.

After almost two months of wrangling over ministerial seats and budget-
cutting measures, the losing SPÖ and the ÖVP were able to agree on the
terms of a "jumbo wedding," which joined the two major parties in coalition government for the first time since 1966.[72] If the coalition can make
good its impressive list of resolutions, the FPÖ will probably lose many
of its protest voters and again become just a gathering point for liberals,
German-nationalists, and assorted malcontents. If however, the SPÖ-ÖVP
coalition is unable to bring significant successes—and in times of serious
economic, resource, and environmental problems the chances are remote[73]—
the FPÖ can continue to thrive. As a party of protest against the "Black-
Red Unity Party" or as a balance on the political scale in an open parliament, the FPÖ can prosper and perhaps even outgrow the tradition that
after forty years still permits the question, FPÖ: liberal or Nazi?

NOTES

1. "FPÖ: Der Aparthaider," *profil* (22 September 1986): 18

2. Adam Wandruzka, "Österreichs politische Struktur: Die Entwicklung der Parteien
und politischen Bewegungen," in Heinrich Benedikt (ed.), *Geschichte der Republik Österreich*
(Vienna, 1954), pp. 291–485.

3. Kurt Steiner, *Politics in Austria* (Boston, 1972), pp. 409–16.

4. *Wiener Zeitung* (3 December 1986), p. 2, reporting the results of polls by the
Sozialwissenchaftliche Studiengesellschaft.

5. Max Riedlsperger, *The Lingering Shadow of Nazism: The Austrian Independent Party Movement since 1945* (Boulder and New York, 1978), discusses the *Lager* theory and closely details the history of the history of the VdU, from which this brief treatment is drawn.

6. Herbert Kraus interviewed in *profil* (21 November 1983), p. 19.

7. See further Steiner, pp. 415–16.

8. Press conference by Dr. Kraus, *Wiener Zeitung* (13 April 1956), p. 2.

9. Kurt Piringer, *Die Geschichte der Freiheitlichen: Beitrag der Dritten Kraft zur österreichischen Politik* (Vienna, 1982), pp. 42–43. These impressionistic recollections are largely supported by an *Institut für empirische Sozialforschung* (IFES) poll done for ORF and published in *Die Zukunft* (July 1979):12. The major difference is that in the 1970s, 29 percent of the FPÖ votes came from workers, which may be attributable to the decline of *Lager* mentality generally but also to the close relationship established between the FPÖ and SPÖ after 1970. Unless otherwise noted, all subsequent details regarding the internal operations of the FPÖ are taken from Piringer, who was responsible for publicity at the beginning of VdU activities and subsequently in all phases of the development of the FPÖ.

10. Piringer, p. 50.

11. See Wolfgang Neugebauer, "Die FPÖ: Vom Rechtsextremismus zum Liberalismus," in Dokumentionsarchiv des Österreichischen Widerstandes, *Rechtsextremismus in Österreich nach 1945*, 5th. ed. by (Vienna, 1981), p. 309. Because of the origins of the third party movement and its makeup, the FPÖ stood alone among Austrian parties in making a distinction between condemning the Nazi era and honoring veterans for their military service. For Neugebauer, this is a sign of right-wing extremism, as is the FPÖ's failure to recognize and honor the Austrian resistance movement. Neugebauer also simply calls attention to the Nazi past of many FPÖ leaders, without making distinctions concerning the nature or degree of their complicity, their postwar behavior, or the record of the FPÖ in dealing with persisting extremism.

12. "Richtlinien freiheitlicher Politik, 1957," in Klaus Berchtold (ed.), *Österreichische Parteiprogramme 1868–1966* (Vienna, 1967), pp. 496–97.

13. Ibid., pp. 509–12, "Das 'Salzburg Bekenntnis' der Freiheitlichen Partei Österreichs, 1964," and for detail on events on the convention itself, see further Piringer, p. 102.

14. Friedhelm Frischenschlager, "Funktions- und Inhaltswandlungen von Parteiprogrammen am Beispiel der FPÖ Programme," *Österreichische Zeitschrift für Politikwissenschaft* (1978):213.

15. Hans Werner Scheidel, 'Die Ära Friedrich Peter', *Die Republik* (1979) No. 1, cited by Bernhard Perching, 'National oder liberal: die Freiheitliche Partei Österreiches', in Peter Gerlich and Wolfgang C. Müller (eds.), *Zwischen Koalition und Konkurrenz: Österreichs Parteien seit 1945* (Vienna, 1983), p. 81.

16. See further Neugebauer, p. 311.

17. "Ischler Parteiprogramm," in Erich Reiter, *Programm und Programmentwicklung der FPÖ* (Vienna, 1982), pp. 84–88.

18. Reiter, p. 72, quoting Albert Kadan, "Die Freiheitliche Partei Österreichs," *Die Republik* no. 1 (1979).

19. Reiter, p. 72. Reiter argues that this statement was intended only to associate the FPÖ with traditional European values, but that there are certain concepts, such as that of Western civilization, which, when used by the FPÖ, become the occasion for polemics.

20. *Salzburger Volksblatt* (17 January 1970), p. 1.

21. Robert Kriechbaumer, *Österreichs Innenpolitik 1970–1975*, a special issue of *Österreichisches Jahrbuch für Politik* (1981), p. 44, estimates that the ÖVP received a seat with about 26,000 votes, the SPÖ 27,000, and the FPÖ 42,000.

22. Ibid.

23. See further Frischenschlager, p. 214.

24. Erich Reiter, "Der Atterseerkreis innerhalb der Freiheitlichen Partei," *Österreichisches Jahrbuch für Politik, 1981* (1982):103–24.

25. Friedhelm Frischenschlager, "Wie liberal ist die FPÖ?" *Österreichisches Jahrbuch für Politik, 1980* (1981):145.

26. On *Freiheitliches Manifest zur Gesellschaftspolitik*, see Reiter, pp. 89–137.

27. See further Frischenschlager, p. 220.

28. Anton Pelinka, *profil* (6 July 1973):20.

29. *Wiener Zeitung* (January 1, 1987), p. 2.

30. Andreas Kohl, "Krise der Parteien–Krise der Demokratie." *Österreichisches Jahrbuch für Politik, 1980* (1981):394, citing a 1980 study by the Paul v. Lazarsfeld *Gesellschaft für Sozialforschung*.

31. Melanie A. Sully, *Political Parties and Elections in Austria* (London, 1981), p. 115, citing H. Konrad (ed.), *Sozialdemokratie und "Anschluss"* (Vienna, 1978), p. 109.

32. John Bunzl and Bernd Marin, "Antisemitismus in Österreich: Historische und soziologische Studien," *Journal für Sozialforschung* 1 (1983):238.

33. "SWS Meinungsprofile: SS-Schatten der Nazi-Vergangenheit," *Journal für Sozialforschung* 4 (1983):505.

34. See further Reiter, pp. 14–18.

35. Franz Sommer, "Die Landtagswahl in Kärnten vom 30. September 1984: Wahlkampf, Ergebnisse, Analyse," *Österreichisches Jahrbuch für Politik, 1984* (1985):67–75.

36. "FPÖ-Abspaltung: Liberale Dreckskerle," *Profil*, (March 1971):24.

37. See further Neugebauer, p. 318.

38. See further Piringer, p. 306.

39. Ernst Gehmacher, Franz Birk, and Herbert Berger, "Nationalratswahlanalyse," *Die Zukunft* 6 (July 1979):10–14, summary of IFES analysis conducted on behalf of ORF.

40. See further Frischenschlager, p. 138.

41. The FPÖ's political color is blue, after the blue flower that symbolized longing for nineteenth-century romantics. Turn-of-the-century German-nationalists in the Austro-Hungarian Empire adopted the blue corn-flower as the symbol of their longing for a truly Greater Germany and Austrian Nazis wore it when Nazi brown-shirts were forbidden during the period 1934–1938 when the Party was banned. The political colors of the SPÖ and the ÖVP are red and black, respectively. The former is the traditional revolutionary symbol, the latter is the mark of the Catholic Church.

42. *profil* (24 January 1983):16–17.

43. "SPÖ-FPÖ Arbeitsübereinkommen," *Österreichisches Jahrbuch für Politik, 1983* (1984):519–27.

44. "Kompetenzprofil der SPÖ-FPÖ Koalitionsregierung nach der Nationalratswahl (Juni/Juli 1983)," *Österreichisches Jahrbuch für Politik, 1983* (1984):902–903.

45. Franz Ferdinand Wolf, "Das eilige Experiment," *profil* (30 May 1983):10.

46. *profil* (26 September 1983):28–29.

47. *profil* (28 January 1984):7, 10; and (4 February 1983):11–21.

48. Alfred Stirnemann, "Das neue Parteiprogramm der FPÖ–eine kritische Analyse," *Österreichisches Jahrbuch für Politik, 1985* (1986):652–80.

49. "Parteiprogramm der FPÖ 1985," *Informationen: Zeitung des Freiheitlichen Bildungswerkes* 4 (1985):13.

50. *profil* (31 December 1984):13.

51. Kurt Traar and Franz Birk, "Der durchgeleuchtete Wähler in den achtziger Jahren," *Journal für Sozialforschung: Sonderheft-Wahlforschung* 1 (1987):20. Steger had a sympathy value of +.3 in 1981 and −.7 in June 1986.

52. *profil* (15 September 1986):25.

53. *Salzburger Nachrichten* (5 September 1986):2.

54. Interview with Dr. Christian Allesch, in *Salzburger Fenster* (1 October 1986):4.

55. Dagmar Felbermayer, "Die blau-braune Schlammschlacht," *Salzburger Fenster* (1 October 1986):4.

56. *Die Presse* (15 September 1986):4.

57. *Die Presse* (16 September 1986):2.

58. *Die Presse* (19 September 1986):4.

59. Traar and Birk, p. 21. In a poll covering the period from September 10 to September 23, during which the leadership change occurred, the number inclined to vote for the FPÖ increased by 1 percent.

60. *Die Presse* (13–14 September 1986):1.

61. *Wiener Zeitung* (24 September 1986):1.

62. *Neue Zürcher Zeitung* (5 October 1986):4.

63. *Die Presse* (19 September 1986):1.

64. *Ein gutes Programm für Österreich* (1986).

65. *Wiener Zeitung* (11 October 1986):2. Haider explained the tax incentive for this conservative family policy in his New Year's message, *Wiener Zeitung* (1 January 1987):2. Here, he also proposed tax incentives for single-income families as a means of returning women to their roles as wives and mothers.

66. *Wiener Zeitung* (12 October 1986):2.

67. *Salzburger Nachrichten* (20 November 1986):1.

68. Bernhard Hütter, "Warum ich Haider wähle," *Salzburger Volksblatt* (11 November 1986):1.

69. *Wiener Zeitung* (25 November 1986):2.

70. *Die Presse* (25 November 1986):3.

71. *Wiener Zeitung* (4 December 1986):2.

72. *Financial Times* (21 January 1987):1. Rumors had been circulating that Mock was attempting to promote the idea of a Swiss-style concentration government, in which all parties represented in parliament would have a proportional share of government responsibilities. Mock was apparently trying to avoid losing supporters to the FPÖ, who might be alienated by a coalition with the SPÖ. Neither the SPÖ nor the FPÖ showed any public interest in such a scheme.

73. Immediately after the announcement of the terms of the coalition agreement, the SPÖ was severely criticized by its own *Grand Old Man*, former, long-term Federal Chancellor, Bruno Kreisky, who resigned his honorary chairmanship of the Party over the appointment of ÖVP chairman Mock as Foreign Minister. In the wake of the negative image brought to Austria by the election of the ÖVP's candidate, Kurt Waldheim, to the Presidency in 1986, Kreisky was protesting the indifference or even ignorance of Party leaders Vranitzky and Sinowatz in appointing to this post someone who could be even remotely identified with the widely reviled Waldheim. *Die Zeit* (30 January 1987):2.

Right-Wing Student Politics in Austria after 1945

REINHOLD GÄRTNER

This paper is concerned with the perennial problem of right-wing student politics in Austria. Its historical roots go back to at least the Revolution of 1848, which historians sometimes call "the revolution of the intellectuals." Radical-liberal students were instrumental in setting in motion the March Revolution 1848, ironically just ninety years before the *Anschluss* of 1938. Ironical, too, was the fact that among its most prominent student leaders was a Jewish medical student, Adolf Fischhof. In 1938, Jewish students were among the principal victims of the *Anschluss*.

Why had Austrian student politics changed so drastically in those ninety years? The short answer lies in the corruption of the forces of early nationalism, basically liberal and humanitarian and primarily directed against autocracy, by the forces unleashed by the Industrial Revolution. In this way, nationalism turned illiberal, was gradually taken over by right-wing forces of a Pan-German hue, and exploited by the new, powerful industrialized State of Germany.

The student movements of Germany and Austria were deeply affected by those developments. During the inter-war period, therefore, right-wing politics was the order of the day at Austrian universities and Mittelschulen (high schools), where the student movement became the focus of anti-Semitism. This paper attempts to show to what extent, if any, that situation has changed since 1945.

279

DENAZIFICATION

Before 1986 it was possible to read an epigraph on a commemorative plaque at the Vienna University of Agriculture and Forestry which read: "As long as there are Germans, they will bear in mind that these were once sons of their people." The reference was to 200 students and teachers of this university who had died at the front during the Second World War. As late as 1986 nobody had realized, or pretended to realize, that these very words had appeared in Hitler's *Mein Kampf*.[1] Whatever the position, no one was in the least upset by the inscription that, to put it mildly, attests to a certain extent of student indifference toward the horrific phenomenon of Nazism.

Immediately after the defeat of the Nazis, Austrian schools and universities were made subject to a process of Denazification. Members of their staffs suspected of a Nazi past were barred from teaching, and Nazi-incriminated students were not allowed to attend university.[2] On 9 September 1946 the *Kleines Volksblatt* gave the following account: "4049 members of the teaching staff were dismissed without notice; 5879 were suspended temporarily; 7730 minor cases had to be left alone to teach in primary school. 12,970 teachers in all were barred from teaching during the school year 1945–1946."[3]

Between 50 and 60 percent of all university teachers were dismissed after 1945.[4] It is as well to realize, however, that even before 1950 many of those rules were relaxed, thus allowing a considerable number of incriminated persons to continue teaching at universities. And soon, too, the Ring Freiheitlicher Studenten (RFS) (literally, Circle of Liberal Students; the term *liberal*, a faint echo still of the Revolution of 1848, but no more than that) and the traditionally right-wing student dueling societies were able to embrace ideologies thought to be safely extinct. Student dueling societies, it ought to be appreciated in a historical context, are an old and basically right-wing institution in both Austria and Germany. A notable feature about them is, however, that while in the Federal Republic of Germany they have been moving away from the Right of the political spectrum toward liberalism, in Austria they have remained in the right-wing.

It is well to bear in mind, however, that more or less Nazi-incriminated persons could not be kept away from teaching indefinitely, with very few exceptions. Besides, despite Denazification, Austria's universities remained meeting places for far-Right groups.[5] In circumstances like these, the influence and spread of neo-Nazi ideas could hardly be avoided, enabling a fair-sized group of students to claim growing support for Nazi-tinted ideologies. Signposts on that road of development were the foundation of the RFS at the beginning of the 1950s, the steady increase in the number of

student duelling societies, the way in which Schiller's birthday was celebrated in 1959, and by way of a tragic climax, the Borodajkewycz incident
in 1965, which claimed the first fatal political casualty since 1945.

THE RING FREIHEITLICHER STUDENTEN

The RFS, "borne from its own idealism to purge the Austrian university student body (Österreichische Hochschülerschaft–ÖH) of corruption
and to assume control over the Catholic Cartellverband (CV),"[6] would
have been illegal without a new University Act passed in 1950, permitting
the formation of formerly proscribed groups.

The history of the RFS may be divided into three periods, as follows:
(1) an early period before 1965 marked by clear-cut, extreme right-wing attitudes; (2) a period of pseudo-liberalism in the course of the following
decade, matched by efforts to shed right-wing politics; and (3) the period
between 1975 and 1988, in which the RFS tended to move back to the
Right. During the last period, the RFS was joined by two serious, but completely different, rivals on the political Right: the Young European Student
Initiative (Junge Europäische Studenteninitiative, or JES, which is non-
Nazi, neo-conservative, and Europhile in outlook), and Action New Right
(Aktion Neue Rechte, or ANR, distinctly on the Right of the RFS). Of
those two, the JES was able to inflict severe electoral losses on the RFS in
the students' parliament. Student parliaments, whether at a local-regional
or at an all-Austrian level, perform certain advisory and consultative functions by law.[7] Though their influence is not to be overrated, it is not wholly
to be dismissed either. Unlike similar bodies in other countries, student
parliaments are not mere debating societies. Elections to them in Austria
are therefore of some importance.

Ironically, the basic intention in founding the JES was to counter the
upsurge of left-wing student strength the world over in the 1960s. And
though it is perfectly true that the members of JES were never overfond
of the politics of the RFS, the electoral inroads made on the latter were almost purely accidental.

The Period 1951–1965

The mere fact that on 11 May 1953 Norbert Burger replaced Erwin Hirnschall as chairman of the RFS significantly illustrates the starting position
of that group.[8] Burger's extreme right-wing attitudes were to be manifest
during the next few years. As candidate for Federal President of Austria in

1980, Burger was to poll a remarkable 3.2 percent of the votes cast. Between 1955 and 1956 Peter Wrabetz was RFS chairman. In 1973 he characterized the *Anschluss* of 1938 as fulfillment of the "Pan-German idea, deeply rooted in all political camps of Austria at that time."[9]

As to the RFS's basic tenets, in 1961 it considered itself committed to the "realization of Western ideals of education" within the framework of liberal principles, strictly defined freedom of teaching and learning, freedom of opinion and religious tolerance in a democratic, constitutional state. The RFS furthermore favored a "cultural connection with the whole German nation," as well as the maintenance of Austria's sovereignty.[10] The injunction to be "unpolitical" figured prominently: "The student representatives' duty is restricted to matters of study alone."[11]

However, practice differed from theory. In 1959 the celebration of Schiller's birthday was already turned into a neo-Nazi occasion. As one report put it: "many had taken out their emblems of the 'Third Reich' . . . former concentration camp inmates . . . people of every walk of life and faith had come to shout 'stop' to this meeting in their anger and resentment."[12] *Die Aula*, mouthpiece of the right-wing Freiheitlicher Akademikerverband (a body not associated with the FPÖ, the right-wing political party), reported the meeting as follows: "one could not be surprised that [on that occasion] a number of street-rowdies dressed in leather-jackets and led by old-time communists experienced in civil war, lined the streets of the torchlight-procession. Regrettably, among these ruffians there were quite a few Socialists who had the nerve to sing the *Internationale* in unison with the communists."[13] No doubt, that Schiller celebration was made the deliberate occasion for a quantitative show of strength of the far Right in Austria.

In February 1961 a student from the United States exercising his "freedom of opinion" was beaten up by members of the RFS and told "Get out of here, damned Jew!"[14] Although cases like these were not everyday occurrences in postwar Austria, they were nonetheless symptomatic of an alarming trend of the time.

The Freiheitlicher Akademikerverband and its organ, *Die Aula*, gave both financial and ideological support to the RFS.[15] Its founder, the late Robert Timmel, was the winner of the European Peace Prize awarded by the *Deutsche National-Zeitung*, a far-Right West German paper, in 1976.[16] Günther Berka, one-time editor of *Die Aula*, attempted to distance himself from the taint of Nazism by making a distinction between anti-Semitic acts, on the one hand, and bombings in the Italian South Tyrol, on the other hand.[17] Yet, those attempts were half-hearted and contradicted by the general attitudes adopted by the Freiheitlicher Akademikerverband, such as its virulent polemics directed against the Slovene minority in Carinthia and its alarming advocacy of "the merciless eradication of anti-social elements."[18] Thus, *Die Aula* of February 1960 gave evidence of its sympathies by lending its support to the "healthy, intelligent, nationally true German or German Austrian" and for a "free South Tyrol." In 1961 Norbert Burger founded the Committee for the Liberation of South Tyrol, thereby encouraging a wave of attacks in that region.[19] Typical also was the selection of topics of importance to *Die Aula*, such as "Talent and Genetics" and the ominous sounding "Genuine Selection or People's Death *(Volkstod)*."[20]

The RFS in ÖH Elections

Considering its ideology and markedly right-wing attitudes, by rights the RFS should not have been able to obtain a significant share of students votes. However, it was able to increase its share steadily from 1953 onward to a plateau of about 25–30 percent of the total votes case. (Table 1). It would nonetheless be misleading to interpret this as representing a far-Right potential of one-third of all students at Austria's universities, mainly because of the absence of electoral competition on the Right. It would be equally misleading, however, to underestimate the dangers inherent in that trend. The fact remains that even far-right-wing ideas were acceptable to some student voters who were right-of-center, proof of a certain lack of political sensibility.

A marked element of the RFS has been its close relationship with student dueling societies, reflected in the personal union of office-holders in them. Another aspect has been the RFS's function as recruiter for FPÖ representatives. Though the RFS emphasizes its formal independence of any political party, a good many RFS members have made their political career within the FPÖ. Their roll-call makes impressive reading: Hirnschall, Frischenschlager, Haider, Gugerbauer, Steger, Krünes, and Bauer–to name only a few.[21] Former RFS members Burger and Bruno Haas, though, started careers in the National Democratic Party and ANR; and Wolfgang Pelikan is Secretary of the United Greens of Austria secretary-general at the moment. There is, however, some doubt whether the RFSs can go on playing this role for much longer, as will be shown.

Until the mid-1960s, the climate prevailing at Austria's universities favored a right-directed course in politics. However, the events connected with the Borodajkewycz affair startled even some extreme right-wing groups, who had second thoughts about their ideas and position. As a result, the RFS was compelled to change direction, embracing pseudo-liberalism, being less rigid in its attitudes, and attempting to shed some of its Pan-Germanism.

TABLE 1
RESULTS OF ÖH ELECTIONS, 1951–1965

Contenders	1951	1953	1955	1957	1959	1961	1963	1965
Wahlblock	6341	5005	5139	5670	8085	12118	13857	14624
	50.8%	46.7%	54.9%	57.3%	54.2%	56%	55.2%	57.6%
	19 seats	14 seats	16 seats	18 seats	17 seats	19 seats	20 seats	19 seats
VSSTÖ (League of Socialist Students)	2200	1752	1119	1047	1987	2896	2884	3089
	17.7%	16.7%	11.9%	10.7%	13.2%	13.4%	11.5%	12.1%
	6 seats	5 seats	3 seats	3 seats	4 seats	4 seats	4 seats	4 seats
RFS	2186	3490	2796	2657	3789	5966	6728	7281
	17.5%	33.2%	29.9%	26.7%	24.8%	27.5%	26.9%	28.7%
	3 seats	10 seats	9 seats	8 seats	7 seats	9 seats	9 seats	9 seats
Votes cast	12480	10570	9363	9889	14909	21599	25812	
Valid votes	11961		9210	9502	14461	21221	25002	25414
Entitled to vote	20441	15348	15082	15166	21457	32611	36828	40035
Participation	61%	68%	62%	65%	68%	65%	70%	70%

Sources: Data from W. Oberleitner, Politisches Handbuch der Republik Österreich 1945–60 (Vienna, 1960) and Politisches Handbuch Österreichs 1945–80 (Vienna, 1981); Khol, Ofner, and Stirnemann, Österreichisches Jahrbuch für Politik, volumes for 1977, 1979, 1981, 1983, 1985; Wiener Tagebuch (May 1975); Marina Fischer-Kowalski, "Zur Entwicklung von Universität und Gesellschaft in Österreich," in Heniz Fischer (ed), Das politische System Österreichs, 2d ed. (Vienna, 1977), pp. 571–624.

The RFS and the Borodajkewycz Affair

Taras Borodajkewycz, professor of history at the Hochschule für Welt-handel (the Vienna School of International Trade, now called Wirtschafts-universität), never attempted to conceal his neo-Nazi thoughts. Time and again he gave proof of his Pan-Germanic, as well as anti-Semitic, views. Thus, the year of liberation from Nazism, 1945, was characterized by him as "replete with meanness and lack of dignity."[22] During the 1961–1962 academic year, Borodajkewycz described Rosa Luxemburg as a "Jewish suffragette and a mass agitator" and Kurt Eisner as a "Polish café-Jew." To add a further point to the venomous outbursts of this man, the constitution of the Weimar Republic was characterized by him as having been drawn up by the "Jewish professor of constitutional law, Hugo Preuss,"[23] as if this illegitimized its existence ipso facto. At a press conference arranged by the ÖH in 1965 to give Borodajkewycz an opportunity to refute some of the charges leveled against him, the very mention of Jewish names was greeted with cynical laughter.[24]

These provocative acts caused demonstrations against him, in the course of which the pensioner Ernst Kirchweger was beaten up on 31 March 1965, dying as a result of injuries received at the hands of Günther Kümel. Notwithstanding that tragedy, the RFS saw fit on the following day to distribute leaflets approving of the pro-Borodajkewycz demonstration. Friedhelm Frischenschlager, then Secretary-General of the RFS, saw matters in a different light. Denying roundly that the pro-Borodajkewycz demonstration was attributable to an initiative taken by the RFS he commented: "The students and I were not concerned about anti-Semitism. We just did not want to have any outside influence. There was a general feeling that anti-Semitic expressions were just a pretext for expelling a politically unwelcome professor."[25] To this day, it has been a matter of some debate why Kümel was given a prison sentence of only ten months, and why Borodajkewycz was allowed to go on teaching until 14 May 1966.[26]

1966–1975: Moving Toward Pseudo-Liberalism

After Kirchweger's death some RFS representatives thought it wise to leave the path of right-wing radicalism. The process was initiated by Holger Bauer, then RFS Chairman, whose attitude toward student dueling societies was much more clear-cut and sophisticated than that of his predecessors.[27] At that moment in time, however, developments within the RFS have to be seen in the wider context of the general changes taking place in society at large. These were summed up and analyzed by Andrew Markovits and Michael Freund as follows:

One can notice a trend to the Left during the past seven years. . . . One of
the main reasons is the weakened and changed – but still dominant – student
Right. Conservative student organizations still show considerable influence
on university life, as well as on the macro-political structure of the country.
Nonetheless, the Right has experienced a basic qualitative change during
those years. The former German-national attitude, racist and anti-Semitic
ideas, "Blood-and-Soil" ideologies and antidemocratic romanticism have lost
out in favor of neo-conservatism.[28]

It was not by any means obvious then that in the long run the RFS
would be unable to cope with those changes. Still, the JES began to appear
an increasingly attractive electoral proposition. Although the RFS managed
to maintain its percentage of student votes, in the mid-1970s the JES was
gaining access to the RFS' voting potential, as may be gathered from the
Table 2.

From 1967 onward the RFS percentage of student votes dropped from
30 to 20 percent. The last time the RFS was able to poll 20 percent was
in 1974. The following year the figure dropped to 15 percent, a drastic loss
of its votes within twelve months. The JES began competing for votes in
1975, polling a mere 7 percent. If RFS and JES percentages are compared
since then a picture emerges: in 1974 the RFS obtained 20.9 percent, in
1975, RFS received 15 percent to the JES 7 percent; in 1977, RFS 8.4 percent and JES 10.2 percent; in 1979, RFS 6.9 percent and JES 14 percent.
The corresponding figures for 1981 were RFS 4.1 percent and JES 16.4 percent; in 1983, RFS 3.1 percent and JES 16.9 percent. In 1985, when the
RFS did not compete, the JES obtained 20.6 percent. In the 1987 elections, a bit surprisingly, the JES share of the vote dropped to 12.3 percent,
while the RFS polled a mere 2.5 percent. The principal beneficiary in 1987
turned out to be the AG-Aktionsgemeinschaft whose share leapt from 30.9
percent in 1985 to 38.6 percent. It is evident, therefore, that the RFS had
been eclipsed.

The RFS's Tenets: A Study in Frustration

In February 1970 the RFS was described as unimaginative.[29] In the run-
up to the 1971 election, in which the RFS once again lost votes, the RFS
"returned to its consevative-German-national, even right-wing position"
after having tried to tread the liberal path. This prompted a long-term discussion about fundamentals, especially in clarifying crucial terms like *liberal*
and *national*.[30] The upshot of this debate, which does not appear to have
been in any way conclusive, was incorporated in *Study Guide 1971–1972*,
published under the auspices of ÖH-Innsbruck. In it, the RFS character-

TABLE 2
RESULTS OF ÖH ELECTIONS, 1967–1987

Contenders	1967	1969	1971	1974	1975	1977	1979	1981	1983	1985	1987
Wahlblock: ÖSU (Austrian Students Union) AG (Aktionsgemeinschaft)	12851 49%	12266 49%	12034 53.5%	10780 41.5%	11328 36.1%	17671 48.3%	13621 38.3%	10438 23.2%	16648 35.3%	14573 30.9%	23828 38.6%
VSStÖ (League of Socialist Students)	3446 13%	3059 12.2%	2379 10.6%	3446 13.2%	5433 17.3%	6278 17%	6422 18%	8779 19.5%	12187 25.9%	10247 21.7%	13360 21.7%
RFS	7871 30%	7122 28.5%	5642 25.1%	5431 20.9%	4710 15%	3091 8.4%	2905 6.9%	1865 4.1%	1499 3.1%	–	1540 2.5%
JES	–	–	–	–	2193 7%	3756 10.2%	4980 14%	7379 16.4%	7960 16.9%	9731 20.6%	7547 12.2
Participation	64%	54.4%	44.2%	34.2%	39%	38.7%	32.6%	25%	36%	30%	34.7%
Valid votes	26283	24977	22425	25998	31363	36333	35574	44900	47100	47160	61600

Sources: Same as Table 1.

ized itself as conservative "if conservative signifies that the present is subject to constant debate and criticsm, devoid of fashionable pressures to yield to every new idea."[31] In 1972, the RFS tried again to review its tenets, as well as a wide range of topics connected with university life.[32] RFS was patently eager to make positive contributions to university reform, but though equipped with a series of reform papers, their representatives proved unable to halt the forward march of the neo-conservative JES. The mild image the RFS tried to project of itself before the 1974 elections bears witness to its auto-reformist intentions. The RFS portrayed itself as "a group of politically engaged students working for freedom. As a student group, RFS represents the interests of students in a liberal-democratic way against party-political or confessional protectionism and against any kind of sociopolitical forms of collective irresponsibility."[33] Yet, despite the avowed intention of RFS subsection "Medicine" to deal with students' problems in as unpolitical a manner as possible,[34] politically inconvenient bookstalls set up in the vestibule of the anatomy theater repeatedly were being attacked and destroyed.[35] Political initiatives taken by the RFS hardly bear witness to any pronouncedly liberal attitudes. Thus, it suggested that the right of non-Austrian students to vote should be abolished on the grounds that "some 300,000 migrant workers"–the figure was deliberately exaggerated[36]–would subsequently and consequently obtain the vote, and in accord with their social position, cast their votes in favor of either the "Socialist or Communist Parties."[37] By way of mitigation of such a measure, the RFS proposed the institution of an advisory board for foreigners. An Innsbruck dueling society invited an attaché of the Republic of South Africa to give a lecture. When some democratic student groups tried to prevent this, a former RFS representative, attributing the protest to "Communist and Socialist cadre groups" suggested darkly that "The democratic sovereign" might shortly "be compelled to prove that it is strong enough to cope with its gravediggers," suggesting that the threat was, as he put it, "a present one."[38]

The RFS after 1975. Challenge by the Aktion Neue Rechte and Steep Decline

High school students traditionally have been politicized to an unusual degree in Austria, even though they were seldom organized as high school students. In 1970 they were able to throw out a markedly right-wing challenge to the RFS. In April of that year the AVM-Arbeitsvereinigung für Mittelschüler (literally, Work League for High School Students) was founded with its own periodical, Richtung. The League arranged lectures for a wide range of far-Right activists, including Robert Verbelen, sentenced to death in absentia in Belgium for Nazi crimes, and Norbert Burger.[39] Though outlawed at the end of 1973 for infringing the Law of Association, its successor, Aktion Neue Rechte-ANR (Action New Right) was founded in January 1974. Like its predecessors (its creator was Bruno Haas), it is probably the most representative of the far Right-wing intellectual group born after 1945, originally a member of the RFS. Though its avowed ambition was to concentrate its activities on universities and high schools, the ANR was barely able to expand its activities beyond the University of Vienna. During the following years, the ANR manifested its racist attitudes on various occasions. Thus, on the "Day of German Unity" it proclaimed the slogan "Not 6 million but only *(sic!)* 200,000 Jews died."[40] Scuffles at ANR meetings were not uncommon occurrences.[41]

The ANR's history before 1980 is amply recorded in the brochure *Am Beispiel ANR. Neonazismus in Österreich*, therefore attention will focus on its activities after 1980.[42] In the late 1970s, it became clear that the ANR would, after all, be unable to gain access to the bulk of former RFS voters, and that some ANR activists would not shrink from engaging in acts of physical violence. These provoked resistance, which built up over the years. In November 1985 a notable decision was handed down by the Constitutional Court that went against the ANR, a warning signal to all neo-Nazi associations.

The charge put in by the League of Socialist Students and Communist Student League was to find out whether the ANR candidature for the student parliament in 1977 was illegal. Another aspect of this Court decision is worth detailing. Between September 1981 and August 1982, Simon Wiesenthal, Edmund Reiss (former Vice-President of the Jewish Community in Austria), Alexander Giese (former head of the science section of Austrian Television), and branches of Schöps and Winter, Austrian chain-stores, were targets of ANR bombs.[43] In that connection, about half a dozen names cropped up time and again. At the neo-Nazi trial that opened in 1983 the chief defendants were three young intellectuals: Bruno Haas, Martin Neidthart, and Hermann Plessl.[44] The trial, which lasted twenty weeks instead of only eight as originally expected, showed up close affinities between the programs of the ANR and the former Nazi Party.[45] Of the nine sentences passed, Ekkehard Weil's share was five years, Attila Bajtsy's three years, Manfred Luxbacher's thirty months, Egon Baumgartner's twenty months, Hermann Plessl's eighteen months (conditional), Martin Neidthart's fifteen months (conditional), Gottfried Heinrich Küssel's 12 months (conditional), Bruno Haas' nine months (conditional), and Michael Witt's three months (conditional). According to the Austria Press Agency, 3 April 1984, the sentences pronounced fell far below of what had been provided in the Law against Reactivation (of the Nazi Party) that envisaged sentences between five and ten years, as well as life imprisonment for bomb attacks considered as acts of such reactivation.

The trial proved that the application of Austrian laws against neo-Nazism were beset with technical difficulties. Thus, only in November 1985, largely because of the decision against the ANR, was it possible to stop neo-Nazi groups from putting forward candidates for elections to the student parliament.[46] And only in January 1986 was appropriate legislation passed in the Austrian parliament that would make it difficult to distribute neo-Nazi leaflets.[47] That legislation should also facilitate the struggle waged against the distribution of far-Right polemical tracts, like *Halt*, in front of high schools.[48]

Laws, though, can be only one—albeit an important—step against neo-Nazi machinations at schools and universities, and it will remain important to fight against radical and extremist groups and ideologies with information of the majority. Despite the fact that in Austria an equivalent of the "Heidelberger Manifest" has not yet been published,[49] some representatives of universities or academic institutions will impede efforts toward more democracy. These are by no means right-wing extremists, but citations like the one made by the then president of the General Medical Council set one thinking: the local students of medicine would be 'lemurs in the hallways of the universities,' their clothes were suitable 'at best for tacky parties,' conditions in Viennese anatomy theatre were like 'a mess as on a Balkan railway station.' And finally: he is concerned about 'these doctors to come who are living in such a filthy milieu and in this atmosphere of a rag culture and even feel comfortable there.'"[50] Heinz Prokop, professor at Innsbruck University, stated in the *Österreichische Ärztezeitung* about drug addicts: "The subculture in which they are living has to be eradicated mercilessly," he suggested taking them in custody for three years, then to transferring them to "rigid ambulatory therapy" and only after these five years they should get their passports back.[51]

There is some evidence that the dual challenge from JES and ANR served to drive the RFS to the far-Right of the spectrum of Austrian student politics. That trend within the RFS was countrywide, which induced some liberal-minded RFS representatives to protest against the new trend, leave the RFS, and continue their political activities as independent members of the student parliament. The electoral decline of the RFS continued relentlessly. Between 1969 and 1983, altogether it had lost no less than 89 percent of its votes. In 1987, it was reduced to the status of a marginal group. Hand in hand with the decline of the RFS went the steady degeneration of student dueling societies, which were reduced to a state of insignificance.

CHANGING STUDENT POLITICS IN AUSTRIA?

The far right-wing scene at Austrian universities has undoubtedly undergone several structural and ideological changes since 1945, while retaining some elements of continuity from the pre-1945 period. Continuity was manifested in some extreme cases in verbal and physical attacks against students holding different views.

The far right-wing scene in Austria's student politics has run through three chronological and ideological phases. Thus, the RFS started out on a markedly right-wing course, attempted to incorporate liberal and neo-conservative ideas after 1965–1966, only to revert to a pronouncedly German-national, right-wing ideology after 1975.

What has changed the sociopolitical attitudes of students who would normally have been found on the Right of the political spectrum during the second half of the 1960s was a move away from both primitive populist notions of "blood-and-soil" and from Pan-Germanism toward a liberally tinged neo-conservatism. This is clearly reflected in student electoral records. The position of the entire spectrum of Austrian student politics, in any case, was considerably to the Right of that in Western Europe and the United States, and it is certain that, with the advent of the JES as a rival to the RFS on the Right, the latter could never be quite the same as before, losing both in general influence and in electoral strength.

The RFS badly misjudged the extent of the changing mood of Austria's student body after 1970 and failed to come up with sufficiently attractive answers to the neo-conservative and Europhile challenge thrown out by the JES. In those circumstances, the tactical response on the part of the RFS, to move back to the far-Right, could hardly have been more ill-advised. The RFS had failed to adjust.

Neo-Nazi student politics in Austria are not by any means dead. There is evidence enough in the activities of the ANR that a neo-Nazi potential exists, and it is doubtful whether, in spite of all that has happened, this potential can be ignored in the future. It seems most unlikely, barring major accidents in history, that neo-Nazism could ever regain the strength it could muster in the years betwen 1945 and 1965, let alone regenerate the full-blooded Nazism of pre-1945 vintage. As far ahead as it is possible to see, right-wing student politics in Austria will be dominated by the neo-conservative JES. Part of the social appeal of the latter for Austrian students with right-wing inclinations lies in its interest in élitist thinking and its concern with social prestige in general as well as with a certain caste-feeling– human propensities that have hardly been affected by any sociopolitical changes that have taken place in Austria and that will continue to present considerable appeal to this kind of student.

At Austria's high schools markedly right-wing agitation is likely to continue, but it is to be hoped that the systematic dissemination of objective political information—now at long last getting into its stride—will ultimately frustrate neo-Nazi endeavors.[52]

NOTES

1. Adolf Hitler, *Mein Kampf* (Munich, 1934), p. 182.

2. The constitutional law banning the Nazi Party was enacted on 8 May 1945. See J. Kocensky (ed.), *Dokumentation zur österreichischen Zeitgeschichte, 1945–1955*, 3d ed. (Vienna and Munich, 1980). Regarding Denazification at Austria's universities, see W. Weinert, "Die Entnazifizierung an österreichischen Hochschulen," in S. Meissl, K. D. Mulley, and O. Rathkolb (eds.), *Verdrängte Schuld, verfehlte Sühne* (Vienna, 1986), pp. 254–69.

3. *Kleines Volksblatt* (15 September 1946).

4. Weinert, p. 261.

5. Dokumentationsarchiv des österreichischen Widerstandes (ed.), *Rechtsextremismus in Österreich nach 1945* (Vienna, 1980), pp. 119 ff.

6. G. Forster, *Die Geschichte der österreichischen Hochschülerschaft 1945–1955* (Vienna, 1984), p. 250.

7. The law regulating the status and rights of Austria's university students (*Hochschülerschaftsgesetz*) was enacted in 1945 and, unlike its predecessor of 1935, provided for secret general elections. See Marina Fischer-Kowalski, "Zur Entwicklung von Universität und Gesellschaft in Österreich," in H. Fischer (ed.), *Das politische System Österreichs* (Vienna, 1974), pp. 571–624, quote from pp. 583–84.

8. W. Oberleitner, *Politisches Handbuch der Republik Österreich* (Vienna, 1960), p. 65.

9. P. Wrabetz, "Das nationalfreiheitliche Lager in Österreich", *Die Aula* (May 1973).

10. Ibid., (September 1961).

11. Ibid.

12. P. Eppel and H. Lotter (eds.), *Dokumentation zur österreichischen Zeitgeschichte 1955–1980* (Vienna and Munich, 1981), pp. 565–66.

13. *Die Aula* (November 1959).

14. Eppel and Lotter, pp. 566–67.

15. *Die Aula* (Janaury–February 1961).

16. Dokumentationsarchiv des österreichischen Widerstandes, p. 137.

17. *Die Aula* (March 1962).

18. Ibid., special edition, (October 1962).

19. Dokumentationsarchiv des österreichischen Widerstandes, p. 123.

20. *Die Aula* (January–June 1960, September 1961).

21. In May 1987 Erwin Hirnschall succeeded Norbert Steger, Vice-Chancellor in the former SPÖ-FPÖ coalition, as head of the Vienna organization of the FPÖ. See *Die Presse* (18 May 1987).

22. Eppel and Lotter, p. 565. On the Borodajkewycz case, see Heinz Fischer (ed.), *Einer im Vordergrund: Taras Borodajkewycz. Eine Dokumentation* (Vienna, 1966).

23. Dokumentationsarchiv des österreichischen Widerstandes, p. 124.

24. *Süddeutsche Zeitung* (26 March 1965).

25. Friedhelm Frischenschlager in an interview printed in *Profil* (4 February 1985).

26. Dokumentationsarchiv des österreichischen Widerstandes, p. 124; F. Keller, *Wien 1968. Eine heisse Viertelstunde* (Vienna, 1983, pp. 29 ff.; Eppel and Lotter, p. 569.

27. *profil* (18 February 1986).

28. A. Markovits and M. Freund, "Studie zur politischen Einstellung Wiener Studenten," *Österreichische Zeitschrift für Politikwissenschaft*, 3–4 (1974):537–46.

29. *report*, vol. 2, February 1970.

30. Ibid., vol. 5–6, February 1971.

31. As regards RFS representation, see *Studienführer 1971–2* (published by the ÖH at the University of Innsbruck), p. 17.

32. *RFS–uni aktuell* (Innsbruck), (April 1972).

33. Ibid., (January 1974).

34. Ibid., November 1973.

35. *Mediziner Zeitung, Zeitung des AKM* (Innsbruck) (December 1973).

36. Bundesministerium für Soziale Verwaltung (ed.), *Forschungsberichte aus Sozial- und Arbeitsmarktpolitik, Nr. 9: Ausländische Arbeitnehmer* (Vienna, 1984), p. 243.

37. W. Flucher, RFS chairman in Graz, in *Die Aula* (June 1973).

38. Letter to the editor of *Tiroler Tageszeitung* by Bernhard Wieser, as cited in *uni-press*, vol. 5 (February 1974).

39. Personal particulars to be found in Dokumentationsarchiv des österreichischen Widerstandes, as well as idem., *Am Beispiel ANR. Neonazismus in Österreich* (Vienna, 1981).

40. Dokumentationsarchiv des österreichischen Widerstandes, *Am Beispiel ANR*.

41. *report*, vol. 4 (June 1976).

42. See note 38.

43. *profil* (4 October 1982).

44. Ibid., (25 July 1983 and 24 October 1983). Other defendants were Michael Witt, Gottfried Heinrich Küssel, Egon Baumgartner, Attila Bajtsy, Manfred Luxbacher, and Ekkehard Weil.

45. Ibid. (20 February 1984).

46. Gabriel Lansky and Georg Zanger, "Das ANR Urteil und seine Folgen," in *Informationen der Gesellschaft für politische Aufklärung*, vol. 8 (March 1986).

47. Ibid.

48. *Halt* is distributed regularly at high schools in Vienna. It promotes strictly neo-Nazi tenets.

49. A group of FRG university professors asked for rigid measures against the "infiltration of German people by foreigners." Other professors answered to this "Heidelberger Manifest" by calling it a disgusting mixture of the dictionary of subhumans and of mean bureaucracy. (*Dokument und Analyse*, vol. 5, Munich, May 1982).

50. *profil* (2 January 1984).

51. Ibid. (19 April 1982).

52. As a first step, the Federal Ministry of Education, Arts and Sports published a brochure on *Wie begegnen wir demokratiefeindlichen Aktivitäten in der Schule?* (How to Counter Antidemocratic Activities at School).

The Waldheim Connection

MELANIE A. SULLY

Kurt Waldheim was born on 21 December 1918 in Sankt Andrä-Wördern, Lower Austria, the son of a school inspector. His grandfather was a blacksmith with the Czech name of Watzlawik but, because it sounded too Slavonic and culturally inferior, his father changed the name after the First World War. After secondary school and twelve-months military service as a volunteer, Waldheim enrolled at Vienna University Law School, simultaneously attending the Consular Academy. Proud of his diligence, he completed his legal studies in 1939 and gained his diploma at the consular academy. With the Nazi occupation of Austria, his father was detained by the Gestapo and subsequently lost his job. During the Second World War, Waldheim served in the German armed forces, a chapter that has provoked much controversy and whose details remain obscure.

The biographical note released by the Press and Information Department in Vienna at the start of the 1986 presidential campaign, laconically stated that, "Injured on the Eastern front, he returned to Austria and embarked on post-graduate legal studies, gaining his doctorate of law in 1944." This followed Waldheim's own story but had to be substantially modified as it became clear that he had neglected to mention his wartime career in the Balkans. The Press Department issued a new revised version just before the election, expanding on the previous bulletin,

Injured on the Eastern front in December 1941, he was exempted from service at the front and was transferred in April 1942 to the Balkans (Army High Command 12). In the summer of 1942 he was stationed in Arsakli in Greece as an interpreter. From 1943 onwards he served as an assistant adjutant with Army Group E (1c). During home leave he was able to continue his legal studies. In 1944 he gained his doctorate of law, then was posted back to Army Group E and returned home in May 1945.

This apparently innocuous addition raised more questions than it answered, since Army Group E was under the command of the notorious Austrian General Alexander Löhr, who was executed for war crimes in 1947. Waldheim insisted that he had neither witnessed nor had been personally involved in any acts of atrocity, but this was insufficient to silence his critics.

After the war he was briefly interned, Denazified, and entered the diplomatic service. From 1948–1951 he was First Secretary of the Austrian Embassy in Paris. For the next four years, he was chief of the Personnel Department in the Foreign Ministry, before becoming permanent observer to the United Nations in New York. He subsequently repesented his country as Ambassador to Canada and, from 1960–1964, was Director of the Department of Political Affairs in the Foreign Ministry, Vienna. From 1964–1968, he was Austria's permanent representative at the UN and chairman of the Outer Space Committee. From 1968–1970 he was Minister for Foreign Affairs in the People's Party government and in 1971 ran for the presidency and was defeated by the incumbent, Socialist Franz Jonas.

Waldheim returned to the United Nations, and in December 1971, was elected Secretary-General; five years later he was re-elected for a second term. He was prepared to run for a third term but was unsuccessful because of opposition from the Chinese. In 1983 he assumed the chairmanship of the Inter-Action Council. His stolid diplomatic career was punctuated by few moments of brilliance or excitement. The picture emerges of Waldheim, the obedient servant, keen to do his duty, serve his country, and keep out of trouble. Until 1986 his efforts were mostly rewarded, but his decision to have a second go at the presidency unleashed a storm of events that have not yet fully run their course.

THE PRESIDENCY

According to the Constitution, the Federal President is directly elected by the people every seven years. Dr. Rudolf Kirchschläger had held the post since 1974 and was ineligible for re-election. He was a nominee of the Socialist SPÖ, who had backed successful candidates for this post since the war. The powers of the President are prescribed by the Constitution, and in an indecisive election, his intervention can be important. Kirchschläger's reign had been uncontroversial and some thought he could have spoken out more on moral issues. The Greens, campaigning for this post for the first time in 1986, suggested that a President should encourage citizen initiatives and open investigations into alleged cases of corruption. They pointed out that, potentially, the President had wider powers than was supposed but that full use had never been made of the post. Waldheim, too, promised if elected to become an "active" President, which caused some consternation and fear that he would become authoritarian, going beyond the moderate consensual tradition. His promise in this respect was to contrast pathetically with his subsequent caricature as a "lame-duck" President.

The previous election in 1980 had aroused considerable anxiety since, although Kirchschläger had won handsomely, one of his opponents had been an extreme right-wing candidate, Norbert Burger of the National Democratic Party. Under the banner "Austria must stay German," he stood for a defence of the fatherland and condemned the "artificial" border along the Brenner Pass that separates the South Tyrol from Austria. Burger had been imprisoned for terrorist activities in his battle to "liberate" Germans South of the Brenner Pass. He made an overt appeal to the Pan-German nationalist vote mixed with a hatred of Communism and promises to reintroduce the death penalty and repeal the abortion laws. One of his election leaflets described how, as a boy of ten, he had experienced the jubilation that, he claimed, was shared by all Austria as Hitler's *Anschluss* united the country with the Reich.[1]

Empirical studies in the late 1970s had already revealed that sections of the population were susceptible to authoritarian attitudes and that an antidemocratic potential existed.[2] Burger's "law and order" platform could be expected to tap this reserve, and it finally won him 140,000 votes (3.2 percent of the electorate). In Carinthia he won 4.4 percent and in some areas in Styria, bordering Yugoslavia, the figure was as high as 6 percent. In Braunau-am-Inn, the birthplace of Hitler, he won 5 percent of the vote. Burger consistently did well in areas of relative economic decline along Austria's periphery, which felt left out of the general affluence.

The Burger votes shocked the complacency of the Second Republic, basking in the halcyon days of the Kreisky era and enjoying international acclaim for its economic success and model democracy. These concerns were to be overshadowed by developments in the 1986 campaign, when much of Austria's unconquered past came uncomfortably into the limelight. Burger's support in 1980 caused widespread concern that democracy could be under threat from the ultra-Right. The daily tabloid *Kurier* even went so far as to announce a "day of mourning" in an article of 20 May, "Republic with Light Brown Edges." This is worth noting since it is possible that Waldheim may have come under more internal criticism if such accusations had not been politically suspect.

The election was an uneasy reminder of the darker side in the normally hyperstable "social-liberal" Republic but provoked little international comment. Kreisky was opposed to banning right-wing groups for fear of driving them underground and preferred to concentrate instead on creating the economic conditions for democracy to thrive. The attitude of Austrians to their past surfaced sporadically during the Second Republic, only to disappear into oblivion until the next salutary encounter. Intellectuals and critics on the Left were disillusioned with the composition of Kreisky's early Cabinets, which included five former Nazis, although nothing exceptional or remarkable was noted by outside observers.[3] Kreisky's ongoing feud with Simon Wiesenthal over the Peter affair in the 1970s was also well known and largely accepted. Friedrich Peter, then head of the FPÖ, continued to be defended by Kreisky even after it had been disclosed that he had served in a company of the Waffen-SS involved in liquidating civilians on the Eastern front. Again, outside interest was minimal and the image of the country at this time was drenched in the glorious Hollywood myths of choir boys, Lippizaners, and the "Sound of Music."

The failure to tackle head on the problem of the past created a complex backlog of unresolved neuroses. The Waldheim case was an unfortunate culmination of deeper problems that involved issues far beyond the escapades of a wartime subaltern. The accusations about Waldheim's past were interpreted as an affront to the integrity of the entire country. The fact that a relentless campaign of "J'accuse" was identified with the World Jewish Congress, only served to heighten the tension. Austrians were accustomed to treating such disputes as a family affair and duly closed ranks against what was perceived to be uninformed foreign "meddling."

In 1983 the aged "sun king," Kreisky, retired from political life wearied by a disappointing election result. The "troubles" then began in earnest that were to erode Austria's cosy and legendary *Gemütlichkeit*. The catalogue included the infamous wine scandal of 1985 which hit exports and shook confidence in the quality of Austrian goods. This followed the "Reder handshake" and a "very important person" (VIP) welcome by the Minister of Defence for a former member of the SS who had been serving a life sentence in Italy for shooting civilian hostages. The "Hainburg incident" demonstrated too that Austria was entering a new era of less tolerance and a higher level of political conflict and violence. Allegations of police brutality were made after demonstrators were forcibly evacuated from the planned site of a controversial power plant. The Establishment was on the defensive, more insecure and unsettled than at any time since the war. Just at this moment, the Waldheim affair broke with devastating results for Austria, its image, and its political leaders.

THE CAMPAIGN

Waldheim was not a member of the conservative People's Party (ÖVP) but had made it clear that his Christian outlook made him sympathetic to its aims and policies. He was adopted as a candidate for the presidency early in 1985 and throughout was given unflinching support. The Socialists at this time were at a loss for a suitable and willing rival and some, to begin with, had even toyed with the idea of backing Waldheim. Eventually in June the SPÖ put forward its own candidate, Kurt Steyrer, a physician and Minister for Health and the Environment. Steyrer was born in 1920 in Linz, Upper Austria, and was portrayed as a sympathetic, humane and socially minded family man. Polls in July 1985 showed that Waldheim had a ten point lead, which he kept all year.[4] The SPÖ was accustomed to winning presidential elections, but fears began to mount that for the first time things could go wrong. Kurt Waldheim had the advantage of not being associated with the scandals and mishaps of the SPÖ-FPÖ coalition, unlike Steyrer, who was in the Cabinet. With international experience and good contacts, Waldheim was billed as "the Man the World Trusts," a slogan that quickly turned sour but at the time demonstrated his superiority over his rival. With Steyrer trailing hopelessly in the polls, rumors circulated that the Waldheim case was dug up with the connivance of the Socialists to ruin the favorite's chances,[5] although this was repeatedly denied by the SPÖ.

As far as the international press was concerned, Waldheim was a colorless bureaucrat, and the Austrian election in its early stages aroused little interest. In ten years at the United Nations, Waldheim had never made much of an impact on world affairs and expectations of newsworthy items were low. A "profile" of Waldheim in the London *Sunday Times* (17 November 1985) was hard-pressed to record anything memorable in his career at all and quoted a senior United Nations official's impression that "the trouble was that in spite of his tremendous input of work and energy, he personified the worst aspects of the old Habsburg empire. He was much too ingratiating, a fault compounded by his B-movie accent and constant obsession with his image." The article continued, "Others are even less charitable. Waldheim has been described as looking and behaving like a head waiter, as the only man who could bend over backwards and forwards at the same time. A fellow Austrian diplomat summed him up with the title of his country's most famous novel, Robert Musil's *Der Mann ohne Eigenschaften-(The Man Without Qualities)*."

Just after this profile was written, Waldheim's autobiography *Im Glaspalast der Weltpolitik* appeared, the first stage in a chain of events which was to alter the world's assessment of the future President. In March 1986 the Austrian magazine *profil* published details about Waldheim's past and it soon became clear that he had omitted references to his wartime activities in the Balkans, apparently in order to spare his readers the boredom of this chapter. Yet Waldheim had underestimated the interest in an area suffering under the merciless occupation of the Germans, in the throes of a partisan war where slaughter of civilians was commonplace and where plans for the genocide of Greek Jews were being launched. Photographs showing Waldheim in the Balkans instead of recovering from wounds, diligently absorbed in his law books in Vienna, all added to the desire to know more about his ventures. The World Jewish Congress in New York as well as the *New York Times* and *profil* all obliged and continued to publicize the missing details on Waldheim's war years. One famous photograph shows Waldheim at Podgorica airport (now Titograd) with an SS and an Italian general in May 1943, the time of "Operation Black", a huge German-Italian offensive in Montenegro against Yugoslav partisans.

These gaps in his memoirs and his lapse of memory lost him credibility abroad and suspicions grew that he was covering up his involvement in the Final Solution. During his time in Greece, rail deportations of Jews to the death camps began on a massive scale and Eichmann himself visited Salonika in January 1943 to oversee the operation. Waldheim's response was unconvincing, muddled, and inconsistent. He denied all knowledge of the deportations, the reprisals against the partisans, and the burning of villages carried out by the German army in retreat. He had always, coincidentally, been on leave or outside of Salonika when the atrocities were committed and claimed to have only just learned about the deportation and killing of the Jews in this area through the newspapers. At crucial times, Waldheim had always flown over the country and had never witnessed the horrors of the conflagration. As a translator and ordinary contact officer with the Italians Waldheim, apparently, had missed just about every major exciting event in the war and many particularly in the United States, finding this difficult to swallow, became sure of his guilt. Waldheim now resembled a more grotesque Habsburg predicament and was trapped in a Kafkaesque "Metamorphosis." Far from being a "man without qualities," he was now to be reviled on placards in the United States as the "butcher of Austria."[6]

At this point the word *campaign* took on a new and sinister meaning and the ÖVP became involved in heated exchanges with what it condemned as a "media tribunal."[7] The World Jewish Congress (WJC) in frequent press releases provided the necessary ammunition, claiming that Waldheim had been involved in brutal interrogations, torture, and so-called "cleansing" (*Säuberung*) operations in Bosnia in 1942. The WJC further reported that Waldheim had distinguished himself and had been decorated following the notorious Kozara battle in 1942, a bloody massacre by the Germans of Yugoslav partisans. Following this the *New York Post* on 26 March 1986 even ran a story entitled "Papers Show Waldheim Was SS Butcher." The article concluded with Waldheim's own comment on the "mopping up" of partisans: "That was a completely normal activity and has nothing to do with atrocities or criminal acts. That was a completely correct and respectable activity." Waldheim modestly replied that his award was a purely routine affair and on Austrian television on 25 March 1986 protested against the description of the Kozara campaign as a "massacre." The election battle had by now become transnational with the media determining the pace and style and Waldheim's supporters searching obsessively for those behind the allegations. The election degenerated irretrievably into an emotional brawl between those who were for, and those who opposed, Waldheim.

What emerges strongly from Waldheim's past is his penchant for accommodation with the mood of the time. His explanation for involvement with the Nazi student league and mounted corps was that he wished to safeguard his own position and that of his family and further his career prospects in the diplomatic service. As far as he knew or could remember, he never formally joined the SA or the Nazi Party and claimed to be mystified by the appearance of documentary material that suggested a different story. Waldheim's selective amnesia personified the dilemma of an entire war generation, of those who were enmeshed in a bestial system not of their making and who felt that they too, just like Waldheim, had simply "done their duty." Waldheim became a symbol for those who realized that they no longer needed to feel ashamed or guilty of the war and the past. For Austrians, the Catholic Waldheim had never looked much like a Nazi war criminal and resentment mounted during the campaign against what was considered to be the unfairness of the attacks.

President Kirchschläger went on television on 22 April 1986 to give his considered opinion on the controversy. The United Nations file on war crimes had been made available in the meantime to assist in determining Waldheim's participation in atrocities in the Balkans. Kirchschläger concluded that in his judgement insufficient evidence was available for the case to stand up in a court of law. The documents suggested, according to the President, that Waldheim had not been an Intelligence officer and had not been in a high enough position to issue orders against the civilian popu-

lation. After perusal of the documents handed over by the WJC, Kirchschläger added that Waldheim nevertheless must have been well informed
abut the entire direction of the war in the Balkans as he was responsible
for writing reports twice a day for his section and as such must have been
aware of reprisals against the partisans. Kirchschläger continued that accusations should be made with caution and that no country, not even the
United States had completely overcome the past.

The furore continued, and for some like Theo Sommer of the West German newspaper *Die Zeit*, "the point is not that Kurt Waldheim is a war criminal but that he is a liar."[8] Sommer also cited passages from Waldheim's doctoral
thesis full of "Nazi clichés" and anti-Slav invective. Others, like Professor P.
Pulzer of Oxford, concluded gloomily that it was a far worse indictment of the
man than if he had been telling the truth. If Waldheim had really only just
discovered the details of the Holocaust, then it showed a tragic inability to ask
questions, understand the past, and learn from its mistakes.[9]

Meanwhile a counterattack had been launched on Steyrer, revealing
that he had left the Catholic Church, had refused military service, and was
under suspicion as a young doctor for having carried out an abortion.
Waldheim, by contrast, was supposed to defend traditional Christian eth-
ics, morals, and values. In one of the most sordid and ugly campaigns of
the Second Republic, the Socialists refrained from open attacks on Waldheim for fear of losing further support. The Party was in a difficult position
and had to appease Left intellectuals and Party workers, critical of Waldheim, without exposing itself to scrutiny on its own handling of the vexed
problem of *Vergangenheitsbewältigung* (conquest of the past).

On the eve of the election, Austrians were divided, confused, and embittered. Many old wounds had been opened, extremism had replaced
tolerance and anti-Semitism was felt to be respectable. The *causa* Waldheim
had become grotesquely distorted and inflated and exposed the Republic's
deficiencies in not coming to terms with the past. "Herr Waldheim ist Herr
Österreicher" commented the political scientist, Professor A. Pelinka.[10]
Like many others he "had done his duty," had never been a committed
Nazi, nor had been in the resistance. When the time came, he was ready
to help in the postwar reconstruction; he was always to be found as a faithful, humble, and obedient servant in the ranks of the majority. He was a
"victim" of Nazism and now, too, was similarly caught up in a pernicious
and slanderous campaign. The events of 1986 had shown the inability of
a system, very much run by powerful economic and party cartels, to accept
or deal with political conflict. Austria's postwar democracy has been directed and controlled from above and the scope for criticism has been limited and discouraged. The reserves and experience were consequently lacking to meet the challenge of something as contentious as the Waldheim affair.

TABLE 1
RESULTS (PERCENT) IN THE LÄNDER

	First Ballot				Second Ballot	
	Waldheim	Steyrer	Scrinzi	Meissner-Blau	Waldheim	Steyrer
Burgenland	47.0	49.4	0.6	3.0	49.3	50.7
Carinthia	43.8	49.0	2.8	4.4	48.3	51.7
Lower Austria	52.5	42.7	0.7	4.1	55.8	44.2
Upper Austria	49.6	44.7	1.3	4.4	53.1	46.9
Salzburg	53.2	39.3	1.7	5.8	58.2	41.8
Styria	50.2	43.8	1.3	4.7	54.3	45.7
Tyrol	63.1	29.0	0.9	7.0	68.7	31.3
Vorarlberg	62.8	25.9	1.3	10.0	70.8	29.2
Vienna	39.2	51.7	0.9	8.2	43.8	56.2
Austria	49.7	43.7	1.2	5.5	53.9	46.1

Note: The turn-out was 89.5 percent in May and 87.2 percent in June.

THE RESULTS

More was at stake on election day, 4 May, than simply the presidency. For many foreign observers, Austria's image had been unhappily tarnished. Waldheim had steadfastly refused to withdraw from the contest, and internal support was unpleasantly emotional and vociferous. Domestic issues, too, played a role in the complex scenario. Toward the end of 1985, a major crisis shook the nationalized steel industry undermining confidence in the Government's handling of the economy. This seriously damaged the credibility of the Socialists to maintain full employment, traditionally one of their strong points. After sixteen years in office, the SPÖ seemed stale and had become associated with suspect deals, mismanagement, and scandals. Just a week before polling day, surveys discovered that 7 percent of the voters were still undecided, a higher number of "late-deciders" than normal.[11] Electoral volatility is on the increase in Austria but the extra pressure resulting from international glare and hostility further unsettled voters. At the beginning of 1986, Steyrer had started to close the gap on his rival and the election promised to have a close finish. The allegations were estimated to have cost Waldheim about 3 percent in support but this was more than compensated by the 8 percent who switched to him in sympathy.[12]

In the first ballot on 4 May, Waldheim failed to secure the presidency by just 16,000 votes. In five provinces, he won an absolute majority and scored over 55 percent of the vote among the young and first-time voter. For the SPÖ, it was the worst result since 1951 and Steyrer could only win an absolute majority in Vienna (see Table 1). Even here there were disturbing signs of high abstentions in the working-class districts. Waldheim received solid backing from the rural areas and also did well among the white collar workers, the new middle class, and the well educated. Of the other candidates, Otto Scrinzi, a former member of the FPÖ who made an overt appeal to the German-nationalist vote, had above average support from those over 70 and men. The Green candidate, Freda Meissner-Blau, did well among the young, women, and the well educated. These two candidates withdrew from the second ballot, which took place on 8 June. This time victory was assured for Waldheim and he won 54 percent of the vote. The Greens split evenly between the two remaining candidates whereas Scrinizi's supporters opted overwhelmingly for Waldheim.

The shock of defeat had an immediate impact on the SPÖ, and Federal Chancellor Sinowatz announced his resignation, to be replaced by the younger, pragmatic Franz Vranitzky.[13] Leopold Gratz, the Foreign Minister, resigned in solidarity with Sinowatz and was succeeded by Peter Jankowitsch. This Cabinet reshuffle proved to be the salvation for the SPÖ, since it was calculated that without these changes, losses in the November general election would have been greater. The ÖVP, mistakenly, saw no urgency for radical improvements at the top, and Alois Mock stayed on as leader. After a poor performance in the November 1986 election, Mock took his Party into coalition with the Socialists assuming for himself the controversial post of Foreign Minister.[14] As such he became responsible for improving Austria's battered image abroad, a task made even more difficult through his unwavering commitment to Waldheim.

THE IMAGE

Experts and academics were consulted on how best to proceed with the planned "correction" of image. Setting up Jewish museums, monuments, and cemeteries was discussed and elaborate schemes were floated to improve relations with Austrian emigrés. Information and propaganda were in future to be geared to portraying the positive contributions of Austria in the fields of culture and human rights.[15] Sensitive issues such as anti-Semitism and the Nazi question were to be set in a wider European context. Conflicting views circulated on the existing levels of anti-Semitism in the Republic and some surveys claimed it had not risen markedly during the presidential campaign. Others, such as Professor Bernd Marin of Florence University, challenged the methodological basis of the questionnaires and suggested that anti-Semitic feeling was stronger.[16]

In the aftermath of the election, Austrians became melancholic and introspective, but still chose for the most part to blame the foreign press and the World Jewish Congress for their troubles. Their President became a lone and tragic figure, snubbed or ignored by world leaders and confined to routine tasks within Austria. Waldheim's isolation entered a dramatic and serious phase toward the end of April 1987 with the decision by the United States government to place him on the "watch list" and so effectively bar him from entering America as a private citizen. This fateful move, coming less than one year after Waldheim's election, resurrected disputes on the war, Nazism, and "conquering the past" and placed a new, intolerable strain on the Socialist-People's Party coalition.

THE UNITED STATES AND THE "WATCH LIST"

After a twelve-month inquiry into Waldheim's wartime activities, the U. S. Justice Department in conjunction with the State Department decided to ban him from entering the United States. Waldheim insisted that he had nothing to hide and allowed the North Americans to inspect relevant documents. U.S. Attorney General Edwin Meese came to different conclusions and, in a 200-page ruling, considered that the evidence collected, "establishes a *prima facie* case that Kurt Waldheim assisted or otherwise participated in the persecution of persons because of race, religion, national origin or political opinion. The Department of Justice has therefore ordered, as required by law, that Kurt Waldheim's name be added to the watch list. His name will be added to a look-out system to alert consular officers as to his *prima facie* ineligibility to enter the United States".

Waldheim is the only head of State to appear on the list, although Pierre Trudeau was banned in the 1950s on suspicion of pro-Moscow sympathies. The "watch list" is designed to exclude, among others, subversives, extremists, criminals, and terrorists. It forms part of the Immigration and Nationality Act and under Section 212 states that,

> the following classes of aliens shall be ineligible to receive visas and shall be excluded from admission into the United States. . . . any alien who during the period beginning on March 23, 1933, and ending on May 8, 1945, under the direction of or in association with—
> (A) the Nazi government in Germany,
> (B) any government in any area occupied by the military forces of the Nazi government of Germany,
> (C) any government established with the assistance or cooperation of the Nazi government of Germany, or
> (D) any Government which was an ally of the Nazi government of Germany, ordered, incited, assisted, or otherwise participated in the persecution of any person because of race, religion, national origin, or political opinion.

Waldheim joined 40,000 others who are banned for various reasons; about a dozen of these cases are included under the regulations of the Holtzmann Amendment of 1978. This was designed to tighten up on war criminals, such as Ivan Demjanjuk and Karl Linnas, seeking refuge in the United States. An Office of Special Investigations was set up in the Justice Department with a research budget of 2 million dollars and a staff of around fifty experts, including lawyers and historians. Suspicion of Nazi atrocities is sufficient reason for being barred or asked to leave the United States. In 1984 the OSI put Franz Hausberger, then Mayor of Mayrhofen in the Tyrolean Zillertal, on the list after discovering his SS past.

After the United States decision, Canada announced that although a visit by Waldheim was not planned, it would be considered nevertheless "undesirable." Britain cautiously stated that there was insufficient evidence to follow the United States example and reiterated its respectful view of Waldheim as a democratically elected head of a friendly State. Robert Rhodes James, Conservative MP for Cambridge and a former private secretary to Waldheim at the United Nations, urged the government in a speech in the House of Commons to take tougher action.[17] He is convinced that Waldheim lied about his war record and is unfit to hold high office.

Austria's isolation was painfully obvious and the President was becoming an increasing burden. The reaction in Austria was a mixture of shock, indignation, and anger. Thomas Klestil, the Austrian Ambassador to Washington, was recalled to Vienna for urgent consultation. The Americans' pious assurance that "close and friendly relations" between the two countries would continue and that the decision in no way reflected "adverse feelings to the Austrian people" was greeted with skepticism. Alois Mock, the Foreign Minister, categorically rejected the decision, claiming that the decree did not conform with a single European legal convention and was tantamount to blackmail. The Austrian authorities demanded immediate access to any supposed incriminating material. The media supported this stance in an amazing display of internal solidarity. Before the announcement, opinion polls had shown increasing dissatisfaction with the coalition government that had been formed in January and only 21 percent of the voters were happy with its performance. Discontent was particularly widespread, with the coalition's bewildering plans for subsidies to the nationalized industries and its confusing policy on the purchase of Swedish fighter aircraft. Squabbles of this kind were temporarily brushed aside in the rush to condemn the North Americans, and one tabloid, the *Neue Kronen-Zeitung*, even referred to a medieval style inquistion and foreign provocateurs.

Federal Chancellor Vranitzky was quick to defend the President, anxious that he should be protected from "unjust accusations." Waldheim made a defiant appearance on television once again to state that he had a clear conscience. He made a strong, emotional appeal to all Austrians to support him in fighting a measure he found "disturbing and incomprehensible." "I am sure that truth and justice will win," he said, recalling that he had actively worked for peace at the United Nations and had even helped United States hostages in Iran.

The United States press was equally of one mind and uncritically backed the decision of the Justice Department. The British press, too, was solid in its anti-Waldheim line, although criticism of the United States bullying tactics and hypocrisy were felt to be in order. According to the *Guardian* of 29 April 1987: "the head of a decent state has to be above suspicion, not just innocent in the sense of not, or not yet, proved guilty," which was exactly what the Austrians repudiated. The *Guardian* also casually remarked in the same issue in a back-page profile of Waldheim that

> there has not yet been any serious concern over his habit of carrying a gun. This was confirmed during the election campaign by his son Gerhardt, who said: 'When I asked about the pistol he told me it was from Greece. He said "My God, those were the days," but would never expand on it'." An editorial in the London *Times* on the same day ran the unambiguous title of "The Ineligible President" and commented in schoolmasterly fashion, "Naturally, many Austrians–probably a majority–are outraged. But if they had wanted to avoid such humiliating treatment of their head of state, they should not have elected him. They made their choice. They must now take the inevitable consequences."

The one-sided foreign reaction gave, paradoxically, a timely fillip to Waldheim's waning image in domestic politics. After almost a year his impact had been insignificant and he had appeared as a withered figure at few functions. The United States ban, like the campaign of 1986, transformed him into a martyr to defend against the alien Goliath. Waldheim announced that a "white book" was well under way which would give a full, unexpurgated account of his war career and prove his innocence. North American reaction viewed the exercise as more of a whitewash and curiously belated. The subject of a "white book" caused some disagreement between the two main parties since the SPÖ, unlike the ÖVP, insisted that it should go beyond a mere listing of events and include Waldheim's own personal rejection of the Third Reich period.

Pressure on Waldheim to do something for his own and his country's good intensified despite obvious sympathy for his plight. Michael Graff, General-Secretary of the ÖVP and a lawyer by training, advised against suing the North Americans because of differences in the legal systems, although Heinrich Keller, Central-Secretary of the SPÖ and also a lawyer, thought legal proceedings were advisable. Simon Wiesenthal, head of the Jewish Documentation Centre in Vienna, criticized Waldheim's bungling of the affair, claiming that the North Americans could have been persuaded against taking such a drastic step. An international historians' commission could have been set up to investigate the case and this would have won more goodwill. The right-wing FPÖ supported Waldheim against the unfairness of the attacks but added that he could have done more earlier to clear his name. For the FPÖ, the honor of an entire war generation and its soldiers was at stake. The Green-Alternative group, represented for the first time in parliament, criticized the North Americans but believed that the onus was on Waldheim to do something positive. The Greens were quick to cite the hypocrisy of the United States that, according to the revelations of the "Paperclip Conspiracy," played a dubious role in enlisting former Nazis in its service.[18]

A revival of the Waldheim affair was an embarrassment for the SPÖ, since a year earlier the Party had put its own candidate forward and now, in government with the ÖVP, it was difficult to explain to the rank and file the need to support the former enemy. Heinrich Keller played the role of appeaser, arguing that Vranitzky, as Federal Chancellor, was obliged to stand by the Federal President but added that this did not mean that Socialists had to identify themselves totally with Waldheim. The President also had a duty, Keller continued, to act on his own behalf. Socialist Deputy Heinz Fischer, leader of the Parliamentary Party, went a step further and called for Waldheim to take a clear position on the entire war period. He was particularly unhappy with the unfortunate and contentious phrase once used by Waldheim that he had merely "done his duty" as a soldier in the German army.

With the President in international quarantine, the responsibility of representing the Republic abroad fell to the Federal Chancellor, Dr. Vranitzky. At the beginning of May he paid an unofficial visit to the Netherlands to open a Jewish Historical Museum, partly financed by Austrain firms and assisted by funds from his government. The ceremony was boycotted by some Orthodox Jews but others believed that the gesture of goodwill should be accepted as a sign of atonement. Austria had contributed 400,000 guilders to the 30 million guilder project.

Toward the end of the month, Vranitzky decided to go ahead with a planned visit to the United States, believing that a cancellation would increase even further Austria's dangerous isolation. His Foreign Minister, Mock, Waldheim, and Jörg Haider, leader of the FPÖ, all expressed reservations about the visit. Relations with the United States had clearly been strained despite the insistence of the Justice Department that the "watch list" decision only applied to Dr. Waldheim as a private citizen. Austrians were outraged that a traditionally good ally should humiliate them in this way. It was recalled that Austria had an impeccable record in providing asylum for refugees from Hungary in 1956, from Czechoslovakia in 1968, and from Poland in 1981. Austrian soldiers had been sent to the Golan Heights as part of a United Nations peacekeeping force and the country had a proud record as a transit stop for Jews leaving Eastern Europe. All these points seemed to have been ignored by the North Americans whose own image had of late been found deficient.

Waldheim's plans to visit Jordan later in the year, his first overseas engagement, were unaffected by the controversy. Hungarian Foreign Minister Peter Varkonyi visited Vienna and intimated that a visit by Waldheim to Budapest had been discussed and was likely to take place in 1988. The Soviet news agency TASS had described the United States' decision as an "unfriendly act" inspired by "Zionist circles." Waldheim had become a political pawn in the complex power game between East and West, and it was ironic that a Catholic conservative should be dependent for support on Eastern Europe and the Arab world. Waldheim was convinced that the campaign against him was part of an elaborate strategy masterminded by enemies he had made as United Nations General Secretary. During his time in New York, the United Nations had passed a resolution condemning Zionism as racist. Others felt that Austria was paying for Kreisky's pro-Arab foreign policy of the 1970s. By now it was clear that more was involved than simply the truth behind Waldheim's memoirs and it was becoming increasingly difficult to find an acceptable escape route.

Pressure to take legal action grew, and an opportunity arose following a meeting in May 1987 of the World Jewish Congress in Hungary. The president of the WJC, Edgar Bronfman, launched a strong attack on Waldheim describing him as "part and parcel of the Nazi killing-machine." According to Bronfmann, Waldheim's lies and misdeeds were so obvious that "it's almost a crime against humanity to have very much to do with this man as an individual." The head of the Israelitic Cultural Community in Vienna, Paul Grosz, doubted that there was sufficient evidence to judge Waldheim and some disquiet was apparent with the lack of prior consultation by the WJC in New York on such a sensitive matter. Waldheim immediately filed a law suit for slander against Bronfmann who seemed unperturbed and declared his willingness to travel to Vienna to answer the charges. This development raised the unpleasant prospect of an emotional battle against World Jewry with Vienna as the stage and added another, dangerous dimension to the saga. Waldheim further declared that he was considering taking legal action against the "monstrous defamations" made by the North Americans. Speaking in Innsbruck on 4 May 1987, he said, "the time has come to counter these calumnies in the courts." Legal experts mentioned the technical difficulties involved in suing the U.S. Attorney General and warned that such action against the media, on past experience, was likely to be expensive and unsuccessful.

At the same time, Alois Mock announced the long-awaited news that an international commission of experts would be set up to investigate the allegations. The commission's job would be to evaluate Waldheim's role as a lieutenant in Army Group E of the Wehrmacht. Academics within Austria, such as Gerhard Botz of Salzburg and Erika Weinzierl of Vienna, were sceptical of the value of such an exercize. Apprehension was expressed about the suggestion that the panel should be appointed by Austrians and that the President should have a veto. Mock adamantly rejected the notion of an external appointment of the commission with the words "we are not a vassal State." The decision to establish such a body was long overdue and taken under pressure in an effort to give the impression of openness. The selection and membership of the commission remained a delicate issue with the esteemed Military History Institute in Freiburg, Breisgau, under Manfred Messerschmidt, put forward as a possible arbiter.

Meanwhile experts headed by Felix Ermacora, professor of law in Vienna, had been dispatched to Belgrade by the Vranitzky government to examine archive material and assess the United States' claims. Professor Ermacora is an ÖVP member of parliament and has a reputation as a United Nations authority on human rights. He was recently doing research into the refugee problem in Afghanistan and had been one of the first to urge Waldheim to take legal action. The team included Kurt Peball and the military historian Rauchensteiner. The publication of Waldheim's "white book" was delayed until the government had been able to study the experts' report. According to details leaked by the press, Waldheim denies in the book all knowledge of deportations and involvement in "Operation Black," the commando action against the partisans in May 1943.[19] The book includes material collected by Waldheim's son that throws light on his movements and duties.

The Austrians called repeatedly for the North Americans to release the documents that had prompted them to put Waldheim on the "watch list." Washington procrastinated and sent a delegation to Vienna to offer a verbal explanation of the decision causing further outrage and insult. They were concerned with Waldheim's role in the Kozara campaign and had been examining anti-Semitic propaganda reputed to have been distributed and initialled by him. He was also under suspicion for handing over civilians to the SS in Bosnia in the spring of 1942. The attitude of the North Americans caused a great deal of offense and resentment and prolonged support for Waldheim. Ultimately the cracks within the coalition began to appear and criticisms of Waldheim became more open and frequent.

EPILOGUE

The two coalition partners, in an effort to show a united front, decided to draw up a joint statement to put before parliament on 14 May. With discontent mounting in the SPÖ a compromise resolution was painfully worked out that condemned the unjustified attacks. The SPÖ withdrew positive support for Waldheim although the ÖVP believed this was implicit in the declaration. Anti-Semitism, religious, political, and racial discrimination were also repudiated. The motion was passed on 14 May 1987 with the votes of the three main parties against the Greens and with some Socialist abstentions.

Jörg Haider, the right-wing populist leader of the FPÖ, sensing the new mood, attacked Waldheim for not doing more and for his memory problems. An opinion poll published in *Die ganze Woche* suggested that most Austrians, wearied by the affair, would not vote for the Waldheim in a presidential election. Vice-Chancellor Mock's speech was greeted with stony silence from the SPÖ, as he drearily referred to his disillusionment with the United States and the important geopolitical role of Austria in East-West relations. A tedious historical account of the "watch list" affair followed and little enthusiasm was evident even among the ranks of the ÖVP. Some of Mock's statements were not politically astute, and he made insensitive references to the "resistance" years 1934–1938 after the murder of Dollfuss by the Nazis. This was a period when many Socialists were in exile or imprisoned. The Party had been outlawed after the civil war in 1934 and regard the following years as a dictatorship that paved the way for Hitler.

Mock also chided the Great Powers for having tolerated the *Anschluss* and reminded his audience that not everyone who had worn a German uniform had been a Nazi. As Heinz Fischer of the SPÖ called for a joint fight against anti-Semitism, he was applauded by deputies from the People's Party. Fischer has made no secret of his disgust with Waldheim's statement that he had only "done his duty" (*Pflichterfüllung*) in Hitler's army. During the debate a Green deputy, Andreas Wabl, caused a sensation by unfurling a swastika protesting that it was a disgrace the President had served under such a flag. In the resulting uproar, the proceedings were suspended until tempers cooled. Shadows from Austria's dark past were continuing to haunt the country in a public parliamentary spectacle.

With relations between the coalition partners deteriorating there seemed little hope of a speedy way out of the dilemma. Foreign Minister Alois Mock started work on a "diplomatic offensive" designed to send envoys to the major European capitals to convince governments that Waldheim was not a war criminal. This was considered insufficient without a change in the President's own attitude and pressure on Waldheim to make a statement that would acknowledge the tragedies and mistakes of the past was intensified. In a speech before a battalion of war veterans, he referred to the years after 1938 under the Germans. He described how he like many other young Austrians had joined the Wehrmacht and had realized only too late the full horrors of the Nazi regime. A few days later, Waldheim appeared on television and confessed that he had made mistakes but that it had not always been easy to talk about such difficult times. He openly condemned the Holocaust and anti-Semitism in a broadcast that many believed was long overdue. The President explained that he had not participated in the war for ideological reasons or through military fanaticism, but that a free decision had not been possible. He regretted the atrocities that had taken place in the Balkans but once against stressed that he had not been personally involved.

Michael Graff, General-Secretary of the ÖVP, praised the speech, but for many others it had come too late to heal the wounds. Graff frequently aggravated the situation by criticising the World Jewish Congress for inciting the campaign against Waldheim. Ultimately, Graff had to resign. Graff's truculent conspiracy theories created enemies within his own party as well as the Socialists. Erhard Busek, the ÖVP's deputy mayor of Vienna, clashed with Graff and worried about a revival of anti-Semitism. An internal power struggle in the People's Party which gained momentum after the November election setbacks, has still not been resolved and continues to be fueled by the Waldheim controversy. The SPÖ is also divided and the leader of the Socialist Youth, Alfred Gusenbauer, has called upon Waldheim to resign. The Party's Central Secretary, Heinrich Keller, has rejected this as a dangerous move that could create a "stab in the back" myth. Political leaders, parties, academics, and the country's democracy have all been severely tested by the Waldheim debate. The scars of this trauma are likely to remain for some time regardless of history's judgement on Lieutenant Waldheim.

An historians' commission was finally set up, headed by Hans Rudolf Kurz, and a report was presented in February 1988. The findings caused a furor in the already shaky coalition government and bitterly divided the country. Whilst no evidence had been found to suggest that Waldheim was a war criminal, the historians believed that he had been well informed of the situation in the Balkans and moreover had done nothing to prevent atrocities from occurring. Mock and Waldheim believed somewhat naïvely that the President was in the clear, but Vranitzky, obviously disturbed by the report, expected a fuller response.

In an interview with the press on Austrian television, the Chancellor hinted that he might resign if the Waldheim affair continued to absorb so much of his time to the detriment of other important official business. Waldheim's own appearance on television failed to address the main problems, and his insistence on staying in office for the sake of the fatherland provoked further hostility. According to the constitution, it is difficult to remove the Federal President without a two-thirds majority in Parliament. Under Mock, the People's Party stood by Waldheim, although public opinion was turning against him and some unease was expressed by leading industrialists and conservative supporters.

Meanwhile the country was becoming increasingly polarised and subject to constant examination by the international press. An additional specter loomed on the horizon with the fiftieth anniversary of the *Anschluss*, and it was considered prudent to do nothing which might further destabilize the domestic scene until the "Ides of March" were over. Waldheim at all costs was to keep a low profile until a calmer, more rational discussion could ensue. The Waldheim case and Austria's failure to confront its past had, by a strange twist of history, coincided to confront the Second Republic with its greatest challenge. Whatever the outcome it will be some time before the wounds and the bitter memories begin to fade.

NOTES

1. *Folge* 62 (October 1979), distributed to households.

2. *Projekt Vergangenheitsbewältigung*, under the direction of Professor K. Stadler, (Institute for Contemporary History, Linz University, 1977).

3. See A. Pelinka, *Windstille* (Vienna, 1985), p. 60.

4. See F. Plasser and P. Ulram, "Das Jahr der Wechselwähler. Wahlen und Neustrukturierung des österreichischen Parteiensystems 1986." *Österreichisches Jahrbuch für Politik*, 1986 (Munich, 1987), pp. 31–80.

5. *Kurier* (22 March 1986).

6. *Wochenpresse*, nr. 18/87.

7. See A. Khol, T. Faulhaber, and G. Ofner, *Die Kampagne* (Munich, 1987), pp. 7–25.

8. Theo Sommer, "An Inch by Inch Striptease," *Newsweek* (2 June 1986).

9. In a "Club 2" broadcast on Austrian television, 24 June 1986.

10. In *Pflichterfüllung*, published by the "Group New Austria" (Vienna, n.d.), p. 4.

11. Plasser and Ulram, p. 41.

12. E. Gehmacher, F. Birk, and G. Ogris, "Die Waldheim-Wahl," *Journal für Sozialforschung* 26 (1986):326.

13. See M. A. Sully, "Austria, Waldheim and After," *The World Today* 42 (August–September 1986):127–29.

14. See M. A. Sully, "Austria at the Crossroads," *The World Today* 43(February 1987): 21–23; and "Austria: The New Partnership," *The World Today* (June 1987):106–109.

15. See *profil* (12 January 1987).

16. Research by C. Härpfer in "Is There Still anti-Semitism?" and published by the Paul-Lazarsfeld Society (Vienna), in *Austria's Way to Democracy*, suggested there was no increase in anti-Semitism, as did an article in the "Focus" section of the *Jewish Week Inc.*, (14 November 1986) by Heinz Kienzl. Differing views were reported in the Spring 1987 *Bulletin* of the Documentations-Archive of the Austrian Resistance, Vienna.

17. *Guardian* (London), (1 May 1987).

18. See Tom Bower in the *Times* (9, 10, and 11 February 1987).

19. See *Die Wochenpresse* (8 May 1987).

Epilogue

F. PARKINSON

In January 1985 the world was treated to the spectacle of an Austrian Minister of Defense shaking hands with former Waffen-SS Major Reder, a convicted Austrian war criminal who had been released from his Italian jail only after prolonged Austrian diplomatic intercession. Nearly a year later, in December 1985, a plaque was erected to the memory of Alexander Löhr, creator of the prewar Austrian air force and colonel-general (*Generaloberst*) – highest German military rank before field-marshal – in the German armed forces in charge of an army group in the Balkans, executed for war crimes by Yugoslavia in February 1947. Early in 1986 it was revealed that Kurt Waldheim, former Secretary-General of the United Nations, had kept secret part of his wartime service in Greece and Yugoslavia that, if revealed earlier, could have caused him major political embarrassment.

On each of those three occasions, there was an uproar, both within Austria and abroad, the cumulative effect of which was to call into question the set of images by which Austria had been beheld by the world after 1945. In particular, questions were raised relating to the role played by the Austrians during the Nazi era. It was those questions which formed the substance of a crisis of confidence that still encumbers the country. The present crisis, then, is not a Nazi crisis but a crisis of identity regarding Austria's Nazi past.

As Pauley has shown in his paper in this volume, Nazism is part and parcel of Austrian history. History will not go away, and neither will the history of Austrian Nazism. This book constitutes an attempt to provide hard and fast evidence about that chapter in Austria's history.

AUSTRIA'S CRISIS OF IDENTITY

Two basic questions have been asked and answered in clarifying the role played by the Austrians under the Nazi regime: Were they Pan-Germans? And, were they Nazis?

It is often asserted that between 1938 and 1945 the Austrians learned their lesson, the implication being that they turned away in revulsion from both Pan-Germanism and Nazism. The truth, however, is that during that period the Austrians learned many lessons. One such lesson concerned the advantages of belonging to an Empire, whether Habsburg or Nazi, in which the German-speaking element was in command.[1]

Three Conceptions

The dilemmas as to their own identity with which the Austrians had to grapple for the best part of the past two centuries were not entirely of their own making. A long history had torn them in three different directions: Pan-German, imperial, and "Little Austrian," each direction giving rise to a separate political conception.[2] In 1945 the choice was made for them by the victorious Allies, as Keyserlingk details in this volume, and an iron Allied grid descended on Central Europe from which there could be no escape and that allowed for no choices in the matter of Austria's orientation.

After 1918, the Pan-German conception prevailed over both the "Little Austrian" (kleinösterreichisch) and the imperial-monarchist one, as Holmes and Pyle inform us in this volume. Such "Austro"-national sentiment as existed after 1945 was born out of fierce anti-Soviet rather than anti-German feelings, which left the Austrians with a perennial ambivalence toward the Germans, while preserving a residue of imperial-monarchist feeling that surfaces from time to time. It is not for nothing that present-day Austria celebrates her "national" holiday on the day the Soviets, and not the Germans, departed from the country.

Moreover, Austria's allegiance since 1945 has been focused on the concept of the State and not on that of the "nation," however defined. To this day the term *nation* and *national* refer automatically and implicitly, without any need for explicit affirmation, to the German nation.[3] Whenever reference is made to Austrian nationalism, the prefix *Austro* has to be inserted in order to avoid ambiguity. The term *patriotic*, current before 1938 to emphasize allegiance to the "Little" Austrian State has been discredited by its overuse on the part of the unpopular Dollfuss-Schuschnigg regime. Occasionally since 1945 the expression *commitment to Austria* has been in use.

To the mass of Austrians today the debate concerning Austria's identity appears irrelevant. The Austrians, like their German neighbors in the North, have had to learn to live with a degree of uncertainty and are no longer willing to commit themselves firmly one way or another. That refusal to make final options is reflected in some recent statistics. Whereas in the early postwar period the majority still professed to adhere to the German nation, in 1965 that majority had shrunk to 52 percent, and in 1979 68 percent professed themselves to be part of a distinctly Austrian nation.[4]

The Attitudes of the Political Parties

Social Democracy The Austrian Social Democrats approached the question of Austria's orientation in a frank and basically rational manner. In two articles in the Party's theoretical organ in exile edited first in Brno and then in Paris, Otto Bauer, the Party's leader and ideologist, treated the *Anschluss* of 1938 as an accomplished fact that had be to accepted and branded the idea of a resurrection of Austria's independence as a "reactionary watchword," adding for good measure the prophetic thought that the only way to resurrect an Austrian State was through a military defeat of Nazi Germany.[5]

In gradually coming around to a moderate "Little Austria" conception, the Party in exile, much to its credit, refused to give in on that point easily in favor of political expediency.[6] Its conversion from 1942 onward nonetheless has been a triumph of pragmatism over dogma. Since 1945 the Party has been playing down its open and consistently liberal Pan-Germanism in the past in order not to be out of tune with post-1945 political realities.

The Catholic Camp Political Catholicism after 1918 adopted an ambiguous attitude toward Austria's orientation. In this volume, Pyle sheds valuable new light on Seipel's attempts to end this ambiguity by coming out in favor of a kleinösterreichisch patriotism that, in the event, never succeeded. When that idea began to be actively promoted by Schuschnigg, its immediate effect was to revive the imperial-monarchist conception (though not necessarily in its pre-1918 form), instead of popularizing the kleinösterreichisch conception.

In an era in which both pro-German and anti-Italian feelings were running high in Austria, the most outspoken "Little Austria" element, constantly and deliberately harping on the theme of Austria's independence, was the pro-Italian, anti-Nazi wing of the Heimwehr under the leadership of the mercurial Starhemberg. The latter was loathed in Austria not only for his various personal escapades but also for his hard "Little Austria" line, for which reason he had to be retired by Schuschnigg from the Vice-Chancellorship in 1936. After the *Anschluss* Starhemberg made a vain attempt to come to terms with the Nazis before finally throwing in his lot with the Allies by joining the French Air Force as an officer and transferring to de Gaulle's forces stationed in Britain after the French surrender of 1940.[7]

The Communists The Communists originally shared the Social Democrats' principled approach towards Austria's Pan-German future. Only between 1937 and 1938 did their spokesman on this issue, Alfred Klahr, expound a theory of Austrian nationhood allegedly in conformity with the four criteria laid down by Stalin in his classical thesis of 1913.[8]

The Nazis As Williams reminds us in his paper, at least the illegal Nazis grouped around Captain Leopold in the 1930s maintained a position that, although not eschewing a merger on a footing of political equality, as distinct from an outright *Anschluss* in which Austria would lose most vestiges of independence, placed some emphasis on Austrian separateness. In a recent detailed study of the events leading to the *Anschluss* by a young Austrian historian and published by the official Austrian publishing house, evidence is provided that the crest of the illegal prewar Austro-Nazi organization "NS-Soldatenring" operating within the regular Austrian Federal Army was red-white-red with a swastika superimposed, mounted by a steel helmet displaying the traditional Austrian field emblem, the twig of fir.[9]

No doubt there was some ambivalence here. Yet, one has to bear in mind that Austrian army officers of Nazi persuasion had to be particularly careful in guarding against the charge of treason to a foreign power (*Landesverrat*), as distinct from that of treason against the government (*Hochverrat*). By and large, however, Austria's Nazis were much wedded to the traditional Prussian colors of red-white-black. All major Austrian Nazi war criminals shouted "Long live Germany!" before being hanged after the war.[10]

In 1938 the majority of Austrians seemed relieved that at long last their prolonged crisis of identity was over. No reliable empirical data exist as to the Austrian feelings of identity during the war. Extravagant claims of a wholesale conversion from a distinctly pro-German to a kleinösterreichisch stance have been made,[11] but based on extremely thin evidence. One instance, cited over and over again as if endless repetition could turn it into an acceptable generalization, is the change of heart experienced by Adolf Schärf, the Socialist lawyer who eventually became President of the Second Republic. According to him, the metamorphosis from Weimar-centered liberal Pan-Germanism to Vienna-oriented Kleinösterreichertum happened in March 1943, just a few weeks after the crushing military defeat at Stalingrad, where four Austrian divisions were annihilated after offering stiff resistance.[12]

Hostility to Prussia? In a recent book, Professor Kreissler of the University of Rouen in France argues that a deep-seated anti-Prussian feeling was part of the Austrian personality, and he invokes dicta by Marx and Engels in order to show that "Preussentum" denotes a particular state of mind in the context of mid-nineteenth century German history.[13]

His point is well taken but, so far as Austria is concerned, it is not by any means the only point that can be made. The traditional Austrian attitude toward Prussia—and, after 1871, Prussian-dominated Germany—has been an amalgam of envy, admiration, subservience, and mild amusement. The term *Piefke* applied by Austrians to Germans north of the River Main is lacking in rancor, akin to the expression *Yank* or *Limey* used by Britons and North Americans (and Australians) in relation to North Americans and Englishmen, respectively.

Contrary to Professor Kreissler's thesis, it could be claimed that the Austrians stood in awe of the Prussian cult of cold efficiency and that moreover they were eager to prove to themselves, as well as to the satisfaction of the Germans, that they could be as *zackig* (tough in a Prussian military way) as the latter. Göring's characterization of the Austrians as *Schlappschwänze* (wimps) hurt them to the quick, coming as the rebuke did from such a greatly admired Prussian who had received a rapturous welcome on his arrival in Vienna in 1938 (*"Unser Hermann!"*).

A number of instances can be cited that alone are of trifling importance but in their aggregate point in the same direction. Thus, in Austria's high schools (*Mittelschulen*) the traditional Austrian military command *Habt Acht* (attention) introduced alongside conscription in 1936 was spontaneously, eagerly, and contemptuously cast aside in favor of the clipping Prussian command *Stillgestanden!* Already at 6 P.M. of 11 March 1938 Austrian SA marched in formation, triple file, according to German military regulation, instead of double file, according to the Austrian one.[14] The Prusso-German acronym *PKW* (Personenkraftwagen) instead of the habitual Austrian *Auto* has been retained to this day. Austrian railway and tramway operators continued for years after the war to use the Prusso-German *Endstelle* before eventually reverting to the traditional Franco-Austrian *Endstation*. Prusso-German military terminology entered deeply and permanently into Austrian usage: *die Deutsche Wehrmacht* (the German armed forces), invariably spelled, contrary to the ordinary rules of German grammar, with a capital *D* to denote sovereign respect, has sunk in so profoundly that even some of the Austrian contributors to this volume have used it unselfconsciously. There is still an awesome reluctance to use the term *Nazi* in preference to the respectful but cumbersome *nationalsozialistisch* or, where this is considered uneconomical, the abbreviation *NS*. Evidently, deep down, the majority of Austrians still feel that *Nazi* sounds not only disrespectful but downright blasphemous.

After the war some half-hearted attempts were made to counter those tendencies. Thus, in 1945 school certificates had to show the degree of proficiency in German under the rubric 'Landessprache'.

The impact was negligible. Even today the *AZ/Tagblatt*, while fulminating about the continued use of Prusso-Germanisms, will mention in the same breath that someone was " . .*mit von der Partie*" (Austrian prewar usage:". . . *war dabei*") and it, like the Communist *Volksstimme*, will habitually refer with a solemn air of reverence to "*the* Federal Republic" when meaning Western Germany, knowing full well that Austria herself is a federal republic.

NAZI AUSTRIA

Nazi Populist Triumph

In 1938 Austria was a plum rotten with Nazism that dropped limply into Hitler Germany's lap, surprising—as Williams shows in his contribution—even the most optimistic Nazi leaders on both sides of the frontier. Whether that could have happened without German pressure and assistance is a hypothetical[15] question, though this editor believes that it could. What has been established beyond all doubt is that the Nazi populist rising, affecting all geographical regions and drawing on all social classes, ensured that the bulk of the country was in Nazi hands before even the first German soldier crossed the frontier.[16] A leading British newspaper characterized what was happening in Austria on 11 March 1938 as "a revolution in full swing," qualifying that statement further three days later, as follows: "There are no signs of the people bowing unwillingly to a foreign yoke"; Vienna looked like a city that had just received news of "a great victory."[17] A leading United States expert on Central European history called it "a popular rising on a broad scale."[18]

Nazi Austria was indeed euphoric. The Austrian majority (Nazi Party members plus the vast mass of Nazi fellow travelers) were able to celebrate a political and psychological victory without parallel in Austria's history. Whatever Seyss-Inquart, his Nazi Party followers, and for that matter, the German Nazi leaders may have had in mind regarding Austria's future status was swept aside by the tidal wave of the Nazi populist rising. The Austrian masses had acted, and who could have stopped them?

Fallen Pillars

What had happened to the two mighty pillars of civilized political life
in Austria: Social Democracy and the Catholic camp? The crumbling of the
reputedly powerful, sophisticated, and mature Austrian Social Democratic
Party, when faced with the prospect of Nazism, must be rated as one of
the saddest moments in Austrian history. Konrad's richly substantiated paper leaves little doubt that the Party was ultimately revealed as a giant with
clay feet, showing a glaring contrast between the mainly urban Marxist leaders and the populist sentiments of the mass, especially outside Vienna,
though Schwarz believes that there was some "silent resistance" to Nazi rule
at any rate during the first year on the part of the grass-roots working-class
Social Democrats.

In mitigation of its signal failure to oppose the Nazis, it must be said
that the Party had been brutally suppressed in 1934 and therefore tended
to side with the enemies of its oppressors. While humanly understandable,
this hardly bears witness to a pronounced sense of political maturity. To
regard the Nazi Party as a labor party is proof enough of the perverted political
values held in Austria at the time.

The Catholic camp degenerated from Christian democracy into clerico-
authoritarianism. Adapting a statement made by Victor Adler on the
Habsburg monarchy, the best that could be said about Austrian clerico-
authoritarianism was that its adverse effects were "mitigated by inefficiency."
Having to fight on two fronts, it lacked the broad populist support on
which such regimes must rely if they are to survive for any length of time.

Austrian Attitudes Toward the War

The mass of Austrians wanted to see Nazi Germany win the war. Doing
one's duty in that context simply meant straining every nerve and muscle
to promote the war effort toward the much coveted "*Sieg.*"

Stuhlpfarrer's cautious analysis of the loyalties of the regular Austrian
officer corps provides some clues to its subsequent behavior during the war,
in which Austrian officers taken over by the German armed forces carried
out their military duties without fail. There could be no question of any
discrimination within the German armed forces against Austrian officers,
professional or not. The highest and most sensitive positions were open to
them. Some Austrian officers' promotions were rapid, some even meteoric.
The overall record of both promotions and decorations conformed to the
all-German average. On the one hand, Austria contributed 7 percent of the
total population of Nazi Germany, but its share of generals was only 5 per-

cent. On the other hand, whereas they could sport no field-marshals, their share of colonel-generals was above the average. Also, all nine commanding Austrian generals were awarded the Knight's Cross to the Iron Cross, at an average of only 83 percent for the German armed forces. Altogether 326 Austrians were awarded the Knight's Cross. There were 220 Austrian generals in the German armed forces, the Waffen–SS, and the police (174 in the army, 27 in the airforce, 6 in the Waffen–SS, and 13 in the police).[19]

Military morale among the Austrians fighting in the German armed forces never cracked. In his memoirs, Schirach recounts how Hans Lauterbacher, Viennese area leader of the Hitler Youth, formed a special battalion of volunteers stationed near Bratislava. When under his war powers Schirach ordered them back, "Lauterbacher and his lieutenants rebelled, as they were eager to fight."[20]

The allegedly sinking morale of the Austrian *civilian* population during the last couple of years of the war has been interpreted as evidence of disillusionment with Nazi Germany. However, this argument lacks logic and ought to be turned on its head. If the Austrians were really getting disillusioned in that way, their morale should have been soaring at the prospect of an Allied victory. If, on the other hand, they were getting depressed at the prospect of a German military defeat, it must have been because, as before, they were still craving for a German victory but despairing of such hope ever materializing. Austrian disillusionment with Nazi Germany on account of disappointed expectations cannot possibly reflect on them with credit, since the recognition of the evils of Nazism never depended on the vagaries of German military fortunes.

The situation in that respect was complicated by the existence of some Austrian Pan-Germans who, while favoring a German victory also wanted to see the Nazi regime overthrown. There may also have been a number of Austrians who were anti-German in sentiment while remaining stoutly pro-Nazi in ideology. Between those two poles there is room for an almost infinite number of permutations.[21]

Resistance

Neither between 1938 and 1939 nor during the war was there—or could there be—a united resistance movement. Hence, the decision to resist the Nazis was taken either by individuals or small groups of individuals acting in terrible loneliness in face of generally prevailing support of the Nazi regime, without any of the political glory enjoyed by the Nazis' opponents in the rest of German-occupied Europe.

In his paper, Hanisch demolishes the notion fostered from time to time by the Catholic Church in Austria, that it had cut a heroic figure between 1938 and 1945. According to him anti-Nazi sentiment was strongest on the lowest rungs of the hierarchy. In the upper echelons, it was ambivalent. The latter is confirmed by Schwarz. Hanisch's paper also carried the suggestion that under the Nazi regime in Austria, in which the Church was never outlawed, active Catholics divided over the issue of whether the Nazi claim to be waging a crusade against Bolshevism was legitimate or merely a pretension concealing the monstrously predatory nature of the military campaign against the Soviet Union. There were small groups of Catholic resisters.[22]

It is a striking fact that among the active resisters on the Austrian Left the Communists did not just outdistance the Socialists, they dwarfed them.[23] This was due to their undoubted dedication and bravery, bearing out Franz Mehring's dictum that Communists are merely dead people on furlough. Nonetheless, the heroism of Communist resistance ought to be seen in perspective. *Voina i Rabochyi Klass*, the relatively outspoken Soviet periodical, noted sourly in November 1943 that "the real underground, nation-wide sabotage against the enslavers, which the [Communist-led] Austrian Freedom Front proclaimed, is still lacking . . . the freedom movement in Austria lags far behind that of other European countries."

One test case of Austrian participation is the conspiracy to overthrow the Nazi regime, which ended in tragic failure on 20 July 1944. Should participation by Austrian anti-Nazis have been made dependent on the previous granting by the plotters of Austrian independence?

In a highly scholarly paper, the late Professor Stadler addressed himself to the question whether the principal German conspirators were willing to grant Austria independence. He arrived at the conclusion that a plebiscite was envisaged in 1940 by Josef Müller, German anti-Nazi intelligence officer in Rome, that between 1941 and 1943 the then head of the conspiracy, Karl Gördeler, wanted both the Sudetenland and Austria to stay with Germany, whereas the attitude of the Kreisauer circle of diplomats and academics was unclear as late as October 1943.[24]

It is well known that a number of Austrian officers were willing to take part in the conspiracy unconditionally. Among the leading Austrian conspirators Lt. Colonel Robert Bernardis, a former member of the illegal "NS-Soldatenring," was Pan-German in outlook and Colonel Nikolaus Uexküll, according to Jedlicka, was a former Nazi of Pan-German conviction. Colonel (later General) Erwin Lahousen, described by a reliable West German postwar journalist as "of Austrian character, Pan-German outlook but without sympathies for the Nazis," happened to be at the front at the time of the attempted coup and was therefore prevented from acting.[25]

What is equally well established is that Karl Seitz, former mayor of

Vienna; Josef Reither, former peasant leader of Lower Austria; and former Federal Chancellor Franz Rehrl agreed to serve as regional political advisers.[26] However, Adolf Schärf, subsequently President of the Second Republic, when approached by Wilhelm Leuschner, the tireless German Social Democratic mover of the conspiracy in March 1943, declined to participate on the grounds that an independent Austria was not being envisaged by the conspirators.[27]

Here, at long last, was an opportunity to take open action against the most loathsome regime in Austria's history, yet a Social Democrat with an unblemished anti-Nazi record of Schärf's standing refused to seize the opportunity. If at least Schärf could have offered a sizable Austro-patriotic force capable of pulling a fair weight by way of an alternative, his refusal would have made some sense. However, nothing remotely resembling such a force was in the offing.

By condemning himself to inaction and by introducing a complication into the scheme of the conspirators, Schärf did nothing to promote the anti-Nazi cause. Surely, a liberal anti-Nazi Germany that included Austria was preferable to continued Nazi rule.

Nazism as the Norm

Between 1938 – at the latest – and 1945, Nazism was the prevailing political norm in Austria. Could the Austrians be blamed for their preference? Sked implies that once nicely in command of the Habsburg Empire, the Austrians had since then suffered a long period of decline and seemingly unending political upheaval. A charitable explanation for the powerful Austrian penchant for Nazism after 1936 must therefore take into account their near-desperate desire to escape from perpetual economic misery and political turmoil into the apparent certainties and political stability of Nazism. In return, a sizable majority of Austrians was prepared to embrace Nazism uncritically, to perpetrate acts of anti-Semitism, as predatory as they were ferocious and cowardly, and combine those activities with a cringing subservience to the Germans that was terminated only by total military defeat in April 1945.

AUSTRIA IN MILITARY DEFEAT

Psychodrama 1945

In 1945 Austria and Germany alike suffered total military defeat. Nazi power was crushed and Allied authority reigned supreme. Most Austrians were as shocked by this outcome of the war as most Germans, and as bewildered about future prospects.

Unlike 1938, 1945 was very far from being seen as a liberating experience. On the contrary, the psychodrama of 1945 was perceived by most Austrians not as nemesis—as the rest of the world regarded it—but as tragedy. But for a series of unfortunate military reverses suffered after the battle of Stalingrad, with the dreaded Red Army closing in relentlessly and the United States Air Force pounding Austrian territory unceasingly, the majority of Austrians never felt conditions under the Nazi regime as unbearable. What was inconceivable was the prospect of permanent Soviet occupation.

An idea of the sheer depth of the Austrian commitment to Nazism may be gathered from a few figures. Before 1 September 1946, the Nazi Party registered 536,660 members, of whom no fewer than 22,729 had been members of the general SS and 61,198 of the SA, amounting to more than 8 percent of the entire population or a quarter of the country's adult population. According to Gruber, the then Foreign Minister, 135,000 civil servants had to be dismissed on account of their Nazi affiliations.[28]

According to a set of figures collected by the Gallup Poll Institute as late as 1985, the question, Whose side were the Austrians on during the war? resulted in 74 percent answering they were on the "losing" and only 18 percent saying they were on the victorious Allied side. Conversely, the poll institute IMAS of Linz established in 1985 that 43 percent of Austrians considered that in 1945 they had been "liberated," 33 percent that they had been "defeated," and 24 percent saying they did not know.[29]

The Public Response It was in this seemingly hopeless situation that the Soviets came to the Austrians' rescue by providing them, like the proverbial deus ex machina, with a way out of their unenviable psychological predicament. That the Soviet forces were giving every cause for complaint is undisputed but, in the present context, not entirely to the point. What impressed observers on the scene was not the volume, shrillness, and constancy of Austrian complaints about the Soviets but the total silence maintained by them about the Nazis and Germans. The contrast was so striking that even the most ignorant observer must have been overcome by the gravest suspicions about what could have caused that absolute partiality so blatantly displayed by the Austrians.

The Establishment Response The newly installed Provisional Austrian Government, itself composed of anti-Nazis of impeccable vintage, had the extremely difficult task of rebuilding an Austrian State capable of engaging the loyalties of the Austrians. Finding itself, through no fault of any of its members, in an acutely embarrassing moral situation, it had no option but create a fiction of history that bore little relation to the historical truth.

Credibility could wait—perhaps for ever.

The Renner Line

> "distanzieren, korrigieren,
> profilieren, integrieren"

All the elements of the Renner line that formed the substance of that fiction and were subsequently promoted in innumerable speeches and government documents, for decades to come, could be found in the Proclamation of the Second Republic of Austria of 27 April 1945, which was signed by the leaders of the three political parties, as well as by the Staatskanzler, as the Provisional Head of Government, Renner himself, was termed. Central to it was this remarkable passage:

> "that the National Socialist Reich government of Adolf Hitler had on account of the complete political, economic, and cultural annexation of the country, led the people of Austria—rendered powerless and impotent (*macht und willenlos*) — into a senseless and hopeless war of conquest that no Austrian ever wanted, or was in a position to foresee or approve, for the waging of war (*Bekriegung*) against nations against whom no true Austrian had ever harbored feelings of hostility or hatred.[30]

Part of what can only be called the ideological line laid down by the Renner government was contained in a memorandum he had drawn up for the benefit of the Soviet authorities of occupation, in which Austrian public opinion during the Nazi era was set forth as follows: "Apart from a few ideologists and academics remote from the real world and certian nonpolitical writers and artists who wanted their daily bread and did not look to see who provided it . . . three months were enough to heal the hearts of real Austrians and to enable them to see clearly."

The perfectly valid objection made by Soviet officers to the effect that the Austrian soldiers and officers had fought as well as those of Germany was cynically rebutted by Renner by attributing this quite simply to Nazi propaganda and SS terror.[31]

The "Opfer" Ideology

Austrian diplomacy's foremost endeavor was to avoid drawing attention to the country's Nazi past and to propagate the new version of history according to which Austrians were the victims of Nazi Germany. In these attempts, the Austrian government clutched tightly to the lifeline thrown it by the Moscow Declaration of 1943, analyzed by Keyserlingk in the present volume.

Even so, the Austrian government's version of recent Austrian history was somewhat contrived and badly needed bolstering by all sorts of special pleading. Thus, the legal adviser to the Ministry of Foreign Affairs maintained in a conversation with a young British diplomat, apparently without as much as batting an eyelid, that the large number of Austrians serving in the German armed forces during the war was explicable on the grounds that it was "precisely those Austrians who were against the Nazi regime" who "had taken refuge in the Germany army, to be safe from Nazi persecution, while at the same time the true Nazis had stayed at home."[32] It was, however, a matter of historical record that 800,000 Austrians served in the German armed forces, of whom the vast majority had answered their call-up papers.

Integration

It is clear that such repression of Nazism as occurred in Austria after the war was mainly due to Allied insistence and not to Austrian revulsion.[33] This is not to say that most Austrians after 1945 continued to be Nazis, simply that the Austrians at large loathed the idea of honestly confronting their Nazi past.

Apart from a number of trials conducted under Allied pressure, Austrian Nazism got away free because, after a brief period of legal proscription, the registered Nazis found themselves the object of an undignified race for their electoral favor by the two main parties. A number of contributors to this volume see this as the turning point in the history of Austrian Nazism. In the event, the Nazi enfranchisement of 1949 portended Nazi absorption rather than Nazi political revival – though nobody was to know that in 1949.

It could indeed be argued on purely factual grounds that the absorption of the Nazis by the two major political parties prevented the formation of a autochtonous, though of necessity somewhat disguised Nazi Party in Austria.

On moral grounds, however, there is a strong case for the claim that absorption has made the Nazis respectable in Austria. Pelinka certainly finds the policy of integrating the Nazis both morally sordid and politically injurious.

The Nazi Response: Indifference and Resignation

After 1945 the Austrian Nazis and their numerous camp followers were reduced to an amorphous mass. Deprived of their emotional focus of loyalty, the German nation, they found in loyalty to an impersonal artefact, the new Austrian State, the only acceptable substitute. Although not exactly recanting their past, many, perhaps most, Austrian Nazis looked upon the new regime as a tolerable alternative to Nazism.

As several contributors to this volume have noted, the Nazis never found a permanent home in any political institution after the war. Though wooed by the two main parties for electoral advantage, they have failed to attain a position from which they could affect the political balance of power. Those who proved to be *"Unbelehrbare"* (unteachables) as distinct from mere *"Ehemalige"* (former ones) have been completely isolated. The Nazis qua Nazis cannot be a menace so long as the general historical context remains unfavorable to them and the psychological climate of optimism continues to prevail in the country.

The FPÖ is a case in point. As Riedlsperger shows, no definite answer can be given to the question whether that Party is "liberal or Nazi" in outlook. Nor should too many conclusions be drawn from the fact that its opposite number in Western Germany, the FDP, has tended to move from the far-Right to the middle of the political spectrum, whereas the opposite seems to be the case with the FPÖ. Both Riedlsperger and Gärtner maintain, or at least imply, that although Austrian Nazism may not have changed too many of its spots, the general improvement in the social and economic environment has made a Nazi revival on any scale much less likely in Austria.

The Military Ethic

The Nazi problem in Austria has been complicated by the mass exposure of an Austrian generation to the military ethic in its most repulsive form. It might consequently be less difficult to root out, or at least to neutralize, the sentiment of Austrian Nazism in its primitive populist form than to cast doubt on the alleged righteousness of the cause for which 800,000 Austrians fought the Second World War. Ideological error is easier to correct than the enduring emotion generated by prolonged military commitment to what was believed to be a noble cause. The very notion of having fought in a war that was subsequently seen as unjust and in a number of ways criminal is bound to produce a deeply disturbing impact on the minds of those involved, and for that reason it will tend to be severely repressed. This does not mean that if, *per impossibile*, the identical situation should recur, those same men and women would once more be prepared to commit themselves unconditionally.

As Stuhlpfarrer is at pains to explain, the great popularity of military reunions in postwar Austria, which go far beyond mere social occasions, is evidence enough of an enduring Austrian affection for prowess in wartime exploits.

Anti-Semitism

Whereas the Nazi past has been at best a matter of indifference to the mass of postwar Austrians, the Jewish issue has not. As an eminent Austrian Jew remarked: "No prominent leader after 1945, whatever his political shade, concealed his displeasure at the prospect of seeing Jews returning from their exile."[34] His observation was substantiated by the first message sent out from liberated Vienna by the leaders of the reborn Austrian Socialist Party to their comrades living abroad as refugees, most of them Jews. It was bluntly stated that the return of Jews to Austria in great numbers would be viewed with "a certain apprehension."[35] Unlike the constituency presented by the numerous Nazis, who could be pressed into the "electoral throng" (the "Stimmpferch," as an Austrian political commentator once called it), the drastically reduced remnant of Austrian Jewry that had survived the Nazi slaughter was of no consequence except as a most unwelcome reminder of Austria's Nazi past. No Austrian politician worth his salt would call for their return. Basic humanity just did not come into it.[36]

It was only under extreme international pressure and in the advanced stages of a crisis of confidence in July 1986 that it occurred to Waldheim to call for their return—forty-one years after the first opportunity for doing so presented itself.[37]

The specifically Austrian form of anti-Semitism, with its venom and greed, is explicable only in terms of the psychological condition in which the Austrians found themselves at the time. Cursed with a rankling inferiority complex towards both Germans and Jews but unable to vent their spleen on the former, the Austrian majority tried to cope by fawning on the Germans while savaging the Jews.

Bukey's closing observations aptly characterize the Austrian psychological condition after 1945, when the random forces of history had changed to rid them of both Germans and Jews, thus tragically bringing their feelings into balance, perhaps for the first time in over a century.

CATHARSIS: CONQUEST OF THE PAST

"Our fate, dear Brutus
lies not in the stars

but in ourselves."
Shakespeare, *Julius Caesar*

After 1945 there was a period of prolonged, embarrassed silence in respect of the history of the *Anschluss* era. In such a climate of opinion, a fearless quest for Austria's Nazi past had no place. Only since the mid-1960s did a change begin. So far, at any rate, Austrian historiography has gone through two, fairly distinct phases.

Phase 1. Forgetfulness

Between 1945 and the mid-1960s a spirit of historical forgetfulness, as unhealthy as it was uncanny, pervaded the country. Whereas in Western Germany a critical historiography of the Nazi period grew up that resulted, inter alia, in the establishment of institutes charged with the scholarly investigation of the phenomenon of Nazism, nothing equivalent happened in Austria, where the historical writing done on the subject was marked by a heavy preoccupation with the predatory designs on Austria exhibited by Nazi Germany and, in places, a focus on the activities of such Austrian individuals and small groups as had resisted Nazism. By and large, however, the impression was conveyed of an Austrian population that was an unwilling party to what had happened between 1938 and 1945, in reassuring conformity with Renner's fiction of 1945.

The weakness of historical writing of that sort was not that the information it conveyed was unreliable – it was not – but that a misleadingly wishful gloss was placed on it. It is significant that the only convincing historical contribution of that period was not a written one but the artfully brilliant solo performance of the satire *Der Herr Karl* by the late Helmut Qualtinger. Although Qualtinger was pulling no punches, this at once captured the imagination of the public who felt that the picture conjured up by Qualtinger was genuine. To prove their delight, the public voted with mass purchase of his record. No doubt, Qualtinger had succeeded in breaking through the wall of hypocrisy by hitting a deeper layer in the Austrian political psyche, producing instant cathartic relief.

Phase 2. The Historians' Finest Hour

The gradual emergence in Austria of a critical in the place of the former conformist historiography since the mid-1960s was accompanied by the advent of a new, investigative journalism in the periodical *profil*, which was to some extent modelled on the successful *Der Spiegel* of West Germany.

A new generation of historians, horrified by the chilling evidence they were unearthing about the *Anschluss* period and puzzled by decades of Austrian indifference to it, began to question the Establishment version of the history of that period, which they suspected was deeply flawed. They certainly managed to inject a dose of realism into that musty version to dispel the delusion of Austrian virtue between 1936 and 1945.

For well over a decade, their impact was confined to Austria but, with the development of the Reder, Löhr, and Waldheim crises in the mid-1980s, it began to command worldwide attention. Austrian historiography was ceasing to be mesmerized by the Renner line of 1945 and coming alive in an atmosphere of continuous, fierce but healthy debate within the profession.

The Establishment Response

Well might those who have tended to denigrate the new generation of historians protest their good intentions. "Let sleeping lions rest and get on with the job" appears to be their message. Many of them genuinely fear that what has been achieved since 1945 could be placed in serious jeopardy by the actions of a minority. In justification they can point to the Austrian social and economic miracle (Insel der Seligen), which has until recently been the envy of the world, and furthermore they claim to have instilled some sense of identity into the postwar generations of Austrians.

Their good faith is hardly in question. What is questionable are Establishment attempts to arrogate to itself the right to decide what version of the history of Nazi Austria is to prevail. Even on the most charitable interpretation, Austria has long passed the point where the Renner fiction of 1945 has to be invoked to help the country over a particularly difficult patch in its history.[38]

The Popular Response

The predominant part of Austrian public opinion tends to look askance at any attempt to revise the Establishment image of Austria's history during the *Anschluss* years. It could not altogether have been a coincidence that the majority voted for Waldheim in the presidential elections of May and June 1986, of which Sully provides a thorough analysis, when the Nazi past was an issue, and for the Socialists in the elections of November of the same year when it was not.

Public hostility also surfaced in Linz in 1985 and 1986. In May 1973 a street in that town was named after SS-Bridgadeführer Franz Langoth, the last Nazi mayor of that city (1944–1945), who had saved the town from suffering war damage by handing it over peacefully to the advancing United States forces in May 1945. However, in 1985 new evidence came to light showing that in addition Langoth had also been among the judges responsible for imposing the death penalty on sixteen Austrians who had engaged in some form of anti-Nazi activity. The then ruling Socialist mayor of Linz decided on the suggestion made by a number of former resistance members to have the street renamed after Franz Jägerstätter, the war hero executed by the Nazis in 1943. (Maislinger, in this volume, provides the full background of this remarkable Catholic peasant son.)

The suggestion, however, was vigorously opposed by local public opinion, and eventually a compromise had to be reached by which Langothstrasse was renamed Kaisergasse, after Mathias Kaiser, local burgess of the seventeenth century.[39]

Austrian public opinion after 1945, it seems, has been non-Nazi rather than anti-Nazi.

A Supplementary Agenda for Historical Research

It would be invaluable for future historical research on Austria's Nazi era, while there is still time, to conduct interviews with former Nazis (in anonymity, if required) Party members as well as fellow travelers, with a view to extracting honest accounts of why they became Nazis, and equally valuable, why they ceased to be such. There is a great scarcity of such accounts, a notable exception being that of Albert Massiczek, former illegal member of the SS who subsequently discarded his Nazi views.[40]

It is a shame that the Gorbach government of the late 1960s imposed a ban on the publication of Alfred Persche's memoirs, because the former leader of the illegal Austrian SA claimed that 80 percent of all Austrians were Nazis. According to Pauley, Gorbach maintained that Persche's claim would "certainly be exploited by the Soviet Union, the Communists and the Socialists," and "would only arouse a violent controversy over the years 1934–1938." And such controversy, apparently, was something not to be tolerated in Austria.[41] The former SA leader is mentioned by Ferenc in this volume as having been among the Nazi administrators of occupied Slovenia.

Stuhlpfarrer complains about Austrian historians working on the Nazi period being hampered in their endeavors by bureaucratic obstruction.[42] It is perhaps worth pointing out that two major sources of Nazi material on that period are still available for exploitation, if that obstruction can be overcome: The *Gestapo files* and, even more important, the *Gauakten*. Both have to be handled with care: the Gestapo material because Gestapo officials had every incentive to exaggerate anti-Nazi activities in the expectation of reinforcing their image as an indispensable pillar of the Nazi regime; the Gauakten, what is left of them after a great part had been destroyed in the early 1960s on the orders of a Minister of the Interior, because applicants for membership of the Nazi Party or one of its formations would overstate their merits in the hope of succeeding.

AN AGENDA FOR A PRESIDENT

In a remarkable interview granted to the diplomatic correspondent of the London *Guardian*, President Waldheim, whose case is analyzed by Sully in this volume, asked the question "What more can I do to show my concern, my sincere interest to make a greater contribution to the understanding of Austria's role under the Nazis?"[43]

Thinking the Unthinkable

In the following a few suggestions will be made to stimulate the President's imagination. They are "unthinkable" because an unhealthy period of forty-three years of Austrian prevarication on the subject has rendered the materialization of these proposals unthinkable. Nonetheless, for the record, here they are:

1. Erecting a monument on the site of the former so-called *Deutsches Eck*, the prewar German tourist bureau that served as focal point of Nazi demonstrations in Vienna's Kärntnerstrasse, in honor of the 65,000 Austrian Jews murdered by the Nazis;

2. Matching of the Austrian national day celebrating the withdrawal of the Soviet troops of occupation in 1955 with one commemorating the departure of the German armed forces in 1945;

3. Instituting an official day of mourning on 11 November (date of the notorious *Kristallnacht* of 1938) for the Austrian Jews murdered;

4. Renaming Schwarzenbergplatz as Franz Jägerstätter-Platz and placing of a Jägerstätter memorial in the main square of all Austrian State capitals;

5. Marking the maturity of postwar Austria with the foundation of a *Dokumentations-Archiv des österreichischen Nazismus* to supplement that already in existence in respect of the exploration of the Austrian Resistance (*Archiv des österreichischen Widerstandes*), with branches in every Austrian capital.[44]

NOTES

1. G. Barraclough, "The German Magnet and the Austrian Way of Life," *The Listener* 52 (18 November 1954):840–41, 867.

2. This is not to be confused with the three Austrias (imperial, republican, and corporate) that were the subject of K. Schuschnigg's book, *Dreimal Österreich* (Vienna, 1937). See also F. Heer, *Der Kampf um die österreichische Identität* (Vienna, 1985).

3. See, for instance, the use of the term by an undoubtedly "Austrian"-committed and lifelong anti-Nazi writer, J. Hindels, "Nationale Strömungen," in J. Hannak (ed.), *Bestandaufnahme Österreichs, 1945–1963* (Vienna, 1963), pp. 83–111. Hindels complained of pro-German and pro-Nazi currents in Austria.

4. Figures in A. Khol, T. Faulhaber, and G. Ofner (eds.), *Die Kampagne. Kurt Waldheim. Opfer oder Täter?* 2d ed. (Munich, 1987), pp. 228–29.

5. O. Bauer (Heinrich Weber), *Der Kampf* (Brno), April 1938 and O. Bauer, *Der sozialistische Kampf* (Paris), June 1938.

Readers might also consult A. L Brancato, "The German Social Democrats and the Question of Austro-German *Anschluss*, 1918–1945," (Ph.D diss., Bryn Mawr, 1975).

6. K. Ausch, "Das London Bureau der österreichischen Sozialisten," *Die Zukunft* 14 (July 1970):16–19.

7. M. Scheuch's article in *AZ/Tagblatt* (14 February 1986) omits Starhemberg's military service in the French Air Force.

8. J. V. Stalin, *Marxism and the National and Colonial Question*, ed. A. Finsberg (London, 1915). In this work, Stalin maintained that a nation is a group of people answering to four criteria: (1) a common territory; (2) a common language; (3) a common economy; and (4) a common historical background.

The editor leaves it to the readers to decide for themselves whether on the basis of those criteria Austria in 1937 could have been considered a nation.

9. Erwin A. Schmidl, *März 38. Der deutsche Einmarsch in Österreich* (Vienna, 1987) p. 54.

10. Only Adolf Eichmann shouted "Long live Germany and Austria."

11. Kohl, Faulhaber, and Ofner, pp. 247–50.

12. A Schärf, *Erinnerungen aus meinem Leben* (Vienna, 1963), pp. 166–68.

13. F. Kreissler, *La Prise de conscience de la nation autrichienne, 1938–1945* 2 vols. (Paris, 1978), pp. 142, 159–61. Kreissler makes mention of a German decree by which a list of foreign expressions were to be expunged. These, according to Kreissler, continued to be used. This may have been true up to a point but to infer from this, as he does, that this represents a form of anti-Nazi resistance is absurd. See ibid. pp. 171–72.

14. Schmidl, pp. 131–32.

15. For a scholarly assessment, see R. Schwarz, "The Nazi Press Propaganda in Austria, 1933–1938," *Duquesne Review* 7 (Fall 1961), pp. 29–38.

16. Schmidl, pp. 89–134.

17. *The Times* (12 and 15 March 1938).

18. Gordon A. Craig, "The Waldheim File," *New York Review of Books* (9 October 1986).

19. Two of the most sensitive posts in German Intelligence went to Austrians: (1) Erwin Lahousen, who in 1936 was appointed deputy head of Austrian Military Intelligence, was taken over to become a colonel on the German General Staff, chief of Section 2 of the OKW dealing with sabotage and special tasks; in 1944 he was given a regimental command, to be promoted major general on 1 January 1945; (2) Otto Skorzeny, SS-Standartenführer (colonel) was in charge of Section IV of the RSHA, where, rather like Lahousen, he was put in charge of directing secret agents in foreign and neutral countries. See C. Whiting, *Otto Skorzeny* (New York, 1972).

Rapid promotions were registered, for instance, in the following cases: Colonel Lothar Rendulic (1939) to Colonel General (1944); Lt. Colonel Julius Ringel (1938) to General of Mountain Troops (1944); Major Maximilian Felzmann (1938) to General of Artillery (1944). See N. von Preradov, *Die militärische und soziale Herkunft der Generalität des deutschen Heeres. 1 Mai 1944* (Osnabrück, 1978), pp. 82–83.

Colonel General Erich Raus began his career in the Austro-Hungarian Empire and became a much-decorated commander of Armored Armies during the Second World War. See B. Perret, *Knights of the Black Cross* (London, 1986), pp. 170–71, 196.

The statistics are to be found in J. C. Allmayer-Beck, "Die Österreicher im zweiten Weltkrieg," pp. 342–75 in J. C. Allmayer-Beck, *Unser Heer, 300 Jahre österreichisches Soldatentum in Krieg und Frieden* (Vienna, 1963), pp. 358–59. Also N. von Preradov, ibid., pp. 82–83.

Major General Franz Böhme was chief of Austrian Military Intelligence when under German pressure, he was appointed head of section III in the Federal Ministry of Defense. See *Times* (4 March 1938), and H. L. Mikoletzky, *Österreichische Zeitgeschichte* (Vienna and Munich, 1962), p. 371. On trial for alleged war crimes while stationed in Southeastern Europe, he committed suicide after the indictment and before the arraignment. See *Trial of War Criminals*, Vol. 11, Case 7: *United States v. List*, "The Hostage Case," Military Tribunal V, Palace of Nuremberg (10 May 1947–19 February 1948), pp. 757–1332. See also L. Jedlicka, *Ein Heer im Schatten der Parteien* (Graz and Cologne, 1955), pp. 157, 176.

20. B. von Schirach, *Ich glaubte an Hitler* (Hamburg, 1968), pp. 312–13. See also R. Ringler, *Illusion einer Jugend. Lieder, Fahnen und das bittere Ende der Hitlerjugend in Österreich* (Vienna, 1977).

21. E. Hanisch, "Gab es einen spezifischen österreichischen Widerstand?" *Zeitgeschichte* 12 (June–July 1985):339–50, quote from p. 345, gives a good example of an anti-German but pro-Nazi lady who remarked that one hundred Jews were preferable to one German (*Piefke*) and that it was a racial crime (*Rassenschande*) for an "Ostmarkian" [sic!] woman to marry a German.

22. Roman K. Scholz was a Catholic priest who led a "Little Austrian" resistance group. See C. Klusacek, *Die österreichische Freiheitsbewegung: Gruppe Roman Karl Scholz* (Vienna, 1968). K. Lederer and J. Kastelic led "Greater Austrian" resistance groups. See R. V. Luža, *The Resistance in Austria, 1938–1945* (Minneapolis, 1984), pp. 29–61.

23. Hanisch, pp. 343, 348.

24. K. R. Stadler, "Die Offiziersrevolte gegen Hitler und die Unabhängigkeit Österreichs," *Die Zukunft* 20 (October 1969):20–25.

25. H. Höhne, *Canaris. Patriot im Zwielicht* (Munich, 1976), p. 305. On Bernardis, see L. Jedlicka, *Der 20. Juli in Österreich*, 2d extended ed. (Vienna and Munich, 1966), pp. 22–25, 43; on Colonel Nikolaus Uexküll, see ibid., pp. 24–25.

26. Stadler, p. 23. Stadler feels that they may have been nominated by the conspirators without their consent; but that is unlikely.

27. Schärf; Kreissler, pp. 314–15; H. Andics, *Die Insel der Seligen. Österreich von der Moskauer Deklaration bis zur Gegenwart* (Vienna and Munich, 1976), p. 29.

28. J. Braunthal, *The Austrian Tragedy* (London, 1948), p. 126.

29. Kohl, Faulhaber, and Ofner, p. 268.

30. Federal Government of Austria, *Für Recht und Frieden. Eine Auswahl der Reden des Bundespräsident Dr. Karl Renner* (Vienna, 1950), pp. 9–10.

31. K. Renner, *Österreich von der ersten zur zweiten Republik* (Vienna, 1953), pp. 207–208. See also idem., *Denkschrift über die Geschichte der Unabhängigkeitserklärung und die Einsetzung einer provisorischen Regierung der Republik* (Vienna, 1945), p. 5.

32. R. Knight, "Dieses schlaffe Land," *profil* 25 (22 June 1987), p. 17. There is an element of truth in the thesis that prominent Austrian Nazis were sent abroad to be replaced by mediocre Germans. See Kreissler, pp. 199–200, and G. Botz writing in *AZ/Tagblatt* (20

May 1987). Thus, Globocnik was first sent to Poland, then to Yugoslavia; Seyss-Inquart to Poland and then to the Netherlands, where he was joined by SS-General Hanns Albin Rauter, formerly of the pro-German and pro-Nazi wing of the Heimwehr, who acted as security chief. (The Dutch referred to that Austrian gang as the "Donauklub"). On Rauter's trial, see Rijksinstituut voor Oorlogdokumentatie, *Het process Rauter* (The Hague, 1952). Former Vienna Gauleiter Alfred Frauenfeld was sent to the Crimea but resurfaced as official Gau-speaker in Vienna during the last year of the war. On Austrians in Slovenia, see Ferenc's paper in this volume.

33. Rudolf Neck, "Innenpolitik," in E. Weinzierl and K. Skalnik, *Das neue Österreich. Geschichte der zweiten Republik* (Graz, 1975), pp. 59–84. As for the prosecution of war criminals, the Austrian Parliament enacted the appropriate legislation "under the close supervision of the four Allied powers," as Reginald Thomas, Austrian Ambassador in Britain, admitted in a letter to the *Times* (16 January 1987).

34. Braunthal, p. 121.

35. Ibid.

36. The claims of recent years that Austrian anti-Semitism was less barbaric than Germany's have been frequent. Most prominently, Waldheim maintained this in his interview with the diplomatic correspondent of *The Guardian* (London) (5 August 1987). Also see Kohl, Faulhaber, and Ofner, p. 185.

There is a clear consensus among the contributors to this volume that the real position was the very reverse. See also, R. Schwarz, "Nazism in Austria," *Syracuse Scholar* 3 (Spring 1982): 17, and Kreissler's emphatic statement to the effect that "le martyre des juifs autrichiens commença dès le 13 mars 1938, et cela d'une manière beaucoup plus brutale que pour leurs coreligionnaires dans le Reich," p. 196.

R. Grünberger, *The Social History of the Third Reich* (London, 1971) cited the SS paper *Das Schwarze Korps* as noting that in the matter of anti-Semitism there was nothing the Austrians had to learn from the Germans that they would not have done "joyfully" on their own (p. 458). For a shocking personal account, see the late Hans Keller, *The Listener*, (28 March 1974):397.

37. *The Guardian* (London) (10 July 1986).

38. See "Armes Österreich: erst Opfer Hitlers, dann der Historiker," *Frankfurter Rundschau* (13 January 1987).

39. For the official report containing the relevant statistics, see *Stadt-Linz* (July 1986). For letters to the editor, expressing indignant public opinion, see *Oberösterreichische Nachrichten* (25 January 1986).

For the general background, see E. B. Bukey, *Hitler's Hometown, Linz, Austria, 1908–1945* (Bloomington and Indianapolis, 1986), pp. 216–17.

40. Massiczek's most valuable contribution is "Zur Nazischuld: Bewertung ist Selbstbewertung," *Die Zukunft* 20 (October 1970):16–18. His chapter "Zweimal illegal," in S. Meissl, K. P. Mulley, and O. Rathkolb (eds.), *Verdrängte Schuld. Verfehlte Sühne* (Vienna, 1986), pp. 302–20 deals mainly with the injustice of formalized Denazification.

Recently there has been a contribution from a former Nazi-diplomat of Austrian origin, R. Spitzy, *So haben wir das Reich verspielt* (Munich, 1986).

41. For a reference to the Persche memoirs, see B. F. Pauley, *Hitler and the Forgotten Nazis. A History of Austrian National Socialism* (Chapel Hill, 1981), p. xiv.

42. On this point, see "Der 'Fall Waldheim' und das Staatsarchiv: Bestände bleiben 'vorläufig gesperrt,'" *Die Presse* (14–15 February 1987).

43. *The Guardian* (London) (August 1987).

44. The Society for Political Enlightenment, founded in September 1982, is engaged mainly in political education. It has been doing valuable anti-Nazi work on a supra-Party level. However, its scope is necessarily confined to passing much needed critical commentary on current affairs.

Index

335

Dr. F. Parkinson was on the teaching staff of the Faculty of Laws of University College London for thirty-five years and is now Research Fellow at the Institute of Latin American Studies of the University of London.

The manuscript was prepared for publication by Gnomi Schrift Gouldin. The typeface for the text and the display is Galliard. The book is printed on 55-lb Glatfelter text paper and is bound in ICG's Arrestox Linen.

Manufactured in the United States of America.

Austrian Nazis

    thoroughly Austrian 34
      back to Hapsburgs
    conversion 36
    antiSemitism / 1920 36
    Sig, then resurgence 38
    H's preference for Linz 38-39
    Outlawed 41, 42-3
    student votes Ø31 41
    illegal Nazi newspapers 48